THE SELECTED WRITINGS OF PIERRE HADOT

CW01024216

Re-inventing Philosophy as a Way of Life
Series editors: Keith Ansell-Pearson, Matthew Sharpe, and Michael Ure

For the most part, academic philosophy is considered a purely theoretical discipline that aims at systematic knowledge; contemporary philosophers do not, as a rule, think that they or their audience will lead better lives by doing philosophy. Recently, however, we have seen a powerful resurgence of interest in the countervailing ancient view that philosophy facilitates human flourishing. Philosophy, Seneca famously stated, teaches us doing, not saying. It aims to transform how we live. This ancient ideal has continually been reinvented, from the Renaissance through to late modernity and is now central to contemporary debates about philosophy's role and future.

This series is the first synoptic study of the re-inventions of the idea of philosophy as an ethical pursuit or 'way of life'. Collectively and individually, the books in this series will answer the following questions:

1. How have philosophers reanimated the ancient model of philosophy? How have they revised ancient assumptions, concepts and practices in the light of wider cultural shifts in the modern world? What new ideas of the good life and new arts, exercises, disciplines and consolations have they formulated?

2. Do these reinventions successfully re-establish the idea that philosophy can transform our lives? What are the standard criticisms of this philosophical ambition and how have they been addressed?

3. What are the implications for these new versions of philosophy as a way of life for contemporary issues that concern the nature of philosophy, its procedures, limits, ends, and its relationship to wider society?

ALSO AVAILABLE FROM BLOOMSBURY

Bergson: Thinking Beyond the Human Condition, Keith Ansell Pearson

The Pornographic Age, Alain Badiou

Happiness, Alain Badiou

The Incandescent, Michel Serres

Hominescence, Michel Serres

THE SELECTED WRITINGS OF PIERRE HADOT

Philosophy as Practice

Translated by Matthew Sharpe and Federico Testa

BLOOMSBURY ACADEMIC

LONDON • NEW YORK • OXFORD • NEW DELHI • SYDNEY

BLOOMSBURY ACADEMIC
Bloomsbury Publishing Plc
50 Bedford Square, London, WC1B 3DP, UK
1385 Broadway, New York, NY 10018, USA
29 Earlsfort Terrace, Dublin 2, Ireland

BLOOMSBURY, BLOOMSBURY ACADEMIC and the Diana logo are trademarks
of Bloomsbury Publishing Plc

First published in France as *Exercices spirituels et philosophie antique* by Pierre Hadot ©
Editions Albin Michel, Paris 2002 and Copyright © Société d'Édition Les Belles Lettres,
2014 and 2010 (for 'La Fin du Paganisme')

First published in Great Britain 2020
Reprinted 2020 (twice), 2021

English-language translation © Matthew Sharpe and Federico Testa 2020

Cover design by Charlotte Daniels
Cover image: Statue of Marcus Aurelius (161–180 AD)
(© Peter Horree / Alamy Stock Photo)

A catalogue record for this book is available from the British Library.

A catalog record for this book is available from the Library of Congress.

ISBN: HB: 978-1-4742-7297-1
       PB: 978-1-4742-7299-5
       ePDF: 978-1-4742-7301-5
       eBook: 978-1-4742-7300-8

Series: Re-inventing Philosophy as a Way of Life

Typeset by RefineCatch Limited, Bungay, Suffolk
Printed and bound in Great Britain

To find out more about our authors and books visit www.bloomsbury.com
and sign up for our newsletters.

CONTENTS

FOREWORD

Transformative Exemplars

Pierre Hadot has transformed our idea not only of ancient philosophy, but of philosophy as such. From his early works on Neoplatonic philosophy to his last book on Goethe and the tradition of spiritual exercises,[1] Hadot has made us see and understand the value of ancient philosophy for the entire history of philosophy. According to Hadot, in ancient philosophy, all philosophical discourses, theories and abstractions are in the service of the philosophical life—the concrete practice of philosophy. Philosophy without flesh and soul, that is, without philosophers, is but an intellectual pastime, since it lacks the dimension of an existential choice to live in a certain way. Hadot summarises his fundamental idea as follows:

> [A]ll ancient philosophical schools refused to consider philosophical activity as purely intellectual, purely formal or theoretical. Rather, the ancients considered philosophy as a choice which committed a person's entire life and soul. This is why the exercise of philosophy was not solely intellectual but could also be spiritual. The philosopher did not finally form his disciples only in the sense of a knowing how to speak or to debate, but a knowing how to live in the strongest and noblest sense of the term. It is to an art of living, a way of life that the ancient philosophers invited their disciples.[2]

This spiritual force of philosophy is not simply located in its ethical dimension. The practice of philosophy is found within each of its traditional disciplines: ethics, logic, physics. Philosophy is at one and the same time a practiced ethics, a practiced logic and a practiced physics. Each part of philosophy comprises a theoretical discourse and a lived practice. Hence:

> lived philosophy is not limited to the practice of moral duties. It also involves a control of the activity of thought and a cosmic consciousness.

Lived philosophy is thus a practice or a way of life which embraces all human activity; it is not only an ethics in the narrow sense of the word.[3]

Living philosophy requires an appeal to the guidance of an exemplary figure who, in antiquity, was called a sage: "The philosopher will ask himself in all circumstances: 'what would the sage do in this circumstance?'"[4] If some ancient philosophical schools considered the sage as "an ideal which is nearly inaccessible, more like a transcendent norm than a concrete figure,"[5] we must not forget that "the ideal figure of the sage has not been abstractly projected in the absolute, it is not a theoretical construction."[6] Rather:

> the figure of the perfect sage ultimately corresponds to the idealisation, the transfiguration or, as we might say, the canonisation of very concrete figures, who are these righteous men [*hommes de bien*], these sages living amongst human beings.[7]

It thus becomes possible to understand why, in antiquity, biography was a philosophical genre of great value. The concept of *figure*, so important for Hadot's interpretation, is strictly linked to this vision of philosophy. The exemplary life of the sage (a state of ideal and transcendent perfection) and the exemplary life of the philosopher (at least a relative perfection, a limited wisdom) delineate not merely an example (too particular and individual) but a figure, namely "a model, an ideal, that orients and inspires the way of life."[8]

As the figure of the ancient sage is a model that orients human conduct, Hadot's own work constitutes for us both the model of a radically new way of writing the history of philosophy, and of practicing philosophy as such. Indeed, in order not to impose our own, modern categories and prejudices on the ancient texts that we read, and thus *allow them* to transform our idea of what philosophy is, we need to consider the activity of reading itself as a spiritual exercise. Hadot teaches us how to re-read the history of philosophy in order to create space for the idea of philosophy as a way of life.

When one reads a philosophical text—whether written by Plato, Marcus Aurelius, Plotinus, Descartes, or Merleau-Ponty—it is critical, Hadot argues, that one tries to "undo oneself from one's subjectivity," thus overcoming one's prejudices, habits and passions. And although a state of perfect objectivity is probably unattainable, it is still (as in the case of the figure of the sage) an "ideal that one must attempt to attain through a certain practice."[9] As with the practice of other spiritual exercises, we can strive for spiritual progress, but without expecting spiritual perfection. Human, all too human, spiritual exercises never come to a definitive end for us; they are existential exercises that continue throughout the stages of our life. Yet objectivity for Hadot is nothing less than a guiding *virtue*, or better, a "spiritual exercise of detachment from the self" which allows one to "undo oneself from the partiality of the individual and impassioned self in order to elevate oneself to the universality of the rational self."[10] If something like wisdom is still possible today, it depends, at least within the practice of philosophy, on the practice of this spiritual exercise.

Learning to read is a spiritual exercise that requires us to move away from the idea of an egoistic reading and to conceive of the practice of reading philosophical texts as essentially *dialogical*—the foundation of a genuine encounter both with others (the authors of the texts) and with oneself that transforms our way of seeing the world and of living. Thus, Hadot invites us to conceive of each philosophical text as a living reality, the result of an intellectual and social practice that we must take into account if we want to be able to really understand the force of the words we read. Just as a sage can be an exemplary figure, so a dialogical text can also become an active exemplar. Self-formation includes reading, meditating on, such exemplary texts. Hadot shows us how to engage in this practice of self-(trans)formative reading. At the end of his article "Spiritual Exercises," quoting Vauvenargues, Hadot expresses the wish that his article be able to make his readers love "a few old truths," and he continues:

> Old truths ... There are some truths whose meaning will never be exhausted by the generations of man. It is not that they are difficult; on the contrary, they are often extremely simple. Often, they even appear to be banal. Yet for their meaning to be understood, these truths must be *lived*, and constantly re-experienced. Each generation must take up, from scratch, the task of learning to read and to re-read these "old truths."[11]

Reading as a spiritual exercise has three main aspects. To understand the meaning and scope of a philosophical text, Hadot argues, one must first ask what the author *must* say—for example, because he belongs to a certain philosophical school, or because of the literary genre being employed, or because he addresses "a particular audience that is more or less formed." Second, one must ask what the author *can* say—for example, he may exaggerate the presentation of a doctrine in order to produce a more striking effect on the mind, or be unfaithful to the dogmas of his own school because he wants "to adapt to a certain audience." Finally, one must ask what the author *wants* to say, his "deep intention," provided however that one does not try to decipher his "more or less secret psychology," but attempts to understand the "choice made with regard to the goal of his work, his mode of presentation, his method, the way in which he has been able to play with all the rules that impose themselves upon him."[12] Thus, by criticising historical psychology, Hadot once again clearly suggests that looking at the past from our own, modern point of view necessarily implies missing its distinctiveness—and its value.

If it is true, as Michel Foucault once claimed, that one of our main tasks, today, is to elaborate an ethics which does not rely on religion, law or science, and that Greco-Roman society provides us with the example of an ethics which does not depend on these points of reference,[13] then learning how to read ancient philosophical texts is one of the most crucial spiritual exercises that we should learn how to practice. Thus, according to Hadot, "there is no point in distorting the meaning of a text in order to adapt it to the requirements of modern life, or to the aspirations of the soul, and so on."[14] What we must learn to do is precisely to overcome our modern demands and our purely personal aspirations. Otherwise, self-transformation will be, at best, limited and superficial. Hadot's lifelong philosophical work, and the exemplary texts collected in this volume, constitute for us a model of this fundamental philosophical task.

January 2020
Arnold I. Davidson[15] & Daniele Lorenzini[16]

Notes

1 See P. Hadot, *Plotinus, or The Simplicity of Vision* [1963], trans. M. Chase, intr. A.I. Davidson (Chicago: The University of Chicago Press, 1993); P. Hadot, *Porphyre et Victorinus* (Paris: Études augustiniennes, 1968); P. Hadot, *N'oublie pas de vivre: Goethe et la tradition des exercices spirituels* (Paris: Albin Michel, 2008).

2 P. Hadot, "Ancient Philosophy: An Ethics or a Practice?" [1993], *infra*, p. 59.

3 Ibid., pp. 68–9.

4 P. Hadot, "The Figure of the Sage in Greek and Roman Antiquity" [1991], *infra*, p. 196.

5 Ibid., p. 193.

6 Ibid., p. 197.

7 Ibid., p. 197.

8 P. Hadot, *The Present Alone is Our Happiness: Conversations with Jeannie Carlier and Arnold I. Davidson* [2001], trans. M. Djaballah and M. Chase (Stanford: Stanford University Press, 2011²), p. 117.

9 Ibid., p. 66.

10 Ibid., p. 67.

11 P. Hadot, *Philosophy as a Way of Life: Spiritual Exercises from Socrates to Foucault* [1987], ed. A.I. Davidson, trans. M. Chase (Oxford: Blackwell, 1995), p. 108.

12 P. Hadot, *The Present Alone is Our Happiness*, pp. 64–5.

13 M. Foucault, *Qu'est-ce que la critique?* suivi de *La culture de soi*, ed. H.-P. Fruchaud and D. Lorenzini (Paris: Vrin, 2015), p. 143.

14 P. Hadot, *The Present Alone is Our Happiness*, p. 67.

15 Robert O. Anderson, Distinguished Service Professor, University of Chicago, USA & Distinguished Visiting Professor of Humanities, The Hebrew University of Jerusalem, Israel.

16 Assistant Professor of Philosophy, University of Warwick, UK.

INTRODUCTION: SITUATING HADOT TODAY

Matthew Sharpe

In a series of works following his 1963 book, *Plotin, ou la simplicité du regard*, Pierre Hadot (1929–2011), the author of these *Selected Writings*, propounded the idea that the practice of philosophy always implicated a *manière de vivre* or 'way of life' in the ancient pagan and early Christian worlds. It did not simply involve the production of theoretical understandings and discourses about language, ethics and the world, as the academic study of philosophy does today. Its practitioners did not necessarily hold down the ancient equivalents of professional chairs (there were no such), although they often enjoyed the patronage of wealthy benefactors and, at different times, of the public purse. Much of the content of the written texts of the ancient philosophers, as such, cannot rightly be understood on the model of the ways that we write and study philosophy as scholars today.

First of all, Hadot observed, there was simply a much greater profusion of literary genres written by ancient philosophers than our papers, reviews, chapters and books: from poems and prayers to epitomes and exhortations, via consolations, diatribes, protreptics, dialogues and a dozen other genres. Second, entire sequences of these texts can appear to the contemporary reader to be rhetorical, literary, repetitive or redundant. All the ancient philosophical schools, perhaps excluding the sceptics, developed highly sophisticated, systematic discourses about the human being, thought, the world and the gods. Yet, rarely did they present these philosophies in what we would consider a systematic manner.

These facts, Hadot came to argue, cannot most plausibly be explained by working with the assumption that the ancient authors were trying but failing to write as contemporary scholars do, wanting always and only to 'make arguments', discover new knowledge or lay claim to some new conceptual terrain. Rather, what was at stake in the ancient philosophical writings, as in their oral teaching, was the attempt to form students, as against merely informing them, to echo one of Hadot's formulations which he borrows from Victor Goldschmidt (see Chapter 3). Ancient philosophy was always pedagogy, for Hadot, in one of its essential dimensions which we will meet in several of the chapters in this collection.[1] Many of the parts of ancient texts we find most puzzling become comprehensible when we see in them the products of attempts to stage or model different types of inquiry or dialogue; to consolidate in the minds of the readers, or of the authors themselves, truths they may already have assented to; or to make these truths come alive again, calling vividly to mind their full implications, so that they could become the living sources of philosophical ways of seeing and being in the world. To evoke Hadot's signature term, associated with perhaps his most famous paper, entire sequences of ancient writings, even entire ancient texts like Marcus Aurelius' *Meditations*, staged 'spiritual exercises': 'voluntary, personal practice[s] intended to bring about a transformation ... of the self".[2] Yet, modern philosophers, with some few exceptions led by Michel de Montaigne and Friedrich Nietzsche, have largely missed this dimension of the ancient philosophical writings.

Perhaps it is still too soon in 2019 to say what the significance of Pierre Hadot and his work will have been, when future generations look back on the history of the philosophy of the twentieth and early twenty-first centuries. Unassuming and restrained, yet prolifically erudite and quietly revolutionary, Hadot's *oeuvre* was not the product of the usual career path of the twentieth-century French *maitre à penser*. Although Hadot was influenced profoundly by Bergson, wrote an early piece on Heidegger and Plotinus,[3] and considered for many years a thesis on Heidegger and Rilke, Hadot's earliest scholarly work was in philology, that most antiquarian of pursuits (albeit one that also cradled Nietzsche). And while Hadot's 1963 study on Plotinus clearly anticipates his later work on ancient philosophy more widely,[4] the notions of philosophy as a way of life and spiritual exercises would only emerge after the later 1960s, including in the groundbreaking 1972 paper we translate here on Marcus Aurelius and physics as a spiritual exercise in the philosopher-emperor's *Meditations* (Chapter 11). The year 1977 saw the publication of 'Exercises spirituels', the piece which the world knows profoundly influenced the later Michel Foucault's turn towards the study of the ancients' technologies of the self. In

1981, the first edition of *Exercises spirituels et philosophie antique* appeared. Hadot was named Professor at the Collège de France in 1982, with Foucault's assistance, where he held the Chair for the History of Hellenistic and Roman Thought until his retirement in 1991. In his final two decades, Hadot continued to produce critical editions and translations of Marcus Aurelius and Plotinus, in the meanwhile completing books on two other of his lifelong loves: the history of Western understandings of nature (research leading to *Le Voile d'Isis*, 2004, translated 2008) and the thought, poetry and spiritual exercises of Johann Wolfgang von Goethe (*N'oublie pas de vivre*, 2008, presently [2019] in translation).[5]

Nevertheless, especially following the translation into English by Michael Chase of *Philosophy as a Way of Life* (1995), *The Inner Citadel* (1998) and *What is Ancient Philosophy?* (2002), Hadot's work has come to exercise an ever-widening influence.[6] It is this influence which principally underlies our decision to translate this selection of crucial Hadotian essays, and our aim to make them available for the first time to an anglophone readership. Hadot's reception hitherto has both scholarly and extra-academic dimensions, each of which we hope will benefit from the new availability of these selected writings.

Within the scholarship, Hadot's work on ancient philosophy as a way of life – in fact, one of four interweaving strands of his work, the others being Neoplatonic studies, Patristic studies and the history of natural philosophy – has a growing interdisciplinary influence. Hadot himself was always clear about the direct link between his scholarly, philological studies and his conception of ancient philosophy as a way of life. As he reflects in a later interview:

> Concerning the genesis of the notion of philosophy as a choice of life or of the notion of spiritual exercises in my work, it should also be said that I began by reflecting on this problem [of] how to understand the apparent inconsistencies of certain philosophers ... This is a rather important point, I believe. I did not begin with more or less edifying considerations about philosophy as therapy and so on ... No, it was really a strictly literary problem ...: for what reasons do ancient philosophical writings seem incoherent? Why is it so difficult to recognize their rational plane?[7]

Reflecting this side to Hadot's persona, it is telling that his works' most favourable reception within anglophone academia has come from historians of ideas like Wayne Hankey, Stephen Gaukroger, Ian Hunter, Peter Harrison, Christopher Celenza and Sorana Corneanu. These figures have taken

Hadot's perspective on ancient *philosophia* as authoritative, and tracked its evolution into later Christian, renaissance and early modern thought.[8] Juliusz Domański's French-language study on medieval and renaissance thought, *La philosophie, théorie ou manière de vivre?: Les controverses de l'Antiquité à la Renaissance*, to which Hadot authored the preface, also deserves special mention here.[9] Readers can find further exemplifications of the 'Hadotian' approach to the history of ideas in the 2013 collection – the only dedicated anglophone collection on his work to date – edited by Michael Chase, *Philosophy as a Way of Life: Ancients and Moderns: Essays in Honour of Pierre Hadot.*[10]

Second, an emerging body of scholarship has begun to use Hadot's understanding of Western philosophical history as the basis to open out new comparative vistas, such as we find in the 2018 volume, *Buddhist Spiritual Practices: Thinking with Pierre Hadot on Buddhism, Philosophy, and the Path.*[11] Hadot himself was notably reticent about the prospects of such comparative philosophy: expressing a philologist's caution about too quickly 'seeing' parallels between different cultural and philosophical traditions. Nevertheless, the reconsideration of Western philosophy as an embodied, intersubjective, social practice characterized by pedagogical and protreptic as well as doctrinal dimensions, evolving sets of literary, rhetorical and argumentative conventions, and the prescription of spiritual exercises to transform the 'entire psychism' of aspirants, itself challenges many of the oppositions in which 'East–West' relations were for a long time framed by Western thinkers. Hadot himself could not altogether refuse the striking parallels between certain Eastern and Western depictions of the figure of the sage, as when he recounts the story of Pyrrho the Sceptic living quietly with his sister, tending pigs, in Chapter 8 below, and adds:

> I cannot deny myself the comparison between this story and that which is reported by Tchouang Tseu about Li Tsu and: 'The three years during which he was locked in, doing housekeeping tasks for his wife and serving food to pigs, as he would have served people. He equally made himself indifferent to all and he eliminated all ornament from his life in order to rediscover simplicity.'[12]

With this much said, the prospects and questions Hadot's refiguring of the history of Western philosophy raise have for comparative philosophical studies have barely begun to be explored.

We will attend (in the next section) to the third component of Hadot's scholarly reception, the criticisms Hadot's work has attracted, notably from Anglo-American philosophers. Before we do this, we should, however, note what is perhaps the most singular feature of Hadot's reception in the Anglosphere. This is that Hadot's readership, since around the turn of the millennium, has in no way remained restricted to professional scholars and students. Hadot himself would report in the interviews of his final years on the letters he received from people around the world thanking him for his work, and the effects it had on their lives. In the last decades of his own life, in fact – and even as academic philosophy has been falling into deeper and deeper crises of confidence and direction – a global network of related, internet-facilitated schools and networks devoted to practicing Stoicism as a way of life has taken shape. These groups now stage annual international conferences, produce podcasts and apps, handbooks and introductions, and champion 'Live like a Stoic' weeks. The leaders of these groups, including professional philosophers like Massimo Pigliucci and Gregory Sadler, and psychotherapists like Donald Robertson, are transparent about the extent of their debts to Hadot's work. To cite just two examples of Hadot's influence in this field: Pigliucci's *How to Be a Stoic* (2017) divides its chapters into the three disciplines of ethics or action, logic or judgement, and physics or desire that Hadot first drew from Adolf Bonhoeffer's work on Epictetus in a key 1978 essay and developed in *La citadelle intérieure* (1992).[13] A 2018 series of podcasts from the 'Traditional Stoicism' group – who are committed to embracing the theological dimensions of Stoicism, unlike those (like Pigliucci) they criticize as 'modern Stoics' – is, nevertheless, likewise divided into the same three Epictetan or 'Hadotian' disciplines.[14]

Many scholars have and will express a profound scepticism about all such attempts to reanimate Stoicism as a live existential possibility as misguided, quaint or wholly a commercial endeavour. For them, philosophy as a way of life remains an approach, powerful and illuminating, to reading texts and interpreting the history of ideas: a position on Hadot's works whose strengths we see amply illustrated in this collection, notably in Chapters 2–4, 6–7, 10 and 11. Yet, it is important to note that Hadot himself did not wholly discourage the idea that at least the ancient Hellenistic philosophies, or their spiritual exercises, could be reanimated as the means to assist modern men and women. Indeed, as he reflected, 'from 1970 on, I have felt very strongly that it was Epicureanism and Stoicism which could nourish the spiritual life of men and women of our times, as well as my own.'[15] At the end of the 'Spiritual Exercises' (1995) article, we read that:

A truly new and truly original book would be one which made people love old truths. It is my hope that I have been 'truly new and truly original' in this sense, since my goal has indeed been to make people love a few old truths ... there are some truths whose meaning will never be exhausted by the generations of man. It is not that they are difficult; on the contrary, they are often extremely simple. Often, they even appear to be banal. Yet for their meaning to be understood, these truths must be lived, and constantly re-experienced. Each generation must take up, from scratch, the task of learning to read and to re-read these 'old truths'.[16]

In several other places, Hadot even indicated that, beneath the historical dimension of his works, he hoped to let an esoteric call sound to people looking for contemporary existential guidance through the study of ancient thought:

> I would say that, for my part, it is a matter of what Kierkegaard calls indirect communication. If one says directly, do this or that, one dictates a conduct with a tone of false certainty. But thanks to the description of spiritual exercises lived by another, one allows a call to be heard that the reader has the freedom to accept or refuse. It is up to the reader to decide. He is free to believe or not to believe, to act or not to act. If I can judge by the numerous letters I have received, written by the most diverse kinds of people, from France, Germany, the United States, who tell me that my books have aided them spiritually – someone has even written 'you have changed my life' – I think that the method is good, and I always respond to these people, with reason, that it was not me, but the ancient philosophers, who have brought them this aid.[17]

Several of the articles included here (for instance, Chapters 6 and 7) are hence every bit as recondite as anyone could desire, reflecting Hadot's comprehensive familiarity with ancient Latin and Greek philosophical, literary and historical traditions. Nevertheless, in line with this other side to Hadot's persona, as both philologist as well as philosopher or even 'spiritual guide',[18] readers can also hear a quiet call to a transformation of attention resounding between many of their lines.

Reception, critique, lacunae

So, our first motivation for undertaking these translations responds to Pierre Hadot's growing influence. It has been a question of trying to make available to anglophone audiences for the first time this series of important and, in several cases, beautiful essays: essays which further address key parameters, features and figures of Hadot's work on philosophy as a way of life, and which add details, nuances and colours to the Hadotian texts already available in the Anglosphere. Our second motivation, however, is somewhat different. It comes from how Hadot has been understood by his scholarly critics, particularly amongst anglophone academic philosophers. This reception has underlain a desire to make available a selection of essays that speak to the criticisms of Hadot's account of ancient philosophy that have been made by leading, broadly 'analytic' scholars such as John M. Cooper, Brad Inwood and Martha Nussbaum.[19]

It is not the place for us in this introduction to examine these criticisms in the detail each deserves: a task which I and others have undertaken elsewhere.[20] Broadly speaking, Hadot stands accused by Cooper and others of misrepresenting ancient philosophy, specifically by underselling its distinctive discursive, rational and argumentative dimensions.[21] What makes philosophy 'philosophy', these critics argue, is exactly its rational, argumentative practices. These cannot rightly be represented as having included, informed or been supplemented in the ancients by what Hadot calls spiritual exercises. In some cases, the criticism is tied to the claim that Hadot's vision of ancient thought, and that of authors who are influenced by him, is a specifically 'continental' one, evoking the 'analytic–continental divide' that has riven twentieth-century academic philosophy.[22]

Hadot's stress on the need for an individual to *choose* to become a philosopher of one kind or another, whether Stoic, Epicurean or Platonic, has in this vein been arraigned by Thomas Flynn, Thomas Bénatouïl and Cooper for importing a specifically *existentialist* vision into the understanding of classical thought.[23] Hadot's use of a language of 'conversion' (Chapter 5) to describe the philosophical aspirant's adoption of a Stoic, Epicurean or other philosophical way of life, some critics have seen as coming too close to collapsing the divide between philosophy, a rational pursuit and religion, a supra or non-rational commitment.[24] Finally, Cooper and Matthew Lamb have presented an historically inflected variant of this critique. They point specifically to Hadot's ongoing engagement with forms of Platonism and Neoplatonism and forms of mysticism, seeing this engagement as determinative of his wider picture of ancient philosophy.[25] Hadot's (Neo)platonic interests and sympathies, these figures contend, inaccurately colour Hadot's image of all of the ancient philosophical schools – despite and *in* his increasing turn after 1970 to a focus on the Hellenistic philosophers. Where Neoplatonism was, Cooper *dixit*, ancient *philosophia* per se cannot come to be.

By including Hadot's important piece on 'Conversion' (Chapter 5), as well as the extended essays on whether ancient philosophy is an ethics or a practice (Chapter 3), on the divisions of the parts of philosophy in the different ancient schools (Chapter 6), and on the place of dialectic and rhetoric in the ancient schools (Chapter 7), we hope that readers will be able to see that these criticisms need to be very carefully parsed, when all of Hadot's production is considered.[26] For one thing that these pieces underscore, amongst many other things, is a point about his own intellectual biography which Hadot would recur to frequently. We have cited it above: the insistence that if he would eventually become widely known for his more-or-less edifying ideas concerning ancient philosophy as a way of life, he only came to this metaphilosophical perspective on the basis of his labours as a philologist trying to understand ancient philosophical writings, by recovering the authors' original intentions. Above all, this work involved the painstaking 'effort to grasp the philosophical process in all of its lived reality, concrete and existential, in all of its dimensions, not solely literary but [also] social, political, religious, institutional, juridical, geographical and anthropological', as Hadot writes in Chapter 2 below.

A different line of criticism of Hadot's work on philosophy as a way of life concerns Hadot's 'interrupted dialogue' with Michel Foucault. Foucault's praise for and debts to Hadot's work, in the lectures and books of the last decade of his life, has played a significant role in making Hadot's works known to wider audiences. The two men developed a friendship which was sadly ended by Foucault's passing. Orazio Irrera, in, 'Pleasure and Transcendence of the Self: Notes on "A Dialogue too Soon Interrupted" between Michel Foucault and Pierre Hadot' (2010), has claimed that Hadot misrepresents Foucault's reading of the ancients. Irrera finds Hadot's remarks concerning pleasure and joy in Foucault's reading of Seneca unjust, showing that Hadot himself does not always closely honour this distinction.[27] Irrera also calls into question, from a critical standpoint, Hadot's claim that the ancient philosophies always pointed towards the ideal of the sage accessing a meaningfully 'universal' standpoint, whether that of the Platonic Ideas, the Stoic *Logos* or the Neoplatonist One. This, for Irrera, invokes 'a normative exteriority that rests on what Derrida would call the metaphysical thought of presence'.[28] Given Hadot's own non-Heideggerian thinking of presence, it would be interesting to reflect upon how Hadot might have responded to this critique.[29] Our inclusion here of Hadot's first article on Foucault aims to make more widely available all the documents in the philosophical exchange between the two thinkers to a new readership.

As well as translating essays that address these important lines of criticism of Hadot's work, it seemed important to us to try to make available to new audiences essays which show elements of Hadot's intellectual persona that are less well known and understood. The first of these is Hadot's relationships with other leading twentieth-century approaches to the study and interpretation of ancient philosophy, history and culture. In interviews, Hadot has been generously open about the different key influences on his *Bildung*: notably including his debts to Paul Rabbow's 1954 study *Seelenführung: Methodik der Exerzitien in der Antike*, which Hadot tells us that he had read by around 1968.[30] Also decisive for Hadot's conception of ancient philosophy as a way of life was his relationship with, and the groundbreaking research of, his second wife, Ilsetraut Hadot, led by her magisterial 1969 German-language study on the Stoic philosopher Seneca and the ancient lineage of spiritual direction.[31] But Hadot's approach to ancient thought, first and foremost, was decisively shaped by his encounter in the late 1950s with especially the later philosophy of Ludwig Wittgenstein, notably in the decisive 1962 piece 'Jeux de langage et philosophie'.[32] As Hadot explained to Arnold Davidson:

> it was also in relation to language games that I had the idea that philosophy is also a spiritual exercise because, ultimately, spiritual exercises are frequently language games … Moreover, in the same context, Wittgenstein also used the expression 'form of life'. This also inspired me to understand philosophy as a form of life or way of life.[33]

In Chapter 2, 'The Ancient Philosophers', Hadot's 'Preface' to Richard Goulet's *Dictionnaire des philosophes antiques* [*Dictionary of Ancient Philosophers*, 1983], we find one of Hadot's most extended reflections on his post-Wittgensteinian interpretive methodology. If we are to understand the literary productions of the ancient philosophers, let alone seek out spiritual orientation in them, we must for Hadot first understand them in terms of the wider literary, institutional and cultural contexts which shaped their authors' intentions. It is a question, in Hadot's formulation, of studying philosophy in its 'totality', in which purview the student 'must consider the philosopher under three aspects: the philosopher living within his school, the philosopher living in the City, the philosopher living with himself (and with what transcends him)'.

This post-Wittgensteinian approach to ancient texts, situating them within historically specific 'forms of life', also saw Hadot throughout his career emphasizing the deep debts of ancient philosophical modes of writing and the predominantly oral, pedagogical nature of ancient philosophy. In anglophone thought, a stress on the proximity of ancient philosophy to forms of spoken teaching is associated most closely with the Cambridge School, and the work of Eric A. Havelock in particular.[34] This stress on philosophy as first of all an oral phenomenon in antiquity also brings Hadot's work into an explicit relationship with the predominant German-language School of Platonic interpretation of the last century: that of the Tübingen School led by the work of Hans Joachim Krämer and Konrad Gaiser on the 'unwritten' Platonic teaching, attested to in Aristotle and several other ancient sources and intimated in the *Seventh Letter*. Chapter 4 of this collection is, in fact, drawn from Hadot's 'Preface' to the first major French-language contribution to this school, Marie-Dominique Richard's *L'enseignement oral de Platon* (1986). In this piece, Hadot takes the opportunity to show the proximity of his approach to ancient texts, in general, to this way of trying to read Plato:

> For the ancient philosopher, at least beginning with the sophists and Socrates, proposes to form men and transform souls. This is why philosophical teaching is delivered, in antiquity, before all else in an oral form, because only living speech in dialogues, in conversations pursued over a long period of time, can accomplish any such work. The written work, however remarkable it may be, is, therefore, most of the time only an echo or a complement of this spoken teaching.

Alongside the relationship between Hadot's way of approaching ancient philosophy, finally, it is remarkable just how little scholarly engagement there has so far been with one further dimension to Hadot's work. This dimension, on the surface, could seem to speak most directly to contemporary concerns and debates. It is Hadot's career-long interest in the history of Western, philosophical understandings of nature. Its premier products are Hadot's last two books, first *Le Voile d'Isis*, published in 2004 (translation, 2008),[35] and then his final study on Goethe, *N'oublie pas de vivre: Goethe et la tradition des exercises spirituels* (2008).[36]

With the exception of reviews by Robert J. Dostal, Alan Kim, Peter Denton, Scott Samuelson, Neil Castree and Ian Hacking, *The Veil of Isis* (2008), for all its magisterial sweep of ancient, medieval and modern literature, has attracted little academic discussion.[37] Yet, this text, in particular, poses fruitful questions to readers: what exactly is the relationship between Hadot's works on Neoplatonism, on philosophy as a way of life in antiquity and beyond, and this work on the history of the philosophy of nature? What forces do its conclusions, notably including Hadot's unveiling of a contemplative, 'Orphic' counter-strain in Western philosophy, pulling against the predominant Promethean, instrumental approaches to nature, have for today's debates about the human relationship to the Anthropocene? Is it possible to conceive and reactivate an Orphic sense of nature today, and would not this seem to be an especially vital task if we are to restore a sustainable balance between human need and ambition and the natural world? It is with such questions in view that we first chose, and then had the pleasure to translate the essays, 'Ancient Man and Nature' (Chapter 8) and 'The Genius of Place in Ancient Greece' (Chapter 9).

Prospectus

The essays included in *The Selected Writings of Pierre Hadot: Philosophy as Practice* are very much, as the subtitle suggests, a selection. And it is worth underlining, before saying more, just how much of a 'selection' these fourteen essays represent, from a body of work of which well over half presently remains unavailable to English-language readers. If we think solely of the *L'Âne d'or* collections of Hadot's essays – and these three volumes themselves represent another, albeit much larger 'selection' of all of Hadot's published works, let alone his lectures – the entire volume of Hadot's essays on Neoplatonism remains untranslated into English, as well as the volume devoted to Patristic studies and the history of concepts.[38] Our selection features many of the pieces from the volume *Études de philosophie ancienne* (2010). Even so, it leaves some seven of eighteen of its essays untranslated.[39] One of our purposes was to make available several of the pieces from the French collection *Exercices spirituels* not included in *Philosophy as a Way of Life*, but which we thought were especially important, namely 'Conversion' (Chapter 5) and 'An Interrupted Dialogue with Michel Foucault: Convergences and Divergences' (Chapter 12). The 2014 Belles Lettres collection *Discours et mode de vie philosophique*, again, whilst containing many of the pieces we translate here, includes many more which remain untranslated into English at this time, including several on Marcus Aurelius, his times and *Meditations*.[40] The Vrin collection, *La philosophie comme éducation des adultes*, which appeared in 2019, contains a further twenty-five untranslated essays, presentations, reviews and interviews. In brief, other criteria, and other selections, than we present here would have been possible and legitimate for such a volume as this. Indeed, it is our earnest hope that a great deal more of Hadot's work will in the near future become available to anglophone audiences.

'My Books and my Research' (Chapter 1) takes its place at the head of the collection for the sake of readers who may be coming to Hadot's work through this collection for the first time. It translates a 1993 lecture, in which Hadot reflected briefly on the course of his career. As such, it provides a concise introduction for people new to his work.

As indicated above, Chapter 2 represents Hadot's 'Preface' to Richard Goulet's monumental, multi-volume, interdisciplinary *Dictionnaire des philosophes antiques* [*Dictionary of Ancient Philosophers*]. After the opening pages, in which Hadot describes and lauds the scope of Goulet's project, he uses the occasion to present one of his more direct, extended reflections on the methodology that governs his own approach to the study of ancient philosophy. As Goulet's *Dictionnaire* highlights, Hadot claims that many elements of ancient philosophy are too often passed over by historians of ideas which are, nevertheless, highly revelatory concerning the phenomena at issue. Thus, we should pay attention to the titles and genres of ancient philosophical writing, Hadot contends, since they differ from those of later modern forms of philosophical literature in revealing ways. Similarly, the doxographic lists of the many lost ancient philosophical works give us a valuable sense of ancient philosophy's vast scope, as well as the different, recurrent *topoi* that shaped philosophers' writings and teachings. A dedicated inventory of the different *questions* the ancients were addressing might also lead to a different sense of the history of philosophy, Hadot muses:

> a history of philosophy which would be a history of problems, which would identify all the questions that were posed by the philosophers of Antiquity, and which would ask why they were posed, under which form they [were posed], in what manner also the posing of the problems evolved.

Again, the ancient lists of the philosophers themselves, including many who never wrote a word or who never taught in a school, should make us pause to consider the social, institutional, pedagogical and oral dimensions of ancient philosophical discourse and practice. In the face of such doxographic testimony, Hadot contends, scholars need to be open to the possibility that, for the ancients, 'the concept of philosophy has a content wholly other than that which it has in the modern world'. We should likewise countenance the extent to which the ancients' concept of the *philosopher* was quite different from our own: above all, naming someone characterized by a distinctive mode or style of life who was trying to gain wisdom by adopting the principles of a specific school, and drawing from them precepts that could guide their everyday life. With such a view of the persona and activity of the philosopher in view, Hadot writes, it becomes imperative to consider ancient philosophy almost as what the great French anthropologist Marcel Mauss called a 'total social fact':[41]

to comprehend ancient philosophy, it will not suffice to analyse the structure of thought which is expressed, for example, in the dialogues of Plato or the writings of Aristotle. To this absolutely indispensable research, it would be necessary to add an effort to grasp the philosophical process in all of its lived reality, concrete and existential, in all of its dimensions, not solely literary but social, political, religious, institutional, juridical, geographical and anthropological.

The foundational importance of the text translated as Chapter 3, 'Ancient Philosophy: An Ethics or a Practice?' is signalled by Arnold I. Davidson in his important introductory essay to Hadot's *Philosophy as a Way of Life*.[42] Here we see Hadot reflecting directly on the research programme that led him to the central notion of 'spiritual exercises'. He also importantly considers the implications of his re-conception of ancient philosophy, involving such exercises, for our understanding of the role of theoretical systematization in ancient thought. The essay's second section develops the key distinction between philosophy as an activity and manner of life as against 'philosophical discourse': a distinction for which Hadot does not claim originality, rather tracing it back to Diogenes Laertius' account of Stoicism in book VII of *The Lives and Opinions of the Eminent Philosophers*. For the Stoics, Hadot claims, the theory–practice distinction did not divide logic and physics on the theoretical side from ethics, as the practical part of philosophy (a broadly Aristotelian schema, as per Chapter 6). Rather, there were 'practiced' forms of logic and physics, as much as of ethics. Each aimed to transform the knower, as well as revealing knowable things. The third part of this programmatic essay is of particular interest, insofar as it sees Hadot applying this sense of philosophy to the philosophies of Aristotle and Plato, before turning to Plotinus and Neoplatonism. Hadot stresses that even Aristotle's prioritization of the theoretical over the practical excellences in book X of the *Nicomachean Ethics* and elsewhere is precisely the valorization of a theoretical *form of life*, characterized by a maximum of contemplative *activity*, over against other possible endeavours.[43] Even in Aristotle, ancient philosophy took aim at the pursuit of a distinct form of life, and a lived *sophia*.

Chapter 4, 'The Oral Teaching of Plato' is Hadot's 'Preface' to Richard's *L'enseignement oral de Platon* (1986). It carries forward from Chapter 2 Hadot's general methodological reflections, once more allowing readers both a better perspective on Hadot's relationship to other schools of interpreting the ancients, and a more developed picture of the bases of his own approach to ancient thought. Until Richard's book appeared, Hadot reflects, 'there did not exist in French language any means of access to the theories relating to Plato's oral teachings' of the Tübingen School, led by Hans Krämer and Konrad Gaiser. Hadot finds highly congenial the Tübingen scholars' way of reading Plato informed by ancient, external testimony concerning the different aspects and levels of his teaching, as well as by Plato's own comments on the status of writing. This approach, for all the methodological and hermeneutic questions it provokes, seems to him to speak to the need to understand Platonic philosophy 'as a phenomenon which engages the whole of human life', an insight in light of which 'one is forced to study this phenomenon in all its concrete aspects'.

Of course, to directly engage with and interpret Plato's specific teachings, as they are presented in the different dialogues and letters, must remain central in Platonic studies. Yet, as he also does in Chapter 3, Hadot takes time here to distance his hermeneutic approach, with Krämer's, Richard's et al.'s, from the structural method of Goldschmidt, which he charges with erroneously looking at the ancient written texts as more or less self-sufficient documents. For Hadot, Goldschmidt is mistaken to suppose that ancient writings can be analysed in isolation from the other social, institutional and pedagogical dimensions of ancient philosophy. For the ancient texts were first of all 'living speech', the teaching of a concrete philosopher to specific students, only written down so as to again ideally become the basis of a future oral reading and pedagogical experience. Writing, as Jacques Derrida has stressed, was, indeed, considered a dangerous supplement to spoken dialogue on this ancient model.[44] This is why, as both the Tübingen and Straussian Schools of Platonic scholarship have taught in the last century, Platonic and other ancient writing was generally esoteric in nature: with external messages for the untrained, interlaced with intimations of more serious, difficult or controversial teachings for those interested and capable of discerning these.[45] We should read Plato's dialogues, Hadot says here, as 'only one aspect of Plato's philosophical activity, and they demand to be' clarified by all that we know of Plato's activity as the head of [the] school', as well as by all that we can glean concerning the pedagogical activities of the school from the testimony its pupils, like Aristotle, and other sources. Only then will we be in a position to fully evaluate Plato's teachings. The same considerations ought also to govern our reception of the works of the other ancient schools.

Part 2 of the collection examines three key 'features' of Hadot's vision of the ancient philosophies: first, his understanding of the 'conversion' at stake in adopting a philosophical way of life in antiquity (Chapter 5); second, his longstanding interest in the different divisions of the parts of philosophy in antiquity (Chapter 6); and third, his vital account of the relationships between philosophy, rhetoric and dialectic in the ancient schools (Chapter 7). As we have indicated, the essays of this part of the collection, above all, can be read today as addressing 'in advance' several of the criticisms that have been made of Hadot's and related works by figures like Nussbaum, Inwood and Cooper.

In Chapter 5, 'Conversion', Hadot distinguishes different forms of conversion in the Western heritage, associated with Greek terms *epistrophê* (meaning a return to an origin or to oneself) and *metanoia* (meaning a change in thought or even repentance). If Hadot's critics claim that he collapses philosophy and revealed religion, this text furnishes direct textual evidence to counter such claims. Hadot maintains that both philosophy and supernaturalistic religions in the premodern world aimed to actualize forms of psychological, existential or, indeed, spiritual transformation in their votaries. Yet, the means, as well as the conceptions of the goal at stake in such conversions, differed. It is not the same kind of thing to 'convert' to a life of philosophy in an ancient school, as to 'convert' to an evangelical religion. Hadot's essay is, in addition, fascinating in its clear-sighted examination of the competing manners in which the different forms of conversion have been conceived and studied in modern historical, sociological and psychological approaches.

In Chapter 6, 'The Divisions of the Parts of Philosophy in Antiquity', the extent of Hadot's continuing engagement with the theoretical dimensions of ancient philosophy is writ large. This chapter, above all, suggests a need for care before we set up an either–or conception of Hadot's renewed attention to the existential dimensions of ancient philosophy, in terms of how it relates to ongoing attempts to understand the ancient philosophical writings and their theoretical claims. Only the third of three kinds of divisions of the parts of philosophy this essay considers (namely, the hierarchical, Platonic–Aristotelian division, the organic Stoic division, and the pedagogical divisions) approximates to what we might imagine Hadot's exclusive focus to have been, as the famous theorist of philosophy as a way of life: namely, a focus on the formation of students, as against the systematic analysis and synthesis of concepts. Both the hierarchical and the organic divisions of the parts of philosophy, Hadot instead shows, responded directly to competing theoretical and ontological visions of the Whole. Neither division was framed with primary regard to questions of how the parts of philosophy might be taught, or their discoveries integrated into a regimen of spiritual practices. For this reason, there is clear doxographic evidence of disagreements in the Stoic School especially as to which parts of philosophy (physics, logic or ethics) should be taught first or last.

Chapter 7, 'Philosophy, Dialectic and Rhetoric in Antiquity', represents invaluable testimony concerning Hadot's vision of the pedagogical life of the schools itself, answering his own call for such studies in Chapter 2. As its title suggests, the essay examines in close detail the relationships between rhetoric, dialectic and philosophy in the different ancient schools, from the classical through to the imperial periods. Yet, as with Chapter 6, the picture which emerges from this chapter is much more nuanced, and much closer to more 'traditional' accounts of the history of ancient philosophy than the criticisms of Hadot might lead us to expect.[46] After considering in detail the different understandings and evaluations of dialectic and rhetoric in Plato and Aristotle, Hadot sets up the following *divisio*, which structures the rest of this dense essay:

> Dialectic can be a pedagogical or school exercise, and Aristotle formulated the rules of this exercise in the eighth book of the *Topics*. Dialectic and rhetoric can also be a method for the teaching of philosophy. And finally, both dialectic and rhetoric can be a constitutive part of philosophy, as subdivisions of logic.

Without having the space here to examine this chapter in the detail it deserves, we merely note that, as it proceeds, there is no simple devaluation of dialectic, and therefore 'rigorous rational argumentation', in Hadot's conception of the pedagogical and wider pursuits of the ancient philosophers. On the contrary, as the essay concludes:

> Even when it was combined with rhetoric, dialectic was no less dominant in the whole of ancient philosophy than rhetoric. We were able to note the importance of the 'question–answer' schema in philosophical teaching, involving either replying to a question by means of a continuous discourse or, on the contrary, by means of questioning dialogically . . . In general, . . . [e]ach work seeks to respond coherently to a given question, to a very precise problem . . . The coherence is situated within the limits of the dialogue between 'question' and 'answer'.[47]

Part 3, 'Nature', contains two revealing essays which reflect Hadot's lifelong research on the history of Western conceptions of the natural world. Their inclusion (as above) hence responds to the comparative dearth of critical responses to this important dimension of Hadot's *oeuvre*. Chapter 8, 'Ancient Man and Nature', provides readers with a glimpse of that other Hadot, author of *Le Voile d'Isis*, who worked continuously on Western conceptions of nature, from the 1960s until his last book on Goethe, which appeared in 2008. Here, we see Hadot working towards what would become in *Le Voile* the distinction between a 'Promethean' attitude towards nature – which tries to wrest nature's secrets from her in order to put them to human use – and what would become, in the 2004 work, the 'Orphic' attitude, which 'consists in contemplating nature as it is: that is to say, of describing it through language, but also of living "according to nature", in an attitude of respect and even of submission'. There is a limpid beauty in this essay that might alone have justified its inclusion, even were it not heavy with a wonderful profusion of citations, anecdotes and *aperçus*, which once more evidence Hadot's quietly understated but extraordinary erudition. We can also remark, as the essay proceeds into consideration of the philosophical sources, the deep intersections Hadot saw between the ancient vision of philosophy as involving a conversion of students' ways of being, and the cultivation of transformed ways of seeing the natural world:

> It is the result of an inner effort, of a spiritual exercise designed to overcome the habitude which make our way of seeing the world banal and mechanical. This exercise aims also to detach us from all interest, egotism or worry which prevent us from seeing the world as it is, because they constrain us to focus our attention upon particular objects in which we find pleasure and utility. It is, on the contrary, by an effort of concentration on the present instant, and living each moment as if it were at the same time our very first or our last, without thinking of the future or the past, awake to the instant's unique and irreplaceable character, that one can perceive, in this instant, the marvellous presence of the world [see Chapter 11].

Chapter 9, 'The Genius of Place in Ancient Greece', can be read as a smaller companion piece to Chapter 8, 'Ancient Man and Nature'. This marvellous little meditation addresses itself to the more specific question of how the ancients understood the Sacred in relation to geographical and spiritual space. The essay begins, 'The first sacred place in Antiquity is the "home", that is to say, the hearth of the house; not the fire of the kitchen, but the sacred altar where the fire consecrated to the gods smoulders continually'. The essay goes on to look at ancient festivals and places of pilgrimage: sacred sites led by Delphi or Delos which remained consecrated to a god or gods over several millennia, continuing to attract crowds of worshippers, tourists, theatre goers and participants in games and festivals. Sanctuaries like Eleusis became associated with specific forms of religious experience, and the first half of Hadot's essay culminates with a consideration of the higher *epopteia* experienced by initiates at Eleusis. By contrast, the piece's second part moves from geographical to spiritual considerations, and from poetic and religious to philosophical sources. The whole ends with a vivid description of the Platonic 'flight of the soul': a turn inwards, which, nevertheless, opens the eye of the soul to the full grandeur of the universe, as if seen from above,[48] and which Hadot presents as the philosophical transformation of the Eleusinian *epopteia*:

> This is the highest summit of the initiation involved in what one could call the mysteries of the spiritual Eleusis. In the mystical experience no less than at Eleusis one does not learn something, but one lives another life: the self is no longer itself, it has become the absolute Other; it no longer knows who it is, nor where it is, and furthermore, Plotinus remarks, it is no longer situated anywhere, but it is carried so far that it is beyond all place, outside of self and of everything.

Part 4, 'Figures', looks at Hadot's engagement with three key figures. Chapter 10, 'The Figure of the Sage in Greek and Roman Antiquity', is an essay of the highest importance in Hadot's *oeuvre*. It arguably features Hadot at his very best, interweaving close scholarly analysis and the lyrical strains present in the two essays on nature of Part 3. As the title announces, 'The Figure of the Sage' looks at ancient accounts of wisdom (*sophia*) in the representations we find across the different ancient schools of the figure of the ideally wise human being or 'sage'. The sage, Hadot tells us here, in a threefold division we can also find elsewhere (see Chapter 12), is a figure who has attained complete inner freedom (*autarkeia*) and tranquillity (*ataraxia, apatheia*), as well as being constantly aware of the nature of, and of his place within, the wider Whole, achieving what Hadot calls a *conscience cosmique*. In the extraordinary final paragraphs of this chapter, we also glimpse a Hadot who, for a moment, steps out from behind the immunity of the commentator, concluding in the first person as follows:

> Above all, this figure of the sage is somehow ineluctable, or so it seems to me. It is a necessary expression of the tension, polarity or duality inherent in the human condition. On one hand, the human being has need, in order to accept his condition, of being integrated into the fabric of social and political organization as well as into the reassuring, comfortable and familiar world of everyday life. But this sphere of everyday life does not entirely enclose us: we are confronted in an inevitable way with what one could call the ineffable, the terrifying enigma of existence, here and now, given over to death, in the immensity

of the cosmos. To become conscious of the self and of the existence of the world is a revelation which breaks open the security of the habitual and the everyday. The ordinary man seeks to elude this experience of the ineffable which seems to him void, absurd or terrifying. Others dare to face it. For them, it is, on the contrary, everyday life which seems empty and abnormal. The figure of the sage responds, therefore, to an indispensable need: that of unifying the interior life of the human being. The sage will be the individual capable of living on two planes: perfectly inserted into everyday life, like Pyrrho, and yet plunged into the cosmos; dedicated to the service of others, and yet perfectly free in his inner life; aware and, nevertheless, at peace; forgetting nothing of the essential and unique; and, finally and above all, faithful to the heroism and to the purity of the moral conscience, without which life no longer merits being lived. This is what the philosopher must try to realize.

Chapter 11, 'Physics as Spiritual Exercise, or Pessimism and Optimism in Marcus Aurelius' translates Hadot's first published article (of 1972) on a figure who would become progressively more central to his work on ancient philosophy: the Stoic philosopher-emperor Marcus Aurelius. This vital article is also amongst the first in which Hadot introduced the key term 'spiritual exercises'. And, although the distinction between lived forms of ethics, logic and physics would await 1978 and 'Une clé des *Pensées* de Marc Aurèle: Les trois *topoi* philosophiques selon Épictète', we already meet here Hadot's account of Stoic physics as implicating a certain spiritual regimen. Hadot focuses in this crucial piece on the Stoic exercises of dividing and defining the physical things that we see according to Stoic categories, in this process denuding them of the emotive and conventional value judgements with which people burden them. At stake is achieving a vivid sense of what Stoic theory describes as the 'indifference' of external things. Hadot is at pains, however, to distinguish sharply this indifference from any idea of 'not caring' for the world, or savouring its presence:

> It consists in not introducing a difference; it is the equanimity of the soul and not any lack of interest or attachment. Indifferent things are not without interest for the sage. On the contrary – and this is the principal benefit of the method of 'physical' definition – from the moment when the sage has discovered that indifferent things do not depend on human will, but on the will of universal Nature, they become infinitely interesting for him. He accepts them with love, but all of them with an equal love. He finds them beautiful, but all with the same admiration.

We know that Michel Foucault greatly admired Hadot's 'Physics as a Spiritual Exercise' (1972). The latter became one source of his own reading of Marcus in *The Hermeneutics of the Subject* (2005). Chapter 12 of the collection, on Hadot's reading of Foucault, hence follows 'Physics' naturally. It presents for the first time in English Hadot's first essay on his personal and intellectual relationship with the better known French philosopher: 'An Interrupted Dialogue with Michel Foucault: Convergences and Divergences'. Here, as in the later piece on this dialogue translated in *Philosophy as a Way of Life*, Hadot takes issue with the Foucaultian notion of an ancient 'aesthetics of existence', insisting on the specifically moral dimension present even in the ancient Greek term *kalon*, and drawing our attention to the relative absence in Foucault's work of engagement with ancient notions of *wisdom* – including the threefold division we met in Chapter 7, between:

> peace of mind (*ataraxia*), inner freedom (*autarkeia*) and, except in the sceptics, cosmic consciousness: that is to say, the process of becoming aware of belonging to the human and cosmic Whole, a sort of dilation or transfiguration of the self which realizes greatness of soul (*megalopsychia*).

Whilst the central parts of this brief essay emphasize these differences with Foucault, it is telling that Hadot both opens and closes the chapter by remarking the two thinkers' proximities. Hadot also stresses their shared sense of ancient thought's continuing force and relevance in the later modern world. As Hadot concludes: 'I consider it as a sign of the times – striking and unexpected in my eyes – that at the end of the twentieth century, Michel Foucault, myself and certainly many others, at the conclusions of totally different trajectories, came together in this vital rediscovery of ancient experience.'

Part 5, 'Ends', begins with 'The End of Paganism' (Chapter 13). This is at once the longest essay in the collection, and a piece which stands out also as the most historical of the chapters – thereby underscoring yet another dimension of Hadot's diverse intellectual output. We include this long piece especially since 'The End of Paganism' so squarely addresses another question which Hadot's understanding of ancient philosophy inescapably prompts readers to ask: *Just when, why and how did this cultural and intellectual phenomenon come to an end?* As several of Hadot's critics have stressed, Hadot began his career working on late antiquity, working for much of his earlier career on the Christian Neoplatonist and rhetorician Marius Victorinus, and Plotinus' pupil, Porphyry. 'The End of Paganism', in an extraordinary panorama, surveys the political, social, psychological, theological and philosophical phenomena that characterized the centuries after Marcus Aurelius, leading to Justinian's eventual closure of the last philosophical school in Athens in 529 CE.

There is, however, a second reason for our inclusion of 'The End of Paganism', leaving aside the intrinsic interest of a learned study of this extraordinary period of social and intellectual history. This reason is that Hadot again shows himself in this long essay as in no way the advocate of any kind of collapse of philosophy into revealed religion, theurgy or magic, such as we find in the Neoplatonists after Iamblichus – and such as Cooper's criticisms of Hadot might lead readers to suppose. Indeed, '[o]ne is surprised to find such credulity, naivety and superstition amongst men who, otherwise, were remarkable logicians and metaphysicians', Hadot tells us here, speaking of the later ancient Neoplatonists. If Christianity had not emerged to reshape the later ancient world, Hadot's essay concludes, the philosophy of the end of antiquity would have increasingly taken on its suprarational dimensions, and ceased being specifically 'philosophical' in the senses we still recognize.

The collection closes with Chapter 14, 'Models of Happiness Proposed by the Ancient Philosophers', another of Hadot's lucid but recondite essays, on the eudaimonism of the competing ancient philosophies. We see here again, as in the Chapter 10 on the figure of the sage, the proximity between ancient philosophical conceptions of the best life and apparently theological considerations. The essay is especially fitting as a concluding text, insofar as its closing section also addresses a further question which critics often address to any notion of philosophical self-cultivation, let alone Hadot's specific contributions to this field. This is the question of whether any such pursuit must not necessarily be an exercise in egotism, in the radically imperfect world in which we find ourselves. 'Let us start with the simplest point,' Hadot commences his reply: 'It is evident that, the Stoics, for whom happiness is found in a moral good which involves, as constitutive parts, the dedication to the life of the community, the practice of justice and love towards other men, cannot be presented in this way.' Hadot's vision of Stoicism, we cannot forget, involves forms of lived or practiced ethics as one of its constitutive parts. And this ethics enshrines the virtues of justice and benevolence towards others. But the Epicurean valorization of friendship, and each of the Hellenistic and Roman Schools' 'missionary' commitments to converting new philosophers also speak for Hadot against any facile equation of the pursuit of wisdom in ancient philosophy with a narcissistic glorying in the 'I' (*moi*), disregarding all others. Notably reprising a theme we find also in Chapter 10 on the figure of the sage, Hadot instead stresses that what is most deeply at stake in the ancient 'love of wisdom' is the search not to enhance, but to transform and *overcome* the ego. It is a matter of striving to attain to greatness of soul, the universal rational core of one's being, or the view from above. As Hadot comments, in a gentle understatement: 'One cannot qualify such an experience as "egoistic".'

On the translations

It is an uncanny moment for translators when they encounter, in the work of an author whom they are translating, a reflection on the strict impossibility of the task of translation. This is a moment which the translators have, nevertheless, experienced, when we read in Hadot's 'Jeux de langage et philosophie' (1960 [1962]) the following reflections:

> We can thus never completely understand a philosophy expressed in a foreign language, above all because it belongs to a linguistic system which is extremely different from our own. Yet, at the same time, it reveals to us a vision of the universe which is absolutely different from our own and which serves to complete our own perspective. This is why the translator must do violence to his own language in order to introduce the distinct traits of the other language into it. And here we are confronted with an impassable limit on the way to clarity and understanding.[49]

Anyone who has ventured to translate a text, let alone a philosophical text, will feel the full force of Hadot's observations here. Even in two languages as closely related as French is to English, with overlapping lexica, there are strictly untranslatable idiomatic expressions and constructions, together with verbs, nouns or even prepositions whose extensions have no direct English equivalents. Again and again as we have proceeded, and experimented with what we termed more or less 'literal' ways of translating Hadot's sentences, we have been confronted with what Hadot calls here the 'violence' (we talked more often of unavoidable 'choices', 'options' or 'decisions') which we found ourselves being forced to introduce in order to convey what we take to have been Hadot's intentions. In truth, as many linguists and philosophers have commented, the very idea of a literal one-to-one translation is at a certain level chimerical. There are only a finite number of different, more or less 'imperfect' translations, whose relative semantic, aesthetic and stylistic values can be weighed on several scales.

We hope, nevertheless, that we have, if not breached, then pushed against Hadot's 'impassable limit' in our efforts to make these *Selected Writings* available for the first time to an anglophone readership. The general simplicity and clarity of Hadot's prose, notably in the chapters on the sage, the ancients and nature, and the models of happiness, have greatly assisted us in this endeavour. To the extent we have succeeded, moreover, it is because we have been able to stand on the shoulders of giants. Michael Chase's translations of Hadot's texts, from beginning to end, have stood as the model, and sometimes as the intimidating ideal, for all our efforts. Chase's translations of Hadot's work are themselves models of simplicity and elegance in English, as many of Hadot's texts are in French. Moreover, they seem to us to well convey what it is as inevitable as it is unsatisfactory to call the 'spirit' of the original in the new language. Accordingly, where Chase has translated Hadot's translations of Greek and Latin texts, notably in Chapter 11 on Marcus Aurelius, we have followed these translations to the letter. Where Hadot uses distinctive formulations, like *conscience cosmique*, we have sought out and followed his advice, as well as his example.

We have also benefited enormously from the generosity of Ilsetraut Hadot, Pierre Hadot's wife and herself an extraordinary scholar of ancient Stoic and classical thought, to whom we humbly dedicate this volume. Although nearly ninety years old, she looked over more than half of the chapters between 2017 and 2018, offering line-by-line reflections and critique. Any virtues which the final text has will then reflect the meticulous attention to detail and love that she has brought to this task. We cannot be too grateful to her for her acuity, attention and assistance.

Our method has always been to begin with as 'literal' a translation as possible (the above provisos accepted). As we proceeded, we then noted strictly 'untranslatable' moments in the text for a discussion between the two of us which in some cases has continued, on and off, over many months and across three continents. From early on in the process, it was agreed that in all cases involving any degree of 'choice' in translating, we would offer the reader the extensive 'translator's notes' that they will find at the foot of most pages, which include the original French expression for the reader's consideration.

The greatest more or less technical translation issue we faced concerns Hadot's distinction, found in Chapter 3, between *théorique*, an adjective qualifying a kind of discourse or way of thinking, and *théorétique*, a term Hadot uses to describe a particular form of life: *viz.* that of the Aristotelian, devoted to the contemplative pursuits of the *bios theorêtikos*. We thank Ilsetraut Hadot for her invaluable advice on this matter, as well again as Michael Chase, whose solution of proposing 'theoretic' for Hadot's *théorique*, and 'theoretical' for Hadot's *théorétique* we have employed in the paragraphs on Aristotle. In this case, we have placed the French words in brackets within the text, so the reader can understand the stake of introducing the unusual term 'theoretic' in this context. The only other place where we put Hadot's original French in brackets is in Chapter 10, where we mark Hadot's uses of the two 'knowledge'-terms, *savoir* and *connaissance*. We did this, given their evident importance in this essay on the figure of the 'sage' or 'wise man', someone whose superlative virtue(s) are related directly to his claims to specific forms of knowledge.

In some cases, we have elected to divide Hadot's longer, more difficult sentences into shorter, simpler English sentences. In doing this, we have aimed in all cases to be scrupulously attentive, so that this process did not have the effect of distorting Hadot's meanings in the attempt to make them clearer. In all cases, the paragraph divisions of our translations reproduce those in Hadot's originals, with the caveat that, in line with an anglophone convention, quotations of over two lines in length we have separated from the body of the text.[50] Where Hadot capitalizes terms for emphasis, like 'the Moon' and 'the Sun' in his description of the Platonic flight of the soul in Chapter 9, we have reproduced his capitalizations. In the cases of Chapters 6 and 11, wherein Hadot's texts are clearly divided into different sections marked in the originals, we have added section subheadings in square brackets. Similarly, in cases where we have, in effect, added English words to make a sentence and its thought(s) parse more readily in English, these words are placed in square brackets.

Remerciements, finally, are due to Dr Chris Pollard for his assistance in the process of editing the text and the footnotes, and to Associate Professor Russell Grigg for his advice on several of the more difficult sentences, notably in Chapter 11. We thank Arnold I. Davidson also for his counsel and advice at various stages of the process. We also thank Daniele Lorenzini for his efforts and enthusiasm for this project, as well as Frédéric Gros for liaising with Gallimard. I would very much like to thank my co-translator, Dr Federico Testa. Translation is, if not a spiritual exercise, then a school of patience, and one in which, like all schools, pupils can sometimes fall short, so that a good part of the process consists in returning and beginning again. Without Federico's exhortations and persistence, as well as his diligence and patience, this volume would not have been possible.

Notes

1   See also the recently published Pierre Hadot, *Philosophie comme éducation des adultes* (Paris: Vrin, 2019).

2   Pierre Hadot, *The Present Alone is Our Happiness*, trans. by Marc Djebillah and Michael Chase (Stanford, CA: Stanford University Press, 2011, 2nd

edn), 87. See Pierre Hadot, 'Spiritual exercises', in *Philosophy as a Way of Life*, trans. by Michael Chase (London: Wiley-Blackwell, 1995), 79–125.

3   Pierre Hadot, 'Heidegger et Plotin', *Critique* 145 (Juin 1959): 339–56.

4   Pierre Hadot, *Plotinus, or the Simplicity of Regard*, trans. by Michael Chase (Chicago, IL: University of Chicago Press, 1996).

5   See Chapter 1 below, 'My Books and My Research'.

6   Pierre Hadot, *Philosophy as a Way of Life*, trans. by Chase; Hadot, *The Inner Citadel: On the* Meditations *of Marcus Aurelius*, trans. by Michael Chase (Cambridge, MA, and London: Harvard University Press, 1998); and Hadot, *What is Ancient Philosophy?*, trans. by Michael Chase (Cambridge, MA: Harvard University Press, 2002).

7   Hadot, *Present Alone*, 59.

8   For a sample of work in the history of ideas that draws from Hadot, see Stephen Gaukroger, *Francis Bacon and the Transformation of Early-Modern Philosophy* (Cambridge: Cambridge University Press, 2001); Peter Harrison, *Territories of Science and Religion* (Chicago, IL: University of Chicago Press, 2014); Sorana Corneanu, *Regimens of the Mind* (Chicago, IL: University of Chicago Press, 2011); Christopher S. Celenza, 'What counted as philosophy in the Italian Renaissance? The history of philosophy, the history of science, and styles of life', *Critical Inquiry* 39, no. 2 (2013): 367–401; John Sellars, '*De Constantia*: A Stoic spiritual exercise', *Poetics Today* 28, no. 3 (2007): 339–62; Wayne J. Hankey, 'Philosophy as way of life for Christians? Iamblichan and Porphyrian reflections on religion, virtue, and philosophy in Thomas Aquinas', *Laval Théologique et Philosophique* 59, no. 2 [*Le Néoplatonisme*] (Juin 2003): 193–224; Ian Hunter, *Rival Enlightenments: Civil and Metaphysical Philosophy in Early Modern Germany* (Cambridge: Cambridge University Press, 2001).

9   Juliusz Domański, *La Philosophie, théorie ou manière de vivre?: Les controverses de l'Antiquité à la Renaissance*, avec une préface de Pierre Hadot (Fribourg, Suisse: Editions Universitaires, and Paris: Cerf presses universitaires, 1996).

10   Michael Chase Stephen R. L. Clark and Michael McGhee (eds), *Philosophy as a Way of Life: Ancients and Moderns – Essays in Honor of Pierre Hadot* (London: John Wiley, 2013).

11   David Fiordalis (ed.), *Buddhist Spiritual Practices: Thinking with Pierre Hadot on Buddhism, Philosophy, and the Path* (Berkeley, CA: Mangalam, 2018).

12   See also Hadot's '"Préface" to Yoko Orimo's translation of the *Shôbôgenzô of Dogen*', in *Philosophie comme éducation des adultes*, 239–46, which Hadot wrote after Orimo approached him, adducing comparisons between Dogen's thought and ancient Western thinkers.

13 See Pierre Hadot, 'Une clé des *Pensées* de Marc Aurèle: Les trois *topoi* philosophiques selon Épictète', in *Exercises Spirituels*, 2nd edn (Paris: Albin Michel, 2002 [1978]), 165–92.

14 See http://www.traditionalstoicism.com (accessed 27 July 2019).

15 Hadot, *Philosophy as a Way of Life*, trans. by Chase, 280.

16 Hadot, *Philosophy as a Way of Life*, trans. by Chase, 121.

17 Hadot, *Present Alone*, 147; cf. Hadot, *Philosophy as a Way of Life*, trans. by Chase, 285. On Hadot's esotericism, see Matthew J. Sharpe, 'Socratic ironies: Reading Hadot, reading Kierkegaard', *Sophia* 55 (2016): 409–35.

18 See Ilsetraut Hadot, 'La figure du guide spirituel dans l'antiquité', in Hadot, *Philosophie comme éducation des adultes*, 323–60.

19 See Martha Nussbaum, *Therapy of Desire* (Princeton, NJ: Princeton University Press, 1993), 5–6, 373. Foucault's work on the Hellenistic philosophers, Nussbaum claims, 'fails to confront the fundamental commitment to reason that divides philosophical *techniques du soi* from other such techniques'. See Bernard Williams, 'Do Not Disturb', *London Review of Books* 16, no. 20 (October 1994), 25–6 (on Nussbaum's defence of philosophy as therapeutic).

20 See Matthew J. Sharpe, 'What place discourse, what role rigorous argumentation? Against the standard image of Hadot's conception of ancient philosophy as a way of life', *Pli* (2016): 25–54; and Sharpe, 'How it's not the Chrysippus you read: on Cooper, Hadot, Epictetus, and Stoicism as a way of life', *Philosophy Today* 58, no. 3 (2014): 367–92.

21 John M. Cooper, *Pursuits of Wisdom: Six Ways of Life in Ancient Philosophy from Socrates to Plotinus* (Princeton, NJ: Princeton University Press, 2012), esp. 17–22, 402–3 n. 4–5. Compare Brad Inwood, 'Review of John Sellars, *The Art of Living: the Stoics on the Nature and Function of Philosophy*', *Notre Dame Philosophical Reviews* 2004.04.04, available at: www-site https://ndpr.nd.edu/news/23760-the-art-of-living-the-stoics-on-the-nature-and-function-of-philosophy/ (accessed November 2015); also Inwood, 'Introduction', in Lucius Annaeus Seneca, *Selected Philosophical Letters*, Clarendon Later Ancient Philosophers (Oxford: Oxford University Press, 2010), esp. xv; Valentin Mureşan, 'Filosofia ca mod de viaţâ sau despre relaţia filosofie-biografi', *Revista de Filosofie Analiticâ* 4, no. 20 (Iulie–Decembrie 2010), 87–114.

22 See Inwood, 'Review of John Sellars'.

23 See Thomas Flynn, 'Philosophy as a way of life: Foucault and Hadot', *Philosophy and Social Criticism* 31, nos. 5–6 (2005): esp. 616–18; Thomas Bénatouïl, 'Stoicism and Twentieth Century French Philosophy', *Routledge Handbook of the Stoic Tradition*, ed. by J. Sellars (London: Routledge, 2015), 541–62; and John M. Cooper, 'Socrates and philosophy as a way of life', in

Maieusis: Essays in Ancient Philosophy in Honour of Myles Burnyeat, ed. by Dominic Scott (Oxford: Oxford University Press), 20–42.

24 See again Flynn, 'Philosophy as a way of life'.

25 See Matthew Lamb, 'Philosophy as a Way of Life: Albert Camus and Pierre Hadot', *Sophia* 50 (2011): 561–76. When Hadot tells us that ancient philosophy in the different schools involved spiritual exercises or forms of *ascesis*, this at most for Cooper describes philosophy in its late antique decline, once it had undergone a fatal 'contamination . . . by religion' in neoPlatonic, then Christian, thought. See Cooper, *Pursuits*, 22.

26 See Sharpe, 'What place discourse?'

27 Orazio Irrera, 'Pleasure and transcendence of the self: Notes on "a dialogue too soon interrupted" between Michel Foucault and Pierre Hadot', *Philosophy and Social Criticism* 36, no. 9 (2010): 995–1017.

28 Irrera, 'Pleasure and transcendence of the self', 1016.

29 See Hadot, '"Only the present is our happiness": The value of the present instant in Goethe and ancient philosophy', in *Philosophy as a Way of Life*, 217–37. Hadot thinks the present ethically, not ontologically. He might well accede to the Heideggerian idea that our ability to perceive present things meaningfully is temporally overdetermined. But how we evaluate what we meaningfully perceive, relative to what we can control and change, invites a different set of reflections.

30 Hadot, *Present Alone*, 35–6.

31 See the expanded French-language version: Ilsetraut Hadot, *Sénèque: Direction spirituelle et pratique de la philosophie* (Paris: Vrin, 2014); and also her 'Épicure et l'enseignement philosophique Hellénistique et Romain', *Actes de VIIIe Congrès de L'Association Guillaume Budé* (Paris: Vrin, 1969), 347–53. As the endnotes to the chapters here underscore, Hadot remained deeply immersed in all of the French-, English- and German-language scholarship on ancient thought, principally including the scholarship on Platonism and later antiquity.

32 Pierre Hadot, 'Jeux de langage et philosophie', R*evue de Métaphysique et de Morale* 67, no. 3 (1960 [1962]): 330–43. This has been remarked too little, excluding from this consideration the invaluable article by Pierre Force, 'In the teeth of time: Pierre Hadot on meaning and misunderstanding in the history of ideas', *History and Theory* 50, no. 1 (2011): 20–40.

33 Hadot, *Present Alone*, 135.

34 Whom Hadot duly cites in Chapter 4 below: see Eric A. Havelock, *Aux origines de la civilisation écrite en Occident*, trans. by E. Escobar Moreno (Paris: Maspero, 1981).

35 See Pierre Hadot, *The Veil of Isis: An Essay on the History of the Idea of Nature*, trans. by Michael Chase (Cambridge, MA: Belknap Press of Harvard University Press, 2006).

36 Pierre Hadot, *N'oublie pas de vivre: Goethe et la tradition des exercises spirituels* (Paris: Éditions Albin Michel, 2008). See Matthew J. Sharpe, 'To not forget: Pierre Hadot's last book on Goethe: Pierre Hadot, *N'oublie pas de vivre: Pas de vivre: Goethe et la tradition des exercises spirituels* (Albin Michel, 2008)', *Parrhesia: A Journal of Critical Philosophy* 15, no. 22 (2015): 106–17.

37 See Robert J. Dostal, 'Pierre Hadot, *The Veil of Isis: An Essay on the History of the Idea of Nature*, Originally published as *Le Voile d'Isis: Essai sur l'histoire de l'idée de Nature* (Paris: Gallimard, 2004)', *Bryn Mawr Classical Review* 2007.03.25; Alan Kim, 'Pierre Hadot, *The Veil of Isis: An Essay on the History of the Idea of Nature*', *Notre Dame Philosophical Review*, available at: https://ndpr.nd.edu/news/the-veil-of-isis-an-essay-on-the-history-of-the-idea-of-nature/ (accessed 4 May 2016); Peter H. Denton, 'Review of *The Veil of Isis: An Essay on the History of the Idea of Nature*', *Essays in Philosophy* 12, no. 2 (2011): 363–71; Neil Castree, 'Review in brief: *The Veil of Isis: An Essay on the History of the Idea of Nature*, by Pierre Hadot, translated by Michael Chase', *Cultural Geographies* 14, no. 3 (2007): 477–8; Ian Hacking, 'Almost Zero', *London Review of Books* 29, no. 9 (10 May 2007): 29–30.

38 Pierre Hadot, *Plotin, Porphyre: Études Néoplatoniciennes* (Paris: Belles Lettres, 2010); and *Études de patristique et d'histoire des concepts* (Paris: Belles Lettres, 2010).

39 Pierre Hadot, *Études de philosophie ancienne* (Paris: Belles Lettres, 2010).

40 Pierre Hadot, *Discours et mode de vie philosophique* (Paris: Belles Lettres, 2014).

41 See Marcel Mauss, *The Gift: The Form and Reason for Exchange in Archaic Societies* (London: W.W. Norton, 1990).

42 Arnold I. Davidson, 'Introduction: Pierre Hadot and the spiritual phenomenon of ancient philosophy', in *Philosophy as a Way of Life*, 1–46.

43 For a contrasting opinion, see John Sellars, 'What is philosophy as a way of life?', *Parrhesia* 28 (2017), 40–56.

44 *Viz.*, on the one hand, it assists memory, and can allow the philosopher to speak to unforeseen others across time and space. On the other hand, and as such, it can come to serve as a substitute for memory, as well as generating myriad erroneous interpretations across different audiences. See Jacques Derrida, 'Plato's Pharmacy', in Jacques Derrida, *Dissemination*, trans. by B. Johnson. Chicago, IL: University of Chicago Press, 1981), 61–3.

45 See Leo Strauss, *Persecution and the Art of Writing* (Chicago, IL: University of Chicago Press, 1948).

46 See Sharpe, 'What place discourse?'

47 And, as above, see Chapter 2 on the place of the questions shaping ancient texts in Hadot's sense of ancient philosophy.

48 Cf. Hadot, 'The view from above', in *Philosophy as a Way of Life*, 240–3.

49 Hadot, 'Jeux de langage', 339.

50 This, even when, as in Chapter 13, some paragraphs range over entire pages, whilst others are as short as one or several lines of text.

PART ONE

KEY PARAMETERS

1 MY BOOKS AND MY RESEARCH[1]

Let me briefly recall the course of my literary or scientific activity for those[a] here tonight who are not familiar with my work.

To begin with, I have produced many editions and translations of ancient texts: in 1960, the theological works of a Latin Christian Neoplatonist, Marius Victorinus; in 1977, Ambrose's *Apology of David*; in 1988 and 1990, two treatises by Plotinus. Furthermore, I have written a number of books: first, in 1963, a short book, *Plotin: ou la simplicité du regard*; then, in 1968, a doctoral thesis devoted to an aspect of Neoplatonism: namely, the relations between Victorinus, this Christian theologian of the fourth century CE, and a pagan philosopher of the same period, Porphyry, Plotinus' disciple.[b] In 1981, I published a work, *Exercices spirituels et philosophie antique*; and, last year [1992], a book with the title *La citadelle intérieure*, devoted to the *Meditations* of Marcus Aurelius. If the Collège philosophique has invited me tonight, it is certainly because of these last two works. In these books, one finds the expression of a particular conception of ancient philosophy, as well as an outline of a conception of philosophy in general.

In a word, in these texts one finds the idea that philosophy should be defined as a 'spiritual exercise'. How did I come to assign such importance to this notion? I think that this dates back to 1959–60, and to my encounter with the work of Ludwig Wittgenstein. I developed a series of reflections

---

[a] [Translator's note] As per endnote 1 below, this chapter was originally a talk delivered in 1993. The French thus addresses *auditeurs*. On the importance of the spoken or oral dimension of ancient philosophy for Hadot, see Chapters 3–4 below.

[b] [Translator's note] Pierre Hadot, *Marius Victorinus, Traités théologiques sur la trinité*, text established by P. Henry, introduction, translation and notes by P. Hadot, 2 vols (Paris: Éditions du Cerf, 1960).

inspired by this encounter in an article in the *Revue de métaphysique et de morale*, entitled 'Jeux de langage et philosophie', which appeared in 1960. In this article, I wrote: 'We philosophize within a language game, that is to say, to quote Wittgenstein's expression, from within an attitude and a form of life which gives its sense to our speech.' I took up Wittgenstein's idea, according to which it was necessary to break with the idea that language always only functions in a single way and always with the same goal: to translate thoughts. On this basis, I claimed that it was also necessary to radically break with the idea that philosophical language always functions in a uniform manner. The philosopher is always, indeed, within a certain language game: that is to say, situated in [the framework of] a form of life, or a certain attitude. It is then impossible to understand the sense of philosophers' theses without situating them within their language game. Moreover, the main role of philosophical language was that of placing the auditors of this discourse within a certain form of life, [or] a particular style of life. This is the origin of the notion of the spiritual exercise as an effort to modify and transform the self.[c] If I have been attentive to this aspect of language, and if I came to conceive of this notion of spiritual exercises, it was because, like many of my predecessors and contemporaries, I was struck by a well-known phenomenon: that of the inconsistencies, even the contradictions that one encounters in the works of the philosophical authors of antiquity. We know that it is often extremely difficult to follow the thread of ideas in ancient philosophical writings. Whether it is a matter of Augustine, Plotinus, Aristotle or Plato, modern historians never cease to deplore the blunders in philosophical exposition, and the compositional defects which are found in their works.[d] In order to explain this phenomenon, I gradually came to observe that it was always necessary to explain the text in light of the living context in which it was born: that is to say, the concrete conditions of life of the philosophical school, in the institutional sense of the word. In antiquity, the priority of the school was never to disseminate a theoretical, abstract knowledge, as we do in our modern universities. Above

---

[c] [Translator's note] Hadot also emphasizes the importance of Wittgenstein for his conception of philosophy in *The Present Alone is our Happiness: Conversations with Jeannie Carlier and Arnold I. Davidson*, trans. by Marc Djebillah and Michael Chase, 2nd edn, (Stanford, CA: Stanford University Press, 2011), 32–3, 58–60, 80–1.

[d] [Translator's note] The phrase Hadot uses, which we have translated as 'the blunders in philosophical exposition', is *maladresses d'exposé*. On the place of interpretive errors in the history of philosophy, compare Pierre Hadot, 'Forms of Life and Forms of Discourse in Ancient Philosophy', in *Philosophy as a Way of Life*, trans. M. Chase (London: Wiley-Blackwell, 1995), 49–70.

all else, it aimed to form the [disciples'] minds[e] in a method and a knowledge of how to speak and how to debate.[f] In one way or another, philosophical writings were always echoes of an oral teaching. Moreover, for the ancient philosophers, a word, phrase or argument was not primarily intended to inform the reader or listener, but rather to produce a certain psychical effect on them, always pedagogically considering their capacities.[g] In this discourse, the propositional element was not the most important one. According to Victor Goldschmidt's excellent formula regarding the Platonic dialogues, one could say that ancient philosophical discourse aimed at forming rather than informing students.

In a word, one could summarise what I have just put forward by saying that ancient philosophy was more a pedagogical and intellectual exercise than a systematic construction. Furthermore, I later situated this observation in relation to the fact that, at least since Socrates and Plato, philosophy also presented itself as a therapeutics.[h] All the ancient philosophical schools, each in its own way, offer a critique of the habitual condition of human beings, a state of suffering, disorder and unawareness,[i] and a method to cure them from this state. 'The philosophical school is a medical clinic,' as Epictetus said. This therapy is situated, above all, in the discourse of the master which has the effect of an incantation, a sting, a violent shock which upsets the interlocutor, as is said of Socrates' discourse in Plato's *Symposium*. Nevertheless, to be cured, it is not sufficient to be moved. One must really will to transform one's life. In all philosophical schools, the teacher is thus a director of conscience. On this subject, I should acknowledge all that I owe to the work of my wife, Ilsetraut Hadot, notably her book on spiritual direction in Seneca,[j] as well as her more general work on the figure of the 'spiritual guide' in the ancient world.[k]

The philosophical school imposed a way of life on its members, a way of life which engaged the whole of one's existence. This mode of life consisted

---

[e] [Translator's note] Translating from the French *esprits* here.
[f] [Translator's note] The knowledge at stake here is closer to the English 'know-how': a practical knowledge about how to speak and discuss in particular contexts.
[g] [Translator's note] See especially Chapters 3 and 5 below.
[h] [Translator's note] Original: *une thérapeutique*. 'Therapy' might be used, but since all ancient philosophy is being described, this more general term has been chosen.
[i] [Translator's note] French: *unconscience*.
[j] [Translator's note] See Ilsetraut Hadot, *Seneca und die Griechisch-Römische Tradition der Seelenleitung* (Berlin: De Gruyter, 1969); [expanded] French translation, *Sénèque. Direction spirituelle et pratique de la philosophie* (Paris: Vrin, 2014).
[k] [Translator's note] See Ilsetraut Hadot, 'The Spiritual Guide', in *Classical Mediterranean Spirituality*, ed. by Arthur H. Armstrong (London: Routledge & Kegan Paul, 1986), 436–59.

of certain procedures or endeavours which we can more precisely call spiritual exercises: that is, practices that aimed at a modification, an improvement and a transformation of the self. At the origin of these exercises, there is an act of choice, a fundamental option for a certain way of life. One then actualizes this option in the order of inner discourse and spiritual activity: that is, in meditation, dialogue with oneself, examination of conscience or exercises of imagination such as the view from above on the cosmos or the earth. One also embodies this option at the level of action and everyday conduct:[l] in self-mastery, indifference to indifferent things, the fulfilment of one's social duties in Stoicism, as well as the discipline of desire in Epicureanism. All these spiritual exercises should be carried out according to the traditional method of each school. From this perspective, philosophical discourse is only one element of philosophical activity, one which is intended to justify or ground an existential attitude which corresponds to the fundamental existential option of the school. The Stoics, moreover, clearly distinguished philosophical discourse from philosophy itself.[m] Philosophy was for them a unique act, a constant everyday attitude. Rather than perfect wisdom, for them philosophy was an exercise aiming at this wisdom, an exercise in which one concretely practiced logic, in thinking reality as it is; ethics,[n] in acting in the service of others; and physics, in living in the awareness of one's place in the cosmos. Philosophical discourse, by contrast, corresponded only to the necessities of teaching: that is to say, to the discursive, theoretical and pedagogical exposition of the reasons one has for living in this particular way. In the other schools, and notably those of Plato and Aristotle – which cannot be examined in detail here – one finds an implicit distinction of this kind, simply because, generally, in the ancient world, the philosopher is considered a philosopher not because he develops a philosophical discourse, but because he lives philosophically. Philosophy is, above all, a mode of life, which includes a certain mode of discourse as one of its integral parts, without being reduced to it.

From this point of view, I think it is important to point out that we can distinguish, in Greek, two meanings of the phrase philosophical 'discourse' (*logos*). On the one hand, it designates discourse, insofar as it is addressed to

---

[l] [Translator's note] The French here reads: *comportment quotidien*. Although the word 'conduct' in English is comparatively unusual, it preserves the sense of the French, suggesting an ordering or orientation of conduct, as well as that conduct itself.

[m] [Translator's note] See Chapter 3 below.

[n] [Translator's note] Hadot uses the term *la morale*, but we follow here the standard English translation of the Stoics' division of philosophy into *ethics* [*êthikê*], logic and physics.

a disciple or to oneself: that is to say, discourse that is bound to an existential context, to a concrete praxis; effectively, this form of discourse is already a spiritual exercise. On the other hand, it refers to discourse considered abstractly, in its formal structure and in its intelligible content. It is this second kind of *logos* which the Stoics considered to be distinct from philosophy, but which generally forms the object of many modern studies in the history of philosophy. However, in the eyes of the ancient philosophers, if one considers this discourse sufficient, one does not philosophize. From the beginning to the end of the history of ancient philosophy, one finds the same critique and the same struggle against those who considered themselves philosophers because they have developed, above all, a dialectical and logical, technical and brilliant philosophical discourse, instead of transforming their kind of life.[o] One could even say that this is where the perpetual danger for the philosopher lies: that is, to confine oneself to the reassuring universe of concepts and discourse, instead of going beyond discourse, engaging in the risk of radical self-transformation.

I should add to this that philosophical discourse is not exceeded[p] solely by the decision to change one's life, but also in certain entirely non-discursive philosophical experiences, whether of an amorous kind, as in Plato, contemplative, as in Aristotle, or unitive, as in Plotinus. Plotinus, in particular, explicitly opposed the theological discourse which speaks of, but does not lead to the Good, to spiritual exercises of purification and unification which lead to an experience of its presence.

In my book, *La citadelle intérieure*, I attempted to apply this conception of philosophy to the *Meditations* of Marcus Aurelius. Indeed, one should understand this text as comprising spiritual exercises, meditations, examinations of conscience, and exercises of imagination. Following the advice of his master Epictetus, Marcus Aurelius strives to assimilate through writing the Stoic dogmas and rules of life.[q] In reading the *Meditations*, we witness a ceaseless effort to formulate the same dogmas and rules of life,[r] always anew and in a striking manner, according to a carefully crafted literary practice. For Marcus Aurelius, it is not a matter of expounding a system, nor even of making notes to remember. His aim is rather to modify,

---

[o] [Translator's note] The French phrase here is: *genre de vie*.

[p] [Translator's note] The verb here is *dépasser*. On this important term in Hadot, see notes on Chapters 10 and 12.

[q] [Translator's note] See Chapter 11 below on Marcus Aurelius.

[r] [Translator's note] Hadot uses the French *dogmas* here, which might be translated as 'teachings'. But sometimes he will use *enseignements*, so we follow his word use. *Dogmata* is the nominative plural of the Greek *dogma*, which does not have the pejorative sense the term has in modern English, a sense which Hadot does not intend here.

when he feels the need, his inner discourse in order to reactivate a certain disposition within himself, so that he can practice the three fundamental rules of Stoicism as formulated by Epictetus: to dare to see reality as it is, to act in the service of others, and to remain aware of oneself as a part of the cosmos, accepting one's destiny with serenity. To put it differently, Marcus wishes to ground himself in truth, justice and serenity. To achieve this, even to reread what has been written will not suffice, since it may not correspond to the needs of the moment. Sometimes, it will perhaps be enough to rewrite what has already been written. For this reason, repetitions are frequent in the *Meditations*. Nevertheless, it is still necessary to write, and to rewrite. For what counts is the very exercise of writing, at any given moment. In this respect, Marcus Aurelius' *Meditations* is perhaps a unique book in the history of literature.

However, Marcus Aurelius is not content to simply formulate the Stoic dogmas and rules of life. He often resorts to imaginative exercises that reinforce the persuasive power of the dogmas. He does not stop, for instance, with saying that all things undergo continual metamorphosis. He places before his eyes all the court of Augustus, engulfed by time, or an entire generation, like that of Vespasian. Thus, shocking images and brutal descriptions of naked reality abound in the *Meditations*. They have struck historians, who please themselves in denouncing the pessimism, resignation, even sadness of the philosopher-emperor.[s] Their error, precisely, has been to not situate these formulae in the context of the spiritual exercises and the true Stoic doctrine. These supposedly pessimistic statements do not express Marcus Aurelius' experiences or impressions but should rather be situated within the fundamental perspective of Stoicism, according to which the only true good is moral good, and the only true evil is vice. There is only one true Value, the purity of the moral intention, which is indissolubly a requirement for truth, the love of human beings and consent to Fate.[t]

The ancient representation of philosophy seems to us very distant from our contemporary understandings of philosophy. How has such an evolution unfolded? What is at stake here is a complex phenomenon, which comprises two main aspects. I have already evoked the first aspect, which is in some way connatural to philosophy: the constant tendency of the philosopher, even in antiquity, to be satisfied with discourse, with the conceptual architecture that he has constructed, without putting his own life into question. The second aspect is contingent and historical: namely,

---

[s] [Translator's note] Again, see Chapter 11 below.
[t] [Translator's note] *Valeur* and *Destin* are capitalized in the original.

the separation between philosophical discourse and the spiritual practice effected by Christianity.

It is, indeed, with the appearance of Christianity that one begins to put the ancient concept of *philosophia* into question. Towards the end of Antiquity, Christianity presented itself as a *philosophia*, as a way of life which, nevertheless, conserved numerous spiritual exercises from ancient philosophy, particularly in monastic life.[u] With the Middle Ages, we witness a total separation of the spiritual exercises (which are, henceforth, a part of Christian spirituality) and philosophy, which becomes a mere theoretical tool in the service of theology (*ancilla theologiae*). From ancient philosophy, only the pedagogic techniques[v] and the teaching procedures remain. In antiquity, philosophy encompasses theology and does not hesitate to formulate counsels on religious practice. Yet, during all the Middle Ages and into modernity, through prudence in view of the Inquisition, we will rigorously separate philosophical speculation on the one hand, and theological thought and religious practice, on the other. Philosophical speculation, in its turn, becomes an abstract construction. It is only with Suarez that the idea of systematic philosophy appears for the first time. To this one must add the functioning of the universities. [In the context of the universities,] the task is no longer that of forming human beings, as [it was] in Antiquity, but rather of forming professors who, in their turn, will form other professors. Such a situation can only favour the tendency, already denounced by the Ancients, to take refuge in the comfortable universe of concepts and discourse, as well as in technical expertise, which is a natural inclination of the philosophical spirit.

However, thanks to the work of my friend, the Polish philosopher Juliusz Domański on the Middle Ages and humanism, I have come to nuance this historical picture[w] First, we can see in the twelfth century, in Abelard, for example, a certain return of the ancient representation of the philosopher. And, above all during the Renaissance, the humanists began to distance themselves from the Scholastics and, to a certain degree, from official

---

[u] [Translator's note] See Hadot, 'Ancient Spiritual Exercises and "Christian philosophy"', in *Philosophy as a Way of Life*, 126–44.

[v] [Translator's note] Hadot uses *scolaires* as his adjective here. In the medieval context, the English word 'scholastic' would describe the teaching techniques of the scholastic dialecticians and theologians, but the French may be less specific, describing any 'school' exercises. Hadot, for instance, uses the term to describe philosophical pedagogy in Chapter 6 of this volume.

[w] [Translator's note] See Juliusz Domański, *La philosophie, théorie ou manière de vivre? Les controverses de l'Antiquité à la Renaissance, avec une préface de Pierre Hadot* (Paris, Fribourg (Suisse): Editions Universitaires, 1996), and Hadot's own 'Preface' to the text.

Christianity; we witness then a return to the ancient conception of philosophy in Petrarch, Erasmus and others. In this perspective, I believe it is possible to detect, alongside the theoretical and abstract current, the permanence of what we might call the 'pragmatist' conception of ancient philosophy:[x] in the sixteenth century, in Montaigne, whose *Essays* are nothing other than spiritual exercises; in the seventeenth century, in Descartes' *Meditations*; in the eighteenth century, in the French '*philosophes*' and, in England, in a figure like Shaftesbury (amongst others), whose extraordinary *Exercises* Laurent Jaffro has published with Aubier.[2] These are again precisely spiritual exercises inspired by Epictetus and Marcus Aurelius, and totally non-Christian. We can also find this conception of philosophy in Germany with the movement of 'popular' philosophy. It is within this perspective that we need to situate what Kant calls 'cosmic' philosophy, which he ultimately considers as the true philosophy. On this subject, my colleague and friend, the sadly missed André Voelke, professor at the University of Lausanne, has developed a remarkable reflection, completely independent of my own, on *Philosophy as Therapeutics*[y] in the Stoics, Epicureans and Sceptics. Like I had done, Voelke also starts with Wittgenstein. However, he rightly stressed the Kantian notion of an 'interest of reason' in order to define what he called the force of a philosophical discourse, according to its power to act; which is to say, its power to interest reason.[z] According to Kant, reason is, above all, interested in the highest ends, which are those of morality,[aa] as Eric Weil has correctly shown.[bb] This is tantamount to recognizing the primacy of practical reason in the search for wisdom. We find here again, in the paradox of an 'interested' reason, the ancient definition of philosophy as the love of wisdom: a ceaselessly renewed effort to achieve a certain state, a way of life which would be that of wisdom. In a text where, in a sliding of language, Kant passes constantly

---

[x] [Translator's note] In English, 'pragmatism' denotes a philosophical tendency that emerged in the later nineteenth century, associated with figures like Charles Sanders Pierce. Evidently, Hadot is thinking not with this modern sense, but with the Greek sense of *pragma* in mind, which has a much broader sense: things in general can be described as *ta pragmata*, and the word is derived from the same stem as *praxis*, usually translated as 'action'.

[y] [Translator's note] André-Jean Voelke, *La philosophie comme thérapeutique de l'âme: Études de philosophie Hellénistique*, Preface by Pierre Hadot (Paris: Vestigia, 1994), in the original.

[z] [Translator's note] Original: *intéresser la raison*.

[aa] [Translator's note] Original: *moralité*.

[bb] [Translator's note] Hadot seems clearly here to be evoking Éric Weil, *Logique de la philosophie* (Paris: Vrin, 1985).

from the figure of the sage to the ideal model of the philosopher – that is to say, as he puts it, to the true idea of the philosopher – he finally emphasises, in the spirit of Platonism and Stoicism, the completely inaccessible character of this ideal model:

> A philosopher corresponding to this model does not exist, no more than a true Christian does. Both [of these] are models. The model should serve as the norm. The 'philosopher' is only an idea. Perhaps we can cast a gaze towards this idea, imitate it in some points, but we will never fully achieve it.

And a little further on:

> The idea of wisdom should be at the basis of philosophy as the idea of Sanctity is at the basis of Christianity ... Certain ancients approached the ideal of the true philosopher ... but even they never accomplished it ... If we consider the ancient philosophers Epicurus, Zeno, Socrates, etc., we realize that it is the destination of man and the means to arrive at it that were the objects of their knowledge [*savoir*]. They thus remained more faithful to the true idea of philosophy than thinkers in modern times, when one conceives the philosopher as an artist of reason [that is to say, for Kant, as someone who only has theoretical and speculative discourse in view, PH].[3]

A movement of return to the ancient conception has thus begun by the end of the Middle Ages. But the scholastic model, the constraints and habits of university life, above all this self-satisfaction of theoretical discourse of which I have spoken, have powerfully obstructed this renaissance.

Finally, it follows from what I have just said that the model of ancient philosophy still remains alive.[cc] This means that a quest for wisdom is always still contemporary and possible.[dd] I ask you not to expect me to develop this difficult and complex theme here tonight. Let me only say that it seems to me that there are universal and fundamental attitudes of the human being, when he searches for wisdom. From this point of view, there is a universal Stoicism, Epicureanism, Socratism, Pyrrhonism and

---

[cc] [Translator's note] Hadot here uses *actuel*.

[dd] [Translator's note] We have rendered *actuelle* here as 'contemporary', to avoid repeating the immediately preceding use of 'alive', and since the French word carries this sense: current affairs or commentaries on the same can thus be called *actuelles*.

Platonism, which are independent of the philosophical or mythical discourses that have claimed to definitively justify them.

And for the final word, I will borrow once more from Kant:

> To an old man, who told him that he attended lessons on virtue, Plato responded: 'and when will you begin to live virtuously?' One cannot always theorise. One must finally aim at passing from thought to exercise. But today we take someone who lives what he teaches to be a dreamer.[4]

Notes

1 This chapter was originally a talk delivered to the Collège philosophique in 1993.

2 Anthony Ashley Cooper, third Earl of Shaftesbury, *Exercices*, ed. by Laurent Jaffro (Paris: Aubier, 1993).

3 Immanuel Kant, *Vorlesungen über die philosophische Encyclopädie*, in *Kant's gesammelter Schriften*, XXIV (Berlin: Akademie, 1980), 8–9.

4 Kant, *Vorlesungen über die philosophische Encyclopädie*, 12.

2 THE ANCIENT PHILOSOPHERS

The work that Richard Goulet has just completed[1] is the first, already monumental volume of an enormous enterprise [the *Dictionnaire des philosophes antiques*], which will not only fill a gap in French research in the field of the history of philosophy and of antiquity more generally. Above all, it will represent an extremely precious work tool for the international scientific community.

The first point of interest of this work is its exhaustiveness, in two senses. [First,] exhaustiveness in the list of philosophers it presents; [second,] exhaustiveness in the presentation of sources. Until now, no philosophy handbook, nor any encyclopaedia, has provided us with a complete index of the philosophers of antiquity. Such a complete index is, nevertheless, indispensable to an integral history of ancient philosophy, as we will have the opportunity to stress. On the other hand, Goulet was not content with simply referring to Greek literary sources. He also looks at iconographical, papyrological and epigraphical documents, and even at Armenian, Georgian, Hebraic, Syriac and Arabic sources. From this perspective, articles such as those dedicated to Aratus, Alexander of Aphrodisia, Ammonius, son of Hermias, Aristides of Athens and Aristotle are extremely interesting. One will thus also find conveniently gathered [a number of] indications which one does not usually find treated in encyclopaedias and handbooks, and which one must usually search for in other works and sometimes even in other libraries!

To carry out this project, Goulet surrounded himself with eighty researchers and academics, French and foreign, often experienced experts in the authors discussed or the epoch in which these authors lived and wrote. Not only do the numerous entries represent the state of the art in the field, but they are also the result of personal and very original researches.

The work will allow us to distinguish philosophers whom we would often confuse, like Albinos-Alkinoos, the two Athenodoruses of Tarsus, as well as to dispel [certain] phantoms, like Actorides [and] Ainesidamus, born of false readings and random conjectures made by papyrologists. But one will also find the names of fictive characters like Alcidamas, Aristainetus, Arignotus, who appear in Lucian. Synoptic tables present us with the families of Aristotle and Plato, as well as the succession of teachers[a] of the school founded by Iamblichus. One will also note the entries dedicated to the Gnostics (notably Apelles) and to the heterodox Christian Platonists (notably Aristocritus), which introduce us to a domain often little explored by historians of philosophy until now, but which day after day shows itself to be ever more important to an understanding of both Christianity and Neoplatonism.

As we have already grasped, Goulet gives us a marvellous work tool for the study of *philosophical texts*. The entries devoted, for example, to Aristotle's treatises are in this regard exemplary. They are precious guides which orient us through the labyrinth of Greek, Syriac and Arab traditions, revealing the extraordinary complexity of the diffusion of Aristotle's work, the impressive number of commentaries that it has provoked and the different classifications it underwent. These entries reassess [our] received ideas on many points and renew the state of the scholarship. A remarkable set of studies notably focus on this mysterious writing which one has traditionally called the 'Theology of Aristotle'. In the same way, the remarkable entry dedicated to Alexanders of Aphrodisias is useful since 'there are few ancient authors whose work is as dispersed as his: direct and indirect traditions; Syriac, Arab, Hebrew, Latin versions; numerous titles recorded by Arab bibliographers, but whose authenticity is sometimes challenged by experts'.

We cannot insist too much on the capital importance of the lists of titles of the works by different authors which have been preserved for us by the ancient historians, above all by Diogenes Laertius. Indeed, it is necessary to underscore that the greatest part of the philosophical production of Antiquity has been lost. We only know a tiny, minuscule part of this production. The Stoic Chrysippus wrote seven hundred works. All are lost. In the present volume [of Goulet's *Dictionnaire*], we learn that ten commentaries which Alexander of Aphrodisias devoted to Aristotle's works, as well as nineteen of his 'personal' works, have totally disappeared. Likewise, we note that the works of Amelius, Antiochus of Ascalon, Antipater of

---

[a] [Translator's note] Literally, *professeurs*, whose direct translation would be anachronistic in English.

Tarsus, Antipater of Tyre, Antisthenes (sixty-five works), Aristippus of Cyrene, and Ariston of Chios have also been completely lost, to only cite some examples of important philosophers. It is probable that, if we knew the totality of this production, for example the works of Xenocrates, Speusippus [and] Chrysippus, the idea which we have of ancient philosophy would be totally overturned. The too-brief fragment of dialogue discovered at Ai-Khanoum,[2] for instance, allows us to surmise the existence of works, now lost, which treated of metaphysical subjects with a rigour in argumentation equal to that of Plato or Aristotle. To compensate for the irreparable loss, these lists of titles of works remain to us and are reproduced in the different entries of this volume.

These lists could be the matter of a further study dedicated to lost philosophical literature. Montesquieu had already thought of a work of this genre:

Since we now have the taste for collections and libraries, some laborious writer who wanted to should make a catalogue of all the lost books which are cited in the ancient authors. He should be a man free of cares and even amusements. He should give an idea of these works, of the genius and the life of the author, as much as one could make of this from the fragments which remain to us and the passages cited by other authors who have defied time and the zeal of emerging religions. It seems that we owe this tribute to the memory of so many learned men. An infinity of great men are known by their actions and not by their works.[3]

Montesquieu's remarks are very judicious. However, I believe one could legitimately think that perhaps he did not see all of the importance and significance of this enterprise. In fact, these lists of titles demand a very detailed study.

First of all, the titles themselves often contain technical terms which can shed light upon the philosophy of their author. This is notably the case for the list of works of Chrysippus, where one notes, for example, the use of all the logical vocabulary distinct to the Stoic School.

They also permit us to know the questions which were submitted to examination in the schools, the habitual themes that the 'theses' (that is to say, the scholarly discussions) took for their subjects, [like] for example, Kingship, friendship, pleasure, the passions.

The lists are indexed, either according to the alphabetical order of the works (for example, the writings of Theophrastus), or according to the parts of philosophy (as one sees very clearly in Chrysippus). In the latter case, one can obtain precious information by examining the order of questions within each part [of philosophy]. The writings of Aristotle are presented according to an order which combines considerations of literary critique (the opposition between writings plainly elaborated and constructed in a literary manner, and simple collections of notes: the opposition between writings where the author stages dialogues between persons other than himself and writings wherein he speaks himself) and scholarly classifications (logical, physiological, mathematical).[4]

These lists of titles thus inform us at the same time of the concerns of those who chose the titles and of those who established the lists. On the one hand, it is very interesting in examining the titles of books where they appear, to register the questions which were posed and discussed in the philosophical schools and those to which these writings were intended to respond. On the other hand, in considering the order in which the titles are presented in the lists, [and] the forced systematization which presided over these classifications, one is sometimes stupefied by the way in which the different school members have radically deformed the thought of the founder of the school.

A methodical inventory, a reasoned classification of the questions posed could lead to a vaster study which will have as its object 'philosophical questions' in general: that is to say, [a study whose object would be] philosophy as inquiry. Historians of philosophy, with some few exceptions, are less interested in the questions themselves than in the architecture of the monuments constructed by the philosophers in order to respond to these questions. But one could also conceive of a history of philosophy which would be a history of problems, which would identify all the questions that were posed by the philosophers of Antiquity, and which would ask why they were posed, under which form they [were posed], in what manner also the posing of the problems evolved. In this research, the study of the titles of the books would very usefully complete the information that one could draw from different philosophical works (notably Aristotle's *Topics*).

Thanks to the titles of the works, as Montesquieu thought, one could form a certain idea of their content, [by] comparing this with the contents of the works of other authors which bear the same title. For, in Antiquity, one did not usually seek to draw the reader in by a strange and surrealist title, like *The Bald Singer, The Dancer and the Chatterton, The Cook and the Man-Eater*.[b] On the contrary, by the title, one indicated in advance the

---

[b] [Translator's note] Hadot adduces these as colourful, but real or plausible examples of French novel titles. The titles are humorous, but the point is quite serious: ancient titles are repetitive because they express a way to do philosophy: responding to specific questions, to which other authors also responded. They also indicate a certain genre of philosophical writing, as in the case of the consolations.

content of the book which would conform in general to the themes which are habitually utilised when it is a matter of treating the subject in question. A 'Consolation', a 'Protreptic', a treatise 'On Kingship' or 'On Tranquillity of Mind', always contain more or less the same arguments, within the same school, and sometimes between different schools. Like Vauvenargues, ancient authors think that 'a truly new and original book would be that which makes [readers] love old truths'.[5]

It is very interesting to note that a tendency to invent seductive titles [–] 'Rays of Honey', 'The Horn of Amalthea', 'Prairies', 'Lamps', 'The Rug', 'The Meadow', 'The Orchard' [–] comes into vogue in the Hellenistic and Imperial period. One can note this in the entry on 'Aulus Gellius', where we learn that this author gave to his work the title *Attic Nights*, reflecting this trend. It is, nevertheless, necessary to note that these titles are distinct to a very specific literary genre: that of collections of memories of conversations, or notes taken during courses. In any case, a history of the way of entitling books would also be extremely interesting.

To compensate for the huge gaps which result from the loss of [so much] philosophical literature, there are also resources, limited but extremely promising, from papyrological research. On this subject, one must mention the remarkable studies of two Italian centres at Florence (the *Corpus dei papiri filosofici greci e latini*) and at Naples (the *Centro internazionale per lo studio dei papiri ercolanesi*). The studies led by these two centres have greatly contributed to the progress in the knowledge of Stoicism and Epicureanism. The results of these works are fully utilized in [Goulet's volume], and it is desirable for French scholars to become aware of the importance of this field of investigation.

Not only will the exhaustive character of the inventory undertaken by Richard Goulet allow us to more easily access philosophical texts. It will also provide the materials indispensable for a study of the *historical phenomenon represented by philosophy as a whole*.

One will be struck, perhaps, to find in this list of ancient philosophers figures that one is not accustomed to seeing appear in textbooks of philosophy: not solely physicians (like Acron of Agrigentum, Adrastus of Myndos, Aiphicianus, Apollonius of Antioch and Apollonius of Citium, Asclepiades), but also musicians (like Agathocles, Agenor of Mytilene), mathematicians (Athenaeus of Cyzicus, Andreas, Andron), or grammarians (Aristophanes of Byzantium). But we need to be clear that the 'extension' of the concept 'philosophy' is completely different in Antiquity than in our times. At different moments in the history of ancient philosophy, the so-called 'liberal' disciplines, like grammar, music or mathematics are considered, either as parts of philosophy, or as a propaedeutic indispensable to philosophy.[6]

But one also finds in [Goulet's volume] figures who are neither scholars, professors of philosophy, nor authors of works within this discipline: women like Arria major, Arria minor (and Arria the Platonist, friend of Galen), political men like Agrippinus, Ariston, a king, Antigonus Gonatas, and finally honoured deceased bearing the title of 'philosopher' on their funerary stelae.

The presence of these figures in Goulet's work seems to me to speak to a healthy reaction against the traditional conceptions of the history of philosophy.

We just said that the concept of philosophy (and of the philosopher) does not have the same 'extension' in Antiquity as today. We could add that it no longer has the same 'comprehension'. One could say, indeed, that the contemporary philosopher is, in general, an academic[c] or a writer; often, both at the same time. As an academic, he is a specialist, a professional who forms other specialists. As a writer, he produces books, objects in which he proposes his interpretation of the world, or of history, or of language, and he is identified in some way with these objects that are his oeuvre. As an academic, he interprets the works of others or comments on his own production. One could thus say with Paul Valéry that 'philosophy, [inasmuch as it] is defined by works that are written, is objectively a particular literary genre, characterized by certain subjects and by the frequency of certain terms and forms', and which, as he adds, 'is deprived of all exterior verification', not aiming at 'the institution of any power', and to be categorized 'not too far away from poetry'.[7] However that may be, it isn't 'striking given these conditions that the history of philosophy, as one generally practises it, consists essentially in the analysis of the genesis of the structures of literary works which have been written by philosophers, notably in the study of the rational ordering and internal coherence of these systematic expositions.

One will ask oneself, however, if such a conception of philosophy and of the history of philosophy could remain valid when one tries to apply it to ancient philosophy. In Antiquity, indeed, the concept of philosophy has a content wholly other than that which it has in the modern world.[8] Probably, under the influence of sophistry, ancient philosophy itself had the tendency, from very early on, to become professorial, scholarly and written. Nevertheless, by a constantly renewed process,[d] it has always striven to be more a living speech than a written work, and more a life than a speech.

---

[c] [Translator's note] That is, a *universitaire*.
[d] [Translator's note] Here: *démarche*.

One knows the celebrated end of the *Phaedrus*,[9] in which Plato lets us glimpse that only living dialogue is enduring and immortal because it is written in living souls and not upon dead pages. And that philosophy is, before everything else, a form of life is the conclusion that one can draw from many of the texts of Antiquity. I will cite only one of these texts, drawn from Plutarch:

> Most people imagine that philosophising consists in lecturing from the heights of one's chair and running courses on texts. But what these people totally ignore is that the daily life in the City is itself also a philosophy which is revealed continuously and equally in works and actions. And, as Dicaearchus has said, such men are happy to say of those who come and go under the porticos that they 'give a philosophical lesson while walking' (*peripatein*). But they do not use this expression when it is a matter of those who walk towards their fields or go to see a friend. Everyday life in the city is, indeed, akin to philosophy. Socrates, for instance, never required an arrangement of steps for his listeners. He did not sit on a professorial chair; neither did he have an established time to walk and debate with his disciples. But it was by joking with his disciples, or by drinking with them, by going to war or to the Agora with certain amongst them, and, finally, by going to prison and drinking the hemlock that Socrates philosophized. He was the first to show that, always and in all places, and in everything which happens to us or that we ourselves do, everyday life can find a place for philosophy.[10]

In Antiquity, the philosopher is thus not necessarily a teacher or a writer. He is, before all else, a man having a certain lifestyle, which he has chosen voluntarily, even if he has not taught or written, such as Diogenes the Cynic or Pyrrho, or such celebrated Roman politicians as Cato of Utica, Rutilius Rufus, Quintus Mucius Scaevola Pontifex, Rogatianus or Thrasea, who were considered true philosophers by their contemporaries.

These figures live in the world, with their fellow citizens. Nevertheless, they do not live like everyone else. They are distinguished from others by their moral conduct, their frank speech, their manner of nourishing and dressing themselves, their attitude towards wealth and conventional values. Here again, Socrates is the very archetype of the philosopher. If he showed that everyday life can accommodate philosophy, he also proved, very clearly, by his life and death, that there is a radical opposition between the habitual life of men and the life of the philosopher. This is why the Platonic dialogues qualify Socrates as *atopos*, that is to say, as 'unclassifiable', not fitting into the habitual frames of everyday life.[11] Such is the paradox of the ancient philosophical life: at the heart of everyday life, it is a more or less profound rupture with everyday life itself.

To adhere to one of the philosophical schools of Antiquity, Platonism, Pythagoreanism (often difficult to distinguish from Platonism), Aristotelianism, Stoicism, Epicureanism, Cynicism or Scepticism was thus to choose a certain form, a certain style of life, a certain behaviour in everyday life. It is thus clearly evident that in order to comprehend ancient philosophy, it will not suffice to analyse the structure of thought which is expressed, for example, in the dialogues of Plato or the writings of Aristotle. To this absolutely indispensable research, it would be necessary to add an effort to grasp the philosophical process in all of its lived reality, concrete and existential, and in all of its dimensions, not solely literary but [also] social, political, religious, institutional, juridical, geographical and anthropological.

If one wishes to understand a phenomenon which engages the whole of human life, one is forced to study this phenomenon in all of its concrete aspects. How could we describe the monastic movement, for example, without speaking of the life of the convent, of exercises of piety or the dietary regime? Now, the philosophical movement in Antiquity presents many analogies with monasticism. (There is nothing striking about this, for Christian monasticism is, in part, the successor of ancient philosophy and even presents itself as a *philosophia*).[12] It is true that the ancient philosopher does not live in a cloister. He is 'in the world'. Very often he effects political action. But, if he adheres with fervour to a school, he must have converted, he must have made a choice which obliges him to transform all of his way of life in the world, he must have entered into a community under the direction of a spiritual master: he will examine his conscience, perhaps confess his faults, as is the custom in the Epicurean School, for example;[13] he will venerate the [school's] founder, often participate in communal meals with the other members of the school.[14] And if he is just a sympathizer, he will make an effort to at least become better, and he will live differently from other people.

One could thus sketch the questions which are posed to the historian of ancient philosophy who wants to take for his object the phenomenon of philosophy in its totality. He must consider the philosopher under three aspects: the philosopher living within his school, the philosopher living in the City, the philosopher living with himself (and with what transcends him).

In order to study the philosopher living within his school, it would be necessary to examine the juridical status of the schools in the ancient world, their internal organization, the problems posed in their functioning and which appear, for example, in the very interesting testaments (notably that of Epicurus) which Diogenes Laertius has preserved.[15] It would also be necessary to enquire about the activity of the teacher. How did the course of philosophy develop? What did the role of the spiritual director consist?[16] What were the relations between written production and oral teaching? Furthermore, what was the situation of the disciple within the school? Was there always a distinction between fervent adepts and sympathizers? What was life like inside of the school, the relations between master and disciples, the reunions, the festivals, the friendship, the freedom of speech? What were the programmes of teaching? What place was reserved for the liberal disciplines?

Concerning the philosopher living in the city, one must, above all, define the relations between the school and the city by recognizing the fact, often neglected, that the philosophical schools never renounced exercising an active influence on their fellow citizens. The means mobilized to achieve this end are certainly different. Some philosophers attempted to effect direct political action, dreaming of seizing power. Others contented themselves with counselling the rulers. Others still put themselves in service of the city, in giving lessons to the ephebes or in attempting to rescue it by becoming ambassadors. Others hoped to make their fellow citizens comprehend what the true life is, proposing to them the example of their own life. All, in fact, think to change the way of life of their fellow citizens. What was the global result of this action? What exactly was the influence that the philosophers and philosophy, in general, exercised over political life and on the evolution of customs in Antiquity?

To study the relations of the philosopher to himself, one must attentively explore the domain of spiritual exercises (examination of conscience, meditations, thought or written) and the inner and mystical life.

Finally, the philosophical works must be interpreted by taking into account these different facts. One must situate the writing in the context of the school in which and for which it is composed, the perspective of the students for whom it could have been addressed. Moreover, it is in the school after all that the writing has been conserved, classed in a *corpus* and commented upon with the aid of traditional rules of interpretation. One must also consider that this form and content could be determined by political concerns: for example, one could draw a portrait of the ideal king in order to advise or criticise a sovereign. Recent research has shown the important role that political concerns and fears played in the elaboration of Plato's work.[17] And finally, one must never forget that theory is never totally separated from the spiritual practice, that philosophical works aimed, above all, to form as well as to inform, and that philosophical discourse is only a means intended to lead to a mode of life which is not different from philosophy itself.

We have just very imperfectly sketched the programme of research for a history of philosophy that would take for its object the phenomenon of philosophy in its entirety. This is precisely the programme that [Goulet's *Dictionary*] puts to work. It brings a precious contribution to this research and it provides abundant material that can be mobilized in future studies.

I will insist very particularly on a significant example: the information that we can draw from this work concerning the relations between philosophy and political activity amongst the followers of Epicurus' school. We encounter here many Epicureans who, contrary to the representation that one has habitually formed of the members of this school, have taken part in political activity. There are, first of all, two Romans: [Titus] Albucius, propraetor of Sardinia, and Cicero's friend, Atticus, who several times became involved in politics. The author of the article on Atticus correctly remarks that his rare interventions in political life do not allow us to doubt of the authenticity of his Epicureanism. But it is interesting to note that this is not a matter of an attitude specific to Roman Epicureanism. For we find in Greek Epicureanism two philosophers whom their city honoured with a statue in recompense for [civic] services which they rendered, and notably in gratitude for an ambassador to Rome: Amynius of Samos and Apollophanes of Pergamum. One must add to these cases, although this is not certain, the tyrant of Athens who resisted Sulla, a certain Aristion (according to Appian, *Mithridatic Wars*, 28). One sees that the question is complex and that, generally, all philosophers, even the members[e] of a school which advocated abstention from public affairs, did not hesitate to render service to their city.

Moreover, one glimpses here all that the epigraphical information can bring to the study of the phenomenon of philosophy in its entirety.[f] Jeanne and Louis Robert wrote in the *Bulletin épigraphique* of 1958 (no. 84, regarding the interesting article of Marcus Niebuhr Tod, *Journal of Hellenic Studies*, 1957: 'Sidelights on Greek Philosophers'):

Starting from the index cards gathered by Tod, it remains to re-examine these inscriptions of philosophers by studying them from an historical or sociological point of view: chronological classification; the geographical centres by which we know them, where they assembled or

---

[e] [Translator's note] Here: *sectateurs*.
[f] [Translator's note] Original: *intégralité*.

where they were honoured; above all, their place in the life of the cities in different periods and in the rich families of magistrates and *euergetes* [benefactors]; their participation in civic life.

[Goulet's] work, particularly by focusing on these inscriptions [and] often very instructive honorific decrees, will provide a valuable resource for future research. There is an entire study still to be made of the geography of philosophy, for example the permanence of philosophical traditions in certain cities like Tarsus, Apameia, Cyrene or Pergamum, not to mention of Alexandria and Athens, the relations between these centres [and] the itineraries of the philosophers.

It is due to this vast inquiry, for which the present work assembles the elements concerning both the writings and the life of the philosophers, that one will perhaps succeed in forming a more precise idea of what ancient philosophy really was.

But for the historian of philosophy, the task will not be finished for all that: or more exactly, he will have to cede the place to the philosopher, to the philosopher who should always remain alive within the historian of philosophy. This ultimate task will consist in posing to himself, with an increased lucidity, the decisive question: what does it mean to philosophize?

Notes

1   From the Preface to *Dictionnaire des philosophes antiques*, published under the direction of R. Goulet (Paris: Editions to CNRS, 1983), po. 7–16.

2   Cf. Claude Rapin, Pierre Hadot & Guglielmo Cavallo, 'Les textes littéraires grecs de la Trésorerie d'Al-Khanoum', *Bulletin de Correspondance Hellénique* 111 (1987): 244–249.

3   Charles-Louis de Secondat Montesquieu, *Cahiers I (1716–1755)*, recueillis et présentés par Bernard Grasset (Paris: Grasset, 1941), 92.

4   Ilsetraut Hadot, 'La division néoplatonicienne des écrits d 'Aristote', in *Aristoteles—Werk und Wirkung. Mélanges Paul Moraux*, vol. II (Berlin, 1967), 249–285.

5   Vauvenargues, *Reflexions et maximes*, sec. 400.

6   Ilsetraut Hadot, *Arts libéraux et philosophie dans la pensée antique* (Paris, 1984).

7   Paul Valéry, *Varieté*, in *Oevures*, tome 1 (Paris: Bibliothèque de la Pléiade, 1957), 1256.

8   Pierre Hadot, *Exercises spirituels*.

9 Plato, *Phaedrus*, 276–277.

10 Plutarch, *An seni res publica gerenda sit*, 26, 796d. [Translator's note: See Chapter 3 below.]

11 Plato, *Symposium*, 215a; *Phaedrus*, 229–230; *Alcibiades*, 106a.

12 Cf. Pierre Hadot, *Exercises spirituels*, 62.

13 Cf. Wolfgang Schmid, 'Epikur', *RAC* 5 (1962), col. 741.

14 On the life of the school of Plotinus, see the very important study of Marie-Odile Goulet-Cazé, 'L'arrière-plan scolaire de la *Vie de Plotin*', in Porphyry, *La Vie de Plotin,* vol. 1, ed. L. Brisson et al. (Paris: Vrin, 1982), 231–280.

15 Cf. John P. Lynch, *Aristotle's School* (Berkeley/London, 1972) (a model of the genre of research that I sketch here).

16 Ilsetraut Hadot, 'The Spiritual Guide', in *World Spirituality*, vol. 15, *Classical Mediterranean Spirituality* (New York, 1986), 444–459.

17 Cf. Konrad Gaiser, 'Plato's Enigmatic Lecture 'On the Good'', *Phronesis* 25 (1990): 517.

3 ANCIENT PHILOSOPHY: AN ETHICS OR A PRACTICE?

1 The notion of spiritual exercises

It was my interpretative work on the philosophical texts of antiquity that led me to an awareness of the importance of what we could call 'spiritual exercises'. In fact, like many of my predecessors and contemporaries, I was struck by a well-known phenomenon, that of the incoherencies, and even the contradictions, that one finds in the works of the ancient philosophical authors. Many modern historians of philosophy begin, in effect, with the postulate that Plato and the other ancient philosophers wanted to construct [theoretical] systems, like the modern philosophers. And, indeed, we can readily suppose that this is what they wanted to do, if we judge by the considerable number of divisions, classifications and hierarchical distinctions that we find in ancient philosophy, from Plato's [dialogues] to Proclus' *Elements of Theology*. Euclid's famous *Elements* represent the accomplishment of the Platonic ideal of axiomatization, and it remained the model of philosophical exposition throughout antiquity, whether for Epicurus or for Proclus. I have myself often been drawn to acknowledge the traces of this ideal [of systematization] in the different philosophers, most notably the Stoics.

It is not, then, a question of denying the existence of a will to coherence or systematization amongst the ancient philosophers. Moreover, as the Stoics clearly saw, all thought, like all reality, cannot exist without striving to be coherent with itself. Nevertheless, when we read the ancient authors, we feel that there is still something disconcerting for our modern mentality about the way in which they conduct their [philosophical] expositions, as well as about the way in which they employ their vocabulary. It would take too long here to list the statements of commentators and historians of ancient philosophy deploring the incoherencies, the clumsiness of exposition[a] or compositional shortcomings of the authors they study, whether it is Plato, Aristotle, Plotinus or Augustine.

It seems to me extremely random, therefore,[b] to apply to ancient authors the structural method[c] of Martial Gueroult and his students Victor Goldschmidt, Fernand Brunner and Jules Vuillemin. This method is very fecund when it comes to modern philosophers who explicitly aimed to construct a system, such as Leibniz, Descartes, Malebranche, Hegel and the German idealists.

I think that this is where the fundamental problem of interpretation of ancient philosophical authors arises. Did the ancients consider the essential task of philosophy to be the production of written texts presenting a conceptual system?

First of all, was writing books the principal task of the ancient philosopher? Victor Goldschmidt seems to have accepted this supposition, when he formulates the postulate upon which the structural method rests.[d] 'The structural method,' he says, 'places the emphasis incontestably on the written work, as the unique testimony wherein philosophical thought is manifested.'[1] Apparently, this sentence states something self-evident. For how, after all, could we know the thought of the ancient philosophers except through their writings?

However, it seems to me that the error here consists precisely in approaching ancient philosophical writing on the model of the modern

---

[a] [Translator's note] Hadot's important phrase here is *maladresses d'exposé*. See Pierre Hadot, 'Philosophy, Exegesis, and Creative Mistakes', in *Philosophy as a Way of Life*, 71–8 and Chapter 1 above.

[b] [Translator's note] Original: *aléatoire*.

[c] [Translator's note] Here the term Hadot uses is *structurale*. We preserve this more literally, as against 'structuralism', given that the latter designates in English a much wider intellectual movement, better known to many English-language readers for its associations with linguistics and anthropology. Here and in what follows, *structurale* is what is translated as 'structural'. The structural method is part of that which, in French, became the position known as structuralism in the history of philosophy. Its main representatives are Gueroult, Goldschmidt, Matheron and others.

[d] [Translator's note] Hadot's relationship to Goldschmidt is complex and goes beyond the critique of the structural or structuralist method in the history of philosophy. Hadot appreciated Goldschmidt's reading of Plato and, to some extent, of other authors and schools, notably including the Stoics, to which he is indebted.

philosophical writing. First of all, these two types of writing are generally very different. As the linguist Antoine Meillet has written: 'the impression of slowness that the literary works of antiquity present is due to the fact that they were made for a spoken reading.'[2] One could say that ancient writing has always a more or less oral dimension. Ancient philosophical writing was particularly tied to orality; it was always tied, in one way or another, to spoken practices,[e] whether because, as in Plato's and many of the ancient dialogues, philosophical writing tried to give the illusion to the reader that they were participating in a spoken event,[f] or whether because, more generally, the written texts were always intended to be read publicly. The text was not written as an end in itself. It was only a point of material support for speech[g] destined to become speech once again, like the modern audio cassette or record, which function as an intermediary between two events: the recording and its replaying.[h] The spatial simultaneity of the modern written philosophical work is opposed to the temporal succession of ancient speech, delivered through writing. Modern philosophical writing resembles an architectural monument, in which all the parts coexist: one can go from one to the other to verify their coherence. By contrast, the ancient philosophical work is more like a musical performance which proceeds by themes and variations.

Ancient philosophical writing is tied, in one way or another, to the event of oral teaching, addressed, first of all, to a group of students who hears the master or debates with him. For this reason, it demands to be understood not only through an analysis of its [written] structure. One must also situate any ancient text in the context of the living *praxis* from which it emanates and within which it is reinscribed. To put it in a different way, in the background of any ancient philosophical writing, one finds, first of all, the life of a school: that is to say, the community of disciples to whom the philosopher, first and foremost, addresses himself, and because of whom the memory of his discourses will be conserved. There is a philosopher who speaks, without aiming primarily to erect an edifice of concepts, so much as to form this group of disciples, whether by the aid of discussions with them or through a lecture course. One could thus say that everything which the moderns consider, from their perspective, as compositional defects, incoherencies or even contradictions in ancient texts primarily stems from

---

[e] [Translator's note] Here: *pratiques orales*.
[f] [Translator's note] Literally: *événement oral*.
[g] [Translator's note] Here: *parole*; 'speech' here specifically designates the 'spoken word'.
[h] [Translator's note] The French here is *reaudition*, so more literally, 'reaudition' or 'rehearing'.

the constraints which are specific to oral teaching. It is the echo of this teaching that one finds, in one way or another, in ancient philosophical writings.

In fact, one must go farther and ask whether the task of the ancient philosopher consisted in constructing a conceptual system, in the first place. Indeed, as we can see, the spoken teachings were not intended to directly and exclusively communicate an encyclopaedic knowledge, under the form of a system of propositions or concepts which more or less reflects 'the system of the world'. 'What happiness there would be,' jests Socrates in the *Symposium*, 'if knowledge was something which, going from the fuller vessel, could flow into what is emptier, so long as we were, ourselves, in contact the one with the other?'[i] But no, this oral teaching and the written works which result from it do not simply communicate a body of accomplished knowledge. They are intended, above all, to form the disciple to a certain *savoir faire*, a knowledge of how to debate and to speak which will allow the disciple to achieve a new orientation in their thinking,[j] in the life of the city or in the world. As René Schaerer has said of the Platonic dialogues:

> The definition [at which one aims in the dialogues, PH] is nothing by itself; the path travelled to attain it is everything. The interlocutor acquires from this process more acuity of spirit, more confidence, more skilfulness in all things.[3]

If this is true to the highest degree of the Platonic dialogues, it is also true of Aristotle's methods, or of Plotinus' treaties, in which long developments can appear to us as totally redundant. The written philosophical work, precisely because it is the direct or indirect echo of an oral teaching, appears to us more as a set of exercises, which aim at putting a certain method into practice, than a doctrinal exposition. Thus, it is possible to note that here we find the emergence of a notion of exercise, even if it is still a matter of an intellectual exercise.

But we must go farther. We might suppose that such intellectual exercises were purely formal, that is to say, purely discursive exercises, totally insulated from life. This is, moreover, what they evidently became for certain

---

[i] [Translator's note] Plato, *Symposium*, 175d.
[j] [Translator's note] Here, Hadot's phrase is *s'orienter dans la pensée*. Hadot may here be evoking an echo of the phrase 'orientation in thinking', associated with Immanuel Kant. Compare the end of Chapter 1 above.

philosophers. Indeed, from the beginning to the end of the history of ancient philosophy, we encounter criticisms of philosophers who only sought renown and wanted to shine by displaying their philosophical discourses. In the third century BCE, the Platonic philosopher Polemon reproached some of his contemporaries for wanting to be admired for their dialectical interrogations, but who contradicted themselves in their inner dispositions.[4] According to Polemon, one should exercise oneself, above all, in the concerns of life.[k] Many centuries later, in the second century CE, the Stoic Epictetus speaks with contempt of 'philosophers' who do not proceed beyond beauty of style and dialectical subtlety.[5] Nevertheless, one can say that, in their principles and fundamental choices, all ancient philosophical schools refused to consider philosophical activity as purely intellectual, formal or theoretical. Rather, the ancients considered philosophy as a choice which committed a person's entire life and soul. This is why the exercise of philosophy was not solely intellectual but could also be spiritual. The philosopher did not finally form his disciples only in the sense of their knowing how to speak or to debate, but in knowing how to live in the most elevated sense of the term. It is to an art of living, a way of life that the ancient philosophers invited their disciples.

It follows that the discourse of the philosopher not only could take the form of an exercise aiming at developing the disciple's intelligence, but also that of an exercise which aims to transform his life. If this is true, then we can also see how it was not only pedagogical constraints, but the demands of psychagogy, the direction of souls, which prevented the ancient philosophical texts from being perfectly systematic. Indeed, the propositions which an ancient text comprises do not always adequately express the theoretical thought of their author but must also be understood from the perspective of the effects that they aimed to produce on the listener's soul. Sometimes, as in Plato's discourses, the intellectual exercise is, at the same time, spiritual, notably when the figure of Socrates is involved, for his speeches are presented in the *Symposium* as being like incantations, bites or shocks which strike the soul of the interlocutor.[6]

It is, however, in the Hellenistic and Roman periods that this phenomenon can be most easily observed. It is in this period that philosophical discourse is only undertaken as a means for the soul to procure *ataraxia* or inner peace. We have on the subject clear texts by Epicurus. 'Our sole occupation must be healing ourselves';[7] 'If we were not troubled by our fears concerning celestial phenomena, then we would have no need to study nature';[8]

---

[k] [Translator's note] Here: *choses de la vie*; literally, 'things of life'.

'Knowledge of celestial phenomena has no other end than *ataraxia*.'⁹ This famous sentence attributed to Epicurus points to the same direction: 'Void is the discourse of the philosopher by which no passion of man is treated.'¹⁰ In this perspective, the history of Apelles' horse, to which the sceptic Sextus Empiricus alludes, is doubly instructive. 'The painter Apelles,' he tells us:

> wanted to reproduce in his painting the foam in the mouth of a horse. He was having no success and decided to give up. At this moment, the painter threw the sponge with which he wiped his brushes at the canvas. And precisely then, striking the canvas, the sponge produced the perfect imitation of the foam of the horse's mouth.¹¹

'The sceptics,' continues Sextus:

> hoped to arrive at *ataraxia* by succeeding to bring a [unifying] judgement on the discordance between what appears to us and that which we think about what appears to us. Not succeeding [in this task], they suspended their judgement completely. And lo and behold! By chance, peace of mind followed the suspension of judgement as the shadow follows the body ...

This text is doubly instructive, as I said, because it shows, on the one hand, that the sceptics had first wanted to imitate the other philosophers; that is to say, they sought to find serenity through the exercise of the faculty of judgement. However, unsatisfied with the arguments of the other schools, they found peace of mind in the very act of suspending their judgement.

On this topic, we might recall also a text from the Stoic Chrysippus, cited by Plutarch:

> There is no other or more appropriate means to reach virtue and happiness than to begin from Nature, by the study of the government of the World [...] Physical theory is only taught in order to teach the distinction between goods and evils [which is the condition of nature and of happiness, PH].¹²

What consequences has this conception of philosophy as a spiritual exercise on the form of philosophical discourse? First, we must underline that this conception of philosophy presupposes the existence of a highly systematic theoretical discourse. Since antiquity, people have admired the extraordinary coherence of the Stoic system, for example. One can also thus recognize the highly systematic character of Epicurean physics. Except that this philosophical discourse takes as its point of departure the formulation of essential vital options; as, for example, the Stoic contention, according to which, 'the moral good is the sole good, and moral good consists in coherence with oneself'. These fundamental options are formulated in a small number of fundamental principles, whose main function is to direct the philosopher's choice of life. These principles are dogmas or rules of life. The philosopher must meditate upon these dogmas and rules of life, he must assimilate them and they must become the substance of his life. As Epicurus says: '*Ataraxia* consists in constantly remembering the general and fundamental principles.'[13]

The spiritual exercises of the disciple will consist precisely in his attempts always to maintain these rules of life present to mind. Indeed, it is from this perspective that the efforts of systematization undertaken by the Stoics and Epicureans should be understood. Their theoretical systems are not elaborated as purely intellectual constructions which would be an end in themselves and which would also, as if by chance, have ethical consequences for the Stoics' or Epicureans' way of life. Rather, the Stoic or Epicurean systems aim at linking the different fundamental dogmas of the school together as strongly as possible. It is not a matter of presenting them in the most developed form, but, on the contrary, of condensing them so that the philosopher can keep them at hand[l] at each instant of his life. The presentation of these dogmas in a systematic form produces certitude, and thus leads to peace of mind and serenity.

This is what Epicurus clearly says both at the beginning and at the end of his *Letter to Herodotus*, when he explains the utility of the systematic summary that he gives to his addressee. This summary will be useful both for those who do not have the leisure to undertake detailed research on natural phenomena, Epicurus says, and to those who are able to make this study. For the latter, it will allow them to quickly return to the essentials: that is to say, to bring to mind the coherence of the system. For those who lack detailed knowledge concerning the subtleties of the system, the systematic summary will allow them to rapidly arrive at the fundamental dogmas needed to achieve serenity.[14]

Let us add that in Stoicism as well as Epicureanism, the system only ties together the fundamental dogmas. As Epicurus underlines, certain details of physical phenomena (rainbows and comets, for instance) are susceptible of multiple explanations, which are not essential parts of the system.[15]

We can see that theoretical and systematic discourse was generally aimed at producing an effect upon the soul of their listener or reader. This

---

[l] [Translator's note] Original: *sous la main.*

is not to say that this theoretical discourse does not respect the demands of logical coherence. Nevertheless, its presentation, literary form and content are all modified by the pedagogical intention to influence the students. With this end in view, the philosopher abundantly employs a host of rhetorical means. Indeed, [in many ancient texts] we find ourselves passing rapidly from theoretical exposition to exhortation, as is the case in Plotinus' treatises. Thanks to Arrian, who has written Epictetus' *Discourses*, we can also form some idea of the latter's teaching. These discourses do not record his integral teaching (which consisted in conducting commentaries on texts, as was always the case in this epoch; these commentaries could themselves be a veritable spiritual exercise). But they do, at the very least, give us an idea of the part of the course in which Epictetus discussed with his students, freely speaking with them.[16] We can see that all of Epictetus' efforts were concentrated on spiritual direction, exhortation and conversion.

To the spiritual exercises of the master correspond the spiritual exercises of the disciple. Whether it be Epicurus or Epictetus, in fact, philosophers exhort their students to meditate upon the dogmas which were exposed to them: 'day and night, meditate upon these teachings';[17] 'These are the thoughts which philosophers must contemplate, which they must write down every day, and which must be the material for exercises';[18] 'Keep these thoughts night and day at your disposal. Put them in writing.'[19]

Marcus Aurelius' *Meditations*, to take another example, represent a written text which is a spiritual exercise, from beginning to end. And, precisely, thanks to this work, we can observe how, in this effort to influence oneself, we can say that every means is good, in a certain sense. To correct mistaken opinions, tenacious prejudices or unreasonable fears, it is necessary, in some way, to twist them in the opposite direction, or to exaggerate to compensate [against their force]. This is why we must not, for example, suppose that Marcus Aurelius was personally 'pessimistic' on the pretext that he so strongly insists, in a manner which is, in fact, wholly consistent with the Stoic orthodoxy, on the 'indifferent' character of things which do not depend on us.[m]

Alongside the exercise of meditation, many other spiritual exercises may be added: inner detachment regarding objects and persons, or the inner preparation which aims at enabling us to overcome future difficulties, for the Stoics; the memory of past pleasures and fraternal correction amongst the Epicureans; and, finally, the examination of conscience, which is common to all the ancient philosophical schools.[20]

---

[m] [Translator's note] See Chapter 11 below.

2 Philosophy as 'practice' in opposition to philosophical discourse in the Hellenistic epoch

It is thus difficult to deny that the philosophies of the Hellenistic and Roman epochs were closely tied to the practice of spiritual exercises. But where exactly were these exercises situated in the ensemble of philosophical activity?

The most tempting response would be to try to situate them within the ethical part of philosophy. The distinction between three parts of philosophy – dialectical, physical and ethical – probably dates back to the ancient Academy, and perhaps it existed even before Plato.[21] In any case, it plays a considerable role in the Stoics.[n] One could thus suppose that logic and physics represent, for the Stoics, the part of philosophy where theoretic [*théorique*][o] discourse is located, and that ethics represents that part wherein the spiritual exercises, exhortations and meditations are situated. However, the line which effectively separates the theoretical and practical domain is not located between ethics and the other parts of philosophy. For at least two of these disciplines, this line is rather situated within each discipline.

This is because ethics itself involves its own theoretical discourse, which expounds the principles of ethics, and their practical applications, which are what we have called spiritual exercises. The theoretical discourse of ethics is not content only with the formulation of precepts or rules of life. It also embraces a whole set of distinctions and very subtle divisions concerning what the Stoics call 'indifferent things', as well as very detailed psychological analyses of the passions, vices and virtues, and, finally, the description of the figure of the sage. It is just that, as the Stoics affirm and repeat, philosophy itself does not consist of these distinctions and

---

[n] See Chapter 6 below.
[o] [Translator's note] Hadot's term here is *théorique,* which is one of two French terms that appear in this essay, the most 'literal' English translation for which is 'theoretic'. Here, as elsewhere in Hadot and other authors, the term *théorique* functions as an adjective describing a kind of discourse, as opposed to any and all forms of practice, action or exercise. The other term is *théorétique,* to which we will see below that Hadot assigns a different meaning, associated with the Greek *theoria,* and describing an activity of contemplation, as against a pure discourse with merely 'theoretic' content. Unless otherwise indicated, the adjective 'theoretical' in this and other chapters, without the French in brackets, indicates '*théorique*', used by Hadot to describe a kind of discourse more or less abstracted from all forms of practice.

analyses, but of the practice of the fundamental rules of life. As Epictetus puts it:

> The carpenter does not say to you: 'hear my argument on the art of carpentry', but he makes the contract for building the house and he builds it [...] Do the same yourself. Eat as a man, drink as a man, [...] get married, have children, take part in the life of the city, know how to endure your injuries, support other people.[22]

In the case of logic or dialectic, things are more complicated. Here it seems necessary to distinguish between four classes of logic. There is, first of all, the abstract theory of logic: that which examines the definitions of the proposition, the different forms of syllogisms and the different ways of refuting sophisms. There is, in the second place, the level of applications, the school exercises which the student will be made to complete in the framework of the logic class. Epictetus tells us that Musonius Rufus, his master, reprimanded him because he had not been able to find what was omitted in a syllogism.[23] Additionally, there was a third level of logic, which involved the application of the rules of logic to the theoretical discourses of the other parts of philosophy, physics and ethics. We can note, for example, the abundance of technical logical terms in the Stoics' ethical theory.

Finally, at a fourth level, there was the application of the rules of logic to everyday life: there was a daily practice of logic, which was supposed to be applied in the domain of judgement and assent.[p] Indeed, this fourth level of logic was essential for the Stoics, since for them our desires, passions and active impulses[q] are all situated, fundamentally, at the level [of our faculties] of judgement and assent. Our desires, passions and impulses are, indeed, shaped by our capacity to give or to refuse assent to a representation, according to whether it is comprehensive and adequate.

Epictetus clearly distinguishes theoretical from practiced logic:

> This is just as if, in the discipline of assent, when representations[r] present themselves, some of which are comprehensive and others not, we were

---

[p] [Translator's note] Hadot uses the term *assentiment*: clearly, the Stoic notion of *synkatathêsis*, usually translated as 'assent' is intended.

[q] [Translator's note] Original: *tendances actives*.

[r] [Translator's note] Ilsetraut Hadot suggested the English phrase *sense-perceptions* as a translation of Hadot's French translation of Epictetus's *fantasia* as *représentations*.

to refuse to make any difference between them and prefer to read theoretical treatises on comprehension instead.[24]

Thus, in everyday life also, there will be a practiced logic, which will consist in withholding our assent to anything that is false or dubious.

Now, one could say: we can understand both what a practiced ethics and even what a practiced logic might be; however, how can we understand what a practiced physics could be? Nonetheless, there is also a practiced or lived physics in Stoicism, and I would also say in Epicureanism. This lived and practiced physics clearly appears in Epictetus and Marcus Aurelius, in particular. Epictetus and Marcus Aurelius after him thus distinguish between three kinds of philosophical exercises.[25] There is the exercise which consists in disciplining our active impulse, the *hormê*,[s] and whose domain of exercise is what the Stoics called the *kathêkonta* or the 'duties'. This is the matter of lived ethics of which we have spoken. Second, there is an exercise which consists in controlling our own feelings, judgements and representations. This is the matter of lived logic, of which we have equally spoken. Finally, there is the exercise which relates to the discipline of our desires and which consists in desiring only what depends on us, and in accepting what does not depend on us as willed by universal Nature, Providence or Fate. Such consent supposes that one understands that the events which befall human beings do not depend entirely on us but result from the necessary enchainment of causes, which is not different from Fate. In all circumstances, Epictetus recommends, you must not upset yourself 'about events which have been disposed by Zeus himself [that is to say, universal reason, PH], which he has defined and ordained with the *Moirai* who, present at your birth, have woven the fabric of your destiny. Would you really ignore what a small part you are in relation to the Whole?'[26]

The discipline of desire supposes, therefore, that the [Stoic] dogmas formulated by theoretical physics concerning the necessary enchainment of causes have been meditated upon and assimilated. These dogmas must become the object of a realization[t] in the light of which the philosopher will perceive himself as a part of the Whole. Lived physics thus consists in this attitude of consent to the will of Nature. We must add, moreover, that one finds in Epictetus an exhortation to contemplate the beauty of the Universe.[27]

---

[s] [Translator's note] *Tendance active* is Hadot's term for the Greek *hormê*, a term widely translated into English as 'impulse'. We follow Hadot's French here and elsewhere, when *hormê* is at issue, and translate this as 'active impulse'.

[t] [Translator's note] The French is: *prise de conscience*.

I believe that we can also find this notion of a lived physics in Epicurus. Indeed, we have already seen how Epicurus' theoretical discourses on physics were intended to procure serenity and peace of mind. Pleasure, the goal of Epicurus' philosophy, can only be pure if the individual is delivered, thanks to the theoretical discourse on physics, from the fear of death and of the gods. However, it does not suffice to say, with André-Jean Festugière, that the science of nature has only a propaedeutic value within Epicureanism.[28] For it also seems that the contemplation of the spectacle of nature itself, as it appears to those who accept the Epicurean dogmas, brings pleasure. We recall the famous text of Lucretius expressing the joy of a soul that acquires a new vision of the universe, thanks to Epicurus' theoretical discourse: 'The terrors of the spirit are dissipated. The walls of the world are cast open. I see, in the immensity of the void, all things unfolding themselves.'[29] It is a sublime spectacle: the observer[u] perceives the peaceful residences of the gods in the ethereal light and catches a glimpse of their inner peace of mind. Lucretius continues:

> Before these things, I am sensibly seized by a divine delight[v] and I shiver at the thought that nature, discovered by your genius [Epicurus], has lifted all her veils to show herself to us.[30]

It is equally an imaginative vision of the totality of the world which seems to be involved in this sentence of the Epicurean Metrodorus:

> Remember that, born mortal and having received a limited life, you have elevated yourself to eternity by the knowledge of nature, and you have seen the infinity of things, those that will be and those which are.[31]

As we can see, these texts present physics as a way of seeing the world. What is at stake is not solely the construction of a physical theory, but a veritable spiritual and lived exercise which gives pleasure and joy to the soul.

---

[u] [Translator's note] Here: *le voyant*.

[v] [Translator's note] Hadot translates Lucretius' term with the French *volupté divine*. Our choice here was based on the translations from Titus Lucretius Carus, *The Nature of Things: A Metrical Translation*, trans. by William Ellery Leonard (London, Paris and Toronto: J.M. Dent & Sons, 1916), Lucretius, *On the Nature of Things*, trans. by W. H. D. Rouse, revd by Martin F. Smith, Loeb Classical Library 181 (Cambridge, MA: Harvard University Press, 1924) and Lucretius, *On the Nature of Things*, trans. by A. E. Stallings (London: Penguin, 2007). In the Italian translation (2010), Laura Cremonesi's choice was *divina voluttà*. In English, the term *voluptuousness* would preserve the Latin root of the word but could create other ambiguities.

Already at the beginning of his treatise *On the Parts of Animals*, Aristotle said that nature offers marvellous enjoyments to those who contemplate it.[32] The same theme existed in the Platonic tradition. In Philo of Alexandria and Plutarch, the contemplation of nature, that is to say, of the earth, sea, air, sky and stars, makes each day for the philosopher like a celebration.[33] In this perspective, one can even see that the discourse on Nature contained in Plato's *Timaeus*, in a certain sense, is not only a theoretical discourse, but is doubly accompanied by a spiritual exercise. First, in presenting this discourse as a game, Plato suggests that it is a game in honour of the gods, a sacrifice for Athena: that is to say, [it is] an activity which brings pleasure, a celebration which responds to divine play. But second, and above all, this offer to the gods is a real, lived movement of the soul, which places itself in the perspective of the Whole and becomes aware[w] of its relationship with the Whole.[34] This is the sense, I believe, of the closing words of the *Timaeus*:

> The movements that attest to our kinship with the divine principle which is within us are the thoughts of the Whole and its revolutions which everyone must follow [. . .] It is necessary to make [the intellectual part of the soul] resemble what it contemplates, in conformity with its original nature, in order to attain, by this resemblance, the perfect realisation of the excellent life proposed by the gods to men, for the present and the future.[35]

Thus, the idea of a physics which is practiced as a spiritual exercise is not unique to Stoicism.[36] It is rooted in a long tradition.

In this way, the frontier which separates theory [*le théorique*][x] and practice was situated *within* each part of philosophy. On the one hand, there is a part of theoretical discourse related to physics, to logic, to ethics. But there is, on the other hand, another part of physics which is practiced, and likewise, a practiced logic and a lived ethics.

These observations perhaps also allow us to understand the distinction which the Stoics – excepting only Zeno of Tarsus, according to Diogenes Laertius – introduced between philosophical discourses (*hoi kata philosophian logoi*) and philosophy itself.[37] The Stoics claimed that *philosophical discourses* themselves were divided into the three parts: physics, logic and ethics. This implied that philosophy itself was not, properly speaking, divided into these parts. I think we can understand this distinction in the following way.

---

[w] [Translator's note] Here: *prend conscience*.

[x] [Translator's note] See translator's note o above. Here, the sense is 'the theoretical domain'.

For the Stoics, philosophy itself, being an exercise of virtue and wisdom, is a single act, renewed at each instant. One can describe it without breaking its unity as involving the practices of lived logic, lived physics and lived ethics. In this perspective, logic, physics and ethics are virtues, of equal value and mutually implicated. It suffices to practice one to practice all of the others. As Émile Bréhier comments:

> It is impossible that the good man would not be a physicist and a dialectician, for it is impossible to realize rationality separately in these three domains, and for example to completely grasp the presence of reason in the unfolding of events within the universe without realizing, at the same time, the demands of rationality in one's own conduct.[38]

In one sense, in this unified act of philosophizing, logic, ethics and physics are not really distinguished, except on the basis of their different relations to their different specific objects: the world, human beings and one's own thought.

Nevertheless, to expound this 'philosophy-bloc', as Bréhier puts it,[39] we are constrained to divide it into three discrete parts in the philosophical discourse used in exposition and teaching, a discourse which will have to be tripartite: physics, logic and ethics.

Here, in this opposition between philosophy and the discourse on philosophy, we find the opposition between, on the one hand, the theoretical discourse on physics, logic and ethics and, on the other hand, physics, logic and ethics as lived practices. The practice of spiritual exercises of which we have spoken is then situated within philosophy itself.

However, we need to specify two further things concerning this fundamental distinction. First, one must not conceive this lived, practiced philosophy as an ethics and a morality. For, as we have seen, on the one hand, the notion of ethics is, by itself, ambiguous: it implies theoretical discourse as much as a lived practice. On the other hand, lived philosophy is not limited to the practice of moral duties. It also involves a control of the activity of thought and a cosmic consciousness.[y] Lived philosophy is thus a

---

[y] [Translator's note] Hadot's expression is *conscience cosmique*. Following Michael Chase, we translate this (more or less literally) as 'cosmic consciousness'. See, for instance, *Philosophy as a Way of Life*, 266–8. Referring to the French original, Arnold I. Davidson uses the same phrase in his introduction to *Philosophy as a Way of Life*: 'Finally, the discipline of physics included not only a theory, but a lived physics, a true spiritual exercise, which involved a way of seeing the world, a cosmic consciousness, and procured pleasure and joy to the soul' (p. 24). This consciousness locates particular experiences within an awareness of the larger, natural or (in forms of Platonism) metaphysical whole in which human life is situated. See Chapter 11 below.

practice or a way of life which embraces all human activity; it is not an ethics in the strict sense of the word.

The second point I would like to underline is that one must not conclude from the opposition between philosophical discourse and lived philosophy that the former is not itself a crucial part of philosophy. Epictetus stresses at the same time the necessity and the dangers of philosophical discourse, in the following way:

> It is necessarily by the means of discourse and oral teaching that one advances towards perfection, that one purifies one's faculty of choice, that one educates the faculty which makes use of representations. But it is necessary also that this oral teaching concerning the theorems of the philosophy adopts a certain style, being developed with much variety and refinements in terminology. Some people are captivated by the style and variety of these discourses and do not go much farther than that. One is fascinated by the style, another by the syllogisms, another by the arguments which change their sense over time.[40]

However, it is evident that the philosopher, who himself practices philosophy, cannot act upon himself and others except through discourse. Philosophy is, therefore, a way of life which brings with it, integrally, a certain mode of discourse. One could even say that philosophy, for those who practice it, consists in mastering their own inner discourse based upon the theoretical discourse formulated in the school to which they belong. This theoretical discourse emanates from a fundamental choice of life, from an existential option, which at the same time involves a vision of the world and a way of life. In turn, the discourse leads those who assimilate it to choose this existential option. The disciple comes to internally repeat the theoretical discourse of the master: putting his own inner discourse in order by grounding it on the fundamental principles and commitments which are the starting point of [the school's] theoretical discourse. Philosophical discourse goes, in this sense, from exteriority to interiority. Beginning with the purely theoretical, this discourse gradually approaches the [disciple's] soul, since the master adapts it to his disciples by practicing spiritual direction.[41] In their turn, they internalize this discourse in dialogue with themselves or with others, or else through writing. Discourse, in this way, plays a vital role in the philosophical life. However, the philosophical life cannot be reduced to discourse, not even to an inner discourse. One could say that the essential element of philosophical life is, indeed, non-discursive, to the extent that it represents a choice of life and a will to live in a particular way, with all the concrete consequences that this choice implies in everyday life.

All of this, which is true to the highest degree of Stoic philosophy, as we have glimpsed, can also be applied to Epicurean philosophy which defined itself as an activity of realizing the blessed life with the help of discourse and discussions.[42]

It is certainly only in Hellenistic philosophy that one finds the distinction between philosophy and philosophical discourse explicitly formulated. Nevertheless, it is possible to say that this distinction was already implicit in the preceding period, in the philosophies of Plato and Aristotle. For these philosophers also, as we will now see, philosophical discourse was never an end in itself. And it could not be confounded with philosophy itself.

3 Philosophical discourse and practice in Aristotle and Plato

Any such affirmations as those I have just presented confront a powerful prejudice which remains alive and well in our times. This prejudice is expressed, for example, at the end of Émile Bréhier's study on *Chrysippus*, when he writes: 'we think that one of the best methods to understand the great systems of the Hellenistic epoch after Aristotle, is to see how they placed in the foreground a concern for the education, much more than that of pure speculation'.[43] The presupposition here is that Plato and Aristotle devoted themselves to pure speculation, and thus to purely theoretical discourse. This prejudice, which is still alive today, consists in believing that the life of the Greek cities suffered decline in the Hellenistic period, and that this decadence led philosophers to renounce the pure and disinterested speculation that had been the essential dimension of philosophy in Plato and Aristotle. This decadence led philosophers to content themselves, instead, with putting forward an art of living for individuals who were, in this period, prey to anguish and isolation.

In fact, recent works by scholars like Louis Robert have shown that the life of Greek cities did not go into the decline attributed to them by nineteenth-century historians. In addition to that, it is difficult to affirm that the allegedly pure and disinterested speculation of classical philosophers was more in harmony with the life of the democratic cities of classical Greece than the pedagogical care which would allegedly have been distinctive of the Hellenistic age.

One could as plausibly affirm that, on the contrary, it was precisely in the epoch of Plato and Aristotle, and precisely in their teaching, that philosophy became, above all, a *paideia*, a work of formation – aiming at 'the harmonious development of the entire human personality, culminating in the acquisition of wisdom as the art of living'.[44] To philosophize is a matter of forming human beings and, as Socrates says already in Plato's *Apology*, of 'making them better',[45] whether in the restricted context of the philosophical school, by means of a philosophical teaching strictly speaking, or in the wider context of the city, by means of a political teaching.

This pedagogical aim has as its first consequence to reduce[z] the purely theoretical character of philosophical discourses. Indeed, philosophical discourses, and particularly the dialectical discourse of Plato and the didactic discourse of Aristotle, have for their mission less to communicate a certain knowledge than to make the interlocutors or the auditors acquire a *habitus*, an intellectual capacity which will, above all, allow them to know how to speak and argue well,[46] but which will also enable them to judge and act well. The Platonic dialogue, first of all – and Plato declares it – does not take place solely to resolve this or that particular problem,[47] but also to improve oneself as a dialectician. One can therefore say of Platonic philosophical discourse what Plutarch used to say of philosophical discourse in general:

> Philosophical discourse does not want to sculpt statues 'immobile on the pedestals' [the beautiful statues which philosophical systems are, we can perhaps add, PH]. It rather aims at making everything it touches active, efficacious and alive; it wants to inspire the desire to act, judgements which generate useful acts . . . [and] engender greatness of soul.[48]

In the same way, one of Aristotle's main concerns is to engender in his auditors the ability to utilize the correct methods in logic, the science of nature and ethics.[aa] Aristotle, in particular, gives us the occasion to specify clearly what we mean when we affirm that ancient philosophy was a practical philosophy. One tends to think that Aristotle's philosophy is essentially 'theoretic', for it truly aims at knowledge for the love of knowledge itself.[bb] There is, in this conception, a confusion between 'theoretic'

---

[z] [Translator's note] French: *diminuer*.

[aa] [Translator's note]. In this case, we have decided to use the English word *ethics* (as, for instance, in the *Nicomachean Ethics*) for *morale* in the context of Hadot's explanation of Aristotle. However, as Ilsetraut Hadot pointed out in correspondence, Pierre Hadot is using the word 'morals' [*morale*] referring to Aristotle for a contextual reason: in Aristotle's time, the tripartition of philosophy in logics, physics and ethics did not exist or, at least, it was not yet systematized.

[bb] [Translator's note] The 'knowledge' in question here is *connaissance*.

[*théorique*] and 'theoretical' [*théorétique*].[cc] The 'theoretic' [*théorique*] is opposed to 'practice'. The 'theoretic' [*théorique*] discourse is opposed to a philosophy which is practiced, lived and, therefore, 'practical'. But the adjective 'theoretical' [*théorétique*] designates the *activity* of contemplation, which is for Aristotle the highest human activity. Such 'theoretical' [*théorétique*] activity is not opposed to practiced or lived philosophy, precisely because it is itself a lived practice, the exercise of a life, and an activity which produces the happiness both of God and men. That such a 'theoretical' kind of activity is not opposed to 'practice', Aristotle says explicitly in the *Politics*:

[cc] [Translator's note] According to Ilsetraut Hadot (in correspondence), the distinction in French between *théorétique* and *théorique* is relatively recent. It was created by Edmond Goblot, at the beginning of the twentieth century. In his *Le vocabulaire philosophique* (Whitefish, MT: Kessinger Publishing, 2009 [1901]), we find the entry *théorétique* (at 472). Although he differentiates between the two terms, Goblot defines *théorétique* differently from Hadot:

> That which regards theory, that which is limited to theory and is not related to practice. Aristotle's *theoretical virtue* consists of the knowledge and contemplation of truth, by contrast to the *practical virtues* which correspond to action; the former is the end of man as a rational being [*zoon logikon*] whereas the latter correspond to the end of man as a citizen [*zoon politikon*] – the *théorétique* is related to theory, while the *théorique* is part of the theory [*fait partie de la théorie*].

For Hadot, the *théorétique*, which appears in Goblot's reference to Aristotle's *zoon logikon*, is not opposed to practice. It designates a practice of a different sort: a theoretical, contemplative practice and the basis of a way of life, the intellectual life or *bios theorêtikos*. As Davidson comments (*Philosophy as a Way of Life*, 29):

> Hadot has distinguished two senses of the term 'theoretical', for which he has employed the terms *théorique* and *théorétique*. The first meaning of 'theoretical' is opposed to 'practical', since it designates theoretical discourse as opposed to lived philosophy. But the adjective *théorétique* which characterizes the life of contemplation, the life according to the intellect, is not opposed by Aristotle to philosophy as practiced and lived.

There is no equivalent of *théorique* in English, since it is a relatively recent French creation. For this reason, following the advice of Ilsetraut Hadot, we have decided to leave *théorétique* and *théorique* untranslated in the text here, in brackets. Following Michael Chase's option in his translation of Hadot's *What is Ancient Philosophy?* (Cambridge, MA: Belknap, 2004, 293 n. 13), we have further tried to convey the distinction by translating *théorique* as 'theoretic' in these paragraphs and the *théorétique* as 'theoretical'. As one reads in *What is Ancient Philosophy?*, 'Insofar as way of life is concerned, it cannot, of course, be theoretic, but it can be theoretical—that is to say, contemplative' (p. 5). In that book, see also chapter 6, especially the explanation at pp. 80–1.

The [word] 'practice' is not necessarily what relates to objects different from ourselves . . .: not only the thoughts which evaluate the outcome of action are [called] practical, but also those which have their end in themselves and take themselves for their object.[49]

For Aristotle, then, the theoretical [*théorétique*] life is not a pure abstraction. It is a life of the mind which can certainly also utilize theoretic [*théorique*] discourse. Yet, it remains a life and a *praxis*, and one which can even lead to an activity of thought which is non-discursive, when it is a matter of perceiving indivisible objects and God himself by noetic intuition. There is another aspect of this pedagogical concern which appears especially in Plato's philosophy. The role played by love in his philosophy is well known. Nevertheless, we perhaps do not rightly appreciate its full significance. According to the *Phaedrus*,[50] the fall of the soul into the body brings with it the consequence that we forget what the soul saw in the intelligible world: that is to say, the values of truth, justice and wisdom. The soul, now fallen into the body, no longer recognizes these values, even in their images here below. As Plato says in the *Statesman*,[51] it can only speak of these things, and try by the hard work of dialectics to define them, but it can no longer [directly] *see* them. The sole vision that the soul can have of a value, an idea here below, is that of beauty, which can be glimpsed in beautiful bodies. The loving emotion[dd] that animates the soul of the lover at this moment is based upon its unconscious remembrance – which can, however, become conscious – of the vision that the soul has had of transcendent beauty in its prior existence.

The experience of physical love,[ee] albeit sublimated, is a constitutive part of Plato's philosophy and it plays a double role in it. On the one hand (as at *Symposium* 209b–c), the love for beautiful bodies and, above all, for the beauty of their souls, Plato tells us, makes the lover's soul fecund: a fecundity which is manifest in beautiful discourse, in philosophical discussion with the beloved. Here, we are apparently led from love to discourse. However, this necessity of the amorous experience[ff] introduces into Platonic dialectic a component which is absolutely irreducible to discourse and to rationality. Dialectic is no longer solely a logical exercise. Rather, it is the dialogue of

---

[dd] [Translator's note] Hadot's expression is *émotion amoureuse*.
[ee] [Translator's note] The adjective is *sensible*, whose literal translation in English is ambiguous, so we have chosen 'physical' here: what is at stake is the experience of the senses, yet 'sensual' connotes erotic or sexual love, which may not be intended here.
[ff] [Translator's note] Quite literally, *experience amoureuse*.

two souls which only elevate themselves towards the Good because they love each other. In the *Symposium*, what counts is less discourse itself than the presence of the beloved. It is less a matter of concluding a process of reasoning through a proposition than of making oneself or becoming better, under the influence of the person whom one loves. The educational influence of the master is exercised in a way which is, to some extent, irrational. There is something magic in the pedagogical power of love.

On the other hand, according to the *Symposium* (210a), the experience of love – if it is well directed, and if it is elevated from the beauty which we find in bodies to that of souls, actions and sciences – will lead the soul to the sudden vision of a marvellous and eternal beauty.[52] It is a vision analogous to the one the initiate enjoys in the Eleusinian mysteries. One notes that at every stage of this ascent, Plato says, the experience of love prompts the soul to engender beautiful and magnificent discourses. Then, at the summit of the ascent, one reaches a vision which goes beyond discursivity altogether, but which enables the soul to engender virtue itself.[53] Philosophy becomes the lived experience of a presence. From the experience of the presence of the beloved, one is elevated towards an experience of a transcendent presence.

Likewise, in the *Phaedo*, the definition of philosophy as the effort to separate oneself from the body, to train the soul to concentrate itself, in a word, the [Platonic] definition of philosophy as an exercise of death, also presupposes a distinction between philosophy and philosophical discourse.[54] Theoretical philosophical discourse is, indeed, different from these lived philosophical exercises by which the soul purifies itself of its passions and spiritually separates itself from the body.

In fact, we find these lived and concrete spiritual exercises throughout the entire course of the Platonic tradition, notably in Philo of Alexandria,[55] but above all in Plotinus. There is, in the latter, a complete lucidity concerning the distinction which separates philosophical discourse from philosophy itself at each level of the soul's ascent towards the beautiful and the good. First, the soul can only become aware of its own immateriality if it undertakes an ethical purification which frees it from everything which is not itself: that is to say, which liberates it from the passions.[56] Then, if the soul wants to be elevated to the level of the Intellect, it must renounce discourse and try to raise itself to an immediate and indivisible intuition of thought itself, an idea that is part of the heritage of Aristotelian thought.[57] When Plotinus wants to describe the ascension of the soul towards the Good, he insists, on the one hand, that there is the discourse, which abstractly instructs us about the Good, that is to say, the abstract discourse of rational theology, with its methods of analogy or negation, for example.

On the other hand, there is that which effectively leads us to the Good, that is, as Plotinus says, purifications, virtues and inner discipline:[88] in a word, spiritual exercises effectively practiced.[58]

Above all, the Plotinian mystical experience prolongs and develops all that the Platonic experience of love represents. The latter gave to the soul the feeling of the presence of beauty. The Plotinian mystical experience gives to the soul the experience of the presence of the Good itself, and it is itself lived as an initiation to the mysteries. There is in this presence a lived dimension which entirely escapes discursive rationality.

***

Let us summarize our argument. There existed throughout antiquity a philosophical tradition which we can find in Plato, Aristotle, Polemon, Epicurus, Zeno, Epictetus and Plotinus. This tradition refused to identify philosophy with philosophical discourse. Certainly, there cannot be philosophy without the inner and external discourse of the philosopher. However, all the philosophers about whom I have talked considered themselves as philosophers not because they developed philosophical discourses, but because they lived philosophically. Their discourse was integrated into their philosophical lives, whether as a pedagogical activity exercised on others or an activity of meditation or as, indeed, the expression or explanation of a contemplative activity which is not discursive in itself. For these ancient philosophers, philosophy itself was, above all, a form of life and not a discourse. It would be possible to maintain that the founder and model for such a conception of philosophy was Socrates, who, when Hippias asked him the definition of justice, answered: 'instead of saying what it is, I make justice manifest in my actions'.[59]

Socrates would remain within this tradition the model of the philosopher who lives more than speaks, and who only speaks for the sake of life. This is shown (amongst many other places) in a text by Plutarch, which opposes philosophical discourse, specially considered as a discourse of the professional philosopher, and the philosophical life which transforms the philosopher's everyday life. And here, also, it is Socrates himself who will appear as the model of the true philosopher.

In this context, Plutarch aims at making clear that the political life is not limited to the professional activities of the politician but permeates all aspects of life as a whole. In this regard, Plutarch contends, politics is

---

[88] [Translator's note] Here, Hadot's words are *mise en ordre intérieure*.

analogous to philosophy, for philosophy is also not limited to the professional discourse of the philosopher. As Plutarch explains:

> Most people imagine that philosophy consists in lecturing [on ideas] from the heights of one's chair and running courses on texts. But what escapes these people totally is the uninterrupted political and philosophical *activity* that we see being exercised every day in such a way that they are always equal to themselves. And, as Dicaearchus has said, such men are happy to speak of someone who comes and goes under the porticos as 'taking a walking philosophical lesson' (*peripatein*). But they do not use this expression when it is a matter of those who walk in their fields or go to see a friend [...] Socrates, who never required an arrangement of steps for his listeners, did not sit on a professorial chair. Neither did he have an established time to walk and debate with his disciples. Socrates has philosophized by sometimes sharing jokes with his disciples, or by drinking with them, by going to war or to the Agora with certain amongst them, and finally by going to prison and drinking the hemlock. He was the first to show that, always and in all places, and in everything which happens to us or that we ourselves do, everyday life can find a find a place for philosophy.[60]

Notes

1   Victor Goldschmidt, 'Remarques sur la méthode structurale en histoire de la philosophie', *Métaphysique et Histoire de la philosophie, recueil d'études offert à Fernand Brunner* (Paris: Neuchatel: Edn. la Baconnière, Dif. Payot, 1981), 230.

2   Antoine Meillet, *Bulletin de la société de linguistique de Paris* 32, comptes rendus (1931): 23.

3   René Schaerer, *La question Platonicienne* (Paris: Neuchâtel, 1969), 87. [Translator's note: 'skilfulness' here translates the French: *habileté*].

4   Diogenes Laertius, *Lives of the Eminent Philosophers*, IV, 18.

5   Epictetus, *Discourses*, III, 23.

6   Plato, *Symposium*, 215d–216c.

7   Epicurus, *Gnomologium Vatacanum,* § 64.

8   Epicurus, *Kuriai Doxai*, 11.

9   Epicurus, *Letter to Pythocles*, 85.

10 Porphyry, *Ad Marcellum*, § 31.

11 Sextus Empiricus, *Hypotyposis*, I 28.

12 Plutarch, *De Repugnantiis Stoicorum*, 9 1035c.

13 Epicurus, *Letter to Herodotus*, 82.

14 Cf. ibid., 35: "For those, Herodotus, who are not able accurately to comprehend all the things which I have written about nature, nor able to investigate those larger books which I have composed on the subject, I have made an abridgment of the whole discussion on this question as far as I thought sufficient to enable them to recollect accurately the most fundamental points; that so, on all occasions, they might be able to assist themselves on the most important and undeniable principles; in proportion as they devoted themselves to speculations on natural philosophy. And here it is necessary for those who have made sufficient progress in their view of the general question, to recollect the principles laid down as elements of the whole discussion; for we have still greater need of a correct notion of the whole, than we have even of an accurate understanding of the details . . ."

15 Epicurus, *Letter to Pythocles*, 86.

16 Cf. Joseph Souilhé, 'Introduction á *Epictete*', *Entretiens* (Paris: Belles Lettres, 1949), xxix.

17 Epicurus, *Letter to Menoeceus*, 135.

18 Epictetus, *Discourses*, I, 1, 25.

19 Ibid., III, 24, 10.

20 Cf. Pierre Hadot, *Exercices spirituels et philosophie antique* 3e édn. (Paris: Albin Michel, [1981] 1992).

21 Cf. Victor Goldschmidt, 'Sur le problème du "système de Platon"', *Revista critica di storia della filosofia* 5 (1950): 171.

22 Epictetus, *Discourses,* III, 21, 4–6.

23 Ibid., I, 7, 32.

24 Ibid., IV, 4, 13.

25 Ibid., III, 2 and III, 12.

26 Ibid., I, 12, 25.

27 Ibid., I, 6, 19.

28 André-Jean Festugière, *Epicure et ses dieux*, 2e édn. (Paris: Presses Universitaires de France, 1968), 54.

29 Lucretius, *De rerum natura*, III, 14–30.

30 Ibid.

31 Metrodorus, fragment 37.

32 Aristotle, *Parts of Animals*, 644b–645a.

33 Philo of Alexandria, *De Specialibus Legibus*, II, 44–48; Plutarch, *Tranquillity of Mind*, § 20, 477.

34 cf. Pierre Hadot, 'Physique et poésie dans le *Timée* de Platon', *Revue de théologie et de philosophie* 115 (1983), 113–133; and in *Études de philosophie ancienne*, 277–305.

35 Plato, *Timaeus*, 90c.

36 Cf. Pierre Hadot, 'La physique comme exercice spirituel ou pessimisme et optimisme chez Marc Aurèle,' *Revue de Théologie et de Philosophie* 3rd ser. 22 (1972): 225–39. [Translator's note: i.e. Chapter 11 below].

37 Diogenes Laertius, *Lives of the Eminent Philosophers*, VII, 39 & 41.

38 Émile Bréhier, *Historie de la philosophie*, tome I, 2 (Paris: Presses Universitaires de France, 1961), 303.

39 Bréhier's term is *philosophie-bloc*. See Bréhier, *Historie de la philosophie*, tome 1, 2, 300.

40 Epictetus, *Discourses*, II, 23, 40. [Translator's note: Hadot's translation differs considerably from the English of Higginson (1890), Long (1890) and Oldfather (1925) and Dobbin (2008). We follow Hadot.]

41 See again Ilsetraut Hadot, *Sénèque* (Paris: Vrin, 2014).

42 Sextus Empiricus, *Adversus Mathematicus*, XI, 169; cf. Hermann Usener, *Epicurea* (Leipzig: Teubne, 1887), sec. 219, 169 n. 5.

43 Émile Bréhier, *Chrysippe et l'ancien stoïcisme* (Paris: Presses Universitaires de France, 1951), 270.

44 Ilsetraut Hadot, *Arts libéraux et philosophies dans la pensée antique* (Paris: Études Augustiniennes, 1984), 15.

45 Plato, *Apology*, 24d, 36e.

46 Compare on Plato in this regard, Wolfgang Wieland, *Platon und die Formen des Wissens* (Gottingen: Vandenhoeck & Ruprecht, 1982).

47 Plato, *Statesman,* 285–286.

48 Plutarch, *Maxime cum principibus*, I, 776c.

49 Aristotle. *Politics*, VII.3.8, 1325b.

50 Plato, *Phaedrus*, 249e.

51 Plato, *Statesman*, 286a.

52 Plato, *Symposium*, 210a.

53 Plato, *Symposium*, 212a.

54 Plato, *Phaedo*, 67d–e.

55 Philo of Alexandria, *Quis rerum divinarum heres sit.*, § 253; *Legum allegoriarum*, III, §18.

56 Plotinus, *Enneads*, IV, 7, 10, 27 ff.

57 Plotinus, *Enneads*, V, 8, 11.

58 Plotinus, *Enneads*, VI, 7, 36, 5 ff.

59 Xenophon, *Memorabilia*, IV, 4, 10.

60 Plutarch, *An seni sit Gerenda Respublica*, 26, 796c–d.

4 THE ORAL TEACHING OF PLATO[1]

A new interpretation of Platonism has been proposed over the last thirty years by what one can call the Tübingen School, since its main protagonists and several of its proponents, in fact, teach in that city. Three key works mark in some way the foundation of this school: the book by Hans Joachim Krämer on *Arête* in Plato and Aristotle, which appeared in 1959, that of Konrad Gaiser on the forms of Platonic dialogue, entitled *Protreptic and Paranêsis in Plato*,[a] also published in 1959, and, finally, that of Gaiser on the unwritten teaching of Plato, dating from 1963.[b]

For a long time, it is true, one has used the ancient testimonies on the unwritten doctrines of Plato, notably Aristotle's, in order to reconstitute their structure.[2] But one generally considered that these unwritten doctrines had appeared late in the evolution of Plato's thought. The dialogues were thus, in the eyes of historians, the unique expression of Plato's thought during most of his life. The novelty introduced by the Tübingen School consisted in refusing to consider the unwritten doctrines as a late phenomenon. On the contrary, it recognizes in them the essential [part] of Platonic thought, because they were the very content of the oral teaching. This oral teaching was for Plato the only valid [form of] instruction. The Tübingen School thus takes seriously the condemnation of writing, that is to say, of his own dialogues announced by Plato in the *Phaedrus* and in the

---

[a] [Translator's note] Original: Konrad Gaiser, *Protreptik Und Paränese Bei Platon Untersuchungen Zur Form des Platonischen Dialogs* (Stuttgart: Kohlhammer, 1959).

[b] [Translator's note] Konrad Gaiser, *Platons ungeschriebene Lehre: Studien zur systematischen und geschichtlichen Begründung der Wissenschaften in der Platonischen Schule* (Stuttgart: Klett-Cotta, 1963).

Seventh Letter. The dialogues express Plato's thought only in an allusive and imperfect way, because they have, above all, a protreptic and paraenetic value, and it is the oral teaching that allows one to understand and to complete them.

The publications of the three books which we have mentioned very soon provoked a gigantic controversy in the scholarly world, a veritable War of the Giants which is yet to be resolved, and which has engendered a very abundant literature, of which one will find the principal titles in the bibliography [of Marie-Dominique Richard's *L'enseignement oral de Platon*]. Indeed, one can affirm that, regardless of the final judgement that one makes of the theories of the Tübingen School, it is impossible to deny that the School has from the start represented an extraordinary renewal in Platonic studies. It has opened new perspectives for the understanding of the dialogues, it has revealed the immense effects which the discussions which took place in Plato's Academy had on the philosophical schools until the end of Antiquity, and it has inspired fruitful researches regarding the history of ancient philosophy as a whole, notably on Hellenistic philosophy and Plotinus.

Around the time of the publication of the works I have just mentioned, several highly remarkable reviews or studies appeared in France between 1960 and 1970, authored by Jean Pépin, Pierre Aubenque, Aimé Solignac and Jacques Brunschwig. The fact remains that the importance and significance of the theses of the Tübingen School are not presently known in our country except by a small number of initiates. Until now, there did not exist in the French language any means of access to the theories relating to Plato's oral teachings and to the controversies which have developed around them, whereas in the Italian language, for example, there exist many extremely important works on this theme.

Marie-Dominique Richard's book, therefore, responds to an urgent need, and fills a significant lacuna in French research. Richard has even made the special effort of writing her work in Tübingen, in the course of a four-year sojourn, during which she was able to follow the 'oral teaching' of Hans Joachim Krämer and Konrad Gaiser, and to converse with them. Her work was thus drawn from the most direct sources. Moreover, because of her remarkable mastery of the German language, she has been able to make accessible to her readers the mass of documents on this question which have been published in the last few years.

It is thus an extremely precious working instrument that [Richard] offers to her readers. They will be able to judge for themselves based on the evidence, since they will find at the end of the book, together with the Greek original text and the French translation, the complete dossier of the main ancient texts relating to the oral teaching of Plato. The book traces the main lines of the history of the controversy which took place around the problem of the oral teaching of Plato, presenting the history and critique of ancient testimonies regarding the unwritten doctrines, carefully distinguishing the translations coming from Aristotle, Theophrastus or the Ancient Academy. Finally, the synthesis that one can extract from these testimonies and thus the structure of the theory of principles elaborated by Plato is presented with great acuity.[c]

***

Richard's book will certainly inspire in its readers the desire to pursue further research, for example on the relationship between Pythagoreanism and Platonism, or on the exact nature of Platonic dialectic, or on the implications of the dualism professed in the oral teaching.

The question of the relation between writing and orality in philosophy, posed by Plato himself in the *Phaedrus* and in the *Seventh Letter*, is a key problem, which one finds very often evoked throughout the pages of this work. The question which is posed to historians is in effect the following: in order to understand Plato's thought, should we trust in fragmentary testimonies of students reporting an oral teaching, rather than in dialogues written by the master and composed by him with an extreme care? Should we not consider that only the writing authenticated by the author has, precisely, an authentic value?

In order to understand what is at stake here, namely the methodology of the history of ancient philosophy as a whole and the very definition of philosophy, I will evoke, first of all, the remarks that Victor Goldschmidt has made, a few years ago, in a work advocating in favour of the structural method in the history of philosophy.[3] Underlining the fact that 'the structural method [...] incontestably stresses the written work, as the unique testimony wherein a philosophical thought is manifested', he goes on to affirm: 'The Greco-Roman civilization early on became a civilisation of writing [...] Philosophy, from its origin, is formulated though writing.'

It is necessary to say this clearly. One cannot maintain that Greco-Roman civilization became early on a civilization of writing. On the contrary, as Eric A. Havelock underlined: 'one could say of Pindar and Plato that they are still part of a world without writing' and that one cannot

---

[c] [Translator's note] The preceding paragraph did not appear in the version of the 'Preface' to Richard's work which appears in *Discours et mode de vie philosophique* (Paris: Les Belles Lettres, 2014) but is found in the 2010 Belles Lettres collection, *Études de philosophie ancienne*, which we follow here.

understand 'their clever compositions[d] [...] without at base examining the oral processes of composition and recording'.[4] Generally speaking, certainly in the epoch of Plato and probably in all of Antiquity, the written work is extremely closely tied to orality. According to the felicitous formula of Arnold J. Toynbee:[5]

> Like the typed text of the speaker on the radio presently, the Greco-Roman 'book' was really a mnemonic system aiming to dispel the evasive power of words and not a book in the sense that we understand today, as a thing made so that one could read it to oneself.

The ancient book was, nearly always, the echo of a speech intended to become speech once again. An echo of speech, as we will see later concerning Plato,[e] the book was destined to once again become spoken word. This is because (during all of Antiquity until the time of Augustine, who was struck, as we know, to see Ambrose of Milan reading with his eyes), the book is read aloud, whether by a slave who did the reading to his master, or by the author in a public reading,[6] or by the reader himself. The constraints that oral literature imposed on literary composition, on the form of the phrase, the rhythm and the sonority which are addressed to the ear and not to the eyes, will thus be rediscovered in [ancient] written works, and these constraints have their consequences in the expression of ideas. In these conditions, indeed, ideas could not be presented timelessly,[f] as in the modern book that one can read in an undetermined order and in which all the parts coexist. They are rather submitted to the time of speech.[g] It is not striking that Plato exposes his ideas under the form of a conversation, of a dialogue which is an event which unfolds itself in time. We will see up to what point he exposes them.

Generally speaking, as speech is tied to real time, insofar as it is an act produced by human beings in relation to others, the ancient book, echo of speech, does not find its meaning exclusively in itself, but in the living *praxis* from which it emanated and towards which it is aimed. No more than the inscriptions that epigraphy studies can it be separated from its spiritual and material site. Thus, as we will have occasion to repeat, the dialogues of Plato cannot be understood in themselves without taking account of all the information which we have on the school of Plato and the discussions and teachings which were practiced there.

---

[d] [Translator's note] More or less literally, "assemblages of words": *agencements de mots*.

[e] [Translator's note] See Chapter 3 above.

[f] [Translator's note] Original: *intemporelle*.

[g] [Translator's note] French: *temps de la parole*.

The written work, therefore, does not suffice to make the 'philosophy' of an author known, and it does not suffice to say, with Victor Goldschmidt 'philosophy, in its origin, is formulated in writing' in order to prove the contrary. One could perhaps think with Havelock[7] that the development of writing enabled the rise of Greek thought by making abstraction possible, by making it possible for a word to correspond no longer to an image but to a concept. But that is not certain. One must not overlook the extraordinary capacities for meditation and memory of the thinkers of Antiquity. We could remark, for example, that Socrates indeed laid claim to search for definitions and concepts solely with the aid of spoken dialogue, and Plato in the *Symposium* depicts Socrates' long, solitary meditation being undertaken without writing. Another testimony of this extraordinary power, at least in certain men, [survives]: we know that Plotinus, before writing his treatises, 'had organised them entirely in his soul',[8] which presupposes that he did not have need of the support of writing to develop his thought.

To speak precisely, it is probably an error to consider abstraction as the main characteristic of ancient philosophy (if not of philosophy in general). For the ancient philosopher, at least beginning with the sophists and Socrates, proposes to form men and transform souls. This is why philosophical teaching is delivered, in antiquity, primarily in an oral form, because only living speech in dialogues, in conversations pursued over a long period of time, can accomplish any such work. The written work, however remarkable it may be, is, therefore, most of the time only an echo or a complement of this spoken teaching.

This is what Plato himself says in the *Phaedrus*.[9] This primacy of the oral over the written is for Plato at the same time an historical necessity and a spiritual requirement. It is, first, an historical necessity because, in a civilization which has political discourse at its centre, it is necessary to form men who possess, above all, mastery of speech. This is the case, even if like Plato, in contrast to the sophists, one wants to found political discourse on a Science which will be mathematical, but above all dialectical, and which will enable philosophers to act and to speak conformably to the Idea of the Good, measure of all things,[10] and to exact definitions which follow from it. Yet, precisely in Plato's school, this dialectic is always practiced in a living discussion, in an oral dialogue. It is also a spiritual requirement. Because, for Plato, the written work only engenders in its reader a false knowledge, a ready-made truth. Only living dialogue is formative: it brings to the disciple the possibility of discovering by himself the Truth because of long discussions, because of a long 'agriculture' which is pursued during his whole life, very different from the ephemeral gardens of Adonis which grow in books.[11] For it is in souls, not in books, that it is necessary to sow [the seeds of philosophy] with the aid of speech.

Living dialogue could only be pursued in a group, not in a school or a university in the modern sense of the term, but in a community of people, united by spiritual love and placing everything in common, above all their ideas: such is very much the spirit of the Platonic Academy. A certain esotericism inevitably results from this: the esotericism inherent in all closed groups which end up having their own tradition, ritual, special language, documents and, in a word, their mysteries. If it is not at all certain, as John Patrick Lynch has shown,[12] that the philosophical schools of Antiquity were not religious thiases, it nevertheless remains [true] that the representation of philosophy as a mystery (at *Symposium*, 210a, for example) could lead [us] to conceive of philosophy as a secret reserved for initiates. As Clement of Alexandria will say much later: 'The mysteries, like God, can only be confided in speech, and not in writing.'[13]

Let us add, to put writing in its rightful, entirely relative place, that true philosophy is neither an oral discourse, nor a written discourse, but a way of being: to philosophise does not consist in speaking or writing, but in being; it is necessary to transform the entirety of one's soul to be able to contemplate the Idea of the Good. Here, one reaches the limits of language.

But then, one will say, why write, why not content oneself with speaking? It is because writing has an advantage over speech, it allows [us] to extend the action of speaking in time and space. For future times, it allows us to conserve the memory of events or ideas which [would otherwise] risk being forgotten.[14] This is also, nevertheless, its danger, for it risks provoking an atrophy of the capacities for memorization (this is what happens to modern man). In any case, writing allows us to amass a 'treasure of memories for old age', as Plato says. One can accept that certain dialogues, for example the *Philebus*, are the echo of certain discussions which had taken place within the Academy. They are thus only the echo of the oral activities of the school. The dialogues thus express the ideas of Plato, but in the perspective of a precise question. One sees there the principles applied to a particular case.

Writing can thus act at a distance, it can be addressed to people who are absent and those who are unknown. The 'discourse will circulate everywhere'[h] and it can reach souls foreign to the school,[15] non-philosophers who, by

---

[h] [Translator's note] Preserving Hadot's translation of κυλινδεῖται μὲν πανταχοῦ from *Phaedrus* 275 d–e, the text would read 'discourse will roll through all sides', which is not felicitous; the translation, in this case, is our own.

reading of the dialogues and putting into question their system of values, can perhaps be converted to philosophy. From this point of view, the Platonic dialogues are literary works of an exoteric character, in the same way as the dialogues of Aristotle. They are only a distant echo of the oral teaching, which aim to make [the latter] known. It is a curious thing, since we still possess the esoteric (acroamatic) works of Aristotle which, like the treatises gathered in the *Metaphysics*, are often a direct and immediate echo of his oral teaching and entail a high degree of technicality, that we do not experience any reticence in considering his dialogues, which are totally lost, as exoteric works intended for the general public, expressing his philosophy under a more accessible form. However, it is necessary to imagine that the same situation is found in Plato: the dialogues, for the most part, are exoteric, addressed to the cultivated public. As for the oral teaching, it [as it were] cannot not have existed. Most likely, the dialectical exercises must have had an important place. But it is impossible that Plato did not then express his own opinions or his methodological reflections. In any case, Plato himself does not seem to have made the effort to ensure that [the oral teaching] was written down. This oral teaching is known to us only through the testimony of his disciples.

To interest readers and eventually convert them, it will be necessary to have recourse to all of those refinements of the art of nascent literature which already appear in Pindar, the tragedians, or Thucydides.[16] One will ask a great deal of the reader, one will pique his curiosity by allusions, subtleties of composition and desired correspondences. There will also be, up to a certain point, an esoteric sense in these exoteric dialogues which will only be discovered by the perspicacious reader.

The protreptic and paraenetic character of the Platonic dialogues has been shown in a remarkable way by Konrad Gaiser in 1959, as we have said. His demonstration is confirmed in a striking and, one could say, sensational fashion by the ancient testimony, nevertheless very close to Plato's times, which is cited by Richard in the Appendix of her book. This text is a 'Life of Plato' written by Dicaearchus, disciple of Aristotle, and it is cited by the Epicurean Philodemus in a writing which forms part of the collection of papyri found at Herculaneum and whose deciphering has recently been considerably improved. Dicaearchus notably writes: 'in composing his dialogues, Plato exhorted (*proetrepsato*) a mass of people to philosophise [...] Due to the influence of his literary activity, Plato encouraged by his books many outsiders [that is to say, strangers to the school, PH] to not personally take account of the opinions of chatterboxes[i]

---

[i] [Translator's note] The French noun being *bavards.*

[probably the sophists, PH]'. Protreptic and paraenesis, exhortation and encouragement, such is therefore the main goal of the Platonic dialogues. We have at least an historical example of this role of the dialogues. We know, indeed, from Themistius[17] that it was after she had read the *Republic* that a woman of Philonthus, Axiothea, came to Athens to become a disciple of Plato, disguised as a man.

The Platonic dialogue thus acts at a distance, but never with the efficacity of living speech. It strives at least to imitate this living speech, to give to the reader the illusion of participating in the dialogue. In this sense, it refers, yet again, to the discussions of the Academy; it is a seductive image of life inside the Academy, an image in which Plato loves to present himself under the traits of Socrates, insinuating that the discussions of the Academy are continuations of the Socratic discussions. As I have said elsewhere, certain dialogues are writings which attempt to make themselves forgotten as writings, which give the illusion of being spoken.[18] Certain others more clearly have the characteristics of written texts, on the contrary, like the *Timaeus*, in which Plato almost completely renounces dialogue. That is, he sees these texts as games, even more so than his other dialogues.

For the literary composition is for Plato a game in honour of the gods: it is, he writes, 'to amuse oneself in a decent and pious manner'[19] that he writes philosophical works. The *Timaeus*, for example, has an affinity with the sacrifice offered in honour of Athena.[20] Like the religious festivals, the literary work is a human game which imitates in some way the divine game of the creation of the world.[21] In the case of the *Timaeus*, it is a likely story which mimics the event of the birth of the God-World. Furthermore, Plato underlines in several places the fact that it is not necessary to take this game too seriously: as Pascal says: 'when they [Plato and Aristotle] entertained themselves by writing their *Laws* and *Politics*, they made them by playing; it was the least philosophical and the least serious part of their lives'.

Plato, therefore, considers with irony his own dialogues as a game that imitates the amusement which the creation of the world was for the gods. A late Neoplatonist has expanded the comparison to the whole of Plato's work.[22] In the same way that the creator God has made certain parts of his creation invisible, like souls for example, Plato delivered a part of his teaching in writing and the other part [was] spoken, namely 'that which he said in his classes (*sunousiai*)'. One sees that, for this Neoplatonist, the unwritten classes of Plato are superior to the written works, as souls are to bodies.

Finally, the Platonic dialogue is to some extent analogous to tragedy, because, on the one hand, it makes characters speak in such a way that Plato never clearly speaks in his own name. On the other hand, the dialogue is not originally intended to be read by a solitary reader but to be recited in a public reading,[23] I would not say in a performance but, in any case, in a spoken form. It is perhaps written consciously in this perspective and the auditor experiences it like a drama, as a momentary event which takes place in time and which is probably only heard once.

All this collection of facts, distinct to Plato or general to his time, obliges us to consider the works that Plato has written as testimonies which, without doubt, have incomparable value in making his thought known to us. But these testimonies do not suffice by themselves. Not only do they refer back to a hidden sense. Above all, they are only a part, only one aspect of Plato's philosophical activity, and they demand to be clarified by all that we know of Plato's activity as the head of [the] school.

But what is the place of the oral teaching in this other part of Plato's activity, that is in his activity as head of the school? What does this systematic schema represent that, in opposing the Dyad to the One, allows the emergence of the Ideas and Numbers? Here, I believe, is a question which also remains open to future research, and I approach it with great caution. Some [readers] will perhaps find this schema very thin or too systematic. But if this theoretical core is relatively thin, it is probably because the system is precisely not an end in itself, it is not intended to deliver all at once a total and exhaustive explanation of reality by the construction of an abstract theoretical edifice, but it has for its end, in each new circumstance, before each new problem which is posed about speech and action, to furnish to the dialectician the means to solve problems in a way that Plato considered to be scientific, recognizing in each case the exact measure according to which the One and the Dyad are mixed, and striving to exactly place each thing under the light of the Idea of the Good. As Konrad Gaiser has clearly shown,[24] this method is an infinite enterprise and it is not at all a renunciation of Socratic aporetic, for it makes philosophy discover the perpetual inadequacy of human knowledge in the face of ultimate reality.

Notes

1   This text was originally published as the French-language Preface to Marie-Dominique Richard, L'enseignement oral de Platon (Paris: Editions du Cerf, 1986), 7–15.

2   Cf. the book by Léon Robin, La Théorie des Idées et des Nombres (Paris: F. Alcan, 1908).

3   In Victor Goldschmidt, Métaphysique, histoire de la philosophie, Recueil d'études offert à F. Brunner (Neuchâtel: Éditions de la Baconnière, 1981), 230.

4 Eric A. Havelock, *Aux origines de la civilisation écrite en Occident* (Paris: Maspero), 14.

5 Arnold J. Toynbee, *La Civilisation à l'epreuve* (Paris: Gallimard, 1951), 53–54.

6 Diogenes Laertius, III, 35–37.

7 Eric A. Havelock, 'Preface', *Plato* (Cambridge [MA]: Harvard University Press, 1961).

8 Porphyry, *Life of Plotinus*, 8, 10.

9 Plato, *Phaedrus*, 276 a–e.

10 Plato, *Republic*, 517c.

11 Plato, *Phaedrus*, 276 a–e, with *Seventh Letter*, 344 b–c

12 John P. Lynch, *Aristotle's School: A Study of a Greek Educational Institution*, 106–114.

13 Clement, *Stromates*, I, 1, 13, 2.

14 Plato, *Phaedrus*, 276 b.

15 Plato, *Phaedrus* 275 d–e.

16 Cf. Jacqueline de Romilly, *Histoire et raison chez Thucydides* (Paris: Belles Lettres, 1956), 89–106.

17 Themistius, *Orat.*, XXIII, 295 c–d.

18 Pierre Hadot, 'Physique et poésie dans la *Timée* de Platon', *Revue de théologie et de philosophie* 115, no. 2 (1983): 126.

19 Plato, *Phaedrus*, 265 c, 276 b.

20 Plato, *Timaeus*, 26 c.

21 Plato, *Laws*, 644 d.

22 Cf. *Anonymous Prolegomena*, edited by Leonard G. Westerink (Amsterdam: Prometheus Trust, 1962), 26–27.

23 Diogenes Laertius, III, 35–37.

24 *Platons ungeschriebene Lehre*, 10.

PART TWO

ASPECTS

5 CONVERSION

According to its etymology, conversion (from the Latin *conversio*) means a reversal[a] or change of direction. The word conversion, therefore, is used to designate any kind of turning around or transposition. This is why the word is also employed in logic to designate the operation by means of which one inverts the terms of a proposition. In psychoanalysis, this word has been used to designate 'the transposition of a psychical conflict and the attempt at resolving it in its somatic, motor and sensitive symptoms'.[b] This article will study conversion in its religious and philosophical sense. It will be understood, then, as a changing of the mind[c] which could go from a simple modification of one's opinion to the total transformation of one's personality. In fact, the Latin word *conversio* corresponds to two different Greek words, meaning different things. On the one hand, there is *epistrophê*, which means a 'change in orientation', and implies the idea of a return (a return to an origin or a return to oneself); on the other hand, there is the word *metanoia*, which means a 'change in thought' or 'repentance', implying the idea of a mutation and a rebirth. Therefore, in the idea of conversion, there is an internal opposition between the idea of a 'return to an origin' and the idea of a 'rebirth'. This polarity between fidelity[d] and rupture has deeply marked Western consciousness since the appearance of Christianity.

Although we often represent the phenomenon of conversion quite stereotypically, it has, nevertheless, gone through an historical evolution and it can manifest itself in many different forms. For this reason, it is

---

[a] [Translator's note] French: *retournement*.
[b] [Translator's note] Hadot cites here from Jean Laplanche and Jean-Bertrand Pontalis, *Vocabulaire de la psychanalyse* (Paris: Presses Universitaires de France, 2007 [1967]).
[c] [Translator's note] Hadot's exact expression is *changement d'ordre mental*.
[d] [Translator's note] The French word *fidélité* evokes fidelity or faithfulness, which is extremely relevant in terms of the religious meaning Hadot is articulating.

necessary to study it from multiple perspectives: psychophysiological, sociological, historical, theological and philosophical. At all of these different levels, the phenomenon of conversion reflects the irreducible ambiguity of human reality. On the one hand, it bears witness to the freedom of human beings, who are capable of completely transforming themselves by reinterpreting the past and future. On the other hand, it reveals that this transformation of human reality is a result of the invasion of forces that are exterior to the self, whether divine grace or psychosocial constraints. It is possible to say that the idea of conversion represents one of the notions that are constitutive for Western consciousness. Indeed, one could describe the whole history of the West as a ceaselessly renewed effort to perfect the techniques of 'conversion': that is to say, to perfect the techniques which aim at transforming human reality, either through bringing it back to its original essence (conversion-return), or through completely modifying this reality (conversion-mutation).

1 Historical forms of conversion

Pre-Christian antiquity

In antiquity, the phenomenon of conversion appears less under the rubric of religion, and much more under those of politics and philosophy. This is because all ancient religions (except Buddhism) are religions of equilibrium, to use Van der Leeuws' phrase. The rituals in these religions assure a sort of exchange of benefices[e] between God and man. The inner experience that could correspond to these rites, and which could in some way be their psychological flipside, does not play an essential role. These religions, therefore, do not lay claim to the totality of their adepts' inner lives and for this reason they are broadly tolerant, to the extent that each admits a multiplicity of rites and other cults beside itself. Sometimes, phenomena of contagion or propaganda take place, like the propagation of Dionysian cults, for instance, or the dissemination of the cult of the mysteries at the end of antiquity. These religious movements give place to ecstatic phenomena, in which the god takes possession of the initiated. However, even in these extreme cases, there is no total or exclusive 'conversion'. Perhaps only Buddhist illumination assumes this character of profound upheaval of the individual's being. This is why the inscriptions of the Indian king Asoka (268 BCE) are so interesting. There, we can see the king alluding

---

e [Translator's note] Original: *échange de prestations*.

to his own conversion to Buddhism, but also to the moral transformation which was operated in all of his subjects after his own illumination.

It is, above all, in the political domain that the ancient Greeks experienced conversion. For them, the practice of judicial and political discussion, in the context of democracy, disclosed the possibility of changing the adversary's mind[f] by means of the skilful manipulation of language through the use of methods of persuasion. The techniques of rhetoric, the art of persuasion, are constituted and gradually codified in this period. One discovers the political force of ideas or the value of 'ideology', to use a modern term. The Peloponnesian war is an example of this political proselytism.[g]

Even more radical, although less widespread, is philosophical conversion. It is, indeed, closely linked to political conversion in its origins. In fact, Plato's philosophy is fundamentally a theory of political conversion. In order to change the city, one must transform human beings. However, only the philosopher is truly capable of accomplishing that transformation, for he is himself 'converted'. One can see appearing here for the first time a reflection on the notion of conversion.[1] The philosopher himself is, as it were, a 'convert', because he has known how to turn his gaze from the shadows of the sensible world towards the light which emanates from the idea of the Good. In this sense, all education is conversion. Every soul has the possibility of seeing this light of the Good. But their gaze is originally misdirected,[h] and the task of education will, therefore, be that of turning this gaze towards the good direction. From this, a radical transformation of the soul will follow. If the philosophers govern the city, then the whole city will 'convert' towards the idea of the Good.

After Plato, in the Stoic, Epicurean and Neoplatonist schools, it is less a matter of converting the city than of converting individuals. Philosophy becomes essentially an act of conversion. This conversion is an event provoked in the listener's soul by the speech of a philosopher. It corresponds

---

[f] [Translator's note] The phrase Hadot uses here is *changer l'âme*, which could also imply a larger persuasive effect than the English expression of 'change of mind'; yet 'change of soul' is unusual in English.

[g] [Translator's note] Hadot's meaning, in direct translation, is arguably somewhat unclear here. To characterize the war itself as involving the proselytizing of persuasive ideological forms would be highly unusual. Although Athens was democratic and Sparta a mixed constitution on a permanent war footing, there is no strong sense that Athens hoped to convert the Spartans to a democratic constitution, or visa versa, albeit that Sparta did impose the notorious regime of the thirty tyrants on the Athenians with the peace. Hadot may be referring to Thucydides' work on the war, in which the historian puts highly rhetorically crafted speeches into the mouths of the rival protagonists.

[h] [Translator's note] French: *mal orienté*.

to a total rupture with habitual ways of living: it implies a change of clothing,[i] often a change in diet, and sometimes the renunciation of political affairs. But, above all, it points to the total transformation of one's moral life and the assiduous practice of numerous spiritual exercises. In this way, the philosopher arrives at tranquillity of the soul, inner freedom and, in a word, beatitude. From this perspective, philosophical teaching tends to take on the form of preaching, in which the means of rhetoric or logic are put in service of the conversion of souls. Ancient philosophy, therefore, never involves the construction of an abstract system, but rather appears as a call to conversion through which a person will find again their original nature (*epistrophê*) through a violent extraction from[j] the perversion in which common mortals live, and a profound disruption of the whole of their being (and here we refer to *metanoia*).

Judaism and Christianity

The inner experience of conversion achieves its point of highest intensity in the religions of the 'unhappy conscience', to quote a phrase from Hegel.[k] That is to say, in the religions like Judaism and Christianity, in which there is a break between man and nature, and in which the equilibrium of the exchanges between the human and the divine is broken. Religious conversion acquires in these religions a radical and even totalizing aspect[l] which is similar to that of philosophical conversion. However, here conversion takes the form of an absolute and exclusive faith in the Word and the redeeming will of God. In the Old Testament, through the mouth of his prophets, God often invites his people to 'convert': that is to say, to turn towards him, to re-actualize the alliance concluded in ancient times at Sinai. Here again, then, conversion is, on the one hand, a return to the origin, to an ideal and perfect state (*epistrophê*). On the other hand, it is the delivery

---

[i] [Translator's note] *Costume* literally means clothing, an outfit, a suit, on the other. Metaphorically, it refers also to a habit, a way of doing. The Latin *habitus* means both a disposition or a habit (*consuetudo*) and a piece of clothing (*indumentum, vestimentum*). Indeed, a way of living is like a series of habits, ways of doing things, of eating, etc.; but it is also something one chooses to endorse, as if wearing a cloak or a specific piece of clothing which corresponds to a certain philosophical or religious option.

[j] [Translator's note] French: *arrachement*.

[k] [Translator's note] Original: *conscience malheureuse*.

[l] [Translator's note] Hadot's adjective is *totalitaire*, which can have the political signification of the English 'totalitarian'. It is not clear that Hadot means to evoke this sense here.

from a state of perversion and sin, penitence and contrition, the total upheaval of being through faith in God's word (*metanoia*).

Christian conversion, too, is *epistrophê* and *metanoia*, return and rebirth. It is situated, however, at least at its origins, within an eschatological perspective: one must repent before the coming judgement of God. The inner event is, moreover, indissolubly linked to an exterior event: the rite of baptism stands for a rebirth in Christ, and conversion is the inner experience of this new birth. Christian conversion is provoked by the faith in the reign of God announced by Christ, that is, by the irruption of divine power which manifests itself in the miracles of the fulfilment of prophecies. These divine signs will be the first factors of conversion. But soon Christian preaching, when addressed to the Greco-Roman world, will revive numerous themes of philosophical preaching, and the two types of conversion will then be superimposed, as the following text by Clement of Alexandria makes clear. Commenting on the evangelical saying, 'he who loses his soul will find it again', Clement writes:

> To find one's soul is to know oneself. This conversion towards divine things, the Stoics say, is made through an abrupt mutation in which the soul transforms itself in wisdom. As for Plato, he says that [this conversion] is made through the rotation of the soul towards the better, and that the soul's conversion turns it away from obscurity.[m]

Missions, religious wars, awakenings

Every religious or political doctrine that demands of its adherents a total conversion aims to be universal and is, therefore, missionary. It uses preaching, an apologetics, and, confident of its right and its truth, it can always be led into the temptation of imposing itself through violence. The link between conversion and mission is already perceptible in Buddhism. However, it appears most clearly in Christianity itself, as well as in other religions that are born after the Christian era. The expansionist movements of Christianity and Islam are very well known. But one should not forget the extraordinary rise of Manichean missions: from the fourth to the eighth century, they will extend their influence from Persia to Africa and Spain, on the one hand, and to China, on the other.

---

[m] Clement of Alexandria, *Stromates*, IV, vi, 27. 3.

The evolution of conversion methods in the history of missions remains poorly known. Christian missions, for example, took over very different aspects depending on the different lands and times. Missionary problems were posed very differently at the time of Gregory the Great, at the time of the great discoveries, of colonialism or, yet again, at the time of decolonization.

The phenomenon of conversion is equally manifest in the movements of reformation and in religious 'awakenings'. The reformation movements originate in the conversion of a reformer who wants to revive and rediscover authentic, primitive Christianity, rejecting the deviations, errors and sins of the established Church. There is, thus, at the same time, a 'return to the origin' and a 'new birth'. The reformer's conversion provokes other conversions. These conversions take the form of an allegiance to a reformed Church, that is, to a religious society, whose structure, rituals and practices have been purified. The conversion of a religious personality who wants to return to the authentic and the essential is also an important factor in the beginning of religious 'awakenings' (such as Methodism and Pietism). But, in this case, conversions involve less the adhesion to a new Church than the entrance into a community in which God becomes sensible to the hearts of believers, and where the Spirit manifests itself. This communal religious experience can give place to phenomena of collective enthusiasm and ecstasy; it is always translated into an exaltation of religious sensibility.

Whenever a political or military force is put in service of a religion or a particular ideology, it tends to use violent methods of conversion which can assume more or less intense degrees: from propaganda to persecution, religious war or crusade. History gives us abundant examples of forced conversions, beginning with the conversion of the Saxons by Charlemagne, passing through the Islamic holy wars, the conversion of the Jews in Spain, Louis XIV's *dragonnades* and ending up in modern political brainwashing. The need to conquer souls by all means is perhaps the fundamental character of the Western spirit.

2 The different aspects of the phenomenon

Under whatever aspect that we approach the phenomenon of conversion, we must use testimonies and documents with great caution. There is, indeed, a 'stereotype' of conversion. This phenomenon is traditionally represented according to a fixed scheme which, for instance, strongly opposes the long trials and errors, the mistakes of [the individual's] life preceding the conversion, to the decisive illumination that he suddenly receives.

Saint Augustine's *Confessions*, notably, played a pivotal role in the history of this literary genre. This stereotype risks extending its influence not only to the way in which we give any account of conversion, but also the way in which one experiences it.

Psychophysiological aspects

The first psychological studies of the phenomenon of conversion date back to the end the nineteenth and the beginning of the twentieth century. Conversion was interpreted by the theories of that time as a complete reorganization of the field of consciousness, provoked by the irruption of forces emanating from the subliminal conscience (William James' view). Many documents and testimonies were gathered at that time.

Contemporary research focuses instead on the physiological aspects of the phenomenon. One studies the influences of physiological conditioning (like the use of conditioned reflexes) or of brain surgery (lobotomy) on the transformations of the personality. Certain political regimes have already used psychophysiological methods for the 'conversion' of their opponents (by brainwashing).

Finally, from a psychoanalytic perspective, the representation of the 'return to the origin' and that of the 'new birth' can be interpreted as a way of aspiring to return to[n] the maternal belly.

Sociological aspects

From the sociological perspective, conversion represents the break with a certain social *milieu* and the adhesion to a new community. This is a key aspect of the phenomenon of conversion. Indeed, this change of social ties can contribute a great deal to giving the event of conversion an aspect of crisis, and, in part, it also explains the upheaval of personality that results from it. The reorganization of the field of consciousness is by no means dissociable from a reorganization of the environment, the *Umwelt*. The modern missionaries had the occasion to experience in its full intensity the drama that Christian conversion involved for members of a tribal society: the extraction from their vital environment. This problem is almost

---

[n] [Translator's note] The verb Hadot uses is *rentrer*.

constantly posed in the history of missions. Generally speaking, this transition from one community to another is accompanied by moral scruples (the impression of betraying a familial or national tradition), and by difficulties of adaptation (the impression of displacement) and difficulties in understanding. On the other hand, it is possible for uprooted individualities, those who, for one reason or another, are temporarily or permanently removed from their original milieu, to be better disposed than others to conversion. Conversely, one must note that one of the most powerful motives of conversion consists in the attraction exercised by the host community, the community which receives the converted; and by the atmosphere of charity or charisma that can prevail within it. That was the case with primitive Christianity and is still the case in certain communities of religious 'awakening'. The radiance° of these communities can provoke a phenomenon of contagion which can develop very quickly.

Religious aspects

The phenomenon of conversion especially characterizes the religions of 'rupture', in which God's initiative irrupts into the world, introducing a radical novelty into the course of history. God's Word which is addressed to man and often delivered in a sacred book, demands absolute adhesion, a complete break with the past, a consecration of one's whole being. These religions are missionary, because they present themselves as universal and because they lay claim to the total being of man. In this context, conversion is a 'repetition', not only in the sense of a new beginning, a rebirth, but also in the sense of a repetition of the original event upon which the religion to which one converts is founded. It is the irruption of the divine within the course of history which is repeated in the individual's history. Conversion thus also acquires the sense of a new creation, if it is true that the original act of creation was one of absolute divine initiative. Augustine, in his *Confessions* (XIII), identifies the movement by which the matter created by God receives illumination and form and is converted towards God with the movement through which his [own] soul was torn away from sin, was illuminated and turned itself towards God.

By situating the theology of conversion in the broader perspective of the theology of creation, Augustine indicated the way to solve the theological problem of conversion: how are we to reconcile human freedom and divine

---

° [Translator's note] Here, we translate more or less literally, from *rayonnement*. One could also think of 'outreach' and 'diffusion' in this context.

initiative? In a theology of the act of creation, everything is grace, because everything relies on the free decision and the absolute initiative of God. The act of conversion is, therefore, completely free, but its freedom, as the totality of its reality, is created by God. The mystery of grace is identified, ultimately, with the mystery of divine transcendence.

Philosophical aspects

In antiquity, philosophy was essentially a form of conversion: that is to say, an act of return to the self by means of a violent extraction[p] from alienation and unconsciousness. Western philosophy stems from this fundamental fact. On the one hand, it has attempted to formulate a physics or a metaphysics of conversion. On the other hand, and most importantly, it has always remained a spiritual activity which has the character of a real conversion.

Ancient philosophy already proposed a physics or a metaphysics of conversion. How is it possible for the soul to return to itself, to turn towards itself, recovering, once again, its original essence? This is the implicit question to which the Stoic and Neoplatonic doctrines responded. For the Stoics, it was sensible reality itself that was endowed with this movement of conversion. The whole universe, which for them was living and rational and animated by the Logos, was endowed with a movement of vibration which went from the interior to the exterior and the exterior to the interior. The conversion of the philosophical soul was thus attuned to the conversion of the universe and, finally, of universal reason. For the Neoplatonists, only true reality, that is to say, spiritual reality, would be capable of this movement, which is the movement of reflexivity. For this movement to be realized, the spirit goes out of itself in order then to return to itself, it reaches ecstasy in life and rediscovers itself in thought. This schema will prevail in all dialectical philosophies.

For Hegel, history is the odyssey of the Spirit, and history as conceived by philosophy, is the return of the Spirit to its own interior [*Erinnerung*]: that is, its 'conversion'. Hegel, who was in this sense loyal to the spirit of Christianity, identifies this conversion with the act of redemption that is the passion of the Man-God: 'history comprehended[q] is the *return to the interior* and the Calvary of the absolute Spirit, the effectivity, the truth and certitude of its throne, without which it would be lifeless solitude' (this is the last

---

[p] [Translator's note] Here, *arrachement*.
[q] [Translator's note] Original: *l'histoire conçue*.

sentence of the *Phenomenology of Spirit*). For Marx, it is human reality which is endowed with this movement of alienation and return, of perversion and conversion: 'Communism is the return of man to himself . . . accomplished consciously and embracing the entire wealth of previous development.'[2]

More and better than a theory of conversion, philosophy still remains essentially an act of conversion. One can follow the forms which this act assumes throughout the whole history of philosophy. For example, one could recognize it in the Cartesian *cogito*, in Spinoza's *amor intellectualis* or in Bergson's intuition of duration. In all its forms, philosophical conversion is the tearing away from and breaking with the everyday, the familiar, the falsely 'natural' attitude of common sense. It is the return to the original and the originary, to the authentic, to interiority, to the essential. It is absolute new beginning, a new starting point which transforms past and future. These very same traits are found in contemporary philosophy, notably in the 'phenomenological reduction' which Husserl, Heidegger and Merleau-Ponty proposed, each in their own way. In any way it presents itself, philosophical conversion is the access to inner freedom, to a new perception of the world, to authentic existence.

The phenomenon of conversion reveals in a privileged way the insurmountable ambiguity of human reality and the irreducible plurality of systems of interpretation that one can apply to it. Some will see in conversion a sign of divine transcendence, the revelation of grace which founds the only true liberty. Others will see in it a purely psychophysiological or sociological phenomenon, whose study would probably allow us to perfect the techniques of suggestion and the methods of transforming the personality. The philosopher will tend to think that the only true transformation of the human being is philosophical conversion.

Notes

1   Plato, *Republic*, 528c.
2   Karl Marx, *Economic and Political Manuscripts of 1844*. We follow here the translation of Martin Milligan (Moscow: Progress Publishers, 1959), section 'Private Property and Communism': Hadot's translation *la retour de l'homme pour soi* would be more literally 'the return of man for himself'.

Bibliography[r]

R. ALLIER. *Psychologie de la conversion chez les peoples non civilises*, Paris, 1925.

A. BILLETTE. *Récits et réalités d'une conversion*, Montréal, 1975.

J. BLOCH. *Les Inscriptions d'Asoka*, Paris, 1950.

L. BRUNSCHVICG, *De la vraie et la fausse conversion*, Paris, 1950.

W. JAMES, 'The Varieties of Religious Experience', in *Gifford Lectures*, 1902; trad. fr., Paris, 1906.

C. KEYSSER, *Eine Papua-Gemeinde*, Neuendettelsau, 1950.

A.D. NOCK. *Conversion. The Old and the New in Religion from Alexander the Great to Augustin of Hippo*, Oxford, 1933.

W. SARGANT, *Physiologie de la conversion religieuse et politique (Battle for the Mind. A Psychology of Conversion and Brain-Washing)*, Paris, 1967.

D. SCHLUMBERGER, L. ROBER, A. DUPONT-SOMMER et É. BENVÉNISTE, *Une bilingue gréco-araméenne d'Asoka*, Paris, 1958.

G. VAN DER LEEUW, *La Religion dans son essence et ses manifestations. Phénomenologie de la religion*, Paris, 1948.

J. WARNECK, *Die Lebenskräfte des Evangeliums. Missionserfahrungen innerhalb des animistischen Heidentums*, Berlin, 1908.

---

[r] [Translator's note] Uniquely amongst the chapters of this book, Hadot provides readers with a dedicated bibliography in this piece, which we reproduce here as it appears in the original text.

6 THE DIVISIONS OF THE PARTS OF PHILOSOPHY IN ANTIQUITY

At the beginning of *The Groundwork of the Metaphysics of Morals*, Immanuel Kant writes:

> Ancient Greek philosophy is divided into three sciences, physics, ethics, and logic. This division perfectly conforms to the nature of things and we can hardly improve it, except by articulating its founding principle, so that we can be certain of its completion, on the one hand, and on the other hand, can determine exactly the necessary subdivisions.[a]

This text of Kant suffices, it seems to me, to show the importance of the role that ancient theories of the division of the parts of philosophy have played in the history of Western thought. I do not intend in the present article to treat all the aspects of this vast theme. It will not be possible for me to speak of all the philosophical schools, nor of all the subdivisions of philosophy that they have proposed. I do, however, think that it could be interesting to characterize the fundamental types of ancient classification by reviewing the conceptual structures, the '*Denkformen*' which underlie them, and the conceptions of philosophy that they imply.

---

[a] [Translator's note] Hadot does not provide the exact reference. Cf. Immanuel Kant, *The Groundwork for the Metaphysics of Morals*, ed. and trans. by Allen Wood (New Haven, CT, and London: Yale University Press, 2002), 3.

These types of classification seem to be reducible to three. These three types, in their own ways, each aim to give a complete classification of philosophy. The first is distinguished by the effort to identify the specificity of the object and the methods proper to each discipline. To do this, it uses a method of division, ordering the subdivisions under the form of a conceptual pyramid. It establishes a hierarchy between the parts of philosophy which corresponds to the hierarchy of their objects. The second type of classification is less interested in the specificity of the parts of philosophy than in the solidarity between them. It tries to grasp the correspondences or the linkages which connect them so as to better show the systematic unity of philosophy. The conceptual structure underlying this type of classification is then no longer the pyramid, but the image of a circle or a living organism. Finally, there is a third type of classification. The latter does not exclude the two others and brings in the temporal dimension, that of the succession of stages the student must pass through; or, in a word, the pedagogical dimension. The classification of the parts of philosophy is made here as a function of the stages of *paideia*: the degrees of spiritual progress of the student. Such a mode of classification will aim at establishing a programme of studies and an order for the reading of certain, specified texts. The underlying metaphor will, this time, be that of the phases of Eleusinian initiation.

These three are the fundamental ancient forms of the divisions of the parts of philosophy that the present essay wants to consider.

[1 The division according to objects and methods][b]

The first kind of classification of the parts of philosophy appears in the Platonic milieu. Its appearance is, moreover, tied to a reflection on the scientific method and on the necessity to introduce a classification of the sciences and their parts. The term 'philosopher', Aristotle notes, is employed like the term 'mathematician'.[1] Aristotle means that in the same way that the term 'mathematician' can designate someone who does arithmetic or geometry or even someone who does astronomy, so the term 'philosopher' can designate someone who does natural philosophy, ethics or theology. As Aristotle adds: 'the science of mathematics also has its divisions:

---

[b] [Translator's note] Here, we add explanatory subtitles, based on Hadot's division of the article.

there is a primary and a secondary mathematics, and other kinds which follow, each in their domain'.² In the Platonic milieu, the division of the parts of philosophy is thus intimately tied to the division of the sciences in general, given that science and philosophy are not yet clearly distinguished, except that Aristotle proposes the principle, according to which a science is more philosophical if it is more theoretical and more universal.³

In Plato, reflection on the scientific method is manifest for example in the *Republic*,⁴ which opposes the method of mathematics to that of dialectic. Plato remarks that the proper task of the dialectician – that is, of the philosopher – is to give us an overview of the different mathematical sciences.⁵ In the *Statesman*, Plato uses the method of division to define the science of politics, beginning from the basic opposition between the theoretical and practical sciences, in a manner which is, nevertheless, somewhat ironic.⁶

But it is in Aristotle that one finds the best example of the first type of classification of which we have spoken. The division of sciences proposed in book Epsilon of the *Metaphysics*⁷ is presented as a conceptual pyramid obtained by the method of division. One again finds there, from the start, a fundamental opposition between theoretical sciences^c and practical sciences. Theoretical sciences relate to those objects which do not depend upon us, and the practical sciences address those objects which do depend upon us, because the principle of their movement is found in us.⁸ The practical sciences are then subdivided into 'practical' and 'poetic' sciences (that is to say, productive sciences^d), based on whether they engender change within the agent or, on the contrary, on works exterior to them. As for the theoretical sciences, these are subdivided into sciences which relate to an unchanging object and sciences which relate to objects capable of motion.^{e9} The first are distinguished according to the following principle. If this unchanging object subsists in itself, it is a matter for theology. But if it is not unchanging, except when it is separated by a process of abstraction

---

^c [Translator's note] Here, the adjective is *théorétique*. See Chapter 3 above on *théorétique* versus *théorique*. Here, Hadot uses *théorétique* not in the specialized sense described there, but as an adjective qualifying a kind of inquiry, as against designating a mode of life.
^d [Translator's note] From here on, we shall translate 'productive sciences', given the specific English association of poetry with written verse, whereas the Greek *poiesis* has a much wider extension, including productive crafts.
^e [Translator's note] The opposition here, in the original language, is between *mobile* and *immobile* objects. Aristotle divides between unchangeable or unmovable objects and objects capable of motion: either of being moved by other objects or initiating movements themselves.

from its matter, then it is a subject for mathematics. The other branch of the division, the science which relates to an object which is capable of motion and which subsists, corresponds to physics.

This classification, which results from applying the method of division, constitutes a hierarchy of the sciences which is founded on the hierarchy of their formal objects:[10] that is to say, on the hierarchy of the modes of being that the mind discovers in reality. This hierarchy of objects corresponds to a hierarchy of methods: the most elevated sciences utilize a method more exact than the inferior sciences.[11] The practical and political sciences are inferior to the theoretical sciences[12] because they relate to contingent objects, human actions; whereas the theoretical sciences relate to being. Amongst the theoretical sciences, the mathematical sciences are superior to the physical sciences, because they abstract from material becoming and retain only an intelligible matter. But the mathematical sciences are inferior to theology because, in the first place, like physics, they relate only to a kind of determinate beings,[13] whereas theology has for its subject 'being *qua* being', and second, because mathematics does not totally abstract from matter. Theology appears, therefore, as the first science, supreme and universal.

This classification does not suppose only the Platonic method of division. It is situated within a Platonic problematic and corresponds to conceptual structures which are typically Academic.[14] One will firstly recognize the fundamental opposition attested to in the *Statesman*[15] between practical sciences and theoretical sciences. On the other hand, one will easily rediscover, in the hierarchy of objects considered by the theoretical sciences, the Platonic hierarchy which ascends from natural objects towards *ta mathêmatika* and from *ta mathêmatika* towards the Ideas, and which appears clearly in the *Republic* in relation to the ascent from *doxa*, via *dianoia* to *noêsis*.[16]

Nevertheless, in presenting the classification of the parts of philosophy which we are examining in book Epsilon of the *Metaphysics*, Aristotle does not purely and simply reproduce a Platonic classification. On the contrary, beginning from the Platonic problematic, he seeks to define the originality of his own doctrine: and, above all, his idea of the supreme science which he elsewhere calls first philosophy and that he here calls theology, which he wants to substitute for Platonic dialectic. One must not represent the classification proposed in book Epsilon as a programme of studies that Aristotle will have defined once and for all, to organize his teaching and to shape the plan of his works. We know that the tradition of Aristotelian commentators understood the text in this manner and that they classified Aristotle's works conformably to what they considered to be a programme of teaching responding to the natural hierarchy of the objects of science. If we accept this supposition, we are compelled also to state that Aristotle himself, nevertheless, does not respect the distinctions which he establishes in this classification. First of all, the exact place of mathematics, and more specifically of astronomy, remains unclearly defined within his oeuvre.[17] Above all, the frontiers between physics and first philosophy are not always distinctly delimited: ontology and physics, theology and physics are often interconnected in Aristotle's physical treatises as in those on first philosophy, so that one often passes almost imperceptibly from one to the others.[18] In addition to that, the scheme of book Epsilon says nothing of the place of dialectic and of the analytics in the ensemble of the sciences; while it is necessary to say that many of the questions concerning first philosophy are equally treated in the treatises dedicated to analytics.[19] Finally, the real complexity of first philosophy does not appear in the schema of book Epsilon. This first philosophy is at the same time general ontology, the theory of substance (*ousia*), the study of principles and theology.[20] To put it differently, the teaching of Aristotle in its concrete reality and the content of his books does not correspond to the rigorous classification proposed in *Metaphysics* Epsilon.

In fact, the goal of the schema of book Epsilon is not to propose a teaching programme. It is to give a definition of the supreme science within the framework of this classification. Through the method of division, Aristotle's classification eliminates everything that does not belong to this supreme science. The latter is not a practical or productive science, because such sciences are inferior to the theoretical sciences.[21] It is not physics, as the pre-Socratics had claimed. In effect, physics has, for its subjects, a determinate genus of being, whereas the supreme science must be universal; and this determinate genus of being is *ousia* in motion,[22] which presupposes an unmovable *ousia* which precedes it. The supreme science can no longer be identical with mathematics, as certain Platonic philosophers had maintained. As Aristotle says elsewhere: 'mathematics has become for today's philosophers the whole of philosophy, even when they say that is necessary to undertake mathematics only in view of another goal'.[23] Indeed, mathematics, like physics, is related only to a determinate genus of being, and if the mathematical sciences consider their objects as unmovable, it is by abstracting them from the sensible *ousia*.[24] That which remains after these divisions and exclusions is the first philosophy or supreme science that will be a science of being, as such, taking account, at the same time, of the essence and existence of all things, on the basis of the affirmation of the existence of a single unmovable, immaterial and eternal *ousia*.[25] By defining the supreme science in this way, Aristotle radically distinguishes his theology from Platonic dialectic. For Plato, dialectic, by means of a technique of analysing discourse tied to dialogue, comes to the definition of things and thus of Forms or Ideas which are the foundations of the structure of all reality. But Aristotle refuses to consider the Ideas as *ousiai*. It follows that Platonic dialogue loses all scientific value in his eyes, because all science must relate either to a genus of being or to being *qua* being. Aristotle thus considers dialectic to be a simple technique of argumentation by questions and answers. It allows us to speak of everything, but never teaches us anything, because it is content to argue beginning from accepted opinions and common notions, without caring for truth. There is thus for Aristotle a radical opposition between dialectic and philosophy.[26] This total change in the content of the definition of dialectic will provoke many confusions in later philosophy.

The first type of classification of the parts of philosophy, which we are exemplifying by reference to Aristotle, is therefore characterized by the attention that it dedicates to defining exactly the specific method of each science. This methodological attention was manifested, as we have seen, in the opposition described by Plato in the *Republic*,[27] between the method of dialectic and the method of mathematics. It is in virtue of the same concern that the *Timaeus* insists on the necessity of resorting to the method of the 'likely story,'[f] when it comes to treating of physical things.[28] This is also the case in Aristotle, for whom the division of sciences corresponds to a methodological concern that is even more developed than in Plato. In effect, Aristotle thinks that each science must develop its arguments starting from its own distinct principles, and by taking account of those aspects peculiar to the object that it considers. Therefore, ethics has its own distinct method,[29] as equally does physics.[30] In the context of the classification proposed in book Epsilon of the *Metaphysics*, Aristotle, for example, insists on the fact that the definition of physics must include a consideration of the matter in which the form is engaged.[31] Aristotle reproaches Plato, therefore, for using the same method everywhere, the dialectical method for the analysis of concepts, whether in ethics or in physics, without taking account of the differences between these modes of being.[32] This is what Aristotle calls reasoning in a purely formal manner: *logikôs*; a method which he opposes to that which begins from the nature of things: *physikôs*, or that which refines the principles proper to a scientific domain: *analytikôs*.[33]

Certain evidences allow us to suppose that the ancient Academy's new classification of the parts of philosophy is simpler than that which we have

---

[f] [Translator's note] Hadot's expression is *fable vraissemblable*.

so far been exposing. In fact, some later testimonies attribute the tripartite classification of philosophy into ethics, physics and dialectics (or logic) to Plato,[34] others to Xenocrates.[35] If we leave aside for the moment the problem posed by the use of the term 'logic', one could think that it is still a matter of a classification obtained by the method of division, opposing first of all practical science (ethics) and theoretical science; then, subdividing the realm of theoretical science into the science of the sensible world (physics) and the science of Forms (dialectic). Effectively, if one considers the catalogue of the works of Xenocrates,[36] one could say that we find an entire group of ethical works, another group explicitly consecrated to physics and, finally, an ensemble of works that corresponds roughly to traditional Platonic dialectic. We must suppose then that the mathematical sciences, by virtue of their objects, belong to dialectic (in the Platonic sense),[37] which is not impossible. It is thus likely that this threefold division of ethics, physics and dialectics existed in the Ancient Academy. We find here, again, the hierarchical system which ascends from the level of human contingency towards that of divine transcendence.

We are therefore enumerating ethics, physics and dialectic. But did the Ancient Academy employ the term 'logic' to designate Platonic dialectic? I think that this is very doubtful, for the following reasons. It seems sure that the Stoics had been the first to employ the word 'logic' (*to logikon meros*) to designate a part of philosophy, and that the presence of the word 'logic' in the later testimonies we have cited only reveals the influence of the Stoic vocabulary. This was the opinion of Rudolf Hirzel, exactly one hundred years ago, in his article, 'De Logica Stoicorum'.[38] In effect, there did not exist before the Stoics any text, any book title, whether Platonic or Aristotelian, which could attest to the use of the word 'logic' to designate a part of philosophy.

One might object to this position by citing the famous text of Aristotle's *Topics*, which distinguishes physical premises from ethical and logical premises. But, despite these appearances, this text could not allude to a true division of the parts of philosophy. First of all, as Aristotle himself says in this context, the division in question is only an approximative method[39] to classify received opinions or different contentions that the future dialectician will glean from the course of his lectures, with the goal of making up a collection of premises serviceable in discussion. It is a matter of the ordering of a file or a notebook. But, above all, we must interpret *logikos* here according to the general sense it acquires with Aristotle.[40] We have seen just now[41] that Aristotle employs the term *logikos* in opposition to a 'physical' or 'analytic' method, to designate a purely formal method, founded on the analysis of a definition (*logos*)[42] and not on the distinct principles of a specific science. The term *logikos* does not designate a discipline on the same plane as that of ethics or physics, but a purely formal process which can be utilized in ethics as well as in physics. Therefore, I think that one can, with Alexander of Aphrodisias,[43] compare this classification of ethical, physical and logical propositions with that of dialectical problems proposed by Aristotle in the *Topics*,[44] some pages earlier. One again finds here, on the one hand, the fundamental opposition between ethical problems and logical problems, and, on the other hand, the indistinct category of problems which are, according to Aristotle, only instruments that allow us to discuss ethical or physical problems. Let us add that it seems unlikely that Aristotle, in a text like the *Topics*, where he treated of dialectic in the *Aristotelian* sense (that is to say, as a technique different from philosophy), would employ the term 'logic' to designate dialectic in the *Platonic* sense (that is to say, as philosophy *par excellence*). Moreover, the word 'logic', in these texts of the *Topics*, is not at all synonymous with 'dialectic', since the 'logical' problems or premises are only one part of the 'dialectical' problems or premises. One could say that Aristotle, the inventor of 'logic' in the modern sense of the word, never employed the word 'logic', but used the words 'dialectic' and 'analytics' to designate his invention.

[2 The organic division or interconnection of the parts of philosophy]

The second type of classification of which we have spoken in the introduction appears with the Stoics. By dividing philosophy into logic, physics and ethics, they perhaps revive a prior classification, but they give it an absolutely new sense, both because of the content of the different parts of philosophy and because of the mutual relations established between them. First, it seems to me that the idea of a 'logic', as part of philosophy bearing this name, is something new. This logic encompasses rhetoric and dialectic. But the dialectic here differs at the same time from both Platonic and Aristotelian dialectics. It is no longer Platonic dialectics, since it does not aim any longer at the Forms or Ideas in themselves.[45] On the other hand, it is no longer Aristotelian dialectic, since, for the Stoics, dialectic (and rhetoric also) is no longer a simple technique of argumentation belonging always to the domain of the probable. It is a science which, beginning from common notions[46] and commonly accepted opinions, elevates itself towards certitude and knowledge of the truth. In any case, this is the position of

Chrysippus, for whom dialectic is the science of true judgement and one of the virtues of the sage.[47] On the other hand, by suppressing Platonic dialectic as a science of Forms, the Stoics situate all theoretical activity in physics. Stoic physics absorbs theology, which is consistent with an enlargement of the notion of *physis*. This now no longer designates a particular domain, as it did for Aristotle, but rather the totality of the cosmos and the force which animates it.

One might think that this Stoic tripartition of philosophy, like the Platonic and Aristotelian classifications, has a hierarchical character. One could say that physics represents the highest discipline because it is related to the world and to the gods; that ethics would be a subordinate discipline because it relates only to human action; and, finally, logic could be thought of as the lowest discipline because it is related only to human discourse. Certain 'pedagogical' presentations of the Stoic system of the parts of philosophy can give us this impression, and we will return to this thought later.[48] But – and this is where we arrive at our examination of the second type of classification – the internal necessity of the Stoic system leads it inevitably to substitute for this hierarchical representation that of a dynamic continuity and reciprocal interpenetration between the parts of philosophy. This unity of the parts of philosophy is founded on the dynamic unity of reality in Stoic philosophy. It is the same *Logos* which produces the world, which illuminates human beings in their faculty of reasoning and which is expressed in human discourse, all the while staying fundamentally identical to itself in all the degrees of reality. Physics thus has for its object the *Logos* of universal nature. Ethics, in turn, has as its object the *Logos* in the reasonable nature of human beings. Finally, logic examines this same *Logos* as it is expressed in human discourse. From one end to the other, it is therefore the same force and the same reality which is simultaneously creative Nature, the Norm of ethical conduct and the Rule of discourse.[49] The method of Platonic dialectic and the Aristotelian method of abstraction allow us to establish a difference of levels between sensible reality and the Forms or Essences. They thereby founded a hierarchy between the parts of philosophy. However, as Émile Bréhier has said, remarkably:

[One finds] no methodological procedure of this kind in the Stoic doctrine;[g] it is not a matter of eliminating the immediate and sensible given, but rather of seeing Reason embodied in it . . . It is in the sensible things that reason acquires the plenitude of its reality.[50]

---

[g] [Translator's note] The French noun is *dogmatisme*, literally 'dogmatism'.

The difference between levels of reality diminishes and, with it, the difference of level between the parts of philosophy. As Bréhier again has said:

> it is one and the same reason which, in dialectic, links consequents to their antecedents, in nature binds all causes, and in human conduct establishes a perfect concord between actions. It is impossible that the good man would not be a physician and a dialectician. In this sense, it is impossible to realize rationality separately in one of these three domains and, for example, to entirely grasp reason in the march of events in the universe, without realizing reason in one's own conduct at the same time.[51]

This reciprocal interpenetration corresponds to a model of relations dear to the Stoics, of which one finds other examples in their physics, regarding the enchainment of causes, as well as in the ethics, concerning the relations between the virtues. This is the relation they called *antakolouthia*.[52] The parts bound by such a relationship are mutually implicated and are only to be distinguished by the particular aspect which gives them their name. Thus, each virtue is all the others, and it is only distinguished by the predominance of a particular aspect. Conformably to this model, one can also say that logic implies physics, because dialectic implies the idea of the rationality of the enchainment of events;[53] and that logic also implies ethics, since, for the Stoics, dialectic is a virtue which itself encompasses the other virtues: like, for example, the absence of precipitation in judgement or circumspection.[54] For, generally speaking, moral good and bad are an affair of judgement.[55] Conversely, physics and ethics presuppose logic since, as Diogenes Laertius says: 'all the themes of physics and ethics can only be examined by resorting to a discursive exposition.'[56] Ethics implies physics because, according to Chrysippus: 'the distinction between goods and evils derives from Zeus and universal Nature.'[57] Physics, finally, implies ethics to the extent that the knowledge of the physical world and of the gods is the end of our rational nature,[58] and since the perception of the rationality of events implies the rationalization of moral conduct. Evidently, in the Stoic system, there is a reduction of all the parts of philosophy to ethics: the three disciplines of philosophy are defined as virtues[59] and it is their reciprocal co-implication which constitutes wisdom.[60] Wisdom is indissolubly ethical, physical and logical. The distinction between the three parts only stem from the relations of the sage with the cosmos [i.e. physics], with other men [i.e. ethics] and his own thought [i.e. logic].[61] Philosophy as 'an exercise of wisdom' consists, therefore, in a constant and simultaneous practice of the three disciplines, as

Marcus Aurelius affirms in this meditation: 'in a constant manner and, if possible, on the occasion of each representation which presents itself in your mind, practice physics, the theory of the passions [that is to say, ethics], and dialectic'.[62] This somewhat enigmatic formulation of Marcus Aurelius is explained, I think, by the evolution of the theory of parts of philosophy in the epoch of Epictetus and Marcus Aurelius: the reduction to ethics is here even more accentuated. Epictetus distinguishes, in effect, three domains of *askêsis*: the discipline of desires, the discipline of impulses,[h] the discipline of thoughts. In the first domain, one exercises oneself in making one's desires conformable to the will of universal Nature; in the second domain, one attempts to make one's actions accord with the will of the rational nature that is common to all men; while in the third domain, one attempts to conform one's thoughts to the laws of reason.[63] We understand, thus, that these three domains correspond, in fact, to the three parts of philosophy: the first to physics, the second to ethics, the third to logic.[64] In all three cases, it is a matter of a spiritual exercise: physics as a spiritual exercise makes us aware of our place in the cosmos and makes us accept events with love and complacency[i] towards the will of the universal *Logos*;[j] ethics as a spiritual exercise aims to make our actions conform to the fundamental tendency of human nature inasmuch as it is rational, that is to say that ethics makes us practice justice and love towards our fellows; finally, logic as a spiritual exercise makes us critique at each moment our representations, so that no unreasonable judgement will be introduced into the chain of our thoughts. In this perspective, the three parts of philosophy are only three aspects of the fundamental spiritual attitude of the Stoic: vigilance. This is the sense of this thought of Marcus Aurelius:

Constantly and everywhere, it depends on you to accept piously the present conjunction of events [this is physics as spiritual exercise], to conduct yourself with justice towards your contemporaries [this is ethics], to apply to your present representations the rules of discernment so that nothing can enter them except that which is objective [this is logic].[65]

Here again, the simultaneity of the three philosophical activities in the present instant appears clearly.

---

[h] [Translator's note] French: *tendances*.
[i] [Translator's note] French: *complaisance*.
[j] [Translator's note] See Chapter 11 below.

The Platonic manuals of the Imperial epoch, probably under the distant influence of Antiochus of Ascalon, attempted a synthesis between Aristotelianism, Platonism and Stoicism. They remained faithful to the spirit of Stoicism when they recognized the threefold structure of philosophy as the foundation of its systematic character. One finds this theme in Diogenes Laertius, Apuleius, Atticus and Augustine.[66] They attribute to Plato himself the merit of having made philosophy a *corpus*, a living organism, complete and accomplished,[k] by binding together dialectic to physics and to ethics. Some of them (Atticus and Apuleius) leave to Plato only the merit of having assembled three pre-existing disciplines: pre-Socratic physics, Socratic ethics and Eleatic dialectic. Others (Diogenes Laertius and Augustine) see in Platonic dialectic a systematizing element invented by Plato in order to synthesize the two elements which Platonism integrates: Pythagorean physics and Socratic ethics. Plato appears, then, as a synthesis of Socrates and of Pythagoras. Indeed, the utilization of the Stoic schema in the presentation of Platonism resulted in a total deformation of the latter. What is most serious is not that the theory of principles (God, the Ideas, Matter) would be placed within physics (after all, the *Timaeus*, considered, in general, as a 'physical' dialogue, could justify this placement).[67] Above all, in the Stoic presentation of Platonism, dialectic loses its character of a supreme science aiming at the absolute principle to become only an art of making distinctions and invention in discourse[68] or an inquiry into the exactitude of denominations, to quote the expressions of these authors.[69] Only Clement of Alexandria, Plotinus and, finally, Augustine[70] preserve the distinction between Stoic and Aristotelian dialectic and Platonic dialectic; and they declare that only the latter has for its object true, that is to say divine, realities.

The unitary and systematic schema of the division of philosophy proposed by the Stoics, taken up in the Platonic manuals, finds its highest form and reveals all of its potential in those theories which present God as the common object of the three parts of philosophy. They carry forward the fundamental intuition of Stoicism, according to which the *Logos* is the common object of the parts of philosophy. According to Clement of Alexandria,[71] physics takes God as *ousia* as its object; ethics has God as the good as its object, while the object of logic is God as intellect. According to Augustine,[72] physics has God as the cause of being as its object, while logic considers God as the norm of thought, and ethics takes God as rule of life. This Augustinian order of physics, logic and then ethics corresponds to the

---

[k] [Translator's note] Hadot's term is *achevé*.

order of divine Persons in the Trinity. The Father is the Principle of Being; the Son, Intelligence; and the Holy Spirit, Love.[73] The systematic unity of the parts of philosophy reflects here the reciprocal interiority of the divine Persons.

[3 The pedagogical divisions of the parts of philosophy]

The third type of classification introduces this time a complex datum:[l] the pedagogical dimension, which implies a method of exposition, a temporal order, a succession of moments, involving an intellectual and spiritual progression. It is a matter of establishing a programme of teaching philosophy which takes into consideration simultaneously the logical order of notions and the capacities of the auditor.

Apparently, this third type of classification adds nothing to the content of the divisions previously established but an extrinsic order of presentation.[m] One might think that the two first types of classification could be considered either in themselves, in a purely formal manner, or in relation to the auditor, in the pedagogical perspective. It is thus that the commentators on Aristotle at the end of antiquity, in their introductions to the *Categories*, on the one hand, faithfully present the Aristotelian division of the parts of philosophy, notably the subdivision of theoretical sciences into theology, mathematics and physics; and, on the other hand, expose the *cursus* which must be traversed by the disciple, a *cursus* which corresponds in principle[74] to the inverse order, since, according to Aristotle,[75] there is a radical opposition between the ontological and the pedagogical orders, between what is more knowable in itself and that which is more knowable for us. It can seem logical that an ascending hierarchy of teachings corresponds to the descending hierarchy of the sciences. In the same way, if one considers the Stoic system, one could say that the pedagogical point of view alone serves to introduce some order between the three parts of philosophy, of which we have shown the intimate solidarity and interpenetration.

Nevertheless, it seems that this third type of classification could really be opposed to the two others. The first two types correspond, in effect, to a purely ideal position: they suppose the totality or integrity of knowledge or wisdom as an already realized accomplishment. By contrast, the third type

---

[l] [Translator's note] Hadot's expression is *donnée complexe*.
[m] [Translator's note] Literally: *ordre exterieur de présentation*.

corresponds to the concrete reality of philosophical activity. Philosophy is not given, once and for all. It is realized in communication: that is to say, in the explication, the 'discourse' which exposes it and transmits it to the disciple. This philosophical 'discourse' introduces the temporal dimension which has two components: the 'logical' time of discourse itself (to take up an expression of Victor Goldschmidt[76]) and the psychological time required by the formation, the *paideia*, of the disciple. The 'logical time' corresponds to the internal exigencies of expression or explication. To be communicated to the disciples, philosophy must be presented in a discursive manner, and thus through a succession of arguments which imposes a certain order. This thing must be said before that other [thing]. This order is that of the 'logical' time. But the exposition is addressed to an auditor, and this auditor introduces another component, namely the phases or stages of his spiritual progress. Here it is a matter of a properly psychological or at least of a pedagogical temporality. To take an example drawn from modern philosophy, we see Descartes[77] consider this pedagogical aspect when he advises his readers to employ 'some months or, at least, some weeks' in the examination of his first and second *Meditations*. What is at stake clearly appears to be a temporality other than the 'logical' time. It is a time for the maturation, the assimilation of the text. As long as the disciple has not assimilated such and such a doctrine, it is useless or impossible to speak to him of other matters. This is why Descartes speaks only of universal doubt in his first *Meditation*, and of the nature of the spirit in the second. Here the pedagogical requirements influence the doctrinal content of the work.

The two components which we have just described, logical time and psychological time, define the third type of classification of philosophy which we will now discuss. These two components, as we can now glimpse, can profoundly modify the content and the sense of the parts of philosophy. It is equally true that there is a permanent conflict between the two components which we are analysing, as we will observe. It is extremely difficult to safeguard the logical order if one wants to take into account the spiritual state of the auditor.

In Plato and Aristotle, we already find these important pedagogical concerns, which will have a great influence in later tradition. However, we do not find a complete classification of the parts of philosophy inspired by the perspective of the spiritual progress of the student. We have already mentioned the Aristotelian opposition between *l'ordo essendi* and *l'ordo cognoscendi*,[78] but we have equally remarked that we do not find in his works a concrete programme of philosophical teaching.[79] In Plato, we find an outline of such a programme, when the *Republic*[80] recommends that future philosophers devote themselves to the mathematical sciences before turning to dialectic. But it is not certain that the concrete teaching of the Academy[81] conformed itself to these theories concerning the organization of education in the ideal State. In any case, Plato is particularly sensitive to the problem of the necessary adaptation between teaching and the spiritual level of the disciple. In the *Republic*, he thus signals the danger to which young men are exposed who begin to practice dialectic too soon.[82] The very idea of spiritual progress is expressed by Plato in two metaphors which will have a considerable posterity: first, the conversion of the prisoners of the cave who are little by little habituated to contemplate the daylight;[83] and, second, the initiation into the mysteries at Eleusis (*telea*, *epoptika*) of which Diotima in the *Symposium* enumerates the degrees, when she describes the ascension of the soul towards the Beautiful itself.[84]

It is with the Stoics that we encounter for the first time an explicit discussion concerning philosophical pedagogy which considers the order and the content of the parts of philosophy. We have mentioned above one important aspect of their doctrine: the mutual implication of the three parts of philosophy whose simultaneous exercise constitutes wisdom. That was only an ideal situation. Let us now turn to another aspect of their doctrine: the distinction and the succession of the parts of philosophy because of the necessities imposed by the requirements of philosophical teaching. It is probably from this perspective that the Stoics claimed that the parts of philosophy are, in fact, not the parts of philosophy itself, but rather the parts of discourse or the *logos* involved in philosophical teaching.[85] It is the discourse of teaching which requires an order and a particular succession. The Stoics are very aware of this pedagogical imperative. Thus, they attempt to fix in a rigorous manner the logical order of the arguments within each part of philosophy,[86] as it appears in the summary of Stoic dialectics given by Diogenes Laertius,[87] as well as in Cicero's exposition of the ethics in book III of *De Finibus*.[88] In this last example, it is striking to note that the rigorous progression of thought is at the same time a spiritual progression which, beginning with a physical theory of natural impulse[n] – that all beings tend to self-preservation – shows how this natural impulse in human beings becomes, at the level of reason, a love of humanity later culminating in wisdom.[89] Above all, the Stoics try to determine an order of teaching of the parts of philosophy. Diogenes Laertius and Sextus Empiricus[90] report to us the different theories which were current in the school. We would generally agree to place logic at the beginning of the *cursus* of studies – although

---

[n] [Translator's note] Hadot's term is *la tendance*; at stake is the Stoic theory of *oikeiosis*, the 'adaptation' of the impulses of natural creatures to their environs.

Epictetus reserves it to those making progress. Nevertheless, one hesitates about the place of ethics and physics, respectively.[91] This hesitation appears clearly in the interpretations that Diogenes Laertius and Sextus Empiricus[92] give of the famous comparisons that the Stoics made between the parts of philosophy and organized ensembles such as the egg, the garden or the living being. If logic is always presented as the part which assures the solidity, ethics and physics often exchange their role. Each differently appears as the most important and indispensable part.°

These discussions and hesitations can be explained, as Adolf Bonhöffer has shown, by the differences concerning the viewpoint – logical or pedagogical – according to which the classifications are carried out.[93] One could equally well say that physics must precede ethics by founding it logically on the knowledge of the rationality of nature, or that ethics must precede physics so as to prepare the soul for the contemplation of nature.[94] Chrysippus himself uses the image of Eleusinian initiation when he places physics last as a revelation (*teletê*) concerning the gods.[95] It is in the same spirit that Sextus Empiricus gives us an account of the order of the parts of philosophy: the spirit must be fortified by logic, then the student's way of living is ameliorated by ethics, before we can finally approach the most divine objects that physics examines.[96]

However, it would be too easy to think that the order of the parts of philosophy is simply interchangeable and that one could easily modify it, according to whether one adopts the point of view of logical necessity or that of spiritual progress. In fact, there is a conflict between the logical and the pedagogical aspect. For example, if in teaching one places ethics before physics, one is obliged to present the former without its logical foundations, which are to be found in physics. Ethics here will no longer be a general theory of the ends of human life but will be reduced to a teaching ultimately concerning the social 'duties'. Bonhöffer[97] has insisted on the twofold aspect of ethics in Stoicism. Yet, if, on the contrary, one places physics before ethics, physics will no longer be deployed in its full scope: there will no longer be the supreme *teletê* of the mysteries of philosophy. Concerning dialectic, it cannot have the same content if it is presented to mere beginners or, on the contrary, if it is exposed to those who have already made progress, as Epictetus wanted. The concrete necessities of the teaching thus conduce finally to important modifications in the content of the parts of philosophy. Unfortunately, we do not know the concrete details of Stoic teaching except from fragments and the doxastic summaries. For this reason, we cannot

---

° [Translator's note] Hadot's expression is: *la partie la plus intérieure et la plus precieuse*.

fully appreciate all the doctrinal variations that this conflict between the logical and pedagogical order was able to produce.

It seems, nevertheless, that the Stoics sought the solution to this conflict in a method of teaching which, while recognizing the necessary distinctions between the parts of philosophy, tried hard to present them all at the same time to the disciple, and always to preserve fidelity to the doctrine as a whole. Indeed, Diogenes Laertius tells us that certain Stoics considered that 'no part has the first place, that all parts are mixed together, and moreover, that they are necessarily interlaced in their teaching'.[98] This is probably what this advice of Chrysippus explains: 'those who commence by the study of logic must not abstain from the other parts of philosophy, when the occasion presents itself'.[99] This method is designed to prevent the danger which not practising logic, ethics or physics during a certain time would represent to the disciple. As has been shown by Ilsetraut Hadot,[100] for the Stoics (and for the Epicureans), the method of teaching strives always to be 'integral' at each stage of spiritual progress. For the beginner, one proposes sentences or summaries which immediately put them in contact with the whole set of fundamental dogmas and which furnish them with the guiding rules of life.[p] For the student who is making progress, one offers more detailed developments and more techniques; but by constantly returning to a focus on the fundamental dogmas, this method would never lose sight of what is essential. The disciple thus remains constantly in contact with the three disciplines, even if he studies one amongst them in a more profound manner. There is always a coming and going between concentration and dilation, between simultaneity and the successive order of teachings.

Nevertheless, this method does not totally eliminate the conflict between the logical and pedagogical ordering of the parts of philosophy. In fact, if one is to adapt the teaching to the spiritual capacities of the students, one can be led to two forms of simplification and adaptation which could seem to transform the doctrine itself. When one addresses oneself to beginners, one can even appeal to formulas that are foreign to the school (borrowed from Epicureanism, for example) if one judges them more likely to have an effect on the disciple. This is the principle enunciated by Chrysippus himself in the *Therapeutikos*.[101] This principle of adaptation to the spiritual capacities of the disciple remains alive in all the schools until the end of antiquity and it will often be necessary to take account of it to understand the incoherencies or the apparent contradictions in different works of ancient philosophers.[102]

---

[p] [Translator's note] French: *grande regles de vie*, an expression whose literal translation in English would be unusual: 'great/grand rules of life'.

In the summaries of Platonic philosophy which we find amongst different authors, from Cicero to Diogenes Laertius, logic is always found in the third place.[103] There is probably a tribute there to the Platonic conception of dialectic as the supreme science even though, in these manuals, the content of logic does not correspond to that of Platonic dialectic. Perhaps it is also a matter of the first glimpse of the classification that one can call 'Neoplatonic', of which we will now speak.

Effectively, beginning from the first century of the Common Era, one notes the emergence of a classification of the parts of philosophy that is essentially founded on the notion of spiritual progress. The three parts distinguished are, respectively, ethics, physics and 'epoptic' (this last word evidently alluding to the supreme initiation in the mysteries of Eleusis). Its first testimony can be found in Plutarch, who, in the *Iside*,[104] affirms that Plato and Aristotle placed, after the physics, a part of philosophy which they call 'epoptic' and which has as its object 'what is first, simple and immaterial'. They think, Plutarch continues, that 'philosophy finds its end, as in a supreme initiation, thanks to a real touch of pure truth which is found in what is first, simple, and immaterial'. In order to describe philosophical formation, Theon of Smyrna uses the technical vocabulary of the Eleusinian initiation, calling *teletê* the study of logic, politics (that is to say, ethics) and physics, and calling *epopteia* the knowledge of true beings.[105] Clement of Alexandria also knows this theory. He enumerates the parts of philosophy in this order: ethics, physics (understood as allegorical interpretation), and epoptic, which he explicitly identifies with Platonic dialectic and Aristotelian metaphysics.[106] Finally, Origen reveals to us the relationship which exists between this tripartition and the stages of spiritual progress.[107] Ethics, according to him, secures a preliminary purification of the soul; physics, by revealing the vanity of the sensible world, invites us to detach ourselves from it; epoptic, finally, opens the purified soul to the contemplation of divine realities. This is why, for him, the three books of Solomon correspond to the three parts of philosophy: the *Proverbs* assures ethical purification; the *Ecclesiastes*, which commences with *Vanitas Vanitatum*, reveals to us the vanity of the physical world; and the *Song of Songs* introduces us to epoptic. In this succession of texts, Origen specifies that logic, as a science of terms or propositions, is not a separate part of philosophy, but is intertwined with the three other parts, according to certain philosophers – namely, the Aristotelians. After Origin, this tripartition founded on spiritual progress reappears in Porphyry, who edits Plotinus' *Enneads* conformably to this schema. The first *Ennead* corresponds to ethics: that is to say, to a phase of preliminary purification; the second and the third *Enneads*, to physics; while the fourth, fifth and sixth *Enneads* correspond to the knowledge of divine realities and thus to epoptic. It is probably through Porphyry that Calcidius knows of the opposition between physics (represented by Plato's *Timaeus*) and epoptic (represented by the *Parmenides*).[108] This entire tradition is characterized by certain number of typical traits: the employment of the Eleusinian word *epopteia* to designate the highest part of philosophy; the identification of Platonic dialectic and Aristotelian theology; the conception of Aristotelian logic as an *Organon* and, therefore, the integration of Aristotelianism into the *cursus* of Platonic studies; and finally, and above all, the idea that each part of philosophy does not correspond to a purely intellectual level, nor to the acquisition of a purely abstract knowledge, but that it represents an inner progress which results in a transformation of the individual, his elevation to an ontologically superior sphere. It is evident that, in this schema, ethics and physics assume a meaning that is entirely different to that which they had for example in Aristotelian philosophy. Ethics is now only a phase of preliminary purification, physics is no longer a scientific research, but speculation aiming to make us aware of the fact that sensible reality is but an image. Moreover, as it appears in the Porphyrian ordering of the *Enneads*, the conflict between the logical and pedagogical order is as acute in Neoplatonism as it is in Stoicism. It is impossible to speak of ethics or physics without considering the whole of the 'epoptic'; and many of the treatises of the first *Ennead*, theoretically destined for beginners, are of an extreme difficulty.

This fundamental schema of ethics, physics, epoptic will be the core of the programme of philosophical studies from the end of the first century CE until the end of antiquity. In the Neoplatonic philosophers after Porphyry, this programme contains, on the one hand, the preparatory study of Aristotelian logic and, on the other, the study of mathematics which is the theoretically indispensable propaedeutic to Platonic dialectic, according to the doctrine of the *Republic*. One thus, finally, has the following scheme: first stage: ethics and logic; second stage: physics and mathematics; third stage: epoptic or theology. We must add that the Neoplatonists interposed into the schema a theory of the stages of spiritual progress which had been outlined by Plotinus and systematized by Porphyry:[109] namely, the hierarchy of virtues. The first stage of spiritual progress was, according to this theory, the practice of 'political' virtues, that is to say, the accomplishment of the duties of social life according to prudence, justice, courage and temperance. After this indispensable preparation which responded in large measure to the ethical part of philosophy, one could rise to the level of the virtues called 'cathartic', which corresponded to a movement of detachment from the body. One passed thus from *metriopatheia* towards *apatheia*. This level corresponded to the physical part of philosophy which, as we have seen, had for its goal to detach the soul from the sensible world. Finally, one attains to the theoretical virtues, when the soul is sufficiently detached from the body and can thus turn towards the divine Intellect and contemplate it. This level was evidently analogous to theology or epoptic. All the levels of virtues had their model in the virtues that are specific to the divine Intellect itself and inaccessible to the soul: the paradigmatic virtues.

We have here the broad outlines of a programme of studies which is at the same time an *ascensio mentis ad Deum*, where one passes by the stages of the purgative way to the illuminative way and the unitive way, respectively.[110] But to what does this programme correspond concretely? To form an idea of it, it is necessary to bear in mind that beginning in a certain epoch, which one can probably situate in the first century CE, philosophical teaching to a great extent consisted in a reading and commentary on the works of the founders of the school. This did not exclude discussions with the master on subjects of a general character or, on the contrary, on very personal subjects. Nevertheless, the essential remained the explanation of the texts.[111] The Neoplatonic programme of studies corresponds, therefore, to an order of reading Aristotle's works and Plato's dialogues. One sees this already outlined by Albinus.[112] If we attempt to systematize the testimonies that we possess, it seems that the schema of the parts of philosophy served, above all, to establish the order of reading Aristotle's work, which represented for the Neoplatonists lesser mysteries: that is to say, a first initiation. It also seems that the scheme of the degrees of the virtues, always intimately tied to that of the parts of philosophy, presided over the establishment of the programme of reading Plato: that is to say, the initiation to the higher mysteries of philosophy.[113]

One can therefore reconstitute the philosophical *cursus* in the following way. The first ethical initiation was to be undertaken by the study of simple and striking texts such as Epictetus' *Handbook* or the *Golden Verses* of the Pythagoreans.[114] The logical formation of the student was then acquired thanks to the study of Aristotle's *Organon*. Then, one studied successively Aristotle's ethical and political treatises, then his *Physics* and, finally, his *Metaphysics*. Marinos tells us that Proclus needed less than two years to be initiated to these lesser mysteries of philosophy.[115] After that, one approached the higher mysteries. After the first introduction to the knowledge of self that the *Alcibiades* represented, the reading of the *Gorgias* and, eventually, of the *Republic* led one to accede to the level of the political virtues. One was then elevated to the level of cathartic virtues through reading the *Phaedo*. Then, at the level of the theoretical virtues, one studied the logical dialogues, namely the *Cratylus* and the *Theaetetus*, the physical dialogues, the *Sophist* and the *Politics*, and the theological dialogues, the *Phaedrus*, *Symposium* and the *Philebus*. A second cycle would, once again, approach physics with the *Timaeus* and theology with the *Parmenides*.[116] It is very evident that the dialogues of Plato could not be placed into any such schema, except by means of a forced interpretation.

***

In the Preface to the first edition of his work, *Die Welt als Wille und Vorstellung*, Schopenhauer writes:

> A system of thought must always have the cohesion of an architectural edifice: in other words, a cohesion such that always one of its parts supports another, without being supported by it: the foundational stone must ultimately support all the others, without being itself supported by any other, and the summit must be supported by the rest, without supporting anything else. On the contrary, a unique idea, although all encompassing, must preserve the most perfect unity. Even if one must divide it into parts in order to communicate it, it remains nevertheless that the cohesion of these parts must be organic, that is to say, that each part contributes to maintain the whole and should be maintained in its place by the whole; none being the first, none being the last: the total idea gains in clarity by the exposition of each part, but also the smallest part cannot be completely understood without previously understanding the whole.[q]

Schopenhauer opposes here 'systems of thought' and a 'unique idea', but one could say as well that he opposes two types of system: on the one hand, the system of an architectural type, or to quote Leisegang's phrase in his '*Denkformen*',[117] the 'pyramid of concepts'; and, on the other hand, the system of the organic type. One recognizes these two types of system in the first two types of classification which we have distinguished. The Platonic-Aristotelian classification supposes a coherence of the architectural type: the inferior degrees of the ontological hierarchy cannot exist without the superior degrees, but these again can exist without the inferior degrees.[118] In contrast, the Stoic classification supposes a coherence of the organic type:

---

[q] [Translator's note] Hadot does not give the citation. See Arthur Schopenhauer, *The World as Will and Representation*, Volume 1. Translated and edited by Judith Norman, Alistair Welchman and Christopher Janaway (Cambridge: Cambridge University Press, 2010), "Preface to the first edition", 5. Compare the translation by R. B. Haldane and J. Kemp at: https://en.wikisource.org/wiki/The_World_as_Will_and_Representation/Preface_to_the_First_Edition (accessed 6 June 2019).

the parts of philosophy, or rather the parts of philosophical discourse, form a system because they are an ensemble of organized thoughts. But they reveal the three aspects of one and the same idea, which is that of the *Logos* and they imitate, in their reciprocal implication, the dynamic unity of this unique *Logos*.[119]

Each of these two types of classification describe a different ideal type of wisdom. For the first, wisdom is a universal knowledge which embraces the architecture of the system of sciences, their methods and the diversity of their objects; for the second, wisdom is a concentrated attention on the presence of the *Logos* within all things. The third type of classification does not describe an ideal type, but an itinerary or concrete method which leads to wisdom. It can authorize different classifications: different orders of the parts of philosophy in the Stoic system, or the tripartition ethics–physics–epoptic in the Neoplatonic system. However, these different classifications remain of the same type because, for them, the parts of philosophy are conceived as stages of an inner path which one must traverse. They are the phases of an evolution and of a transformation which one must realize. This third type is properly *philo-sophical*, in the etymological sense of the term, since it corresponds to an effort, a search, an exercise[120] which leads to wisdom. It is this properly philosophical aspect which prevents it from being totally systematic and which explains the hesitations, the incoherencies and the internal contradictions which characterize it.

Notes

1   Aristotle, *Metaphysics*, 1004 a8.

2   Aristotle, *Metaphysics*, 1004 a8. We follow Tredennick with the translation of "primary" and "secondary" mathematics here.

3   Aristotle, *Metaphysics*, 982 a5, 982 b10.

4   Plato, *Republic*, 510b.

5   Plato, *Republic*, 537c.

6   Plato, *Statesman*, 258e.

7   Aristotle, *Metaphysics*, 1025b3 ff.

8   Aristotle, *Metaphysics*, 1025b20: nature in itself has the principle of its own movement, whereas the principle of technical productions or of actions is found in the human agent.

9   Aristotle, *Metaphysics*, 1026a10 ff. on the critical problems posed by this passage, cf. Philip Merlan, *From Platonism to Neoplatonism* (The Hague: Nijhoff, 1960), 62 ff.

10 On these problems, cf. Heinz Happ, *Hyle: Studien zum Aristotelischen Materie-Begriff* (Berlin: Walter de Gruyter, 1971), 565–569.

11 Aristotle, *Metaphysics*, 982a26.

12 Aristotle, *Metaphysics*, 1026a23.

13 Aristotle, *Metaphysics*, 1025b9 & 19 [Translator's note: 'kind' here translates the French *genre*].

14 Cf. Hans-Joachim Krämer, *Der Ursprung der Geistmetaphysik* (Amsterdam: Grüner, 1967), 146, n. 66.

15 Plato, *Statesman*, 258e.

16 Plato, *Republic*, 510–511; cf. Happ, *Hyle*, 267. On the association between the soul and the *mathêmatika*, cf. Merlan, *From Platonism to Neoplatonism*, 11 & 82.

17 Aristotle, *Metaphysics*, 1073b5 & *Physics*, 193b22 ff.

18 Cf. Happ, *Hyle*, 477 & 36, n. 149.

19 For example, the theory of science or of definition.

20 Cf. Happ, *Hyle*, 311.

21 Aristotle, *Metaphysics*, 1026a23.

22 Aristotle, *Metaphysics*, 1025b19 [Translator's note: 'Genus' here translates the French *genre*].

23 Aristotle, *Metaphysics*, 992a33.

24 Aristotle, *Metaphysics*, 1026a14. One will remark that the text (1026a8 and a14) refuses to define in a general manner the ontological status of mathematical objects but aims only at certain branches of mathematics.

25 Aristotle, *Metaphysics*, 1025b10–19 & 1026a30–33.

26 Aristotle, *Topics*, 105b30; cf. John D. G. Evans, *Aristotle's Concepts of Dialectic* (Cambridge: Cambridge University Press, 1977), 7–55

27 Plato, *Republic*, 510b.

28 Plato, *Timaeus*, 29d.

29 Aristotle, *Nicomachean Ethics*, 1094b11.

30 Aristotle, *Physics*, 193b22; *Parts of Animals*, 639a1.

31 Aristotle, *Metaphysics*, 1025b28.

32 Aristotle, *Parts of Animals*, 642b5; *Generation of Animals*, 748a8; *Nicomachean Ethics*, 1107a26.

33 Aristotle, *Physics*, 204b4 & b10; *Nicomachean Ethics*, 1147a24 ff.; *Generation and Corruption*, 316a11; *De Cielo*, 280a32; *Posterior Analytics*, 84a8; cf. Mario Mignucci, *L'Argomentazione Dimonstrativa in Aristotele*, tome 1 (Padova: Editrice Antenore, 1975), 484 ff.

34 Cf. *infra* n. 66–69.

35 Sextus Empiricus, *Adversus Mathematicus*, VII, 16.

36 Diogenes Laertius, *Lives of Eminent Philosophers*, IV, 11 ff.

37 Cf. Krämer, *Der Ursprung der Geistmetaphysik*, 146, n. 66.

38 Rudolf Hirzel, 'De Logica Stoicorum', *Satura Philologica, Festschrift Hermann Souppe* (Berlin, 1879), 64 ff.

39 Aristotle, *Topics*, 109b19.

40 Aristotle, *Topics*, 105b19: *hôs tupôi*.

41 Cf. note 33 above.

42 Aristotle, *Topics*, 105b19: *hôs tupôi*.

43 *Alexandri Aphrodisiensis in Aristotelis Topicorum Libros octo commentaria*, ed. Maximilianus Wallies (Berlin; G. Reimer, 1891), 74, 26 & 94, 7.

44 Aristotle, *Topics*, 104b1.

45 Cf. Hans-Joachim Krämer, *Platonismus und Hellenistische Philosophie*, 114, n. 35.

46 Cf. Émile Bréhier, *Chrysippe et l'ancien stoïcisme* (Paris: Presses Universitaires de France, 1951), 59 ff., esp. 65.

47 Hans von Arnim, *Stoicorum Veterum Fragmenta [SVF]*, tome II, 97–106.

48 See Pierre Hadot, 'Marc-Aurêle: Était-il opiomane?', in *Études de Philosophie Ancienne*, 97–106.

49 Max Pohlenz, *Die Stoa* (Göttingen: Vandenhoeck & Ruprecht, 1959), 34; Krämer, *Platonismus*, 114, n. 35; Andreas Graeser, *Zenon von Kition* (Berlin: de Gruyter, 1975), 21 ff.

50 Émile Bréhier, *Histoire de la philosophie*, tome I, 2 (Paris: Presses Universitaires de France, 1961), 303.

51 Ibid.

52 Cf. Victor Goldschmidt, *Le Système stoïcien et l'idée de temps* (Paris: Vrin, 1977), 66; Hans-Jürgen Horn, 'Antakolouthie der Tugenden und Einheit Gottes', *Jarbuch fur Antike und Christentum*, tome 13 (1970), 3–38; Pierre Hadot, *Porphyre et Plotin*, tome 1 (Paris: Études Augustiniennes, 1968), 239 ff.

53 SVF tome II, §952: the determinism of destiny and the principle of contradiction are intimately bound up together.

54 SVF tome II, §§130–131; Cicero, *De Finibus*, III, 21, 72; Diogenes Laertius, *Lives of the Eminent Philosophers*, VII, 46.

55 SVF tome III, §456 ff.

56 Diogenes Laertius, *Lives of the Eminent Philosophers*, VII, 83.

57 SVF tome III, §68; Cicero, *De Finibus*, III, 22, 73.

58 Cicero, *De Natura Deorum*, II, 14, 37.

59 Cf. Cicero, *De Finibus*, III, 21, 72.

60 Philo of Alexandria, *De Ebrietate*, §§ 90–92.

61 Cf. Marcus Aurelius, *Meditations*, VIII, 27.

62 Marcus Aurelius, *Meditations*, VIII, 13.

63 Epictetus, *Discourses*, I, 4, 11; III, 2, 1; II, 8, 29; II, 17, 15 & 31; IV, 4, 16; IV, 10, 13.

64 Cf. Pierre Hadot, 'Une Clé des *Pensées* de Marc Aurèle: les trois *topoi* philosophiques selon Marc Aurèle', *Les Études Philosophiques* (1978): 65–83.

65 Marcus Aurelius, *Meditations*, VII, 54.

66 Diogenes Laertius, *Lives of the Eminent Philosophers*, III, 56; Apuleius, *De Platone*, I, 3, 186; Atticus, in Eusebius, *Praeparatio Evangelica*, XI, 2, 1; Augustine, *Against the Academics*, III, 17, 37; *De Civitate Dei*, VIII, 4 ff.

67 Diogenes Laertius, *Lives of the Eminent Philosophers*, III, 76; Apuleius, I, 3, 190.

68 Atticus, in Eusebius, *Praeparatio Evangelica*, XI, 2, 1.

69 Diogenes Laertius, *Lives of the Eminent Philosophers*, III, 79.

70 Clement of Alexandria, *Stromata*, I, 28, 176, 3; Plotinus, *Enneads*, I, 3, 5, 12; Augustine, *Against the Academics*, III, 17, 37; *De Civitate Dei*, VIII, 7.

71 Clement of Alexandria, *Stromata*, IV, 25, 162, 5.

72 Augustine, *De Civitate Dei*, VIII, 4; *Epistles*, 118, 3, 20.

73 Augustine, *De Civitate Dei*, XI, 25 in liaison with the triad *natura, doctrina, usus*; cf. Pierre Hadot, 'Etre, Vie et Pensée chez Plotin et avant Plotin', *Entretiens sur L'Antiquité Classique*, tome V (Genève: Fondation Hadt, 1960), 123–125; Olivier de Roy, *L'Intelligence de la Foi en la Trinite selon Saint Augustine* (Paris: Ětudes Augustiniennes, 1966), 447.

74 For example, *Simplicii in Aristotelis Categorias Commentarium*, ed. Karl Kalbfleisch (Berlin: Reimer, 1907), 4, 23 & 5, 3; *Eliae in Porphyrii Isagogen et Aristotelis Categorias Commentaria, Commentaria in Aristotelem Graeca*, ed. Adolfus Busse (Berlin: Georgii Reimeri, 1900), 115–119, which enumerate diverse Aristotelian claims concerning the order of teaching, showing that, even in Aristotelianism, the problem was not very (*si*) simple to resolve.

75 Aristotle, *Posterior Analytics*, 72a; cf. Mignucci, *L'Argumenazione dimostrative di Aristotle*, tome I, 30.

76 Victor Goldschmidt, 'Temps historique et temps logique dans l'interprétation des systèmes philosophiques', *Acts du X1eme Congrès International de Philosophie*, XII (Bruxelles 1953), 7–13.

77 I draw this example from Victor Goldschmidt. 'Temps historique et temps logique', 11. He cites Descartes, 'Réponse aux Seconds Objections (contra les [. . .] *Meditations)*", in *Oeuvres de Descartes*, tome IX, edited by Charles Adam et Paul Tannery (Paris: Léopold Cerf, 1904), 103–104.

78 Cf. note above on Aristotle, *Posterior Analytics*. One finds in the work of Aristotle certain pedagogical notations: for example, in *Metaphysics* 1005b4: one cannot understand certain questions of first philosophy without having previously studied the analytic: or better, in *Nicomachean Ethics*, 1095a1 ff., young men cannot study ethics and politics if they have not already begun improving their lives.

79 Cf. notes 18–21 above.

80 Plato, *Republic*, 521c ff.

81 Cf. Harold Chemiss *Die Altere Akademie* (Heidelberg: C. Winter, 1966), 82–83.

82 Plato, *Republic*, 539b. We note thus in the *Phaedrus* 271b the idea of a rhetoric which adapts the species of discourse to the different species of souls.

83 Plato, *Republic*, 514a ff.

84 Plato, *Symposium*, 210a.

85 Diogenes Laertius, *Lives of the Eminent Philosophers*, VII, 39: "tripartite, they say, is the discourse of philosophy (*ton kata philosophian logon*)", and *ibid.*, VII, 41: Zeno of Tarsis, as opposed to the other Stoics, thought that the parts in question were the parts of philosophy, and are not parts of philosophical discourse. [Translator's note: see Chapter 3 above.]

86 Cf. Goldschmidt, *Le Système stoïcien*, 61–62. On the subdivisions of ethics, cf. André Mehat, *Essai sur les Stromates de Clement of Alexandria* (Paris: Éditions du Seuil, 1966), 77 ff.

87 Diogenes Laertius, *Lives of the Eminent Philosophers*, VII, 49, VII, 84, VII, 132.

88 Cicero, *De Finibus*, III, 4, 14 ff.

89 Cf. Goldschmidt, *Le Système stoïcien*, 62.

90 Diogenes Laertius, *Lives of the Eminent Philosophers*, VII, 40–41; Sextus Empiricus, *Adversus Mathematicus*, VII, 16–19.

91 Epitetus, *Discourses*, III, 2,5; IV, 8, 4.

92 Sextus Empiricus, *Adversus Mathematicus*, VII, 17–19; Diogenes Laertius, *Lives of the Eminent Philosophers*, VII, 40.

93 Adolf Friedrich Bonhöffer, *Epiktet und die Stoa* (Stuttgart: Verlag von Ferdinand Enke, 1890 [reprint 1968]), 13 ff.

94 Cf. Ilsetraut Hadot, *Seneca und die Greichisch-Romische Tradition der Seelenleitung* (Berlin: Walter de Gruyter, 1969), 115.

95 SVF, tome II, §42.

96 Sextus Empiricus, *Adversus Mathematicus*, VII, 23.

97 Bonhöffer, *Epiktet und die Stoa*, 19.

98 Diogenes Laertius, *Lives of the Eminent Philosophers*, VII, 40 (I read *pokekrosthai* with the manuscripts).

99 SVF tome II, 20, 10 (= in Plutarch, *De Stoicorum Repugnantiis*, 1035a).

100 Ilsetraut Hadot, *Seneca*, 52–56; and her 'Épicure et l'enseignement philosophique hellénistique et romain', *Actes de VIIIe Congrès de L'Association Guillaume Budé* (Paris: Vrin, 1969), 347–355.

101 SVF tome III, §474.

102 Ilsetraut Hadot, *Seneca*, 21; and by the same author, *Le Problème du Néoplatonisme Alexandrin* (Paris: Études Augustiniennes, 1976), 190.

103 Cf. Émile Bréhier, *Études de philosophie antique* (Paris: Presses Universitaires de France, 1955), 215–217. I do not think that Bréhier had good reasons to attribute this third place "to a disdain for logical technique." On the contrary, this third place is probably a place of honour.

104 Plutarch, *de Iside*, 382d.

105 Theon of Smyrna, *Expositio Rerum Mathematicarum ad Legendum Platonem Utilium*, ed. Eduard Hiller (Leipzig: Tuebner, 1878 [1966]), 14.

106 Clement of Alexandria, *Stromata*, I, 28, 176, 1–3.

107 Origen, *In Canticum Canticorum*, in *Origenes Werke*, Vol. 8 (GCS 33), ed. W. A. Baehrens (Berlin: C. Hinrichs, 1925), prol., 75, 6. Cf. Évagre le Pontique, *Traité pratique ou Le moine*, §1 Gaullamont.

108 Calcidius, *On Plato's Timaeus*, 170, 7 and 277, 5 Waszink.

109 Porphyry. *Sententia*, ed. Erich Lamberz (Leipzig: Teubner, 1975), 32. Cf. Wilhelm Theiler, *Gnomon* 5 (1929): 307–317; also Ilsetraut Hadot, *Le Problème du Néoplatonisme Alexandrin*, 152 ff.

110 Cf. Henri van Leshout, *La Théorie Plotinienne de la Vertu: Essai sur la genèse d'un article de la* Somme theologique *de Saint Thomas* (Freiburg, Switzerland: Broché, 1926).

111 Cf. Epictetus, *Discourses*, I, 4, 7; I, 17, 13; II, 16, 34; II, 21, 10–11; III, 21, 7; Cf. Georg H. I. Bruns, *De Schola Epicteti* (Kiel, 1897), 14; Aulus-Gellius, *Attic Nights*, I, 9, 9; Porphyry, *Life of Plotinus*, §14; Marinus, *Vita Procli*, ed. Jean François Boissonade (London, Rome, Paris: Lipsiae: Weigel, 1814), 157, 7 ff. See also *Eliae in Porphyrii Isagogen et Aristotelis Categorias Commentaria*, 115–119, on the order of study of the parts of philosophy.

112 Albinus, *Eisagôgê*, in Karl Friedrich Hermann, *Platonis Opera*, VI (Leipzig: Novi Eboraci Apud Harperos Phatres, 1853), 147–151; cf. René Le Corre, 'The Prologue of Albinus', *Revue Philosophique* 81 (1965): 28–38. Albinus proposes an order of reading founded on the dispositions of the disciple and on his spiritual progress.

113 Compare Marinus, *Vita Procli*, 157, 41; *Simplicii in Aristotelis Physicorum Libros Quattuor Priores Commentaria*, ed. Hermann Diels (Berlin: G. Remeiri, 1882), 5, 29 and *Simplicii in Aristotelis Categorias Commentarium*, 5, 3 ff.; *Anonymous Prolegomena to Platonic Philosophy*, 10, 26, 49, I.

114 Cf. Ilsetraut Hadot, *Le Problème du néoplatonisme Alexandrin*, 160 ff.

115 Marinus, *Vita Procli*, 157, 41.

116 Cf. André-Jean Festugière, "L'Ordre de lecture des dialogues de Platon aux Ve/VIe siècles", *Mus. Helv.* 26 (1969): 282–296.

117 Hans Leisegang, *Denkformen*, 2e ed. (Berlin: Walter de Gruyter, 1951), 208, which cites the text of Schopenhauer of which we are speaking.

118 The metaphor of Schopenhauer is in effect reversed: it is this time the superior which makes the inferior exist. But the essential component of the metaphor is safeguarded: the relations between the parts of the system are not reciprocal.

119 Goldschmidt, *Le système stoïcien*, 64 makes allusion, concerning Stoicism, to the text of Schopenhauer's that we have cited.

120 Cf. Pierre Hadot, 'Exercises Spirituels', *Annuaire de la Ve section de l'École des Hautes Études* 84 (1977): 25–70. [Translator's note: i.e. 'Spiritual exercises', in *Philosophy as a Way of Life*, trans. by Michael Chase (London: Wiley-Blackwell, 1995), 79–125]. On philosophy as quest of wisdom, cf. Plato, *Symposium*, 203 d, where it coincides with the figure of Eros, that of Socrates and of philosophy.

7 PHILOSOPHY, DIALECTIC AND RHETORIC IN ANTIQUITY

The following study can only be a very general sketch:[1] one would need a whole work to treat this topic in all its details. Our exposition will especially focus on the relations between philosophy and dialectic; rhetoric will only appear to the extent to which it is intimately related to dialectic. On the other hand, we will not analyse all philosophical schools: to be more specific, we will leave the Epicureans aside.[2] After having presented the relations between philosophy, dialectic and rhetoric in Aristotle, which will allow us to evoke the Platonic background [of Aristotle's position], we will then study the evolution of these relations in Hellenistic and Neoplatonist philosophy. We will thus be led to a set of methodological conclusions.

1 The three disciplines in Aristotle

It is in the work of Aristotle that we find the most elaborated ancient theory on the relationship between the three disciplines.[3]

First of all, what are the common points between rhetoric and dialectic? They both suppose an initial situation marked by conflict: that is, a situation where two contradictory responses can be given to a theoretical, juridical or political question (or problem).[4] However, rhetoric and dialectic are not interested in the response as such. They are only concerned with the means which will allow an adversary, a judge or the people to accept one of the two. What counts, therefore, is not so much the theme of the discussion, but rather the interlocutor[a] himself, who must be persuaded.[5] In order to conduct the listener to a given conviction, one must start from those things of which the listener is already convinced; that is to say, one must start either from his own opinions or, more generally, from opinions that are universally accepted, common and natural notions, admitted by everyone.[6] This point, for Aristotle, is what radically distinguishes rhetoric and dialectic from the sciences such as mathematics, for example.[7] The latter have, indeed, their own principles and techniques which are only understood by specialists, and they are applied to one specific domain of reality. Rhetoric and dialectic, on the contrary, are 'common' and universal. They do not have any specific and determinate domain of reality on which they focus; rather, they can be applied to any subject of discussion, and they start from principles which are accessible to all. They do not bring knowledge concerning any specific issue. They seek only to persuade the interlocutor, with the help of what he already knows. This is why they are both able to prove the positions 'pro' and 'contra':[b8] this is what Cicero will call argument *in utramque partem*. This does not deprive them in any way of logical rigour. From the moment that one admits a certain point of departure, the necessary chain of syllogisms will inexorably lead to the conclusion. The syllogistic reasoning is the same in science and dialectic.[9] It is solely the principles which differ between them: in each science, its own specific principles; in rhetoric and dialectic, common notions. Furthermore, rhetoric and dialectic, as we have already said, are not concerned with the conclusion in itself, but rather with the means that lead to the conclusion.

Despite this fundamental kinship, rhetoric and dialectic are different from one another. Let us first speak about the characteristics that are specific to dialectic. Dialectic is the art of discussing; that is to say, it formulates the rules of the dialectical joust,[10] in which an attacker[c] argues against the thesis of an adversary in order to oblige the latter, through skilful questions, to necessarily admit the thesis which contradicts his own. 'To interrogate' (*erôtan*), this is the task of the attacker; to construct a syllogism, starting from the premises (questions posed to the adversary) which will lead (if he concedes the truth of these premises) to a conclusion which involves the contradictory proposition to the adversary's thesis. The attacker himself does

---

[a] [Translator's note] French: *auditeur*. Sometimes we will translate this more literally as 'auditor' or 'listener', in the context of a dialogue or discussion, the addressee of a philosophical discourse participates in discourse and is, therefore, an 'interlocutor'.
[b] [Translator's note] French: *le pour et le contre;* more literally: the positions 'for' and 'against' a certain thesis.
[c] [Translator's note] Literally, from Hadot's *attaquant*.

not have a thesis. However, he is capable of arguing in such a way that he who defends a thesis will be inexorably constrained to contradict his own thesis. One recognizes here the Socratic situation. As Aristotle says: 'Socrates asked questions, he did not provide answers, since he confessed to know nothing.'[11] Not only does dialectic teach one how to ask questions. It also teaches how to respond; that is to say, it teaches one how to defend a thesis against the traps[d] of the questioner.[e12] The respondent defends a thesis, but only for the sake of the exercise: he must be able to defend the thesis and the thesis that contradicts it. He thus only appears as if he knew.

This game of questions and answers and its tortuous itineraries, which often puts off the readers of Plato's dialogues, cannot be found in rhetoric. The latter uses continuous discourse;[13] that is, an exposition which is not interrupted and structured in questions and answers. This was the method of the sophists. The listener who must be persuaded does not participate in the argumentation, as was the case in dialectic. In dialectic, the questioner and the respondent specify, at each step of the discussion, the points on which they agree. And this is exactly the danger for the respondent, who can let himself be led to imprudently agree to a premise (that is, to say 'yes' to a question) in such a way that the logical consequences of the premise thus conceded will constrain him to admit as true the contradiction to his own initial thesis. In rhetoric, the discourse is developed with no obstacles, starting from the positions that the listener is supposed to accept.

Moreover, dialectic is more universal than rhetoric. The former treats all possible subjects, and does so in the most universal way, without the intervention of concrete data.[f] On the contrary, rhetoric takes as subjects, above all, concrete problems[14] (Did this man commit murder? Should we go to war?). What is at stake for rhetoric is the kind of problems that the ancients called 'civil' or 'political'[15] which are, by definition, contingent. One should not be surprised to find the phrase 'civil questions' in the Latin rhetoricians, employed to designate the problems of rhetoric.[16] There will always be a close link between rhetoric and ethical and political problems. This opposition between the generality of dialectic and the particularity of rhetoric corresponds to the opposition between thesis and hypothesis. As Boethius will say:

---

[d] [Translator's note] French: *pièges*.

[e] [Translator's note] The French is *interrogateur*, which we render as 'questioner', given the historical and legal associations in the English 'interrogator'. 'Inquirer' might also have been used but it is specifically someone charged with asking questions according to certain rules that is at stake here. Inquiry may involve asking questions, but it also has a wider denotation.

[f] [Translator's note] French: *données*.

Dialectic is only concerned with the 'thesis'. The thesis is a problem (*questio*) without any concrete or particular circumstances (*circumstantiae*). Rhetoric concerns itself with discussing hypotheses, which is to say, discussing problems which presuppose a multiplicity of concrete circumstances (Who? What? Where? When? Why? How? By what means?)[17]

For Aristotle, there is a fundamental opposition between philosophy and these two techniques of rhetoric and dialectic. In effect, this position reflects the novelty of his conception of philosophy, compared to that of Plato. One knows that in the *Phaedrus*, after having criticized the rhetoric of the rhetors, Plato proposed a philosophical rhetoric.[18] This would not be a rhetoric of mere appearance, but one which would be founded on the knowledge of truth[19] and on the differentiation of possible relations between different kinds of souls and the kinds of discourses capable of affecting each of these types of souls.[20] In Plato's mind, this philosophical rhetoric presupposes dialectic, which for him means philosophy, and which is what will allow rhetoric to be founded on the knowledge of truth. Dialectic is defined in the *Phaedrus* as a twofold movement of thought. On the one hand, it reduces the multiplicity of notions to the unity of a Form, that is, of an Idea in the Platonic sense. On the other hand, dialectic re-descends from this Form, distinguishing and organizing the subordinated forms which it implies.[21] In Plato, this method is closely linked to the practice of dialogue. Indeed, as one notes in Plato's dialogues, it is in the game of questions and answers, through the slow progression of the interlocutors' reflection on their own discourse, that the ideal Form gradually emerges, together with the division of particular forms which are enveloped in this first Form.[g] The logical architecture of reality is discovered by discourse and by the discourse about discourse. As Léon Robin excellently writes: 'The reflective and free adhesion to a thesis subject to examination is essential to dialectic, i.e., the dialogical method of research in common by questions and answers conducted according to an order.'[22]

This is precisely what Aristotle refuses. For him, Platonic dialectic is a purely formal method which is incapable of leading us to a truly scientific form of knowledge. Indeed, Platonic dialectic starts from common notions, whereas for Aristotle each science must start from principles specific to the domain of reality it studies. In addition to that, Platonic dialectic moves within the homogenous and universal domain of discourse, whereas each science has as its object a determined *ousia*, which it must attain through

---

[g] [Translator's note] Original: *cette Forme première*.

specific methods, ultimately relying on observation from the senses. Platonic dialectic cannot exit the domain of discourse. It only attains abstract notions rather than *ousias*, which, for Plato, would be the Ideas subsisting in themselves.[23] The refusal of the theory of Ideas and the refusal to consider dialectic as a philosophical science go hand in hand in Aristotle. Generally, Aristotle employs the term *logikôs* either to designate this purely formal way of arguing which relies on the ordinary meaning of the words, or to designate the analysis of what is logically implied in a definition.[24]

In Aristotelian philosophy, there should then be a radical separation between rhetoric and dialectic, on the one hand, and the philosophical sciences, on the other.[25] Since the status of science is denied to dialectic in the Platonic sense, and since dialectic is preserved only as a technique of persuasion, indifferent to the pursuit of the truth, there should be no room for it in philosophical science. In fact, Aristotle often distinguishes with great clarity dialectical from demonstrative premises: the former have an interrogative form, to which one could respond with a 'yes' or 'no'. One will ask the interlocutor: 'Is pleasure a good? Yes or no?' The rest of the discussion will depend on the answer that the interlocutor gives. Demonstrative premises, on the other hand, are not interrogative; they are already choices between the contradictory alternatives. For example: 'pleasure is a good'. One can, then, extract the consequences from this affirmation. Therefore, they allow us to build up a science. Since the consequences are themselves a result of the principles proper to that science, they lead us to determinate conclusions; whereas if dialectical premises are taken as [the] starting point by the questioner, they can only lead to a refutation of the respondent's position.[26] Aristotle thus distinguishes didactic from dialectical arguments:

> we call didactic those arguments which reach their conclusions starting from principles that are specific to each discipline, instead of beginning from the opinions of the person who responds. We call dialectical those arguments that reach a conclusion which contradicts the given thesis starting from premises that are probable.[27]

With this fundamental opposition posed, Aristotle still recognizes that dialectic has a role to play in philosophy.[28] First of all, it is a sort of intellectual gymnastics, which one should practice in the scholarly[h] exercise of the dialectical joust. Aristotle formulated the rules of this kind of joust in the eighth book of the *Topics*. And the practice of dialectic will remain

---

[h] [Translator's note] Hadot's adjective is *scolaire*.

prestigious for a long time in the philosophical schools, as we will see in what follows.

Dialectic (and eventually rhetoric) represents a means to adapt oneself to one's interlocutors. Moreover, dialectic and rhetoric can play a protreptic role in philosophy: inviting someone to a philosophical conversion, starting from common notions that every man can understand and accept.[29] They can also have a polemical mission. We can, for instance, surmise that the Aristotelian dialogues, today lost, which according to Cicero presented successive arguments for and against a thesis, were precisely aimed at refuting a doctrine after having clearly exposed it.[30] One can often find this procedure in Cicero. One can also note that, in the *Metaphysics*, Aristotle – who reproached Platonists for developing non-scientific and merely formal arguments – claims that he can refute Platonic doctrines by using arguments even more formal than those of his rivals, and therefore beating them on their own terrain, thanks to dialectic.[31] In general, the knowledge of common notions, accepted by everyone, or the knowledge of the theories of one's adversary, allow one to take as one's starting point in the discussion the adversary's prejudices and presuppositions, in order to lead him to detach himself from them. The technique of refutation which characterizes dialectic will make it possible to persuade one's interlocutors to renounce their own untenable positions.

Finally, within philosophical science itself, when a particular science such as physics is led to speak about absolutely universal principles, it will be constrained to call upon dialectic, to the extent to which the 'axioms' that it supposes are founded on universally accepted opinions. As Aristotle said:

> It is impossible to speak of first notions in each science while at the same time relying on the specific principles of this science, because principles are precisely that which is first in relation to all the rest. It is thus necessary, if one wants to examine them, to make recourse to what exists in terms of generally accepted ideas concerning each of these notions. This task is proper to dialectic.[32]

Dialectic, then, comes onto the scene when a science reaches its original limit and cannot reflect on its own principles. This is why first philosophy cannot explain the use of the identity principle, which is the fundamental axiom of all science, except by resorting to a dialectical method.[33] Another boundary of science appears when one finds affirmations of existence. For example, physics poses the problem of the existence of time.[34] Now, science has as its object the essence and not the existence of things: one does not know, properly speaking, an existence; rather, one can only be convinced of it (or not). On the other hand, as Wolfgang Wieland[35] correctly remarked, rhetoric, and especially judicial rhetoric, is prepared to face this sort of issue, since it must often convince people of the existence of a certain fact. When treating of problems of existence, Aristotle uses, then, a mode of rhetorical argumentation, which he calls 'exoteric'. Simplicius, when commenting on this phrase, explains: 'That which is exoteric is not specialised (*koinon*), and that which reaches a conclusion starting from reasons accepted by everyone (*endoxon*).'[36]

In principle, in his scientific works, Aristotle should have used only the apodictic methods he had proposed in his *Analytics*. However, like many theorists of methodology, he is often disloyal to his own principles. His procedures of argumentation sometimes happen to be dialectical, and even rhetorical. Like every science, philosophical science should go from the premises to the conclusion; that is to say, it should start from general principles, specific to the science in question, and advance towards consequences which would be more and more distanced from these premises. On the contrary, rhetoric and dialectic correspond to an inverse movement of thought: they lead us from the conclusion to the premises. Indeed, in rhetorical or dialectical argumentation, one knows the conclusion in advance. In judicial rhetoric, the lawyer knows from the start whether he will answer 'yes' or 'no' to the question: 'did this man commit murder?' In dialectic, the attacker and the respondent have defined positions from the start. To the question: 'is pleasure a good?', one answers 'yes', the other answers 'no'. What one must find are not the conclusions, but rather the premises; that is, the propositions from which one will be able to ground a conclusion which is already known. Aristotle's *Topics* and his *Rhetoric* precisely provide the 'places' (*topoi*), that is, the typical schemas[i] of argumentation that will allow one to find, concerning any given issue, the premises that will necessarily lead to some conclusion. The dialectical and the rhetorical method are therefore hypothetical; they lead us back to the necessary conditions which make the conclusion possible. Now, as Wieland has shown, it is precisely the rhetorico-dialectical method that one finds applied in many points of Aristotelian philosophy, rather than the deductive method defined in the *Analytics*.[37] That which Aristotelian science seeks to discover are the principles on the basis of which syllogistic deduction can take place. These principles often constitute general schemas of argumentation that are, indeed, analogous to the *topoi* of dialectic.

Must we go further and say, with Pierre Aubenque, that the first philosophy that Aristotle wanted to substitute for the Platonic dialectic

---

[i] [Translator's note] Hadot's phrase is *schémas-types*.

remained at a stage of a purely aporetic dialectic?[38] Given the limited scope
of this article, we can only raise this problem which shows the importance
of dialectic in Aristotle's philosophy.

2 Dialectic as a pedagogical exercise[j]

To describe the relations between philosophy, dialectic and rhetoric in post-
Aristotelian ancient philosophy, it would be necessary to clearly distinguish
three main domains of application of dialectic and eventually of rhetoric.[39]
Dialectic can be a pedagogical or school exercise, and Aristotle formulated
the rules of this exercise in the eighth book of the *Topics*. Dialectic and
rhetoric can also be a method for the teaching of philosophy. And finally,
both dialectic and rhetoric can be a constitutive part of philosophy, as
subdivisions of logic.

In what concerns pedagogical dialectic, we have already seen that
Aristotle formulated in the eighth book of the *Topics* the general rules of
dialectical discussion, opposing for the sake of intellectual gymnastics a
questioner and a respondent. It is probably to the pedagogical exercise that
Polemon,[40] Xenocrates' successor at the Academy in the third century BCE,
referred when he said that it was better to exercise oneself in the difficulties
of life than in dialectical questions, since he criticized those whom one
admires for their argumentative performances (*erôtêseis*), but who
contradict themselves in their inner dispositions.[41]

Moreover, it is to the dialectical joust that we can link the habit of using
the word 'interrogate' (*erôtan* in Greek, *interrogare* in Latin) to designate
all forms of syllogistic argumentation until the end of antiquity. This is
because, in dialectical exercises, it is he who interrogates[k] who puts
forward syllogisms.[42] Approximately four centuries after Polemon, we find
a parallel between the dialectical exercise and the exercise of virtue in
Epictetus:

---

[j] [Translator's note] Here, *exercise scolaire*: we translate the adjective as 'pedagogical' to
avoid the association of the term 'scholastic' in English with specifically medieval forms of
university teaching. 'Scholarly' in English also carries a different set of connotations than
those in play here; Hadot's term designates something closer to a 'school exercise', which
we will accordingly sometimes use.

[k] [Translator's note] Literally, *celui qui interroge*.

In the same way that we exercise ourselves in responding to sophistical interrogations, we have equally to exercise ourselves daily to confront representations, for they also pose interrogations to us.[43]

Aulus Gellius, who writes in the first half of the second century CE and who had been the disciple of the Platonist Taurus, mentions the pedagogical exercises in dialectic when he evokes one of the fundamental rules of these exercises: that which established that the respondent could only reply by saying 'yes' or 'no'. But he remarks that one had the right to refuse to answer sophistical questions such as: 'have you stopped committing adultery, yes or no?'[44] In the fifth century, we find Proclus, in his *Commentary on the Alcibiades*, perfectly informed about the fundamental rules of the dialectical exercises.[45]

Throughout the Middle Ages and into the twentieth century,[46] the dialectical exercise of argumentation will, in fact, continue to be an important element in the formation of future philosophers.

We have less details concerning rhetorical exercises. However, we know from Cicero that both Academics and Peripatetics attributed great importance to the training of speech.[47] For this reason, they practiced exercises in which arguments for and against a thesis were successively developed. Generally speaking, it seems that philosophical education included as one of its constitutive parts the composition of 'theses', in the rhetorical sense of the word: that is to say, the composition of continuous speeches (in contrast with dialectic) and expositions on general topics, such as: 'should the sage get married?' Such exercises seem to have formed part of the exercises proper to philosophical formation in the Platonic, Aristotelian and Stoic schools.[48]

3 Dialectic and rhetoric as methods of philosophical teaching

The problem we now pose is effectively different [from the preceding]. Here, we are not concerned with knowing if one practiced dialectical or rhetorical exercises during philosophy courses, but rather if the master used a method which would involve dialectical and rhetorical traits in order to communicate the content of his philosophy to his students. From this perspective, one can say that the period between the third century BCE and the fourth century CE corresponds to a triumph of dialectic and rhetoric in philosophical teaching. Evidently, the use of the two disciplines acquires multiple forms and meanings; the phenomenon is, nevertheless, a general fact.

On this topic, we possess a very interesting text from Cicero specifically on the teaching methods of the Academy. There, we can clearly see the fundamental importance of the question–answer schema, but also the more dialectical or rhetorical orientations of different pedagogical methods.[1] It will be very useful to analyse this text with precision. At the very moment when he begins speaking in the dialogue of *De Finibus* in order to refute the Epicurean position,[49] Cicero warns his interlocutors: 'First of all, I ask you to understand that I will not develop a *schola* as a philosopher,[m] which is something that I have never appreciated in a philosopher.' By *schola*, Cicero understands a continuous discourse, and thus a rhetorical type of discourse.[50] Indeed, he continues:

> When has Socrates, who we could rightly call the father of philosophy, done such a thing? That is rather the custom of those who one used to call 'sophists'. Among the latter was Gorgias of Leontium, who challenged Socrates to propose to him any topic on which he wanted to hear him speak: a daring enterprise, I would say even a temerity, if this practice was not later transmitted to our philosophies.

Cicero specifies what could be understood as a rhetorical form of teaching: a listener poses the question and the master replies by means of a continuous discourse. He suggests that the philosophers of his time also used this form of teaching, before coming back to this detail later in the text. To this rhetorical method, the rest of Cicero's text opposes the dialectical method:

> However, this Gorgias I have just named as well as the other sophists, as we can learn from Plato, we see them played with by Socrates. Because the latter, asking questions and interrogating, had the habit of leading those with whom he discussed to reveal their own opinions, so that he could himself argue, if it seemed interesting for him, against that which they had proposed.

---

[1] [Translator's note] Original: *méthodes d'enseignement*.

[m] [Translator's note] Rackham in the Loeb edition of the text translates *schola* as 'formal lecture', at Marcus Tullius Cicero, *On Ends*, trans. H. Rackham (Cambridge, MA, and London: Harvard University Press, 1931), 79.

One is clearly speaking here of the dialectical method, since a dialogue takes place between a questioner and a respondent. 'This method,' Cicero continues:

> was not preserved by Socrates' successors, but Arcesilaus revived it, establishing the following rule: those who wanted to hear him speak should not ask him what he thought, but should themselves speak what they thought; when they said this, he would himself argue against them; his listeners, however, could defend their own opinion whenever possible for them.

According to Cicero, then, the Ancient Academy ('that which comes after Socrates') had renounced dialectical method as its means of teaching until Arcesilaus reintroduced it. In Arcesilaus' school, the master, who is the questioner and the attacker, has no thesis. It is rather the student, the respondent, who defends a thesis. Cicero stresses the difference between this dialectical method, in which the respondent engages in a dialogue with the master, and the rhetorical method of teaching, in which there is no dialogue:

> For other philosophers, he who posed a question then holds one's tongue: this is the current practice nowadays in the Academy. He who wants to hear the master speak, tells him, for instance: 'pleasure, it seems to me, is the sovereign good'. The master, then, argues against this opinion by giving a continuous speech, in such a way that one can conclude that those who say 'it seems to me ...' are not completely convinced of what they say, of the opinion they express, and want to hear the contrary.

This is the rhetorical method, therefore, because the master's discourse is continuous. Nevertheless, one can also note the point in common between the dialectical and rhetorical methods of teaching: namely, the teaching is always realised *contra thesim*: that is, against a thesis that one refutes.

With the support of this text, and of others that complement it, one could, in effect, present the different aspects of the teaching of philosophy in that period in the following way:

1 The teaching is always done *contra theism*:[51] which is to say, it proceeds against a determinate position interrogatively or affirmatively presented by a listener: 'in my view, death is an evil' or, again: 'can the sage be angry?'[n]

---

[n] [Translator's note] The French expression is *se mettre en colère* ...

2   Regarding this thesis, the master can then develop his teaching either in a dialectical or in a rhetorical way.

3   If the teaching is done in a dialectical way, then a dialogue takes place through questions and answers between the master and his listener. Against the thesis presented by the listener, the master argues syllogistically, by posing to the listener questions whose responses will necessarily lead him to accept the contradictory thesis to the one he had earlier proposed to the master. This is Arcesilaus' and Polemon's method.[52]

4   If the teaching is done following the rhetorical method, no dialogue follows the initial question, the *thesis* proposed by a listener. But regarding this thesis, the master develops either only one continuous discourse of refutation, or two antithetical discourses, one for and the other against.[53] In this latter case, the method of argumentation employed is that of *in utramque partem*. These two types of rhetorical argumentation were used by Xenocrates,[54] Arcesilaus,[55] Carneades[56] and Cicero[57] himself.

All this concerns only the method. However, it is evident that common methods can acquire different meanings, depending on the philosophical orientation of the masters who use them. One could, in fact, distinguish three fundamental orientations. The Ancient Academy (for instance, Xenocrates or Polemon) uses dialectic or rhetoric in a still Platonic spirit. This means that, whether rhetorical or dialectical, the argumentation is always already pre-directed. As Cicero says, the listener who poses the questions knows in advance what the master will say. Additionally, he does not maintain the thesis he proposes to the master: in truth, he shares the master's position. The question proposed is then purely formal. It only serves as a pretext for the master to expose his own doctrine, either by means of dialectical refutation or rhetorical abundance. Arcesilaus, on the other hand, has very different intentions. He claimed to not uphold any determinate thesis himself. Arcesilaus considered himself an inheritor of Socrates, who knew only that he knew nothing. Both when he argues dialectically against a thesis in order to destroy it, and when he rhetorically develops two antithetical discourses, his aim is not that of teaching any particular content. His teaching has no doctrinal content, he only aims at provoking an *epochê*, the suspension of judgement. 'He suspends the assertion,' Diogenes Laertius says, 'because of the contradictions between discourses.'[58] Finally, the third orientation is that of the probabilistic academic sceptics. For them, the rhetorical method is that which is most important, especially under the form of *in utramque partem* discourse.

Indeed, while remaining loyal to Arcesilaus' ideas concerning the impossibility for the human spirit to reach truth, they also think it is possible for people to choose among opposed opinions that which will seem to be closer to the truth: the most probable one.[59] From this perspective, the use of rhetorical means will allow one to be more persuasive. But one should seek equally to present the 'pro' and 'contra' so as to leave the listener the free choice.

There evidently was a sort of pre-established harmony between the Ciceronian ideal of the philosopher-orator and this tendency in the Academy of his time to grant a preponderant place to rhetoric in the teaching of philosophy. As Cicero himself puts it: 'we use this philosophy that has engendered oratorical abundance and which expresses ideas which do not differ that much from common opinion.'[60] Rhetoric, dialectic and philosophy here come together in order to allow the listener or interlocutor to discover by himself that which seems more probable to him: that is to say, that which is more likely to correspond to common notions admitted by humankind.

In what concerns the ancient Stoics, we do not know much about their method of teaching. We do know, however, that Chrysippus firmly opposed Arcesilaus' method, and that he refused to drag the listener, especially the beginner, into the dangers of the *in utramque partem* argumentation. He wanted philosophers such as the Stoics who developed a science which should lead one to live a life in accordance with itself, to begin by acquiring the basic principles and by studying the doctrine as a whole.[o][61] The polemic with adversaries which played a key role in teaching for the Academics was for the Stoics reserved for a later stage of the philosophical education.[62] However, dialectical interrogation was a procedure of exposition dear to the Stoics. Cicero tells us, indeed:

They sting you as with darts, with small sharp interrogations. But those who respond 'yes' to them are not transformed in their souls, and they leave in the same way they came. This is due to the fact that, even if the thoughts they express can be true and surely sublime, they are not handled as they should be, but rather, narrowly.[63]

For Cicero, the continuous and ornate discourse of rhetoric has more psychagogic power than the brevity of dialectical interrogations. Elsewhere, Cicero tells us that Cato, as a good Stoic, does not develop the subject matter

---

[o] [Translator's note] Hadot's expression is, more literally, 'from one end to the other' (*d'un bout à l'autre*).

which he treats, but that he proves his thesis by short interrogations.[64] Effectively, for the Stoics, dialectic was not only used to 'sting'[p] the interlocutor's attention. Through its sharp questions, it should above all allow one to address the interlocutor beginning from that which he already accepts. Émile Bréhier had correctly shown the importance of this key aspect in Stoic dialectic:

> The goal to be pursued by the Stoics is, first of all, to create a steadfast belief within the disciple's mind; by a peculiar postulate, they superimpose the objective conditions for persuasion and a strong subjective conviction. However, the aim of the dialectician is not exactly the invention [or] the discovery of new theses; all his effort centres upon the discussion of theses which naturally present themselves to the human mind. Once they pass the test[q] of discussion, from uncertain and unstable opinions, they become firm and systematic beliefs. Thus, the Stoics only seek to prove theses which they consider common opinions or those which they link, by a kind of artifice, to the general beliefs of humanity: the existence of the gods, the truth of divination. Moreover, they seek to prove, less to establish the validity of a thesis than to establish a conviction capable of resisting all opposing argumentation. For this reason, dialectic is here a defensive weapon which allows one to escape one's adversaries. This is why it contains a theory of sophisms.[65]

After the first century CE, the method of philosophical teaching is modified in all schools, to the extent that the master's teaching in large measure involves an exposition of the main texts of the school founders. One can note this phenomenon equally in the Platonists, the Aristotelians and the Stoics.[66] In truth, as Hans-Georg Gadamer remarked,[67] one can detect in the hermeneutical relationship of the exegete with the text that he explains the same fundamental situation of dialogue that exists between an interrogator and a respondent which characterizes dialectic. This is true to the extent that the commentary generally presents itself in the form of *zêtêmata*;[68] that is to say, under the form of questions that are put to the text, so to speak.

However, the game of questions and answers in philosophical teaching does not completely disappear. After the explanation of the text made by the master or by a student in front of the master, the students had the chance to ask questions. Here we find, once more, the ancient traditions. We know

---

[p] [Translator's note] Original: '*piquer*'.
[q] [Translator's note] Here: *épreuve*.

from Aulus Gellius that, when attending a course of the Platonist Taurus, he asked the master: 'does the sage ever get angry?' One can here recognize the situation we have already seen described by Cicero. A student poses a question with the intention of hearing the master responding 'no'. Aulus Gellius wanted to give Taurus the occasion of demonstrating that the sage does not get angry. Taurus, however, will propose a distinction between impassibility and insensibility, giving a nuanced response. In any case, Aulus Gellius specifies that Taurus' answer was *graviter et copiose*: that is, abundant and noble in style. This means that his exposition was a putting to work of the rhetorical method.[69]

We find the same kind of practices[r] in Neoplatonism. Porphyry tells us that Plotinus would seek to stimulate the listeners to pose questions, after having explained Platonic and Aristotelian texts as he would usually do in his courses. That created a situation of disorder, according to Porphyry, opening the space for pointless questions.[70] Porphyry kindly underscores how, after his arrival at Plotinus' school, the latter chose him as a privileged interlocutor, which did not please everyone. For three consecutive days, he was the one interrogating Plotinus about the union of body and soul. A certain Thaumasius complained about it, saying he could not stand this game of questions and answers with Porphyry, but that he rather wanted to hear Plotinus himself developing a general thesis, speaking in a way which would allow one to take notes.[71] Plotinus would respond that: 'if we did not have to respond to the *aporias* that Porphyry's questions present, we would not have anything to say that could be worthy of noting'.[72] We find here, once again, the opposition between dialectical and rhetorical methods. The dialectical method is that which Plotinus employs: it consists in the 'game of questions and answers' mentioned by Thaumasius. The rhetorical method is that which Thaumasius wanted to see Plotinus practicing. The epithet employed by Thaumasius to designate the kind of discourse he wished to hear is *katholou*. This is a technical term to designate the 'theses' in the rhetorical sense of the term; i.e. the general questions developed in a continuous discourse.[73]

The Stoic Epictetus also divided his classes between the explanation of texts by Chrysippus or Antipater and discussions with his listeners. The *Discourses* published by Arrian are nothing other than these discussions with the students.[74] In them, we find the trace of both continuous speeches, and thus of the rhetorical method as well as of dialogues, and thus of the

---

[r] [Translator's note] Hadot's term is *usages* here: *viz.* customs, usages, manners, fashions, customary or habitual practices.

dialectical method, more frequently. Epictetus knows the Socratic technique of dialogue very well, and he makes explicit reference to it.

The dialectical method still occupies an important space in the teaching of the Christian, Origen. For him, dialectical discussion between master and disciple plays an essentially critical role. According to his disciple Gregorius, Origen asked questions and listened to his students' answers so as to test them:[s]

> In a way that was effectively Socratic, he made us stumble by his discourse, when he saw us completely indolent[t] ... In the beginning, it was not without pain and difficulty that we subjected ourselves to these conversations, for we were not yet accustomed or trained to follow reason, and therefore he purified us.[75]

These different texts confirm, then, the importance of dialectical and rhetorical methods in the philosophical teaching of antiquity.

4 Dialectic and rhetoric as parts of philosophy

We have presented above the radical opposition between Plato and Aristotle regarding the relations between rhetoric and dialectic, on the one hand, and philosophy, on the other. For Plato, philosophy was essentially dialectic: that is to say, communal research in dialogue, of the Truth of the forms which founds the very possibility of dialogue (and a philosophical rhetoric can only be grounded on this dialectic). For Aristotle, on the contrary, dialectic and particularly rhetoric are absolutely exterior to philosophy, given that they are but techniques of persuasion, and not sciences that would investigate a specific realm of reality. They start from common opinions rather than scientific principles. Instead of dialectic, philosophy should normally use the analytic,[u] a special method for scientific demonstration. Is it necessary to recall *en passant* that the creator of logic, in the modern sense of the word, never uses in his work the term 'logic' to designate a particular discipline, either dialectic or analytic?

---

[s] [Translator's note] Again: *les éprouver.*
[t] [Translator's note] Original: *réstifs.*
[u] [Translator's note] French: *l'analytique.*

The use of the word 'logic' to designate a specific part of philosophy only appears, for the first time, with the Stoics, who put it on the same plane as ethics and physics.[v] This Stoic logic, the science of human discourse, comprises two parts. On the one hand, there is rhetoric, defined by the Stoics as the science of speaking well; that is, of continuous discourse. On the other hand, there is dialectic, defined as the science of 'discussing with rectitude'; which is to say, the science of dialogue or of discourse, insofar as it is broken down into questions and answers.[76] The theory of this dialectic contains the following chapters, organized in a rigorous way:[w]

[1] one begins by establishing the cognitive relationship between man and the events of the world, a cognitive relationship designated by the name of *phantasia*, which we could translate as 'representation';

[2] next, one examines the criteria of truth of this representation;

[3] then, one proceeds to the expression of this representation in discourse, initially considering this expression as sound, as voice, and then examining its value in terms of meaning[x] or as 'signified';

[4] finally, one studies the propositions that express events and the reasonings which link these propositions among themselves.[77]

The theory of dialectic thus enunciates the rules which allow us to speak of reality in an exact way. True dialectic, as part of philosophy, is not this abstract theory, however. It is, rather, the practice of this theory, the lived philosophy which is a permanently vigilant attention to retain in thought and discourse an exact representation of reality. From this perspective, Stoic dialectic retains essential characteristics of the Socratic–Platonic dialectic. It is fundamentally a critique which is exercised through interrogation, addressed to oneself and others, and which aims at detecting errors in our representations and in those of others. It is a critique, but it is also a maieutic which helps us to develop the natural notions that we already have within ourselves which, through a suitable approach, can be organized into a coherent and systematic vision of reality: the human *logos* asks only to be in harmony with the *logos* of nature. Understood in this way, dialectic is then a spiritual exercise and only the sage is truly a dialectician, because he is the only one capable of avoiding errors in judgement.[78]

---

[v] [Translator's note] See Chapter 6 above.
[w] [Translator's note] We have added the indentation and enumeration of Hadot's inventory here, for purposes of clarification. The original is continuous text.
[x] [Translator's note] The French is: *valeur de sense*.

In the Academy, from Arcesilaus to Cicero, both rhetoric and dialectic, probably joined together under the name of 'logic' (as in the Stoics), are constitutive parts of philosophy. More precisely, they constitute the totality of philosophy, to a certain extent. This is particularly true for Arcesilaus, but also for the Academics of Cicero's time and for Cicero himself.

We know that, for Arcesilaus, dialectical or rhetorical argumentation was exercised against every dogmatic thesis, and that it should lead to the total suspension of judgement. The other traditional parts of philosophy, namely physics and ethics, would disappear to the extent that they would not have specific contents anymore, since *every* thesis is refutable, as is any physical or ethical doctrine. Nevertheless, logic would assume a sort of ethical value to the extent that it would operate an *epochê*, a suspension of judgement leading to *ataraxia*,[79] peace of mind. From this perspective, the practice of this rhetorico-dialectical logic had an existential significance.

Equally, in Cicero's time, there is a preponderance of rhetorico-dialectical logic among the Academics. This time, however, the other parts of philosophy are not completely eliminated. Certain physical or ethical theses are admitted as being more probable than others. However, the method which permits recognizing them as probable, or of being convinced of them, is an essentially rhetorico-dialectical one. It is no longer a matter of completely suspending judgement, but of seeking that which is closest to the truth, as against the truth itself, and of thus producing a subjective conviction. It is a matter of finding out what one can reasonably admit. Therefore, one will seek to dialectically criticize theses that are doubtful and obscure, and to expose rhetorically – that is to say, with persuasive force – the possible solutions of a problem, with the aim of choosing that which is more probable. In this way, the disciplines of rhetoric and dialectic, which Aristotle considered foreign to philosophy, become essential to it. As for Plato, dialectic is philosophy. But the dialectic of the Academics is no longer the dialectic of Plato, the way of accessing the universe of Forms. Rather, paradoxically, it corresponds to the persuasive techniques that Aristotle rejected from the domain of philosophy, because they would be situated uniquely in the domain of the probable and of common opinions.[y]

It is this rhetoric–dialectic logic that we will find in Cicero. For him, logic (*ratio disserendi*)[80] implies a dialectical part (*ratio disputandi*) and a rhetorical part (*ratio dicendi*).[81] As a technique of discourse by questions and answers, dialectic implies a theory of the criteria of distinction between truth and falsity, as well as of the relations of opposition and consequence,

---

[y] [Translator's note] See section 1 above.

a science of definition and division, and a teaching concerning the figures of reasoning.[82] Rhetoric, on the contrary, is the technique of continuous discourse and implies a theory of invention, of disposition and of style. What is at stake in rhetoric is finding the arguments, then disposing and presenting them in such a way that the listener would be moved and persuaded.[83] It is evidently this latter rhetorical part which interests Cicero, the orator. Dialectic is only valuable for him to the extent to which some of its precepts can be used by rhetoric. For that matter, Cicero reproaches the Stoics for having almost wholly neglected rhetoric.[84] And by rhetoric, Cicero understands especially the theory of invention: the 'topics'.[85] He even divides logic no longer into dialectic and rhetoric, but into dialectic (*ratio iudicandi*) and topics (*ratio inueniendi*).[86] For him, the Peripatetics are the masters of this art of invention. Cicero seems to believe that his *Topics* are a summary of Aristotle's *Topics*.[87] As a matter of fact, Cicero had to use a post-Aristotelian handbook which marks a clear evolution of the Aristotelian doctrine of the *Topics*, originally dialectical, in the direction of a rhetorical use.[88] In particular, one notes that, in the second part of Cicero's short treatise on the *Topics*, referring to the 'theses' (*proposita*) which one will be able to deal with thanks to the theory of the places, Cicero gives as examples theses which are surely not dialectical, since they do not admit only 'yes' or 'no' as an answer, which is characteristic of that discipline.[89] Cicero's *Topics* are, therefore, a characteristic example of the evolution that leads to a predominance of rhetoric over dialectic in philosophy. The 'theses' of which Cicero speaks correspond to Platonico-Aristotelian dialectical argumentation, in which a thesis having been proposed by a defendant,[z] a questioner would then seek to make the defendant accept the contradiction within it. However, Ciceronian theses are no longer dialectical arguments. The initial theme remains of the same kind: 'should the sage get involved in public affairs?', or again: 'can virtue be taught?' But the way in which the issue is handled is completely different. This will now be dealt with through a rhetorical exercise, of an exposition which takes the form of continuous discourse. This is the meaning of Cicero's work, the *Stoic Paradoxes*. Cicero explicitly tells us, in the Preface, that his aim was to present the Stoic theses using the rhetorical method: which is to say, to rhetorically present these positions that were treated dialectically within this school.[90]

The ambiguous position of Cicero's *Topics* sheds light on the hesitations of the encyclopaedists of late antiquity concerning this work. Martianus Capella places the Ciceronian theory of places in his *Rhetoric*.[91] Cassiodorus,

---

[z] [Translator's note] Original: *défenseur*.

on the contrary, places Cicero's *Topics* in the corpus of dialectical authorities that he establishes for the library of Vivarium.[92]

In the work of one of Cicero's contemporaries, Antiochus of Ascalon,[93] who claims to return to the doctrines of the ancient Academy, logic always entails the two parts that we referred to above: dialectic and rhetoric. However, as in Stoicism, rhetorico-dialectical logic becomes again a means to achieve and express the true and the necessary.[94] The same tradition is found in Alcinous,[95] a Platonist from the second century CE. Antiochus and Alcinous divided dialectic into the theory of division, the theory of definition and the theory of demonstration:[96] a subdivision that will continue to take pride of place in Neoplatonism.[97]

With Neoplatonism, a new turning point in the evolution of the concept of dialectic takes place. This phenomenon occurs due to the integration of Aristotelian logic into the Neoplatonic system, and because of a new awareness regarding the originality of Plato's dialectic. Dialectic in the Aristotelian sense, understood as an art of discussion which starts from accepted ideas, regains its place in the Aristotelian system of logic, alongside analytic, which represents a theory of specifically philosophical reasoning. This Aristotelian logic, which is but a tool (*organon*) of philosophy and a propaedeutic to it,[98] is evidently distinct from Platonic dialectic.[99] The latter is considered as the supreme part of philosophy which fixes our gaze on the 'intelligible', that nourishes our soul on the plane of truth,[100] and through which we exercise contemplation of the intelligible. In the Neoplatonists, dialectic is practiced according to Plato's own methods: division, ascension to first kinds,[aa] synthesis and analysis.[101] However, an aspect of Plato's dialectic disappears in the Neoplatonists. Indeed, for Plato, it was through dialogue that philosophers could experience the reality of Forms, which, in their turn, made dialogue possible and gave it its validity. On the contrary, for the Neoplatonists, dialectic becomes a monologue.[102] It preserves only a very vague trace from the dialogical structure: it is perceived as a path (*diexodos*)[103] and even an errancy which is fulfilled through the Forms. It follows the movements of procession and conversion, the phases of distinction and reunion, and the stages of internal multiplication in which the intelligible world is constituted. These procedures of analysis and synthesis, of affirmation and negation, aim at making us catch a glimpse of the reflection of the transcendent One in the intelligible multiplicity. And, for the Neoplatonists, this Platonic dialectic is but one of the methods of theology amongst others.[104]

[aa] [Translator's note] Original: *la remontée aux genres premiers.*

[Concluding remarks]

Let us then conclude this too-brief sketch by making some general remarks. First of all, we have seen that the term 'dialectic' in antiquity can have many different meanings which correspond to the different stages of this lively history. After having been identified by Plato himself with philosophy, that is, with science, dialectic is then excluded from philosophy and reduced to a technique of persuasion by Aristotle. This technique of persuasion will be, once again, identified with philosophy by the probabilist Academics, whereas the Stoics would come to elevate the same technique of persuasion to the dignity of a scientific method, as a constitutive part of philosophy. In Neoplatonism, this Aristotelian–Stoic dialectic will again be excluded from philosophy strictly speaking; whereas Platonic dialectic is reduced to a monologue, becoming a theological method. In the Latin West, on the contrary, it is dialectic as a method of persuasion, drawn from Aristotelian and Ciceronian sources, which will be bequeathed to the high Middle Ages.[105]

This dialectic, as we have also seen, tends more and more to mingle with rhetoric after Aristotle. One renounces, in teaching, the technicality[bb] of dialogue, which is extremely hard to operate, becoming satisfied with the simpler means offered by continuous discourse. One contents oneself with integrating into rhetoric some elements of dialectic which can be useful to the former.[106] From this perspective, one should evoke the problem of this so-called literary genre that modern historians call the 'diatribe'. As Hermann Throm had shown,[107] the 'diatribe' is just a thesis. And a thesis is originally part of a dialectical exercise, in which one poses a dialectical problem (that is to say, a question), a problem with a broad scope to which the dialogical argumentation will have to answer. The 'diatribe' is, therefore, a thesis that is treated in a rhetorico-dialectical way. The only thing that survives from dialectic are the outlines of fictional dialogues (moreover, this is the reason why the philosophical works of Cicero and Seneca are called *dialogi*).[108] It is rhetoric, however, that provides the main means of amplification and persuasion. Additionally, the themes of the 'diatribe' correspond to the traditional set of issues which were the object of theses.[109]

Even when it was combined with rhetoric, dialectic was no less dominant in the whole of ancient philosophy than rhetoric. We were able to note the importance of the 'question–answer' schema in philosophical teaching, involving either replying to a question by means of a continuous discourse

---

[bb] [Translator's note] Original: *technicité*.

or, on the contrary, by means of questioning dialogically. This fundamental structure, inherited from Socrates and Plato, is of capital importance for Aristotle. Concerning the latter, Ingemar Düring correctly underlined:

> What characterizes Aristotle's method is the fact that he is always in the process of discussing an issue. Every important outcome of his investigations is almost always the answer to a question posed in a clearly determined way, and it is only valid as a response to this specific question.[110]

Similarly, Wieland notes that 'it is so essential for the Aristotelian structure of thought to answer to specific questions that the detailed explanation of the meaning of the question becomes itself a philosophical task'.[111] In fact, one must recognize that, in this characteristic, Aristotle does not differ from the whole of the ancient philosophical tradition. As we have seen, for the Academics, teaching consisted in replying to a question, and we know that Plotinus' treatises, for example, were written in order to respond to the questions that were posed to him in the course of his teaching.[112] The Stoic doctrine could seem to present itself in a more systematic way. However, one must not forget that it is known to us by means of doxographic summaries, and that we are completely ignorant of what the works of the school founders could have been. In any case, in the Stoic works that have been preserved, as, for instance, those of Epictetus and Seneca, the question–answer structure plays a fundamental role. In general, the philosophical works of antiquity, the different treatises written by an author never present themselves as the parts of a system that would aim at being perfectly coherent or complete. Each work seeks to respond coherently to a given question, to a very precise problem. This does not exclude the incoherencies that can emerge between the different responses to different issues given by the same author. The coherence is situated within the limits of the dialogue between 'question' and 'answer'. To put it in a more profound way, this 'question–answer' structure imposes upon thought ethical exigencies and a logic that Gadamer admirably analysed.[113] Let us add that this centrality of the 'question–answer' schema could invite us to investigate what we might term the 'problematics' in ancient philosophy:[cc] that is to say, a reflective inventory of the types of questions to which it sought to answer.

---

cc [Translator's note] Original: *la problématique dans la philosophie antique*. See Chapter 2 above.

In the 'question-answer' schema, the reference to the listener or interlocutor plays a central role. The philosopher always addressed someone. In the *Phaedrus*, Plato already wanted to constitute a philosophical rhetoric that would be able to adapt the different types of *logoi* to the different types of souls. In ancient philosophy, a doctrine is never completely separated from pedagogical care and philosophy, to a large extent, is identified with its teaching, which means to say that it is fundamentally formative. Teaching must always adapt itself to the exigencies of the disciples' spiritual progress and spiritual level. Cicero, as we have seen, considered rhetoric as more efficient than dialectic to produce the conversion of his listeners. By contrast, Proclus, in his *Commentary on the Alcibiades*,[114] affirms precisely the opposite. Either way, one must take into consideration this 'pedagogy' of the master if one wants to understand the precise meaning of this or that work. One would need, for instance, to determine whether it was addressed to beginners or to progressing students,[dd] to adversaries or to laymen.[ee]

This reference to the listener which corresponds to the dialectical and rhetorical aspects of ancient philosophy, invites us also to recognize the capital role played by the recourse to common notions admitted by all people. This is, even still, an important topic for reflection. Given that philosophy always implies a radical conversion from the natural attitude,[ff] a break with the 'quotidian' view of things, it is, nonetheless, concerned with addressing as its starting point what is evident and natural to man. The total transformation of one's worldview will only be accomplished by a deepening and a systematization of these common notions.

Finally, the reflections we have developed here concerning the relationship of rhetoric, dialectic and philosophy in antiquity remind us once more that philosophy has never been pure theory; or, to put it differently, even when philosophy sought to be pure *theoria*, as in Aristotle, it was still the concrete choice of a life dedicated to *theoria*.[gg] In other words, philosophy, at least since Socrates, has always implied a conversion, a total transformation of one's way of living and thinking.[115] From this perspective, dialectic and rhetoric correspond to the psychagogic power of language.

[dd] [Translator's note] Hadot's expression is *progressants*, and it is possible to surmise that he had in mind here the Greek *prokoptonta*, 'those making progress' in the Stoic texts.

[ee] [Translator's note] French: *les profanes*.

[ff] [Translator's note] Hadot's expression is, exactly, *attitude naturelle*. Given his awareness of Husserl's work (see Chapter 1 above), it is probable that Hadot wanted to evoke the Husserlian connotations of this term here.

[gg] [Translator's note] See Chapter 3 above, where Hadot develops this reading of Aristotle's conception of *theoria*.

Notes

1   This chapter appeared in *Studia philosophica* (1980), 139–166. It formed
    the object of an exposition before the *Groupe vaudois de philosophie* on the
    18th of June, 1979.

2   One will find valuable indications on this subject in Petrus Hermanus
    Schrijvers, *Horror ac divina voluptas. études sur la poétique et la poésie de
    Lucrèce* (Amsterdam: A. M. Hakkert, 1970).

3   Cf. Hermann Throm, *Die Thesis* (Paderborn: F. Schöningh, 1932); Antje
    Hellwig, *Unterschungen zur Theorie der Rhetorikbei Platon und Aristoteles*
    (Göttingen: Vandenhoeck & Ruprecht, 1973); John D. G. Evans, *Aristotle's
    Concepts of Dialectic* (Cambridge: Cambridge University Press, 1977). See
    also the important systematization given by *Alexandri Aphrodisiensis in
    Aristotelis Topicorum Libros octo commentaria*, ed. Maximilian Wallies
    (Berlin; G. Reimer, 1891), 4, 6.

4   Cf. Aristotle, *Topics*, 158a16; *Prior Analytics* 24a, 22ff. In rhetoric this
    situation is that of the *amphibêtêsis*, for example Aristotle, *Rhetoric*, 1416a9.
    See also ibid. 1357a4.

5   Cf. Theophrastus, in Andreas Graeser, *Die Logischen Fragmente des
    Theophrast* (Berlin: de Gruyter, 1973), 4.

6   Aristotle, *Rhetoric*, 1354a3, 1355b27; *Topics*, 100a25–30; *Refutation of
    Sophisms*, 183a36.

7   Aristotle, *Rhetoric*, 1355b8 and 25-34; 1358a10–35 and 1359b8–10;
    Posterior Analytics, 77a 26 ff.

8   Aristotle, *Rhetoric*, 1355a29 ff.

9   Aristotle, *Prior Analytics*, 24a25.

10 Cf. Paul Moraux, 'La joute dialectique d'après la huitième livre des
    Topiques', in *Aristotle on Dialectic: The Topics*, ed. Gwilym E. L. Owen
    (Oxford: Oxford University Press, 1968). Cf. Aristotle, *Topics*, 104a8.

11 Aristotle, *Sophistical Refutations*, 183b8.

12 Ibid., 183b6.

13 Aristotle, *Rhetoric*, 1357a1–4.

14 Ibid., 1354b4; 1355b25.

15 Cf. Hermann Throm, *Die Thesis: Ein Beitrag zu ihrer Entstehung und
    Geschichte (Rhetorische Studien)* (Université de Lyon: Persée, 1938), 92–94.

16 Cf. Heinrich Lausberg, *Handbuch der literarischen Rhetorik* (Munich: Max
    Hueber Verlag München, 1960), p. 41.

17 Anicius Manlius Severinus Boethius, *De Topicis Differentiis*, trans. Eleanore
    Stump (Ithaca: Cornell University Press, 1978), IV, cols. 1173–222, 1205c.
    We will see below, notes 89–90, that the theses do not always remain

dialectical in the strict sense, but that they take on a rhetorical aspect to the extent that they have renounced argumentation by question and response.

18 Plato, *Phaedrus*, 257b; 276e.

19 Plato, *Phaedrus*, 262c.

20 Plato, *Phaedrus*, 271b.

21 Plato, *Phaedrus*, 265c–266c; 277b.

22 Léon Robin, *Platon, Phédon* (Paris: Belles Lettres, 1952), 12, n. 2. It seems difficult to admit the theory of Gilbert Ryle, 'Dialectic in the Academy', in *New Essays on Plato and Aristotle*, ed. Renford Brambough (London: Routledge & Kegan Paul, 1965), 55 and Hans-Joachim Krämer, *Platonismus und Hellenistische Philosophie* (Berlin: De Gruyter, 1971), 21, according to which the word 'dialectic' will have had two senses in Plato's Academy: the first will have designated *Ideendialektik*, that is to say the science of ideas; the second will have related to the technique of dialectical jousting of which the *Topics* of Aristotle had fixed the rules. One will rediscover the traces of this dialectical gymnastics in the divisions which play a great role in the last dialogues of Plato. But in this hypothesis the vocabulary of Aristotle becomes incomprehensible. We see indeed at the beginning of the *Topics* the distinction between dialectic (which operates conformably to opinion) and philosophy (which seeks after the truth); so why does Aristotle not distinguish between these two senses of the word 'dialectic' which, according to the hypothesis of Ryle and Krämer, existed in the Academy? If the word 'dialectic' had two senses, he would have had to say: I admit dialectic as a technique of discussion, but I do not admit dialectic as the science of Ideas. In fact, all the work of Aristotle shows clearly that what he refuses in Platonism is precisely a dialectic which will be at the same time ontological and 'dialogical': it is precisely the confusion between two methods that he denounces: the scientific method and the method of discussion. It seems very clear that the allusions which Plato makes to dialectic in his dialogues imply an identification between science and the technique of discussion.

23 Aristotle, *Metaphysics*, 992b18 ff.; 1004b18; 1025b5 ff.; cf. Evans, *Aristotle's concept of dialectic*, 7–52. See also Aristotle, *Sophistical refutations* 172a12–40.

24 Aristotle, *Physics*, 204b4 and 10; *De Caelo*, 280a32; *Posterior Analytics*, 84a8; *Metaphysics*, 1029b13; *Generation of Animals*, 747b28. For allusions to the danger of the dialectical method, see *Parts of Animals*, 642b5; *Generation of Animals*, 748a8; *Nicomachean Ethics*, 1107a28.

25 Aristotle, *Topics* 105b30; a neat distinction between philosophy, which treats of things according to truth, and dialectic, which treats them conformably to opinion (*pros doxan*).

26 Aristotle, *Prior Analytics*, 24 a22; *Sophistical Refutations*, 172 a16.

27 Aristotle, *Sophistical Refutations*, 165a38.

28 Aristotle, *Topics*, 101a25 b4.

29 Aristotle, *Topics*, 101a30.

30 Cicero, *De oratore*, III, 80; *De Finibus*, V, 10; cf. Ingemar Düring, *Aristoteles* (Heidelberg: Bibliothek der Klassischen Altertumswissenschaften, 1966), 134, n. 59 and 155.

31 Aristotle, *Metaphysics*, 1080a10.

32 *Topics*, 101a37.

33 *Metaphysics*, 1006a12; *Prior Analytics*, 43a38.

34 *Physics*, 217b30.

35 Wolfgang Wieland, 'Aristoteles als Rhetoriker und di Exoterischen Schriften', *Hermes* 86 (1958), 332-346.

36 Simplicius, *On Aristotle's Physics*, 695, 33 Diels.

37 Wolfgang Wieland, *Die Aristotelische Physik* (Gôttingen: Vandenhoeck & Ruprecht, 1962), 216. Cf. also Jean Marie Le Blond, *Loqique et méthode chez Aristote* (Paris: Vrin, 1939).

38 Pierre Aubenque, *Le problème de l'être chez Aristote*, 2e édn (Paris: Presses Universitaires de France, 1966).

39 On the 'continuity of academic dialectic', cf. Hans-Joachim Krämer, *Platonismus und Hellenistische Philosophie*, 14–58.

40 Diogenes Laertius, *Lives of the Eminent Philosophers*, IV, 18. The expression *dialektika theôrêmata* which we have translated by 'dialectical questions' recalls Aristotle, *Topics*, 104b1 where the 'dialectical problem' is defined as a *theôrêma*.

41 Diogenes Laertius, *Lives of the Eminent Philosophers*, IV, 19.

42 Some examples: Teles, *Teletis reliquiae*, 2nd ed., ed. Otto Hense (Tübingen: G. Olms, 1909), 35, 9 (and the note); Epictetus, *Discourses*, II, 18, 18; II, 19, 1; 111, 21, 10; 1, 7, 1; Diogenes Laertius, *Lives of the Eminent Philosophers*, II, 108; Sextus Empiricus, *Hypotyposis*, I, 20; II, 185; Cicero, *De Fato*, 12 (*interrogare* = to argue).

43 Epictetus, *Discourses*, III, 8, 1.

44 Aulus Gellius, *Attic Nights*, XVI, 2.

45 Proclus Diadochus, *Commentary on the First Alcibiades of Plato*, ed. Leendert G. Westerink (Amsterdam: North-Holland Publishing, 1964), 283: in dialectical interrogations, the questions must be formulated in such a way that one can respond to them by 'yes' or 'no', and it is the respondent who 'says' something, that is to say who has a thesis.

46 Cf. Marie-Dominique Chenu, *Introduction à l'étude de Saint Thomas d'Aquin* (Paris: Institut d'études Medievales, 1954), 73–77 (the *disputatio*).

The exercise of dialectical argumentation was still practiced recently in the teaching of Thomist philosophy.

47 Cicero, *Orator*, 46; *De Finibus*, V, 10; *Tusculan Disputations*, II, 9. Cf. Diogenes Laertius, *Lives of the Eminent Philosophers*, V, 3; Quintilian, *Institutes of Oratory*, XII, 2, 25.

48 For the academic and peripatetic schools, see the preceding note; for Stoicism, one finds indications which give us glimpses of the existence of this practice in Epictetus, *Discourses*, II, 1, 30 & 34; II, 17, 35; II, 6, 23.

49 Cicero, *De Finibus* II, 1, 1–3. [Translator's note: The ensuing quotes from Cicero all come from this textual location.]

50 As the ensuing text shows, the *schola* is exactly a continuous discourse improvised in order to respond to a question posed to the improviser by an auditor; cf. Cicero, *Tusculan Disputations*, I, 7 and *Laelius, On Friendship*, 17. One finds an analogous process in the *disputatio quodlibet* of the middle ages.

51 Cf. Diogenes Laertius, *Lives of the Eminent Philosophers*, IV, 19; IV, 40; V, 3; Philodemus, *On Rhetoric*, II, 173, 5 Sudhaus.

52 Diogenes Laertius, *Lives of the Eminent Philosophers*, IV, 19; Polemon taught while on his feet, making a continuous discourse in response to a thesis. He argued while walking.

53 Cicero, *Lucullus*, 7; *Tusculan Disputations*, II, 9; *De Fato*, 1.

54 Plutarch, *Apothegmata laconica*, 220e, where we see Xenocrates develop a thesis—only the sage is a good general (which assumes the question: is the sage a good general?) In what concerns the arguments *in utramque partem*, one can suppose in light of the testimony of Cicero that it was a current usage amongst the Academicians and Peripatetics.

55 Cf. Diogenes Laertius, *Lives of the Eminent Philosophers*, IV, 40; Arcesilaus makes continuous discourses (*legein*) contra the theses.

56 Lactantius, *Institutes of Oratory*, V, 14; this is the story of the two discourses for and against justice upheld in Rome by Carneades; cf. equally Cicero, *De oratore*, II, 161.

57 For discourse against a thesis, see the five *scholae* which constitute the five books of the *Tusculans*; for discourse *in utramque partem*, see the *De divinatione*, according to the *De Fato*, 1.

58 Diogenes Laertius, *Lives of the Eminent Philosophers*, IV, 28.

59 Cf. Cicero, *Lucullus*, 7: 'Ut … exprimant aliquid quod aut verum sit aut ad id quam proxime acedat.'

60 Cicero, *Parodoxa Stoicorum*, Proem, 2: 'Nos ea philosophia plus utimar quae peperit dicendi copiam et in qua dicuntur ea quae non multum discrepent ab opinione populari.'

61 SVF, vol. II, §127 (Plutarch, *De Repugnantiis Stoicorum*, 1036 a).

62 Cf. Ilsetraut Hadot, *Seneca und die Griechisch-Römische Tradition der Seelenleitung* (Berlin: De Gruyter, 1969), 55: the exposition and the discussion of adverse theses only comes in the third and last stage of the teaching, if one can judge from the order of the letters from Seneca to Lucilius.

63 Cicero, *De Finibus*, IV, 7.

64 Cicero, *Parodoxa Stoicorum*, Proem, 2.

65 Émile Bréhier, *Chrysippe et l'ancien Stoicisme* (Paris: Presses Universitaires de France, 1951), 63.

66 For example, Epictetus, *Discourses*, I, 4, 7; I, 17, 13; II, 16, 34, etc.; Aulus Gellius, *Attic Nights*, I, 9, 9.

67 Hans-Georg Gadamer, *Wahrheit und Methode*, 2nd edn. (Berlin: Akademie Verlag, 2011), 351 ff.

68 On the history of the word *zêtêma*, cf. Heinrich Dörrie, *Porphyrios 'Symmikta Zetemata'* (Munich: Beck, 1959), 1–60. A great part of the treatises of Porphyry and Plotinus are *zêtêmata* concerning the texts of Plato.

69 Aulus Gelius, *Attic Nights*, I, 26, 1–11; *Copiose* marks well the rhetorical character of the exposition, for example at Cicero, *De oratore*, II, 151.

70 Porphyry, *Life of Plotinus*, 3, 36.

71 Or more probably: 'to speak on the texts', cf. Porphyry, *La vie de Plotin*, vol. II, ed. Luc Brisson et al. (Paris: Vrin, 1992), 155. [*Addition of 1998*].)

72 Porphyry, *Life of Plotinus*, 13, 10-17, cf. the preceding note.

73 Cf. Throm, *Die Thesis*, 28, 87, 94, 130. The thesis, as exposed on a general theme (without consideration of the particular circumstances) is an exercise theoretically reserved to the philosophers, even though many rhetoricians practiced it.

74 Cf. *Epictète, entretiens, livre I*, ed. and trans. Joseph Souilhé (with the collaboration of Amand Jagu) (Paris: Les Belles Lettres, 1943), préface, xxix.

75 Gregory the Thaumaturge, *Prosphônêtikos (Address of Thanks to Origen)*, VII, 97–98.

76 SVF, vol. II, §48 (= Diogenes Laertius, *Lives of Eminent Philosophers*, VII, 41).

77 Cf. Diogenes Laertius, *Lives of Eminent Philosophers*, VII, 43–44.

78 SVF, vol .III, §548 = *Ioannis Stobaei Anthologium*, Vol. 2, Curtius Wachsmuth & Otto Hense eds. (Berlin: Weidmannsche Buchhandlung, 1909), 111, 18. On the development of natural notions, cf. Victor Goldschmidt, *Le système Stoïcien et l'idée de temps*, 2e édn (Paris: Vrin, 1977), 159. On the critique of representation, cf. Goldschmidt, ibid., 118.

79 SVF, vol. II, § 48 = Diogenes Laertius, *Lives of the Eminent Philosophers*, VII, 41.

80 Cicero, *De Fato*, 1; *De Finibus*, 1,7, 22 and IV, 8, 7; *Orator*, 113: *dissenere* embraces *disputare* (dialectic) and *dicere* (rhetoric); *Prior academics*, 30.

81 Cicero, *Orator*, 113.

82 Cicero, *Orator*, 114–117; *Brutus*, 152; *Lucullus*, 91.

83 Cicero, *Orator*, 43 ff.; *De oratore*, II, 115; *Brutus*, 185.

84 Cicero, *De Finibus*, IV, 3, 7 ff.

85 Cicero, *De Finibus*, IV, 4, 8. The theory of invention is one of the five Roman rhetorical canons. See *Orator*, 44; *Parts of Oratory*, 5. See also *De oratore*, II, 157.

86 Cicero, *Topics*, 6.

87 Cicero, *Topics*, 1–5.

88 The *Topics* of Cicero (53) nevertheless integrates the Stoic theory of reasoning, which underscores their post-Aristotelian character.

89 Cicero, *Topics*, 83; the theses related to the *descriptio* are of the type: what is a miser? What is a flatterer? On the other hand, the 'practical' theses (86) involve exhortations or consolations, both psychagogic techniques which are evidently not dialectical.

90 Cicero, *Paradoxa Stoicorum*, Proem, 5: "I transpose in our oratorical style what one calls *thetica* in the schools." On the relations between rhetoric and philosophy in Cicero, see the fundamental work of Alain Michel, *Rhétorique et philosophie chez Cicéron* (Paris: Presses Universitaires de France, 1960).

91 Martianus Capella, *De nuptiis philologiae et mercurii*, V, 474–501.

92 Cassiodorus, *Institutions of Divine and Human Learning*, II, 15–17.

93 Cf. Cicero, *Prior Academics*, 32 (a summary of Platonic philosophy inspired by Antiochus of Ascalon).

94 Cicero, *Prior Academics*, 30–32.

95 Albinus (Alcinous), *Didaskalikos*, in *Platonis dialogi decundum thrasylli tetralogias dispositi*, ed. Karl F. Hermann (Leipzig: Teubner, 1880), Vol. 6, 154, 7–156, 20.

96 Cf. Reginald E. Witt, *Albinus and the History of Middle Platonism* (Cambridge: Cambridge University Press, 1937), 36 and 61. Cf. Albinus (Alcinous), *Didaskalikos*, 153, 26.

97 Cf. Porphyry, *Porphyrii Isagoge et in Aristotelis categoris commentarium* ed. Adolfus Basse (Berlin: G. Reimer, 1887), 1, 5–6; Proclus Diadochus, *Commentarium in Platonis Parmenidem*, In *Procli Opera Inedita*, ed. Victor Cousin (Paris: Augustus Durand, 1864), 982, 11.

98 Cf. Proclus, *Theologie Platonicienne*, ed. and trans. Henri-Dominique Saffrey & Leenert G. Westerink (Paris: Les Belles Lettres, 1968), 1, 10, 18.

99 The opposition appears clearly in Plotinus, *Enneads*, I, 3, 4, 18, but already in Origen, *In Canticum Canticorum*, in *Origenes werke*, Vol. 8 (GCS 33), ed. Wilhelm A. Baehrens (Berlin: C. Hinrichs, 1925), 79.

100 Plotinus, *Enneads*, I, 3, 4, 10 and 5, 9.

101 Plotinus, *Enneads*, I, 3, 4, 12–16; cf. Werner Beierwaltes, *Proklos*, 2nd ed. (Frankfurt-am-Main: Klostermann Vittorio GmbH; 1979), 248 ff.

102 Cf. Beierwaltes, *Proklos*, 240, n. 1.

103 Proclus Diadochus, *Commentarium in Platonis Parmenidem*, 993, 9.

104 Proclus, *Theologie Platonicienne*, 1, 20, 6 ff.; the modes of theological exposition are the Orphic mode, which utilises symbols, the Pythagorean mode, which utilizes numerical symbols, the Chaldean mode, which is the direct revelation under divine inspiration, and the dialectical mode proper to Plato.

105 Abelard for example is still very close to the Ciceronian tradition of the *Topics*, as I have indicated in *Marius Victorinus* (Paris: Collection des Études Augustiniennes, 1967), 197, n. 36.

106 Cicero says that dialectic is a contracted rhetoric and that rhetoric is a dilated dialectic, at *Brutus*, 309.

107 Throm, *Die Thesis*, 77 and 149. Throm is perhaps wrong to tie too exclusively dialectic in 'general' to rhetoric in 'particular'.

108 Cf. Hadot, *Marius Victorinus*, 211–214.

109 Throm, *Die Thesis*, p. 78–79.

110 Ingemar Düring, 'Aristoteles und die Platonische Erbe', in *Aristoteles in der Neueren Forschung*, Paul Moraux ed. (Darmstadt: Wissenschaftliche Buchgesellschaft, 1968), 247.

111 Wieland, *Die Aristotelische Physik*, p. 325.

112 Porphyry, *Life of Plotinus*, 4, 11 and 5, 60.

113 Gadamer, *Wahrheit und Methode*, 345: 'Fragen heist ins Offene stellen. Die Offenheit des Gefragen besteht in dem Nichtfestgelegtsein der Antwort . . . Nun ist die Offenheit der Frage keine uferlose. Sie schliesst vielmehr die bestimmte Ungrenzung durch des Fragenhorizont ein.'

114 Proclus Diadochus, *Commentary on the First Alcibiades of Plato*, 172, 6: the dialectical genre obliges the audience to pay more attention than continuous discourse; it obliges the interlocutor to seek and to find for themselves.

115 Cf. Pierre Hadot, 'Spiritual Exercises', in *Philosophy as a way of life*, 79–125 [and Chapter 4 above].

PART THREE

NATURE

8 ANCIENT MAN AND NATURE

The words *physis* and *natura* do not encompass all of the senses and affective values that we moderns ascribe to the indefinable word 'nature'.[1] These terms originally signified the process of growth of particular beings or the results of this process. It is only beginning with Stoicism that the two terms come to designate all beings and the productive force of the universe. But even then, the ancients never explicitly attached to 'nature' the aesthetic sentiment that they could experience before some particular landscape or spectacle within nature.

One can distinguish two fundamental attitudes of ancient man concerning nature. The first can be symbolized by the figure of Prometheus. Prometheus represents the ruse which steals[a] the secrets of nature from the gods who conceal them from mortals or the violence which tries to vanquish nature in order to improve human life. The theme already appeared in ancient medicine (in the *Corpus Hippocraticum: Treatise on the Art of Medicine*),[2] but, above all, in ancient mechanics.[3] The word *mêchanê*, indeed, designates ruse. And the mechanic, the 'Prologue' of the Hippocratic *Treatise on the Art of Medicine* says, aims to utilize mathematical knowledges in order to trick nature:

> In many cases, nature produces effects which are contrary to the interests of men. For nature acts always in the same manner and without detours, whereas our interests often change … We call the part of art which is aimed at assisting us in such difficulties ruse (*mêchanê*).

---

[a] [Translator's note] The verb is *dérobe*, and the noun is 'la ruse', which can indicate a single trick, but here a capacity to repeatedly 'trick' or 'trick with' nature is intended.

Mechanical ruse is never disinterested. It aims, on the one hand, to relieve human toil (for example, by the invention of the watermill) and, on the other hand, it fundamentally aims to satisfy the passions, notably the passions of kings and wealthy men (through the invention of machines of war, magnificent monuments or luxurious residences). Philosophers will, in general, be hostile to such artifices.

This Promethean attitude can also be found in magic and the occult arts. Mechanics, however, reflected a rational process put into the service of human passion: the application of mathematical science to the production of motions that the ancients considered to be contrary to nature. Magic, by contrast, bases its practices on the belief in invisible powers, gods or demons, who can produce such movements contrary to the normal unfolding of natural processes. It is a matter of employing formulae and performing rites which can constrain the god or the demon to become a servant of the magician. Finally, in the cases of both mechanics and of magic, men aimed to deceive nature or the powers of nature, dominating them and submitting them to their will. The Promethean relationship to nature is hence never disinterested.

Opposed to this 'Promethean' attitude, which aims to put artifice in service of the needs of men, there existed in antiquity a second, wholly different type of relationship towards nature. The latter, which could be qualified as poetic or philosophical, is that of 'physics' as a spiritual exercise.[b] This attitude consists in contemplating nature as it is: that is to say, of describing it through language, but also of living 'according to nature', in an attitude of respect and even of submission.

This attitude is, first of all, translated into the desire for a return to the 'simple life'. The theme is sketched by Xenophon's Socrates (in the *Memorabilia*).[4] Perfection, and notably the perfection of the gods, consists in having no needs. It is thus necessary to train oneself[c] in a life of endurance so as to habituate oneself to diminish one's material needs and to deliver oneself from the insatiable desires engendered by the passions. The same theme is reprised by the Cynics,[5] especially Demetrius,[6] and then again by the Stoics:[7] it is a matter of living 'according to nature'. The Epicureans also have for their ideal *autarkeia*, and independence with regards to the needs which are born from desires which are neither natural nor necessary.[8] With Lucretius and Horace, this ideal is tied to that of the pure pleasure provided

---

[b] [Translator's note] In Pierre Hadot, *The Veil of Isis*, trans. by Michael Chase (Cambridge, MA: Harvard University Press, 2008), Hadot will speak of an 'Orphic' approach to nature, opposed to that of the Promethean. This term does not yet appear in this essay.

[c] [Translator's note] Original: *s'exerciser*.

by the rustic life in the countryside in a landscape which is agreeable and charming (*locus amoenus*):

> Nature cares not a bit when the house does not shine with silver or glitter with gold, or when there are no panelled and gilded roofs to echo the sound of harps. Men who lack such things are just as happy when they spread themselves in groups on soft grass beside a stream of water under the limbs of a high tree, and at no great cost pleasantly refresh their bodies, especially when the weather smiles and the seasons sprinkle the green grass with flowers.[9]

The ideal of the simple life is rediscovered in the Neoplatonic philosophers[10] and even amongst the Sceptics, to the extent that the ideal of indifference – that of Pyrrho, for example – is conducive to living the most humble and simplest life, so long as this life is characterised by a state of total inner liberty.[11]

A certain number of mythical, poetic or even utopian representations crystallized around the notion of the simple life.

The first depicts the golden age or age of Kronos: a time of peaceful abundance which characterized the life of primitive humanity: without work or war; an age characterized at the same time by the reign of justice and the absence of all civilized refinements – and, for the Pythagoreans, by vegetarianism. This myth of the golden age is intimately tied to the critique of technical progress characteristic of the age of iron.[12]

There is equally the eulogy for the simple, virile and rustic life. One projects this ideal of life into the mythical past of different peoples, whether the ancient Spartans or Romans, or in the description of the customs of the Barbarians. On this subject, we must acknowledge that an entire philosophical lineage insisted upon the value of working in the fields. One finds this theme, for example, in the Stoic Musonius, in Dion of Prusa and Synesius.[d]

This ideal of the simple life was not solely a matter for poetic or philosophical developments. It had a certain influence on political reforms, such as those of Agis and Cleomenes of Sparta in the third century BCE and those of the Gracchi in second century BCE Rome, or again in the revolt of Aristonicus.[13]

---

[d] [Translator's note] There is also, of course, *De Agri Cultura* by Cato the Elder, although Hadot does not name this text here.

This attitude towards nature which we are describing also implies a disinterested regard upon it: a way of seeing which can for example circumscribe[e] what we would call a 'landscape'.

What are the characteristics of a 'landscape', in general terms? It is, first of all, that which corresponds to a gaze focused aesthetically, that is to say, disinterestedly upon nature. The field or the stream becomes a 'landscape' when we look at them not as the demarcations of frontiers, nor as a means of production or commerce posing technical problems, but when we look at them for themselves, without a practical finality. This gaze of the spectator carves out a privileged field from the totality of nature. But it not only delimits the landscape. It also unifies it, giving it a certain structure, and organizes it. This way of seeing perceives the landscape as a sort of expressive physiognomy from which emanates a certain atmosphere, sentiment or character. In this perception of what we could call a corner of nature, in this portion it separates from the whole, this gaze of the spectator simultaneously senses the totality of nature. In other words, the landscape makes us sense our situation as terrestrial beings. As Carl Gustav Carus has said, the art of the landscape is the art of representing the life of the earth (*Erdlebendildkunst*).[14]

There is thus no landscape in itself, but solely in relation to a spectator: in relation to the human being who knows how to see it, to circumscribe it from the whole of nature in such a way as to, once more, find this whole within the delimited, circumscribed space. This is true in the art of landscape painting, in the literary description of landscapes, but also in the perception of nature in general. In other words, that which has been called a 'landscape' in painting or in literature since the seventeenth century is nothing else, in life, than the aesthetic perception of nature, the perception of the life of the earth, as Carus puts it. And like art, such a perception supposes a certain way of seeing.

One can distinguish two sorts of landscapes in antiquity: the charming place (*locus amoenus*), and the grandiose or sublime landscape. The model of the charming landscape (*locus amoenus*), which will dominate the imagination and sensibility of antiquity, is the Cave of Calypso.[15] In the Homeric description, the perceiving subject is the God Hermes, whose senses (of smell, hearing and sight) are enchanted and whose soul is veritably ravished by his contemplation of the beauty of the place. The components of the charming place will always be woods of different kinds, birds, meadows, murmuring springs, flowers, perfumes, the breeze, fruits: in short, pleasures for all the senses. This whole will embody a divine

---

[e] [Translator's note] Original: *delimiter*.

presence. The theme can also be found in Sappho (in her 'Prayer to Aphrodite'), in Sophocles,[16] in the celebrated prologue of Plato's *Phaedrus*, in Theocritus (*Thalysies*), Lucretius,[17] Horace[18] and Quintilian.[19]

If the 'charming place' is indisputably an object of aesthetic contemplation in antiquity, can we say the same of those grandiose or wild or terrifying spectacles that nature can offer to man? Many historians have doubted this. As has been shown by Marjory Hope Nicholson in her *Mountain Gloom and Mountain Glory: The Development of the Aesthetics of the Infinite*,[20] it is true that until the middle of the eighteenth century, one considered rocks and mountains to be terrifying or ugly. It was only then that a change in sensibility took place in Europe: what had been considered horrible was now experienced as sublime. This transformation contributed notably to the distinction that Immanuel Kant establishes in his *Critique of Judgment* between the beautiful and the sublime.[21] In this distinction, the sublime corresponds to the disposition by which our spirit strives to become equal to the grandeur of the power of the immense force of nature.

In fact, antiquity already knew the idea of the sublime. In the anonymous treatise *On the Sublime*, which probably dates to the first half of the first century CE, there is a brief paragraph which is extremely revealing:

> Nature has introduced us into life and the universe ... so that we could contemplate all that takes place within her; from the beginning, she has given birth in our soul to an invincible love for all that is eternally great ... Also, the world does not suffice, not even in its universality, for the impulse[f] of contemplation and thought in human beings ... From this, it comes about, by a sort of natural inclination, that our admiration is not directed to small streams, despite their translucency and utility, but to the Nile, the Danube or the Rhine, and even more so again to the Ocean ...[22]

In the treatise *On the Sublime*, we find the idea of an aesthetics of the infinite already expressed. Our admiration before the Ocean or the Etna, spectacles which announce the power and grandeur of nature in the highest degree, respond to a need for transcendence[g] and the infinite that is close to the heart of human beings. It is, moreover, this theme, dear to Aristotle and the Stoics, that underlies the proof of the existence of God from the beauty of the world which we will later find in Saint Augustine in *The City of God*.[23]

---

[f] [Translator's note] Here: *élan*. In French, this can mean a momentum or an impetus, a movement or an impulse.

[g] [Translator's note] The French is *dépassement*, which we have elsewhere translated as 'going beyond', following Michael Chase. See especially Chapter 10 below.

The aesthetic sentiment of the sublime is also linked to an aesthetics of life and existence. For Aristotle[24] as for Marcus Aurelius,[25] Seneca[26] or Plotinus,[27] beauty consists less in the symmetry of proportions than in the upsurge of life,[h] in the fact of being and of living, in the miracle of presence itself:[i] 'an ugly man, if he is alive, is more beautiful than a man whose beauty is only represented in a statue';[28] 'there is no less pleasure to contemplate, in their naked reality, the gaping mouths of wild beasts than all the imitations proposed of them by painters and sculptors'.[29]

This admiration for the magnificent spectacles of nature is well attested in all of antiquity, from Homer[30] to Augustine: '[a]nd men admire the tops of mountains, the gigantic waves of the sea, the wideness of the courses of rivers, the immensity of the ocean, the revolutions of the heavenly bodies . . .'[31]

These sublime spectacles also, like the sight of charming places, make us sense a divine presence. In his *Letter 41*, aiming to show that the [figure of the] sage makes us glimpse something sacred, Seneca compares the sublimity of virtue to the sublime in nature. In this context, he evokes then the sentiment of astonishment and of admiration, a sacred emotion, that the spectacle of deep, remote forests provokes [in him], or inexplorable caves, lakes or the springs of great watercourses. It seems that in Horace also, the sentiment of the sublime has a distinctly Dionysian tonality:

> To where do you lead me, Bacchus, when I am filled so completely with you? Into what forests, into which caves does this sudden inspiration take me . . .? Just like the sleepless Bacchae, on the tops of mountains, fall into ecstasy . . ., in the same way I love, far from beaten paths, to admire the rivers and the solitary woods.[32]

This Dionysian land is that of the *Bacchantes* of Euripides: the mountains, the dense forests, the gorges flanked by escarpments, savage nature.

We have already indicated that the sentiment of the sublime could be inspired as much by the spectacle of nature as by the spectacle of the soul of the sage.

This theme is particularly clear in Seneca, for example in his *Letter 89*, to Lucilius:

> If only, in the same way as the entire face of the universe presents itself to our eyes, philosophy could present itself before our eyes as a whole,

---

[h] [Translator's note] Hadot's verb is *jaillissement*.
[i] [Translator's note] Hadot's expression is simply *la présence*.

replicating the spectacle of the universe! It would, then, delight all mortals with admiration.[33]

And, above all, there is this in *Letter 64*, 6: 'I find no lesser ecstasy in contemplation of wisdom than the one I find, in other moments, in the contemplation of the world, which I often see as a spectator who looks at it for the first time.'[34] The sublime is thus at the same time in Seneca perceived in the external world and within conscience.

One could also imagine that these two Stoic sources of the sublime are the model behind the famous phrase of Kant, written at the beginning of his conclusion to *The Critique of Practical Reason*:

> Two things fill the soul with ever new and increasing admiration and awe the oftener and the more steadily we reflect on them: the starry heavens above and the moral law within. I have not to search for them and conjecture them as though they were veiled in darkness or were in the transcendent region beyond my horizon; I see them before me and connect them directly with the consciousness of my existence.[j]

But let us return to the phrase of Seneca's *Letter 64*: 'the world itself, which I often behold as if I saw it for the first time'. We encounter here a completely extraordinary thought: at once highly revealing and very rare in antiquity. Seneca tells us that he comes before the world as if he were a *spectator novus*: that is to say, he casts on the world an entirely renewed gaze.[k]

However, this new perspective does not involve a gratuitous and unexpected intuition. It is the result of an inner effort, of a spiritual exercise designed to overcome the habitude which makes our way of seeing the world banal and mechanical. This exercise aims also to detach us from all interest, egotism or worry which prevents us from seeing the world as it is, because these things constrain us to focus our attention upon particular objects in which we find pleasure and utility. It is, on the contrary, by an effort of concentration on the present instant, and living each moment as if it were at the same time our very first or our last, without thinking of the future or the past, awake to the instant's unique and irreplaceable character, that one can

---

[j] [Translator's note] See Immanuel Kant, *Critique of Practical Reason*, trans. and ed. by M. Gregor (Cambridge: Cambridge University Press, 1997), 133. We have followed the translation of this famous passage here of Thomas Kingsmill Abbott.

[k] [Translator's note] Original: *il pose sur le monde un regard neuf*. In the following sentence, we render '*ce regard nouveau*' as 'this new regard'.

perceive, in this instant, the marvellous presence of the world. Let us add that in Cicero,[35] Seneca,[36] Lucretius[37] and Augustine,[38] one rediscovers the idea that it is only habit, the routine of everyday life, which prevents us from perceiving the world as a miracle. And this perception of the world is precisely sublime because, like the figure of the sage himself, it involves a 'paradox', something which transcends habitual human experience.

Did the Greeks know landscape painting? It seems that it only really appears in the Hellenistic period, whether to illustrate a narrative scene (like the mythological landscapes in which the episodes of the *Odyssey* are situated) or in the décor for the theatre. While the tragic stage setting contained columns, pediments and statues, and the setting for comedies depicted the houses of ordinary men and women, the scenery of the Satyric (*viz.* Dionysian) dramas was decorated by mountains, caves, trees and rustic elements.[39] The Imperial period saw the custom of painting on the walls of the rooms of houses, based on the stage settings of the theatre, notably the Satyric décors.[40] These décors each came to reflect the others. Gardeners imitated the sets of the theatre and landscape painters imitated gardeners in order to give the illusion that the room they were decorating opened out onto a garden.[41]

Landscape painting does not seem at all tied to eremitism, as seems to have been the case in China, where painters remained often in the solitude of high mountains in order to contemplate nature. However, it is perhaps not quite accurate to say with Paul Friedländer that the Greeks did not accord any positive value to solitude, and that to be seen and heard was the indispensable precondition of the life of Greek man.[42]

The Pythagorean tradition seemed to have recommended practices of isolation in deserted places. Porphyry, in his *Life of Pythagoras* section 32, tells us that Pythagoras would choose for his walks 'the most solitary and beautiful locations'. 'The Pythagoreans took their morning walks alone', Iamblicus writes:

> in the places where one could find solitude and retirement, like temples, sacred woods, and all other places which give joy to the heart. For they thought that one must not encounter anyone before having established peace in one's soul and having put our thought into a harmonious state. It is solitude which suits this appeasement of the soul.[43]

The *Thêrapeutês* described by Philo of Alexandria likewise lived in gardens and isolated places in pursuit of solitude.[44]

Outside of this Pythagorean tradition, the desire for solitude in nature was widespread amongst the philosophers and even amongst non-philosophers. Marcus Aurelius notes that 'one is accustomed to seek out retreats in the country, by the sea, and in the mountains' – although he adds that this is naive, because, at any moment, one can retire into oneself.[45]

Many ancients also wondered if solitude in nature was propitious to meditation. Quintilian recognized that being alone is indispensable for writing, but:

> This is not to say that it is necessary to listen to those who argue retreat into the woods or the forests is most conducive to this end, on the pretext that the open sky and the charm of landscapes elevate the spirit and procure a more joyful inspiration.[46]

For Quintilian, the pleasure of 'the flowing rivers, the breath of the breezes in the branches of trees, the song of the birds, and the grandeur of the view' diminishes the vigour of thought, rather than fortifying it. This was, nevertheless, the opinion of Horace, [namely] that: 'The whole choir of poets loves the woods, and flees the city, true followers of Bacchus, lovers of the sacred holy sleep under the shade of trees.'[47]

If one compares the text of Quintilian to that of Horace, we can glimpse the idea that solitude in nature leads rather to a sort of dissolution in nature, to a Dionysian ecstasy (as Rousseau would later extol in his *Reveries of a Solitary Walker*: 'he loses himself in a delicious fervour in the immensity of this beautiful system with which he feels identified'[48]), rather than to the precise work of the advocate preparing his pleas of whom Quintilian was thinking.

In any case, Jackie Pigeaud has demonstrated that, at least in the Hellenistic epoch, the philosopher was represented as meditating in solitude.[49] For example, in the twelfth *Letter* attributed to Hippocrates (a forgery of the first century BCE or CE found in the ninth volume of the *Oeuvres* of Hippocrates), one reads that:

> It is not madness, it is excessive vigour of soul which is manifested in this man ... concentrated on himself, day and night, living isolated in caves, in solitude, under the shades of woods, on the soft grass or alongside running waters.[50]

All of this must also be situated alongside the very rich theme of ancient theories on the 'melancholy' of the man of genius.

This tradition culminates at the end of antiquity in the practice of Christian eremitism, illustrated by the famous *Letter 14* of Basil of Caesarea to his friend Gregory of Nazianzus. It describes a solitary and inaccessible mountainous landscape, which offers a marvellous view when one contemplates it from the heights of the summits. It is at the same time the solitude of this place, and its beauty, which bring peace and tranquillity of mind (*hêsuchia*)⁵¹ to the soul of the one who lives there. In this *Letter*, Basil makes no allusion to Christianity. On the contrary, he compares this place to the island of Calypso: that is to say, to the classical model of all beautiful landscapes. This allows us to conclude that it was very much the poetic and philosophical tradition of antiquity, at least of the Hellenistic period, and not Christianity, which accorded this privileged value to the solitary contemplation of nature.

Generally speaking, from the fact that the ancients spoke little, or at least with great sobriety, about certain experiences that we moderns describe with such emphasis and abundance, we must not conclude that they did not live these experiences, or that they experienced them only in a vague and imperfect manner. On the contrary, it is this half-silence which betrays the importance that such experiences had for them. There was in ancient culture a tendency to remain silent about what was essential. We have, unhappily, become more talkative, more attentive to words than to reality. As Goethe reflected:

> The ancients represented existence, whereas we represent its effect. They described that which is terrible, while we describe terribly; they described that which is agreeable, we describe things agreeably. This is the source of all our exaggerations, our mannerisms, our false elegance and our pomposity.⁵²

Notes

1   This chapter first appeared in *Annuaire du Collège de France*, 1988–1989 (Paris: Collège de France, 1989), 371–379, then in *Études de philosophie ancienne* (Paris: Les Belles Lettres, 2010), 307–318.

2   *Corpus Hippocraticum, Traite de l'Art*, XII, 3.

3   'Prologue' des *Problêmata mêchanica*.

4   Xenophon, *Memorabilia*, I, 6, 1–10.

5   See Diogenes Laertius, *Lives of the Eminent Philosophers*, VI, 105.

6   Seneca, *On Benefits*, VII, 9, 1.

7   Ibid.

8   See Epicurus, *Letter to Menoeceus*, 130–131.

9   See Lucretius, *De natura rerum*, II, 17 ff.

10 See Porphyry, *Of Abstinence*, I, 51, 3.

11 See Diogenes Laertius, *Lives of the Eminent Philosophers*, IX, 66.

12 See Ovid, *Metamorphoses*, I, 129 ff. or Seneca, *Letters to Lucilius*, 90, 4 ff.

13 Cf. Ilsetraut Hadot, 'Tradition stoïcienne et idées politiques au temps des gracques', *Revue des études latines* 48 (1970): 133–179.

14 Casper David Friedrich and Carl Gustav Carus, *De la peinture de paysage* (Paris: Klincksieck, 1988), 118.

15 See Homer, *Odyssey*, V, 55–73.

16 See Sophocles, *Oedipus at Colonus*, 668.

17 Lucretius, *De natura rerum*, II, 29 & V, 1392.

18 Horace, *Epistles*, I, 16.

19 Quintilian, *Institutes of Oratory*, X, 3, 22.

20 Marjory Hope Nicholson, *Mountain Gloom and Mountain Glory: The Development of the Aesthetics of the Infinite* (New York: Cornell University Press, 1959).

21 Immanuel Kant, *Critique of Judgment*, trans. W. S. Pluhar (Cambridge, MA: Hackett Publishing, 1987), § 23 ff.

22 *On the Sublime*, XXXV, 2.

23 Augustine, *Civitate Dei*, XXII, 24, 5.

24 Aristotle, *Parts of Animals*, 664b31.

25 Marcus Aurelius, *Meditations*, III, 2.

26 Seneca, *Moral Letters to Lucilius*, 41, 6.

27 Plotinus, *Enneads*, VI, 7, 22.

28 Plotinus, *Enneads*, VI, 7, 22, 31.

29 Plotinus, *Enneads*, VI, 7, 22, 1.

30 Homer, *Iliad*, VIII, 555 or IV, 442.

31 Augustine, *Confessions*, X, 8, 15.

32 Horace, *Odes,* III, 25, 1.

33 Seneca, *The Moral Letters to Lucilius*, Letter 89, 1.

34 Seneca, *The Moral Letters to Lucilius*, Letter 64, 6.

35 Cicero, *De Natura Deorum*, III, 38, 96.

36 Seneca, *Naturales quaestiones*, VII, 1.

37 Lucretius, *De natura rerum*, II, 1023a ff.

38 Augustine, *De utilitate credenda*, XVI, 34.

39 Vitruvius, V, 6, 9.

40 Pliny, *Naturalis historia*, XXXV, 116 & Vitruvius, VIII, 15.

41 Compare Pierre Grimal, *Les jardins Romains* (Paris: De Boccard, 1943), 93 ff.

42 Paul Friedlander, *Plato* (Princeton: Harper & Row, 1973), 155.

43 Iamblichus, *Life of Plotinus*, §96.

44 Philo Judaeus, *De Vita Contemplativa*, §20.

45 Marcus Aurelius, *Meditations*, IV, 3.

46 Quintilian, *Institutio oratoria*, X, 3, 22.

47 Horace, *Epistles*, II, 2, 77 [Translator's note: Hadot uses the translation by A. S. Kline]. Compare Horace, *Epistles*, I, 4, 4; Tacitus, *A Dialogue on Oratory*, 9 & 12; Pliny the Younger, *Letters*, I, 6.

48 Jean-Jacques Rousseau, *Reveries of a Solitary Walker*, trans. Peter France (London: Penguin, 1979), 7, 108.

49 Jackie Pigeaud, *La maladie de l'âme* (Paris: Les Belles Lettres, 1981), 452 ff.

50 Hippocrates, *L'oeuvre de Hippocrate*, tome IX, trans. Émile Littré (Paris: J. B. Baillière, 1861), 330.

51 *Letter 14* of Basil of Caesarea to his friend Gregory of Nazianzus.

52 Goethe, *Voyage en Italie*, 17 May 1787. [Translator's note: See Johann Wolfgang von Goethe, *Italian Journey*, trans. W. H. Auden and E. Meyer (London: Penguin: 1962), 310.]

9 THE GENIUS OF PLACE IN ANCIENT GREECE

The first sacred place in Antiquity is the 'home',[a] that is to say, the hearth[b] of the house; not the fire of the kitchen, but the sacred altar where the fire consecrated to the gods smoulders continuously. This is where the goddess Hestia is present, 'seated at the centre of the house', as the *Homeric Hymn to Aphrodite* says.[c] The hearth is thus in some way rootedness in the Earth,[d] which is itself Hestia, the immobile centre of the Universe. But the hearth is also the point of contact with the higher gods, the point from whence the smoke of the incense or the sacrifices rises. Hestia is, nevertheless, not solely the figure of the Earth, but the figure of the woman who remains by the hearth, whereas the man will work outside.[1] Our civilization has perhaps been profoundly marked by the poem, *The Odyssey*, which describes the pilgrimage of the exiled man who strives to come back to the hearth[e] where the woman whom he loves awaits him: return to the native land, which is at base a return to oneself.

However, as Gerardus Van der Leeow says very well, 'the place of pilgrimage is, also, a sort of native country or home, elevated to the second

---

[a] [Translator's note] In French, 'chez-soi'.

[b] [Translator's note] The French is *foyer*, which has no direct English equivalent. This term can designate the home, the marital home (as below, concerning Odysseus), the hearth, or (as in *foyer d'incendie*), the areas of a fire. See Fustel de Coulanges, *The Ancient City* (Botache: Kitchener, 2001), especially chapter 3, 'The Sacred Fire', 17–29. In Latin, as Coulanges shows, the expression is *lar*, which designates the home, the domestic sphere, the dwelling, while at the same time it means the fireplace, the hearthside, the sacred fire or altar.

[c] [Translator's note] *Viz.*, at line 30 of the poem.

[d] [Translator's note] The original reads: *l'enracinement dans la Terre*.

[e] [Translator's note] Here again, it is *foyer* at issue, whilst the context suggests the home more widely, where Penelope faithfully awaits Odysseus' return.

power'.[2] This place corresponds, like the hearth of the house, to a privileged point of contact with the divine power. One said of Delphi that it was the navel of the Earth. There is an extraordinary stability about these sacred places. Before the cult of Apollo, which appeared at Delphi around the ninth–eighth century [BCE], there existed already, exactly in the same place, a cult of the Mother-Goddess identified as Gaia [*Gê*], the Earth, and whose first traces look back to the second millennium BCE. In the same way, the origins of Eleusis, Delos and Ephesus are lost in the night of prehistory. Beyond the diversity of divinities brought to these places by different civilizations, the sanctity of the place remains always the same. Immense crowds converged upon the sanctuaries, travelling the sacred way on fixed dates which often were deemed to reproduce the itinerary that the god himself had followed in order to come to establish his presence in this place (like the Pythaid of Athens to Delphi, for example). These crowds come to venerate sacred and mysterious objects such as the *Omphalos* (navel) of Delphi, they came to consult the oracles, to implore cures. They deposited innumerable votive offerings, testaments of miracles accomplished and of graces obtained. These gatherings gave place to festivals of all kinds: sporting contests, songs, dances, theatrical representations, markets. The festive atmosphere is thus closely associated with the cult of the gods.[3]

It is impossible to evaluate the fervour, the religious emotion of all the pilgrims, for we possess few literary testimonies on this subject. It seems, in any case, that from this point of view, Eleusis occupied a special place. The pilgrims, coming from Athens in procession, were initiated there by participating in mysteries which lasted over many days. This experience provoked, it seems, a real shock in the soul. According to Aristotle's famous text,[4] the initiates at Eleusis *learned* nothing (one thus did not reveal to them any secret concerning the divinity and the beyond), but they *experienced* a certain impression. It is true that all that we can reconstitute about the rites practiced in the sanctuary of Eleusis, with the aid of some allusions by ancient authors, can appear quite banal: ritual cries, the exhibition of an ear [of corn], effects of light; one can only poorly explain the extraordinary renown of these mysteries. Dario Sabbatucci[5] has given what seems to be a plausible explanation of this enigma in stressing the fact that the Eleusinian experience was that of a pilgrimage, in the sense of a 'sacred parenthesis' provoking a break with everyday life: at Eleusis, 'the initiate did not *learn* his other-worldly destiny, but in a brief space of time, he *lived* this supra-individual, other-worldly life'. The true secret of Eleusis is hence this very experience, this moment where one is plunged into the wholly-other, this discovery of an unknown dimension of existence.

We have only spoken up to now, albeit too briefly, of pilgrimages. However, by evoking the sacred festival, we have glimpsed how the religious need is often intertwined with the desire to travel and for entertainment in the psychology of the ancient pilgrim. One passes rapidly from pilgrimage to tourism, from [religious] enthusiasm to curiosity, above all in the Hellenistic and Roman epochs: [in] one of the mimes of Herodas, *The Women at the Temple of Asclepius*,[f] the protagonists certainly fulfil their vow to the healer god, but they [also] profit from the occasion to admire the paintings of Apelles which are found in the temple. One makes the journey to Olympia to contemplate the Zeus of Phidias.[6] One visits the pyramids of Egypt, the tombs of Troy, the shores of the Hellespont,[7] and islands like Chios, Lesbos and Samos.[8] Philosophers and rhetors make pilgrimages to sacred places of history and the spirit:[g] in Athens, they go to see the Academy, where Plato and other illustrious men taught: 'we are more moved then than when we read their books'.[9] There are also places where one will search for health. The *Sacred Discourses* of Aelius Aristide transport us to the sanctuary of Asclepius at Pergamum, town of healing and centre of pilgrimage, where devotion and hypochondria are given free reign.[10]

In this need to go to distant places in order to find happiness or strong emotions, the philosophers identified the symptom of an inner uneasiness and evil: 'who strives to change places strives to flee himself";[11] 'the evil which we suffer comes not from the place, but from ourselves';[12] 'we unjustly accuse the place, [when] it is in our soul that the fault is found';[13] 'those who run beyond the seas change the sky but not the soul';[14] 'happiness is not attained through ships or horses'.[15] For true happiness, according to the ancient philosopher, is not found in the places which we visit to change scenery,[h] but in inner displacement,[i] in the spiritual transformation which brings peace of mind and a new way of seeing the world.

---

[f] [Translator's note] The mime in question is mime 4 by Herodas.

[g] [Translator's note] The French is: *de l'histoire et de l'esprit*.

[h] [Translator's note] French: *dépaysent*. The term 'dépaysé' can be used to characterize he who is out of his homeland, who feels far from home, who is displaced or uprooted. It could also designate a break in routine and habits. It could also mean to be disoriented. All of these meanings contribute to the weight of this expression in Hadot's text.

[i] [Translator's note] French: *dépaysement*. See previous translator's note.

To change the soul, rather than the place

It is interesting, moreover, to note that, in order to symbolize in some way this state of mind, Epicurean poets like Lucretius and Horace[16] evoke, once again, the image of a sacred place, inhabited by Muses and Nymphs, but very close, easy to reach, precisely because it is less an objective place than a state of mind projected into nature. I am referring to the rural and bucolic countryside that traditional poetry often described, from the cave of Calypso to the idylls of Theocritus. This countryside is, first of all, the symbol of pure pleasure, since it delights the five senses: sight, by the form of the trees or the rocks, the clarity of the sky and the finery of the flowers; hearing, by the bird's song and the cicadas and the murmur of the waters; smell, by the perfume of the flowers; taste, by the freshness of the water and the riches of the orchard; touch, by the impression that the shadow of trees produces and the caress of the wind. A symbol, therefore, of peace of mind, this idyllic place signifies the return to the simple life, the moderation of desires, the tranquillity of the humble life. It is a symbol, finally, of the poetic life, the rural countryside, the woods, its springs inhabited by the Muses and the Nymphs. The aged Hesiod[17] had already seen the Muses dancing 'around the source with dark waters', he had seen them bathe their gentle bodies, sinking in the mist, and he had heard them sing at night the praise of the gods. It is at the foot of the Helicon, grazing his lambs, that Hesiod had received his poetic mission from the Muses. Similarly, it is in the 'fresh grove'[18] inhabited by the Muses that Horace received his divine inspiration. But this sacred place, for Lucretius as for Horace, did not bring him its graces and benefits by itself. It is only in being converted to the simple life, in knowing how to be satisfied with the present moment, that one can discover the beauty of nature and find peace of mind and poetic inspiration there.

The Stoics and Platonists invite us also to change our soul, rather than to change locations. It is not necessary to voyage to the ends of the world to see wonders,[19] but it suffices to open one's eyes to contemplate the totality of the Universe, the Sun, the Moon, the stars and the Earth. The Cosmos is at the same time the place proper to man, citizen of the world, and the sole sacred place, [a] temple which is not made by the hands of man, but which the divinity inhabits: man passes his life there and this is why each day is a festival, the sole true festival for those who know how to comprehend the splendour of existence.[20]

Even more precisely, for the Platonists, the journey is entirely interiorized: it is accomplished within the soul which, in thought, hovers over the surface of the globe, traverses the sea, accompanies the Sun, the Moon and the stars in their revolutions. The flight of the soul unfolds over the entire Cosmos.[21] This movement is not one of dispersion, but, on the contrary, the journey of the soul is directed towards the centre of the soul,[22] towards the most profound [level] of the self. This is its odyssey, its return to its homeland, its inner pilgrimage. For it is there that the soul finds the Forms of all things and it is there that it finally finds the mystery at the origin of all existence. 'We flee towards our dear homeland,' exclaims Plotinus:

> but what is this flight? That of Ulysses escaping from Circe and from Calypso ... Our homeland is the place where we come from and where our father is. It is not with our feet that we must flee, for our feet always take us from one land to another. It is not a matter any longer of preparing horse and carriage or a ship, but, closing the eyes, we must awaken our inner eye.[23]

This is the highest summit of the initiation involved in what one could call the mysteries of the spiritual Eleusis. In the mystical experience no less than at Eleusis one does not learn something, but one lives another life: the self is no longer itself, it has become the absolute Other; it no longer knows who it is, nor where it is,[24] and furthermore, Plotinus remarks,[25] it is no longer situated anywhere, but it is carried so far that it is beyond all place, outside of self and of everything.

Notes

1   Cf. Jean-Pierre Vernant, *Mythe et pensée chez les Grecs*, tome 1 (Paris: F. Maspero, 1971), 124–170.

2   Gerardus Van der Leeow, *La Réligion dans son essence et ses manifestations* (Paris: Payot, 1970), 393.

3   On ancient pilgrimages, cf. Fred Raphael, Gérard Siebert et al, *Les pélerinages de l'Antiquité biblique et classique à l'Occident medieval* (Paris: Gauthner, 1973); Jean Chelini & Henry Branthommer (eds.), *Histoire des pélerinages non chrétiens. Entre le magique et la sacré* (Paris: Hachette, 1987), 94–135.

4   Cf. Jeanne Croissant, *Aristote et les mystères* (Liége: Droz, 1932).

5   Dario Sabbatucci, *Essai sur le mysticisme grèc* (Paris: Flammarion, 1982), 134 ff.

6   Epictetus, *Discourses*, I, 6, 23.

7   Maximus of Tyre, *Dissertationes*, XXII, 6 Däbner.

8 Horace, *Epistles*, I, 11, 1.

9 Cicero, *De Finibus*, V, 1, 1–6.

10 Aelius Aristide, *Discours Sacré* (Paris: Macula, 1986).

11 Lucretius, *De rerum natura*, III, 1059 & 1068.

12 Seneca, *Of Tranquillity of Mind*, II, 15.

13 Horace, *Epistles*, I, 14, 12–13.

14 Horace, *Epistles*, I, 11, 27.

15 Horace, *Epistles*, I, 11, 28–29.

16 Lucretius, *De rerum natura*, II, 29–33.

17 Hesiod, *Theogony*, 1–34.

18 Horace, *Odes*, I, 30.

19 Epictetus, *Discourses*, I, 6, 23.

20 One will find the texts commodiously collected in André-Jean Festugière, *La Révélation d'Hermès Trismégiste*, vol. II, *Le Dieu cosmique* (Paris: Les Belles Lettres, 1948), 233 ff. and 555 ff.

21 See again the texts assembled in Festugière, *La Révélation d'Hermès Trismégiste*, 444 ff.

22 See, for example, Proclus, *Théol. Plat.*, I, 3, 15–16, ed. & trad. Saffrey-Westerink (Les Belles Lettres: Paris, 1968).

23 Plotinus, *Enneads*, I, 6, 8, 16.

24 Plotinus, *Traité 38* (VI, 7), 34, 15, 22 (pp. 171–172 of the edition edited and translated by Pierre Hadot (Paris, 1988)).

25 Plotinus, *Traité 38* (VI, 7), 35, 41, see p. 175 of Hadot's translation, and the commentary at p. 345.

PART FOUR

FIGURES

10 THE FIGURE OF THE SAGE IN GREEK AND ROMAN ANTIQUITY

We live in a civilization where the domain of science is totally autonomous, and independent of ethical and existential values.[1] This is precisely the problem, if not the drama of our times, as Georges Friedman has clearly shown in his book, *La Puissance et la Sagesse* (*Power and Wisdom*).[2] How will the modern world rediscover wisdom, that is to say a form of knowledge or a consciousness which does not bear solely upon the objects of knowledge [*connaissance*],[a] but upon life itself taken in its lived everydayness[b] and the way in which we live and exist?

This separation between science and wisdom did not exist in Greek and Latin antiquity. The words *sophos* and *sophia*, which we translate, respectively, as 'sage' and 'wisdom', appear very early on in the poetic and philosophical literature of ancient Greece. In that context, they designate technical ability as much as excellence in musical or poetic art, and the texts make allusion to a know-how which is at the same time the result of education by a master, the fruit of long experience and a gift of divine inspiration.[3] It is to the advice of Athena that the carpenter in the *Iliad* (15, 411) owes his *sophia*, his skill and knowledge of the art of building. And it is thanks to the muses that the poet knows what and how he must sing.[4] Indeed, we recognize here a constant trait of the ancient doctrine of wisdom:

---

[a] [Translator's note] Hadot uses both *connaissance* and *savoir* in this essay, which we translate equally as 'knowledge'. To mark the difference, especially important in this context, we will place the French word in brackets as here, after the translation.

[b] [Translator's note] The French is *dans son vécu quotidien*.

the latter is pre-eminently the privilege of the gods, even the principal mark of the distance which separates gods from human beings.

The words *sophos* and *sophia* are equally applied to political know-how. This is notably the case when the ancients speak of the Seven Sages: historical figures of the seventh and sixth centuries BCE. These figures rapidly became legendary for their possession of both technical and political know-how. They were legislators and educators like Solon. The maxims that were attributed to their wisdom were engraved near the Temple at Delphi, and the custom of inscribing them on stelae at the centre of towns was extremely widespread.ᶜ We find them, for example, in ancient Bactria, at Ai-Khanoum on the frontier of Afghanistan, upon the stele which was engraved by Aristotle's disciple, Clearchus, probably in the third century BCE. Amongst these maxims were the celebrated formulae: 'know thyself', 'nothing to excess', 'recognize the opportune moment', 'moderation is best', and 'everything is a matter of exercise'.⁵

These Delphic maxims, alongside others, were intended to make men aware of the distance which separated them from the gods and of the inferiority of their knowledge and wisdom. The highest wisdom of a man consisted in recognizing his own limits. Or, more exactly again, as Socrates would say, citing the oracle from Delphi: 'O men of Athens! the one amongst you is most wise (*sophôtatos*) is he who, like Socrates, know that in truth he is worthless in what concerns wisdom (*sophia*).'⁶

In the fourth century, or more precisely, with Socrates and Plato and their reflection on the use of the word *philosophia* (the love of wisdom), a decisive shift took place in the representations of the Sage. With this turning point, indeed, one becomes aware of the superhuman character of wisdom: a divine and transcendent state, in relation to which human beings can only recognize the immense distance which separates them from it. At the same time, wisdom comes to be increasingly identified with *epistêmê:* that is to say, a certain and rigorous knowledge. This knowledge, however, is never conceived exactly like our modern scientific knowledge [*savoir*], because it always involves a know-how [*savoir faire*],⁷ a knowledge about how to live [*savoir vivre*] and, ultimately, a certain way of life. In effect, after Plato, the Greeks profoundly felt that there is no true knowledge [*savoir*] which is not a knowledge embracing one's whole soul, thereby transforming the total being of the person who exercises it.

ᶜ [Translator's note] *Stelai* were monumental stone or wooden slabs, on which commemorative or funerary inscriptions were recorded.

Isocrates the orator, Plato's contemporary, already conceived wisdom as a transcendent state. He writes, for example, in his discourse, *On Exchange*, §271:

> Since it is not in the nature of men to possess a knowledge (*epistêmê*) such that, if we possessed it, we would know how to act and what to say, I consider as sages (*sophoi*) those who, within the limits of what is possible, can most often attain the best solution thanks to their conjectures. I call 'philosophers' those who devote themselves to studies thanks to which they will acquire, as quickly as possible, such a capacity of judgement.[8]

Here we find an ideal wisdom, a *savoir faire* perfectly founded upon a total and certain knowledge [*savoir*], distinguished from wisdom compatible with human nature and, finally, from the exercise which leads towards wisdom: that is to say, philosophy. For Isocrates, these different levels of wisdom and philosophy are related to the art of living in the City; that is to say, to political efficacy and rectitude of action at the same time.

In Plato's *Symposium*, the figure of the sage is even more ideal, and the distance between philosophy and wisdom likewise becomes more radical. Socrates appears here, once more, as 'the wisest sage'[d] because he knows that he is not wise: indeed, because he knows that he knows nothing. This situation places him in between the gods, who are truly wise, and who know all things purely and simply, and men who believe that they are wise and who remain ignorant of the fact that they are not. This intermediate situation is that of the philosopher who aspires to wisdom, precisely because he knows that he does not yet possess it. This intermediary status recalls that of Eros, who loves Beauty precisely because he does not possess it. Eros is neither God nor man, but an intermediary between them. Therefore, the figure of Socrates coincides with that of Eros and philosophy itself. As we read in the *Symposium*:

> Eros is between knowledge (*sophia*) and ignorance[e] ... Indeed, no God philosophises [that is to say, etymologically, they do not experience love for a knowledge of which they would be deprived, PH] nor do the gods wish to become wise. And if there is another sage apart from the gods, it

---

[d] [Translator's note] *Le sage qui est le plus sage*, in the original.
[e] [Translator's note] In this quote from the *Symposium*, the 'knowledge' at issue is *savoir*, and we have translated Hadot's 'non-savoir' in this context as 'ignorance'.

is true that he does not philosophise and does not desire to become wise either. This is the misfortune of ignorance: to believe that one is beautiful, good and wise when, in reality, one is none of those things. For the man who does not feel himself deprived of something has no desire for what he does not think that he needs.[9]

Only the one who, lacking wisdom, knows that he is deprived of it, desires to acquire this wisdom. This is a philosopher. In the class of those who are not sages, there are two categories: those who lack awareness of their ignorance,[f] and those who are aware of it, the philosophers. Thus, philosophy is defined from the start by its relationship to that good of which it is deprived, namely wisdom, which is the prerogative of the gods.

Isocrates, as we have seen, distinguished between the ideal sage, the sage insofar as he can exist amongst men, and finally the philosopher. Plato, for his part, apparently leaves us with only two extremes: the ideal sage identified with God and the philosopher. Evidently, the divine wisdom of which Plato speaks is no longer a political and practical *savoir faire*, as it is for Isocrates. It is rather a universal knowledge [*savoir*] which has for its object not solely human things or the affairs of the City, but also divine things, that is to say, the entire Cosmos. For Plato, moreover, political knowledge [*savoir*] must be founded on such a universal knowledge, capable of seeing all things in the light of the idea of the Good.

The sage, identified here with God, thus appears as a transcendent and almost inaccessible ideal. This conception, as we will have occasion to repeat, will have a great influence on the Stoic conception of the figure of the sage.

Isocrates, as we were saying, distinguished between three terms: the ideal sage, the 'human' sage and the philosopher. We have also said that apparently Plato distinguished only the ideal sage, identified with God, on the one hand, and the philosopher, on the other. Nevertheless, in fact, certain signs allow us to glimpse that the 'human' sage, the sage living amongst men, also exists in Plato. Indeed, at the end of the *Symposium*, if Socrates wins the competition over wisdom according to the judgement of Dionysus, this is not only for the apparent reason that he alone remains awake after that night of debate and drinking. It is, above all, because he appeared as a sage throughout the whole dialogue.[10] Alcibiades, in praising him, has shown that Socrates possessed to the highest degree a sage-like concentration of mind, strength and temperance.[11] Moreover, Plato affirms

---

[f] [Translator's note] Here, *non-sagesse*. See previous note.

elsewhere, in the *Theaetetus*, that the task of the philosopher consists in assimilating himself to God, and thus in coming to resemble the ideal sage, within the scope of what is possible (and this restriction leaves open all of the distance between human and divine reality). 'To assimilate oneself to God,' Plato specifies, 'is to become through reflection just and pious.'[12] Spiritual progress is thus possible. The philosopher can aspire to become, not the ideal and divine sage but a sage amongst men, always conscious of the distance which separates him from the gods. This is a highly uncomfortable position, as the fate of Socrates reminds us.

Hence, the task of the philosopher will consist in exercising himself, in his life, to attain wisdom and, in his philosophical discourse, to describe the ideal sage. This description will be the theme of oral exercises practiced in the philosophical schools and also the subject of numerous treatises. The posing of philosophical problems will often be conditioned by this figure of the ideal sage. Thus, in book I of the *Metaphysics*, when trying to describe what the first philosophy must be like, Aristotle sets as his point of departure the traditional opinions concerning the sage. The sage knows everything, even the most difficult things; his knowledge [*savoir*] is accompanied by certitude; and it is related to the very cause of things; his knowledge is determinate, it governs over all other knowledges [*savoirs*] and knows the end to which each thing is directed.[13] In the same way, the later disputes on the possibility of a certain knowledge [*connaissance*] between the Stoics and the Academics, their contemporaries (which means those of Arcesilaus' school) turn upon weighing the degrees of assent that the sage can give to different representations.[14] We know that, in all the schools, one discussed the conduct of the sage in the decisive circumstances of human life: must he participate in politics? Should he marry? Can he be angry?[15] Moreover, we have ancient philosophical texts at our disposal which are devoted to the discussion of this or that particular aspect of the figure of the sage; for example, that of Philo of Alexandria on the liberty of the sage or that of Seneca on the constancy of the sage, or again, several of the books of Cicero's *Tusculan Disputations*. Additionally, in the fragments of the first Stoics which remain to us, there are numerous allusions to this theme.

What descriptions are given of the sage in the different philosophical schools? The fundamental point, as we have seen concerning Plato, is the following. One identifies the figure of the sage with that of God, with the result that the description of God in the different schools corresponds to the idea that each one has of the sage. One represents the sage, it is true, with all the human traits and as living a human life. However, one projects onto God the ethical traits peculiar to the sage. We could thus name these descriptions of God the 'theology of the sage'. Michelet spoke profoundly on this subject in his *Journal*, dated 18 March 1842: 'Greek religion culminates in its true God, the sage.'[16] It is true that, for Plato, but also in Aristotelianism, Epicureanism and Stoicism, the figure of God is, above all, an 'ethical paradigm', to use Klaus Schneider's excellent expression.[17] The Greeks had always attributed to the gods both transcendent and superhuman knowledge [*savoir*] and power. But in the fourth century BCE, to this element of divine power, that of moral perfection is added. One remains, nevertheless, within the framework of anthropomorphism, since this perfection is imagined as a human perfection elevated to its highest point.

Plato himself conceived God as endowed with moral qualities. In book 3 of the *Republic*, Plato tells us that He is good, truthful and simple. In the *Phaedrus*, God is qualified as beautiful, wise and good;[18] and the Demiurge of the *Timaeus* is good, devoid of envy,[g] desiring to produce everything that is best.[19]

The same passage from the figure of the sage to the figure of God can be observed in Aristotle. He represents the sage in the figure of the contemplative man, and of the scholar who devotes himself to the study of natural phenomena and their ultimate causes. However, Aristotle remarks that the human condition makes this exercise of thought fragile and intermittent, spread over time and exposed to error and forgetfulness. Nevertheless, one can imagine a spirit for whom thought would be exercised in an eternal present by passing beyond these limits. This would be thought which thinks itself in an eternal act.[20] Aristotle's God appears as the perfect sage and the model for human wisdom. According to the *Nicomachean Ethics*, the philosopher or the sage among men only rarely succeeds in exercising his activity of thought and contemplation. These rare moments represent the most pleasing and happy that are accessible to human beings.[21] To those rare moments, book XII of the *Metaphysics* opposes the eternal joy of divine thought.[22] Moreover, these rare moments of pure thought, according to book X of the *Nicomachean Ethics*,[23] seem to be beyond the human condition. They represent a divine life surpassing human life which nevertheless corresponds to what is most essential to human beings, the life according to the Spirit.[h] This is a fundamental theme that we find again and again: wisdom is a state in which man is at the same time essentially human

---

[g] [Translator's note] Hadot's phrase is *sans envie*. The French *envie* can mean a natural need or desire, more widely, as well as the English sense of 'envy'. We follow W. R. M. Lamb here, who translates the Greek *phthonos* as 'envy'.

[h] [Translator's note] The French, with capitals, being *Esprit*. In the theological context of this passage, we have elected to translate the term as 'Spirit', rather than 'Mind'.

and goes beyond the human, as if the human essence consisted in being beyond itself.

For Epicurus, the figure of the sage also comes to coincide with that of God. Wisdom, however, no longer consists in the exercise of pure thought but in peace of the soul and the purity of pleasure. This is why the atomistic and materialistic theory of the universe is so important for him. This theory allows us to affirm that the gods are not involved in any way in the creation and administration of the world. In this sense, the essence of divinity does not reside in the power of creation but in a mode of being: that of peace, pleasure and joy. As Lucretius puts it:

> The divine nature necessarily enjoys an eternal duration in the most profound peace and it is separated and distant from our worries. It is exempt from all sadness and all perils, it is strong in itself and by its own resources, never having any need for our aid, this nature is not seduced by gifts nor touched by rage . . .[24]

Nevertheless, for the Epicureans, the distance between gods and men tends to be reduced. In a sense, it is only a spatial and temporal distance. The gods live in what the Epicureans call the inter-worlds: the void spaces between the worlds, escaping thus from the corruption inherent in the movement of atoms. Their subtle bodies are of human form and eternal. The gods are but immortal sages and the human sages mortal gods. Sages, and first of all Epicurus himself, are equal to the gods, similar to them in decisive respects and therefore they are like gods amongst men.[25] We have on this subject a highly interesting testimony which is found in one of Epicurus' letters.[26] One day, probably during one of his courses, Epicurus was expounding his theory of nature. Suddenly, his disciple Colotes fell to his knees:

> In your veneration for what I was saying, Epicurus tells us, you have been taken by a desire little conformable to the philosophy of nature to embrace me, draping yourself on my knees, to give me kisses like to those which people are accustomed to give in their devotions and prayers. Thus, I am forced to render you the same sacred honours and the same marks of reverence. Go therefore on your way, as an immortal god, and hold us as immortals also.

Epicurus means that Colotes is also a sage himself and has the right to divine honours. In any case, Epicurus' disciples considered their master a veritable saviour and as the bringer of a message of salvation. They felt for him an intense love which inspired them to imitate him.[27] It is necessary to do all things, Epicurus himself said, as if Epicurus was there witnessing them.[28] Moreover, the adherents of the Epicurean school surrounded themselves with portraits of the master. Each year, the community of disciples celebrated his birthday by a frugal meal like the one evoked by Philodemus in one of his epigrams.[29] This cult of Epicurus has nothing solemn or magnificent about it. It is completely imbued with the atmosphere that Epicurus knew how to give to the spiritual movement of which he was the founder: serenity, smiling, benevolence, friendship, simple pleasures, frugality and relaxation. These are moreover the sentiments which animate the Epicureans' piety towards their gods. For them, the gods are models of serenity, peace and simple joys. They are our friends, our equals, whom we invite to joyously celebrate on the occasion of religious festivals and who, in their place, invite the sages to participate in their blessed life.[30] To live like the gods is extremely simple, at least in appearance. 'Not to be hungry,' says one Epicurean sentence, 'not to be thirsty, not to be cold. Whoever enjoys this state and can hope to conserve it can rival Zeus Himself in happiness.'[31] As I said, this is extremely simple: apparently. But how could one be the equal of Zeus by not having hunger or thirst, nor feeling cold? It is by knowing how to enjoy this state. However, in order to know how to enjoy this state, one must fulfil two difficult requirements. On the one hand, one must suppress in oneself all superfluous desires which, according to the Epicureans, are neither natural nor necessary. This involves an ascesis, a renunciation of all the things that ordinarily captivate men: riches, glory, luxuries and disordered voluptuousness. On the other hand, even if the Epicureans do not say this explicitly, this presupposes that one is capable of knowing how to enjoy all the pleasures of divine existence: that is to say, at base, the pleasure involved in the [very] awareness of existing.[i]

As has been noted by Eva Hoffmann, because of the very fact that he considers existence as pure chance, as an unexpectedly successful conjunction of events, the Epicurean welcomes it as a sort of miracle, as something divine, and with immense gratitude.[32]

The sage of the Stoics is also an equal of Zeus. But this time it is not a matter of an equality of pleasures, but of an equality in the purity of moral intention and virtue: which is to say, ultimately, equality in the perfection of reason. The virtues of God are not superior to those of the sage.[33] The Stoic God is nothing other than Reason conceived as an organising force, immanent to the world, producing and ordering all cosmic events. Human

---

[i] [Translator's note] Here: *le plaisir de la conscience d'exister.*

reason is an emanation from, and one part of this universal Reason. However, it can be skewed or deformed in the course of life in the body, in particular by the lures of pleasure. Only the sage succeeds in bringing his reason to its perfection and in making it coincide with the universal Reason.

It is with the Stoics that the paradoxes implied by the ancient figure of the sage appear in the most striking manner. First, for the Stoics, the sage is an exceptional being: there are very few of them, perhaps only one or none at all. The figure of the sage is for them an ideal which is nearly inaccessible, more like a transcendent norm than a concrete figure, in contrast with the figure of Epicurus. This is why the Stoic Chrysippus wrote in the third book of his treatise *On Justice*: 'because of their [the sages'] excess of grandeur and beauty, the things we say seem to resemble fictions and to be foreign to human beings and human nature'.[34]

Here, we once more find the same paradox which we have already encountered in Aristotle. Wisdom corresponds to what is most essential in the human being:[j] [yet] to live according to reason and the mind appears to the human being as something strange and superhuman.

For the Stoic, as for Socrates in Plato's *Symposium*, there is an immense distance between the philosopher and the sage for the simple reason that the philosopher, since he exercises himself in wisdom,[k] is not yet a sage. Therefore, there is an opposition or contradiction between the sage and the non-sage: either one is a sage or one is not a sage, and there is no middle ground. In relation to wisdom, there are no degrees in the state of non-wisdom. It makes little difference, say the Stoics, whether one sinks a cubit or five hundred arm's-lengths beneath the surface of the water: one drowns either way.

As a result, and this is a new paradox, since the sage is extremely rare or even non-existent, it follows that all of humanity is effectively foolish.[l] Human reason itself is an emanation of the divine reason. But the lure of pleasure and the force of the passions provoke in people a corruption or an almost complete deviation of reason.

---

[j] [Translator's note] Hadot uses the masculine singular, with definite article, *l'homme*, to signify all human beings, or what is common to all.

[k] [Translator's note] The French is *s'exerce à la sagesse*, and while the meaning is clear – the philosopher is training himself in order to achieve a wisdom he has not yet attained – we have followed Hadot's phrase more or less literally. The verb 'to exercise' is obviously particularly important in Hadot's conception of ancient philosophy. See, for example, 'Spiritual Exercises', in *Philosophy as a Way of Life*.

[l] [Translator's note] Hadot uses the term: *insensée*. Often, this Stoic thought is translated as suggesting that all non-sages are 'fools', 'mad' or 'crazy'.

This radical opposition between wisdom, being wise and non-wisdom leads to a further paradox. One cannot become a sage little by little, nor progressively. It must be a sudden, radical and substantial transformation, so abrupt that even the sage himself is not aware of the exact moment when this event occurs.

Still, and here again we find a new paradox, the Stoics invite people to philosophize: that is to say, to exercise themselves with a view to achieving wisdom. Therefore, they evidently did believe in the possibility of spiritual progress. This is because, if it is true that there is an insurmountable contradiction between wisdom and non-wisdom – so that, in this perspective, there are no degrees in non-wisdom itself – nevertheless, within the condition of non-wisdom, there are the two categories which we have seen in Plato's *Symposium*. First, there is the category of those non-sages who are not conscious of their state (most human beings). Second, there are also non-sages who are conscious of their state and who attempt to make progress. These are the philosophers in quest of inaccessible wisdom. From the logical point of view, there is then an opposition of contrariety between the sages and those who are unconscious [of their own lack of wisdom], considered as senseless or foolish. Yet, this opposition of contrariety admits of a middle ground: the philosophers.[35] The satirical writer Lucian, in his *Hermotimus* mocks this apparently endless quest:

But what are your hopes in pursuing philosophy, then? Because you see that neither your master, nor his, nor his again, and so on to the tenth generation, has been an accomplished sage ... It will not serve you to say that it is enough to get near happiness. To what end? A person on the doorstep is just as much outside and in the air as another a long way off ... the greatest portion of your life slips from you, while you are sunk in self-denial, in dullness and wakeful weariness. Nevertheless, you say you will toil on it for twenty more years at the least, so that when you are eighty (and who can assure you that you will reach that age?) – you will take your place in the ranks of the not-yet-happy.[36]

However that may be, this ideal sage will be he who is capable, at each instant, of recognizing the divine Reason at work in each event in the universe and in his life. He will be capable of perceiving the necessary rational order which governs the enchainment of events, so that he can give his full consent to this order at each instant. And yet, more precisely, he will intensely *will* each event and each effect produced by the divine Reason. This is what the famous Stoic motto expresses: to live according to Nature. To live according to Nature is to actively will this rational universal order.

The liberty of the sage consists in accepting or in willing this order, and in thus making his reason coincide with the universal Reason. This is the only thing which effectively depends only upon ourselves. All the rest – sickness or health, poverty or wealth, obscurity or glory, life or death – does not depend upon us, but upon circumstances independent of our will, of the enchainment of events in the world. All this is indifferent to the sage or, more precisely, the sage does not differentiate between these things. Instead, he accepts them and loves them equally, because they are ineluctably tied to the order of the world.[m] Virtue, and thus the moral good, consists of this act of liberty which depends on us and which makes our will coincide with that of universal Reason. There is no other happiness than this moral good, no other happiness than virtue. The Stoic sage practises a heroism of moral conscience.[n]

One understands, then, to what extent the Stoic figure of the sage presupposes such a state of perfection that it is rather a transcendent ideal than a concrete reality. Such a figure is strange and paradoxical, if we consider him from the perspective of everyday life and the concerns and options of the average person. This is why the description given by the Stoic Zeno of the natural state of society in his *Republic* certainly has something scandalous about it, precisely because it describes this society as a community of sages.[37] In Zeno's *Republic*, there is only one true homeland, the world itself. In Zeno's description, there are no laws, since the reason of the sage suffices to prescribe to him what he ought to do. There are no courts, since he commits no crimes; no temples, 'since the gods have no need of them and because it is a nonsense to understand the works of the hands of man as sacred', no money, no laws concerning marriage, complete liberty to make love with whomever one wants, even in an incestuous manner. Even laws concerning the burial of the dead are absent from Zeno's description. One notes here how the attitude of the sage with regard to social conventions is bound up with a certain refusal of civilization, and the ideal of a state of nature superior to all social or political organization; a state of nature where it will be possible to live only because all the citizens are sages. Civilization and culture as we know them are only of use to human beings who are no longer sages.

---

[m] [Translator's note] See Chapter 11 below.

[n] [Translator's note] Hadot's phrase being *conscience morale*, which could also be 'moral consciousness' or 'moral awareness', or even perhaps 'ethical conscience/consciousness'. The adjective here suggests 'conscience', and we follow Chase, at 'Spiritual Exercises', 88 and 108 here.

The wisdom of the Stoic sage, moreover, suffices in all things. The sage, according to the Stoics, is not simply infallible, impeccable, unshakable, happy, free, beautiful and wealthy. He is also the only true statesman, legislator, general, poet and the only true king. These statements mean, first of all, that the sage is the bearer of the sole true liberty and the only real wealth. However, these statements also mean that, if it is a matter of political or cultural activity, since wisdom is the perfection of reason, the reason of the sage will allow him to perfectly exercise all of these activities, if need be.

The Stoic philosopher knows that he can never realize this ideal figure of the sage. Nevertheless, its very conception exercises an attraction upon him, giving rise in him to enthusiasm and love, allowing him to hear the appeal of living a better life, and to become aware of the perfection that he attempts to attain. The Stoic philosopher will ask himself in all circumstances: 'what would the sage do in this circumstance?' It is for this philosopher, engaged in everyday life, a citizen of a terrestrial city, that the ancient Stoics – not solely the late Stoics, as has sometimes been proposed – elaborated the theory of duties or functions which are meant to prescribe what is reasonable to do in one's relations with the gods, with other people, and with oneself. However, the ethical life for the Stoics does not consist in the scrupulous accomplishment of these prescribed rules, but rather in utilizing these practices as the material by means of which one exercises reason and virtue. This morality of duties absolutely does not eclipse the superior norm that the sage represents. Indeed, only the sage can fulfil these duties with perfection, without having any need of guiding precepts. This is why, as we have seen, the sage is the sole true magistrate, the sole true general, and the sole true king.

This ethics of duties therefore does not eclipse the figure of the sage, but it allows us to reintroduce the more human sage whom Isocrates had placed between the ideal sage and the philosopher below the absolutely perfect sage: this 'relative sage' who most often attains the best or most satisficing solution in an imperfect, conjectural manner. We see the idea of the human sage reappear in both Cicero and Seneca.[38] Indeed, the latter speaks of good men of a 'second class' (*secundae notae*) for, he adds, good men of a truly 'first class', that is to say men like the ideal sage, are 'born perhaps, like the Phoenix, once in every 500 years'.° For Cicero, the good man of the second class can be a political man or a soldier like those celebrated in Roman history for practicing certain virtues like courage, righteousness or honesty, in a particularly striking manner. One certainly senses here the realistic

---

° [Translator's note] Seneca, *Moral Letters to Lucilius*, 42.1.

reaction of the Romans against what they saw as the philosophical abstractions of the Greeks. But I am not sure that such a notion of the good man, in opposition to the ideal sage, was only invented by Roman Stoicism. What is specifically Roman here is not the conception itself but the examples that are chosen to illustrate it. I would propose that this notion [of the admirable non-sage] is born out of the very logic of the Stoic system. From the moment that one admits the possibility of spiritual progress, it is necessary to admit that this progress can reach a certain result, an at least relative perfection. For this reason, people making progress could legitimately aspire to become, if not sages, then good men. Moreover, and this is very important, we thus see how even the ideal figure of the sage has not been abstractly projected in the absolute. It is not a theoretical construction. Rather, as we can note in the case of Plato with the figure of Socrates or in Seneca with the figure of Cato of Utica – whom he considered as one of those rare sages who appear once every 500 years – the figure of the perfect sage ultimately corresponds to the idealization, the transfiguration or, as we might say, the canonization of very concrete figures, who are these righteous men, these sages living amongst ordinary human beings.

***

After this brief exposition relating to the representation of the sage in the great philosophical schools of antiquity, I would like now to attempt to draw out its historical and anthropological significance.

First of all, I would say that the appearance of the figure of the sage corresponds to an increasingly acute awareness of the I,[p] the personality, and of interiority. This movement of becoming aware is inaugurated by the famous Socratic formula: 'take care of yourself',[39] which reveals to the individual that he can govern his life and that his self has its own value which may be as important as that of the entire City. Platonism, Aristotelianism, Epicureanism and Stoicism all agree in recognizing inner liberty. The sage is precisely he who has known how to conquer this inner freedom: this liberty to think according to the norm of Reason and Nature. He can thus be opposed every bit as much to the opinions, prejudices and imperatives of the City as to the caprices of desire and passion. This core of inexpungible liberty is situated by the ancient philosophers in the faculty of judgement. This is stated most strikingly by Epictetus in his *Handbook*: 'it is

---

[p] [Translator's note] Here: *moi*. In the ensuing paragraph, the '*moi*' is what is translated as 'the self'.

not things that trouble human beings, but the ideas that they form concerning things'.[40] Or, as Marcus Aurelius concurs: 'things do not constrain us to make such and such a judgement upon them. None of them forces itself upon our judgement; they remain immobile'.[41] To put it differently, things only have an effect upon the self to the extent that we transform them into representations. Now, I am actually free to choose the representations I wish. The great Stoic distinction between those things which depend upon us (our judgements) and those which do not depend upon us (external things) precisely defines this inexpungible inner core of the personality.

The figure of the sage allows the self to become aware of the power that it has to free itself from all that is external to it, to be independent. Here we encounter, finally, the famous *autarkeia*:[q] that quality that all the schools claim for their sage and that the philosophers aim to acquire.

Freedom and independence also assure to the sage inner peace or *ataraxia*. This peace, this tranquillity of soul, is the highest value in antiquity, fascinated as it was by the image of the man who could remain imperturbable in the midst of adversities and all the troubles of the city, or even amidst cosmic catastrophes:

> The man who is just and firm in his resolution can be affected neither by the fury of the citizens … nor by face of the tyrant. This affects him no more than Auster, turbulent chief of the stormy Adriatic; any more than the great hand of Jupiter casting down lightning; for as the world breaks and falls apart, its fragments will strike him without frightening him …[42]

The philosopher who exercises himself in wisdom will attempt to constitute this core, this inner freedom, by spiritual exercises of vigilance and attention to self, by the examination of his thoughts and representations, by efforts of will and memory which will shore up in him the liberty to judge and an independence with respect to his desires and passions. It is a whole inner life which is developed in this way and which, in the Platonists, the Aristotelians and the Stoics, is concentrated around the Spirit or the *daimôn* present within man.

---

q [Translators' note] I.e. αὐτάρκεια, independence is related but different to/from αὐταρχέω, to be autocratic in the political arena, an absolute ruler or aspirant to the same. Hadot is using the former, which is clear in the transliteration *autarkeia* in the French original.

Nevertheless, we must understand correctly what this becoming aware of the self to which we are referring involves. Indeed, I do not think that one can agree with Michel Foucault[43] concerning this relationship of the self to itself when he says: 'In place of this kind of violent, uncertain and conditional pleasure, access to the self is capable of providing a form of pleasure that comes, in serenity and without fail, of the experience of oneself.'[44] Foucault cites Seneca's *Letter 23*, 6–7 to illustrate his purpose. I believe there are several inaccuracies here.[r] First of all, in the text that Foucault cites from Seneca, the philosopher speaks not of pleasure, but of joy, not of *voluptas*, but of *gaudium*, and the difference is decisive for the Stoics. Above all, if one reads the text of Seneca, one sees that, a little further on, he says the very opposite of what Foucault makes him say: 'Turn your gaze (*specta*) towards the true good and be happy (*gaude*) with what is truly yours. And what do I mean by "what is truly yours"? I mean your very self, that which is the best part of you.'

If one compares this text with that of *Letter 124*, 23, we thus have a series of equivalences: the true good is what belongs peculiarly to the self. What belongs exclusively to the self is the very self and the best part of the I. Now, this best part of the self is nothing other than perfect reason; that is to say, divine reason, as we have already seen. The best part of the self is thus a transcendent self, the *daimôn* of which we have spoken earlier, or, for Aristotle, the Spirit,[s] which is something divine and superhuman within us. Therefore, Seneca does not find joy so much 'in' Seneca, as in the transcendent Seneca, in discovering that he can elevate himself, Seneca, to a superior level of existence where he is no longer just this 'Seneca' limited in time and space, but universal Reason, Spirit or even the *daimôn* which is within Seneca – which he has become, with which he is now identified.[t] One could also say that he has become the transcendent sage which was in Seneca and which is, in some way, the superior self of Seneca. Here again, the human being appears, in what is most proper to him, as something which is more than human. Or, to speak more precisely, the true self of each individual transcends each individual.

One evidently does not find the idea of a transcendent self in the Epicurean doctrine. It, nevertheless, remains true that the Epicurean sage, no more [than the Stoic sage], does not find his pleasure in himself. On the contrary, he finds pleasure in something else: in friendship with other

---

[r] [Translator's note] See also Chapter 11 below, for Hadot's 'interrupted dialogue' with Foucault.

[s] [Translator's note] Translating from the French: *l'Esprit*. Hadot presumably intends the Greek *nous* here.

[t] [Translator's note] In this sentence, in which two 'Senecas' are in play, we have added the inverted commas to try to disambiguate the meaning.

philosophers, in the contemplation of the immensity of the world, and in his astonishment in this sort of unexpected grace which is existence.

This brings us precisely to what seems to us to be one of the most important elements of the figure of the sage in antiquity: that is, his relationship to the world or to the cosmos. Bernard Groethuysen has stressed this point:

> The sage's consciousness of the world is peculiar to him alone. Only the sage never ceases to have the whole constantly present to his mind. He never forgets the world, but thinks and acts with a view to the cosmos . . . The sage is a part of the world; he is cosmic. He does not let himself be distracted from the world, or detached from the cosmic totality . . .[45]

The motto of the ancient sage is therefore expressed in Seneca's formulation:[46] '*toti se inserens mundo*', 'to plunge himself completely into the cosmos'. In the *Timaeus*, Plato already demands that we redress the movements which take place in our souls by placing them in harmony with the movements of the Whole.[47] As for the Stoic sage, he places each moment of his life within Nature, in the perspective of the cosmos. He consents to the will of Nature, he says to the universe, like Marcus Aurelius: 'I love *with* you', which is to say, I love what you love to produce.[48] And he asks, as Marcus Aurelius asks himself:

> What is this universe? For such a universe, what is the utility of this object which presents itself to me? What is the value that it has in relation to the whole and in relation to human beings?[49]

The Epicurean sage, as Léon Robin has said in his commentary on Lucretius' poem, 'is placed in the immobility of eternal Nature, independent of time'.[50] Thanks to Epicurus' physical doctrines, the sage is, in effect, plunged into the infinity of worlds, the void and the cosmos. As the Epicurean Metrodorus says:

> Remember that, having been born a mortal, with a limited life, you have elevated yourself, through the theory of Nature, towards eternity and the infinity of things and that you have seen all that has been in all that will be.[51]

It is precisely here that we can glimpse the marvellous possibility represented by the figure of the ancient sage. Life, too short in itself, perhaps allows us some kind of access to the infinite; the sage, thanks to those instants of life which are granted to him by Nature, becomes in some way the consciousness of the cosmos itself. He is dilated into the immensity of the cosmos, he accedes at last to a vision of the splendour of universal existence. The ancients have very well described the unconsciousness in which most people live or what one could call their blindness with regards to the universe, which allows us to suppose that only the sage knows how to see the cosmos. As Lucretius again says, after having evoked the blue of the sky and the brilliance of the sun:

> If today the whole world appeared to mortals for the first time, so suddenly, unexpectedly, surging up before their eyes – what could be more marvellous than this whole, far beyond anything which the imagination of human beings could conceive? And yet no one deigns any longer to raise their eyes towards the luminous regions of the sky, because one is weary and jaded about this spectacle.[52]

The figure of the sage thus implies two dimensions which are totally foreign to quotidian life: inner liberty, on one the hand, and cosmic consciousness,[u] on the other. This figure of the sage allows the philosopher to discover that there are things more essential, more vital, more urgent than the occupations and conventions of social and political life. As Nietzsche will say, much later: 'Are not all social institutions designed to prevent men from feeling their life, constraining them to the constant dispersion of their thoughts?'[53] We have seen, for example, that in the *Republic* of Zeno, which is conceived as a Republic of sages, the figure of the sage is closely tied to the representation of a state of nature in which man has no need of the constraints of laws and institutions to know what he ought to do: the state of nature in which human beings are no longer separated from the universe by the barriers of habit and convention.

Yet, the sage must live amongst other human beings in the City. He can evidently refuse social constraints, according to the ideal of the Cynic sage, and cultivate the shamelessness of a Diogenes. Without impudence but with firmness, he can also act as a Roman senator in the third century: like Rogatianus, Plotinus' disciple, who on the very day that he was to take up his functions as a praetor, renounced all his charges, abandoned all his goods, freed all his slaves and decided to no longer eat except once every two days.[54] He could also, like the emperor Marcus Aurelius, habituate himself to practice a spiritual exercise of 'natural' or 'physical' definition of things,

---

[u] [Translator's note] French: *conscience cosmique.*

aiming to reveal what things are in themselves, independently of the prejudices and conventions of civilisation. 'This purple [robe],' he says, 'is but sheep's wool dyed with the blood of a shell-fish; this elaborate dish is but the corpse of a fish, a bird or a pig.'[55] He will then preserve his freedom of judgement in the midst of what could be called the human comedy.

Certain sages have moreover adapted an attitude of apparent conformism to human life as it is commonly lived by ordinary human beings. This outer attitude corresponds, from an inner perspective, to a total indifference that preserves their serenity and inner peace. Such is the case of Pyrrho, who the Sceptics claim as their inspiration, and about whom an ancient historian relates the following anecdote: 'He lived piously with his sister who was a female sage: sometimes, he went to sell the chickens and pigs, and with equal indifference did the cleaning and bathed the pigs.'[56] Here, apparently, the sage is not distinguished from the common man, except in what regards his inner liberty. And I cannot deny myself the comparison between this story and that which is reported by Tchouang Tseu about Li Tsu:

> The three years during which he was locked in, doing housekeeping tasks for his wife and serving food to pigs, as he would have served people. He equally made himself indifferent to all and he eliminated all ornament from his life in order to rediscover simplicity.[57]

This return to the simplest and humblest life, above all if it is lived in this state of indifference and of absolute inner liberty, is in a certain sense a return to the state of nature, the stripping bare of all artifice, of all formal rules. We find in Epicurus an analogous movement. The renunciation of superfluous desires, of desires which are neither natural nor necessary, leads us to the simplicity of nature. 'Thanks be to blessed Nature,' Epicurus could say, 'that has made necessary things easy to attain, and difficult things to attain unnecessary.'[58]

In a certain sense, the theory of duties or functions for the Stoics also appears as a sort of conformism which preserves inner freedom completely. The sage will practice his duties as a father and a family man, a citizen and even a political man. But in doing so, he will take them as matter through which to realize the one thing necessary, the life according to Nature and universal reason.

Contrary to a very widespread and tenacious opinion, the ancient sage does not necessarily renounce political action. The sage has not abandoned the desire and hope to exert an influence upon others, in any of the philosophical schools of antiquity. And if on the one hand, the amplitude that the sage attributes to his action differs between the schools, on the other hand, the goal is always the same: to convert, liberate or save human beings. Epicurus tried to do this by creating small, faithful communities where a cheerful friendship reigned. The Platonists, Aristotelians and Stoics did not hesitate to try to convert entire cities, acting upon their constitutions or upon the king. And let us say, in closing, that in all the schools, one finds descriptions of the ideal monarch which are more or less inspired by the model of the ideal sage. As for the Cynics, they attempted to act upon their contemporaries by the striking example of their own way of life.[v]

It would, in any case, be an error to think that the figure of the sage which the philosopher describes and imitates could authorize a conduct of escape and evasion of everyday reality and the struggles of social and political life. First of all, the figure of the sage invites the philosopher to action, and not solely inner action, but external action as well: 'to act according to justice in service of the human community', as Marcus Aurelius says.[59]

Above all, this figure of the sage is somehow ineluctable, or so it seems to me. It is a necessary expression of the tension, polarity or duality inherent in the human condition. On one hand, the human being has need, in order to accept his condition, of being integrated into the fabric of social and political organization as well as into the reassuring, comfortable and familiar world of everyday life. But this sphere of everyday life does not entirely enclose us: we are confronted in an inevitable way with what one could call the ineffable, the terrifying enigma of existence,[w] here and now, given over to death, in the immensity of the cosmos. To become conscious of the self and of the existence of the world is a revelation which breaks open the security of the habitual and the everyday. The ordinary man seeks to elude this experience of the ineffable which seems to him void, absurd or terrifying. Others dare to face it. For them, it is, on the contrary, everyday life which seems empty and abnormal. The figure of the sage responds, therefore, to an indispensable need: that of unifying the interior life of the human being. The sage will be the individual capable of living on two planes: perfectly inserted into everyday life, like Pyrrho, and yet plunged into the cosmos; dedicated to the service of others, and yet perfectly free in his inner life; aware and, nevertheless, at peace; forgetting nothing of the essential and unique; and, finally and above all, faithful to the heroism and to the purity of the moral conscience, without which life no longer merits being lived. This is what the philosopher must try to realize.[60]

---

[v] [Translator's note] See Chapter 14 below.

[w] [Translator's note] Hadot's term is *être-là*, also the French-language translation of Heidegger's term, 'being-there' or *Dasein*.

Notes

1   This chapter first appeared in *Les Sagesses du Monde*, an interdisciplinary colloquium under the direction of Gilbert Gadoffre (Institue Collégial Européen, Paris: Éditions Universitaires, 1991), 9-26.

2   George Friedman, *La Puissance et la Sagesse* (Paris: Gallimard, 1970).

3   George B. Kerford, 'The Image of the Wise man in Greece before Plato' in Carlos Laga et al eds., *Images of Man in Ancient and Medieval Thought: Studia Gerardo Verbeke ab Amicis Dedicata* (Leuven: Leuven University Press, 1976), 18–28; Friedrich Maier, *Der Sophos Begriff. Zur Bedeutung, Wertung und Rolle des Begriffs von Homer bis Euripid* (Munich: Dissertation, München, 1970): Burkardt Gladigow, *Sophia und Kosmos* (Hildesheim, Georg Olm, 1965).

4   Hesiod, *Theogony*, lines 35–115.

5   Bruno Snell, *Leben und Meinungen der Sieben Weisen. Griechische und lateinische Quellen* (München: Heimeran-Verlag, 1952); Louis Robert, 'De Delphes à l'Oxus. Inscriptions grecques nouvelles de la Bactriane', *Comptes Rendus de l'Académie des Inscriptions et Belles Lettres* (1968): 416–457.

6   Plato, *Apology*, 23b.

7   Cf. the important work of Wolfgang Wieland, *Platon und die Formen des Wissens* (Göttingen: Vandenhoeck & Ruprecht, 1982). On the transformation of the soul, cf, Plato, *Republic*, 518c.

8   Isocrates, *Discours*. Tome III, dir. & trad. Georges Mathieu (Paris: Budé, 1966), 169.

9   Plato, *Symposium*, 203e–204a.

10 Ibid. 175e & 223d.

11 Ibid., 215d–223e.

12 Plato, *Theaetetus*, 176b. [Translator's note: Here, as elsewhere, we follow Hadot's translation into the French, which translates the *meta phronêseôs genesthai*, omitted, for instance, in the English of Harold N. Fowler's 1921 translation.]

13 Aristotle, *Metaphysics*, I, 982a.

14 Cf. Cicero, *Lucullus*, §57, 105, 115. See George B. Kerford, 'What does the Wise Man Know?', *The Stoics*, ed. John M. Rist (Berkeley: California University Press, 1978), 125–136.

15 Cicero, *Topics*, 81; Aulus Gellius, *Attic Nights*, I, 26.

16 Jules Michelet, *Journal*, tome 1, ed. Paul Veillaneix (Paris: Gallimard, 1959), 383.

17 Klaus Schneider, *Die Schweigenden Götter* (Hildersheim: G. Olms, 1966), 31.

18 Plato, *Phaedrus*, 246d.

19 Plato, *Timaeus*, 29e–30a.

20 Cf. Aristotle, *Metaphysics*, XII, 1074b35.

21 Aristotle, *Nichomachean Ethics*, X, 1177b.

22 Cf. Aristotle, *Metaphysics*, XII, 1075a7 & 1072b15.

23 Cf. Aristotle, *Eth. Nic.*, X, 1177b26.

24 Lucretius, *De nat. rerum*, II, 646.

25 Cf. Lucretius, *De nat. rerum*, V, 8; cf. Epicurus, *Letters to Menoeceus*, tome III, 135.

26 Cf. Plutarch, *Contra Colotês*, 1117b. See the translation in André-Jean Festugière, *Épicure et ses Dieux* (Paris: Presses Universitaires de France, 1968 [2nd ed.]), 67–68.

27 Cf. Lucretius, *De nat. rerum*, III, 5.

28 Cf. Seneca, *Letters to Lucilius*, 25, 5.

29 Cf. Marcello Gigante, *La Bibliothèque de Philodème et l'Épicurisme Romain* (Paris: Les Belles Lettres, 1987), 110–122.

30 Wolfgang Schmid, '*Götter und Menschen in der Theologie Epikurs*', *Rheinisches Museum* 94 (1951): 97–156 (notably, 120); Festugière, *Épicure et ses Dieux*, 34; Wilhelm Schmid, 'Epikur', in *Reallexikkon fur Antike und Christentum*, tome V, col. 748.

31 *Gnomologium Vaticanum*, §33, cf. Festugière, *Épicure et ses Dieux*, p. 44.

32 Ernst Hoffman, 'Epikur', in M. Dessoir, *Die Geschichte der Philosophie*, vol. 1 (Wiesbaden: Ullstein, 1925), 223–225.

33 Cf. SVF, tome III, §§245–252; cf. Seneca, *Letters to Lucilius*, §92.

34 Plutarch, *De Stoicorum Repugnantiis*, 17, 1041.

35 Cf. Otto Luschnat, 'Das Problem des Ethischen Fortschritts in der Alten Stoa', *Philologues* 102 (1958): 178–214.

36 [Translator's note: Translation adapted from Lucian, *Hermotimus, or the Rival Philosophies*, trans. by H. W. Fowler and F. G. Fowler, in *The Complete Works of Lucian* (Oxford: Clarendon Press, 1905), 77; Hadot cites from *Hermotimus ou les Sectes,* trans. by Eugène Talbot (Paris: Hachette, 1857), 33.]

37 Cf. Ilsetraut Hadot, 'Tradition Stoïcienne et Idées Politiques au Temps des Grecques', *Revue des Études Latines* 48 (1970): 150–179.

38 Cicero, *De Officiis*, I, 4, 13–17; Seneca, *Letters to Lucilius*, 42, 1.

39 Plato, *Alcibiades*, 102 d4; *Apology of Socrates*, 36c.

40 Epictetus, *Handbook*, §5.

41 Marcus Aurelius, *Meditations*, XI, 16, 2.

42 Horace, *Odes*, III, 3, 3–8.

43 Michel Foucault, *Le Souci de Soi* (Paris: Gallimard, 1984), 83.

44 Ibid. [Translator's note: Michel Foucault, *The Care of the Self: History of Sexuality*, Vol. 3 (London: Penguin, 1990), 66. Orazio Irrera (in 'Pleasure and transcendence of the self: Notes on "a dialogue too soon interrupted" between Michel Foucault and Pierre Hadot', *Philosophy and Social Criticism* 36, no. 9 (2010): 995–1117) has notably contested Hadot's criticism, as we have commented in the Introduction.]

45 Bernard Groethuysen, *Anthropologie philosophique* (Paris: Gallimard, 1952), 79–80.

46 Seneca, *Letters to Lucilius*, 66, 6.

47 Plato, *Tim.*, 90d.

48 Marcus Aurelius, *Meditations*, X, 21.

49 Marcus Aurelius, *Meditations*, III, 11.

50 Alfred Ernout & Léon Robin, *Lucrèce, De la nature, Commentaire*, vol. II (Paris: Les Belles Lettres, 1962), 151.

51 In Clement of Alexandria, *Stromates*, V, 14, 138, 2.

52 Lucretius, *De Rerum Natura*, II, 1054. [Translators note: Here as elsewhere, we have translated Hadot's translation of this ancient text.]

53 Friedrich Nietzsche, *Considérations inactuelles*, tome III, 4, trad. Geneviève Bianquis (Paris: Aubier-Montaigne, 1966), 79.

54 Porphyry, *Vie de Plotin*, c. 7.

55 Marcus Aurelius, *Meditations*, VI, 13.

56 Diogenes Laertius, *Lives of the Eminent Philosophers*, IX, 61.

57 Tchouang-Tseu, c. 7, dans *Philosophes taoistes* (Paris, Gallimard: Bibliothèque de la Pléiade, 1980), 341.

58 Cf. Hermann Usener, *Epicurus* (Leipzig: Teubne, 1887), 300, §469.

59 Marcus Aurelius, *Meditations*, VIII, 54 & IX, 6.

60 In closing, permit me to return to the luminous study of Jacques Perret, 'Le Bonheur du sage', in *Hommages à Henri Bordon* (Bruxelles: coll. Latonus, tome 187, 1985), 291–298.

11 PHYSICS AS SPIRITUAL EXERCISE, OR PESSIMISM AND OPTIMISM IN MARCUS AURELIUS

Leafing through the collection of the *Meditations* of Marcus Aurelius, one is struck by the abundance of pessimistic statements which one finds there. Bitterness, disgust, 'nausea' before human existence is expressed in striking formulations. Take, for example, this: 'Just as your bath appears to you – oil, sweat, filth, sticky water, and all kinds of disgusting things – such is each part of life and every object' (VIII, 24).[a]

This kind of contemptuous expression is, first of all, directed at the body, the flesh, called 'mud', 'earth', 'impure blood' (II, 2). It is also directed at things that people consider valuable:

'This is the corpse of a fish, this other thing the corpse of a bird or a pig.' Similarly: 'This Falernian wine is just some grape juice', and: 'This purple vestment is some sheep's hair moistened in the blood of some shellfish.' When it comes to sexual union, we must say: 'This is the rubbing together

---

[a] [Translator's note] Due to frequency of citation of the *Meditations*, we will in this chapter include references to the book and section numbers of Marcus Aurelius' famous work in brackets within the text. Unmarked references to book then section numbers in notes also will refer to Marcus Aurelius' *Meditations/Ta Eis Heauton*.

of abdomens, accompanied by the spasmodic ejaculation of a sticky liquid.'

VI, 13[b]

The same disillusioned gaze is directed at human activities:

> Everything to which people attach so much importance in this life is empty, rotten, and petty; little dogs that nip at one another; kids who fight, laugh, and then suddenly burst into tears; laughing, and presently weeping again.

V, 33, 2

The war in which Marcus Aurelius defends the frontiers of the Empire is like a hunt of the Sarmatian, comparable to the fly's pursuit by the spider (X, 10). On the disordered agitation of human marionettes, Marcus Aurelius casts an unpitying gaze:

> Imagine them as they are when they are eating, when they are sleeping, when they are making love, or going to the toilet.[c] Then imagine them when they are putting on airs; when they make those haughty gestures, or when they get angry and upbraid people with such a superior air.

X, 19

Human agitation is even more ridiculous in that it lasts only a moment and is reduced to the smallest of things: 'yesterday, you were a bit of phlegm; tomorrow, you will be ashes or a skeleton' (IV, 48, 3).

Two words suffice to summarize the human comedy: all is banal, all is ephemeral. Everything is banal because there is nothing new under the sun:

---

[b] [Translator's note] Here, as elsewhere in this chapter, we will generally follow Michael Chase's translation of Hadot's translations of quotations from Marcus, as found in *The Inner Citadel: The Meditations of Marcus Aurelius*, trans. by Michael Chase (Cambridge, MA, and London: Harvard University Press, 2001), here from 104–5. For Hadot's procedure in translating Marcus, see 'Preface', x, to the same text, with 'Notes on transliteration and quotation'; and for Chase's procedure of translating Hadot's translations of Marcus, see the 'Translator's note' that immediately follows in *The Inner Citadel*. With quotations which do not feature in *The Inner Citadel*, we translate Hadot's translations, with one eye on the Greek original.

[c] [Translator's note] Hadot uses the expression *aller à la selle*. Francis Hutcheson and James Moor in their translation used 'easing nature'; Maxwell Stanifroth opted for 'excreting'.

Think constantly about this: how all events which are similar to those which are happening now, have also happened in the past; and think that they will happen again. Place entire dramas, and homogeneous scenes, which you know through your personal experience or through ancient history, before your eyes: for instance, all of Hadrian's court; or that of Antoninus; the whole courts of Philip, Alexander, or Croesus. For all of that was similar; only the actors were different.

X, 27

This banality and boredom reaches to the point of nausea:

What you see in the amphitheatre and similar places makes you sick: it's always the same thing, and such uniformity makes the spectacle tedious; you feel the same way about the totality of life. From top to bottom, it is always the same thing, made up of the same things. Where will it all end? For how long are we still to look at these things?

VI, 46

However, not only are human affairs banal, they are also ephemeral. Marcus Aurelius forces himself to revive through imagination the human swarming of entire epochs of the past (IV, 32); for example, that of Vespasian or of Trajan: the marriages, illnesses, wars, festivals, commerce, agriculture, ambitions and intrigues. All of these human multitudes and their activity have faded away, and nothing more than a trace remains of them. This incessant process of destruction, Marcus Aurelius strives to represent to himself as at work on those who surround him (X, 18 and 31).

Can man console himself for the brevity of his existence in the hope of surviving in the name he bequeaths to posterity? But what is a name? 'A simple sound, as weak as an echo' (V, 33). And this poor fugitive thing is only transmitted to generations that will each endure for a flash[d] in the infinity of time (III, 10). Rather than nourishing this illusion, is it not better with Marcus Aurelius to repeat: 'And how many men know not even your name; how many will quickly forget it?' (IX, 30). Better yet: 'The time approaches when you shall forget all things, and be forgotten by all' (VII, 21).

What, therefore, is the human world in the whole of reality? A small corner of the earth encompasses it, and [the] earth itself is but a small dot in the immensity of space, whereas human life is only a fleeting instant in the twofold infinity which extends before and behind us. In this immensity,

---

[d] [Translator's note] The French being *éclair*.

all things are mercilessly carried away by the impetuous torrent of metamorphoses, by the endless river of matter and time (IV, 43).

Thus, all human things are nothing but smoke and nothingness (X, 31). Across the centuries and differences of culture, Marcus Aurelius seems to echo *Ecclesiastes*: 'Vanity of vanities, all is vanity.'

[1 The literary form of the *Meditations*][e]

One must therefore not be surprised that many historians have spoken with some complacency of Marcus Aurelius' pessimism. Paul Wendland evokes 'his gloomy resignation',[1] John Michael Rist his scepticism,[2] Eric Robertson Dodds emphasizes the perpetual self-criticism Marcus Aurelius exercises upon himself.[3] He situates this tendency in relation to a dream of the emperor which is related to us by Dio Cassius.[4] On the night of his adoption, Marcus dreamed that he had shoulders of ivory. All of this, according to Dodds, suggests that Marcus Aurelius went through what modern psychologists call an acute identity crisis.[5] Recently, Dr Robert Dailly, an expert in psychosomatics, and Henri Effenterre have attempted, in a co-authored study, to diagnose the forms of psychological and physiological pathologies of 'The Case of Marcus Aurelius'.[6] Drawing on the testimony of Dio Cassius,[7] they propose that Marcus Aurelius suffered from a gastric ulcer and that the personality of the emperor corresponds to the psychological correlates[f] of this malady:

> The sufferer of ulcers is a man folded in on himself, unsettled, preoccupied ... A sort of hypertrophy of the self overshadows his neighbours ... it is ultimately himself that he seeks out in others ... Conscientious to the minute, he is more interested in the technical perfection of administration than the human relationships of which this perfection should be the result. If he is a man of thought, he is inclined to look for justifications, to create superior personas[g] and to [take on] Stoic or Pharisaic attitudes.[8]

---

[e] [Translator's note] Here, as in other chapters, we add explanatory section headings, based on the internal divisions in Hadot's text. We note that in the version of the text published in the *Revue de théologie et de philosophie* 22 (1972), Hadot introduces section breaks at several of the points where we have suggested subheadings to English readers.

[f] [Translator's note] The original being: *corrélations psychologiques*.

[g] [Translator's note] Here, *à la composition de personnages supérieurs*, which one could read as 'creating superior characters'.

In the eyes of the authors of this study, the *Meditations* respond to a need for 'self-persuasion' and of 'justification in his [Marcus Aurelius'] own eyes'.[9]

It is precisely here, I believe, that the interpretive error emerges, by virtue of which one believes that we can draw conclusions concerning the psychology of the Stoic emperor from the reading of his *Meditations*. One represents this work as a sort of intimate journal, in which the emperor unburdened his soul. One then romantically imagines the emperor in the tragic atmosphere of the war against the Barbarians, writing or dictating by night his disillusioned reflections on the spectacle of human things or continually attempting to justify or persuade himself, as a remedy for the doubt that gnawed away at him.

But this is not right. In order to understand what the *Meditations* are, we must recognize the literary genre to which they belong, situating them in the general perspective of the teaching and philosophical life of the Hellenistic era.[10] In this period, philosophy is essentially spiritual direction: it does not aim to give an abstract teaching. Rather, every dogma is intended to transform the soul of the disciple. This is why philosophical teaching, even if it is developed in extended studies or vast syntheses, is inseparable from a continual return to the fundamental dogmas, presented, if possible, in brief, striking formulations, in the form of the *epitomê* or catechism that the disciple must know by heart, to remember them constantly.[11]

An important moment of the philosophical life is thus the exercise of meditation: 'Meditate day and night,' as Epicurus says in his *Letter to Menoeceus*.[12] Thanks to this meditation, one has constantly 'at hand',[h] that is to say, present, the fundamental dogmas of the School so that they can exercise their powerful psychological effect upon the soul. This meditation can take the form of a written exercise[13] which will be a true dialogue with oneself: *eis heauton*.[14]

A large part of Marcus Aurelius' *Meditations* corresponds to this exercise. It is a matter of having the fundamental dogmas of Stoicism present to the mind in a living manner. What Marcus Aurelius repeats 'to himself' are fragments of the Stoic system.[15]

To this 'memorization' of dogmas by the philosopher-emperor other written spiritual exercises are added, which are also absolutely traditional. First, there is the examination of conscience in which one observes one's own spiritual progress.[16] Then, there is the exercise of the *praemeditatio malorum* aimed to prevent the sage from being surprised by unexpected events.[17] One represents oneself as already experiencing the most untoward

---

[h] [Translator's note] French: *sous la main*.

events which could take place, so as to demonstrate to oneself that they are not truly fearsome.

Marcus Aurelius' *Meditations* are therefore an extremely precious document. Indeed, they conserve for us a remarkable example of a genre of writing which must have been very frequent in antiquity, but which was prone to be readily lost, by its very nature: the written exercises of meditation. As we will see now, the pessimistic formulae of Marcus Aurelius are not the expression of the personal views of a disillusioned emperor, but spiritual exercises practiced according to rigorous methods.

[2 The exercise of physical analysis and definition]

In the present study, we will concentrate our attention on a very characteristic spiritual exercise. This consists of making for oneself an exact 'physical' representation of objects or events. Its method is defined in the following text:

> One must always make a definition or description of the object which is presented in a representation, so as to see it in itself, as it is in its essence, in its nakedness, in its totality, and in all its parts, following the method of division. One must say to oneself the name which is peculiar to it, as well as the names of the parts which compose it, and into which it will be resolved.
>
> [For] nothing is more capable of producing greatness of soul than the power to examine methodically and truthfully every object which may present itself to us in life, and to look at this object always having in mind the following questions: 'What is this universe? For such a universe, what is the utility of this object which now presents itself? What is its value in relation to the Whole and in relation to man?'
>
> III, 11

The exercise then consists, first of all, in defining the object or event in itself, as it is, separating it from all the conventional representations that people habitually form of it. At the same time, one will apply a method of division which, we will see, may assume two forms: division into quantitative parts, if the object or event is continuous or homogenous; or, in most cases, division into constituent parts, that is to say, distinguishing the causal and the material element. Finally, we will consider the relation of the object or the event with the whole of the universe, its particular place in the causal fabric of the world.

The part of the method which consists in defining the object 'in itself' and in saying to ourselves its true name can clarify certain apparently pessimistic texts which we cited at the beginning of the present study. In this way, the definitions of foods, wine, the imperial purple and sexual intercourse (VI, 13) aim to be purely 'natural', technical or medical definitions of the objects in question. Notably, the definition of sexual intercourse recalls the formula: 'sexual union is a small epilepsy' attributed by Aulus Gellius to Hippocrates, and by Clement of Alexandria to Democritus.[18] In the same way, when Marcus Aurelius unpityingly imagines the intimate lives of arrogant men, 'when they are eating, when they are sleeping, when they are making love, or excreting' (X, 19), he strives to give a physical description of the human reality. The same method is applied to the representation of death:

> He who considers the fact of dying in itself, in isolation, stripping it by the analysis of the concept of those false representations which are tied to it, would judge death to be nothing but a work of nature.
>
> II, 12

The attempt to give a 'scientific' name to this work of nature recurs many times in the *Meditations*, in a manner which is conformable to a general theory of cosmic physics: 'either dispersion, if the theory of atoms is true; or else extinction or transformation, if the theory of the unity of all is true'. (VII, 32)[19]

Such representations, Marcus Aurelius notes, 'reach the thing itself':[i]

> Even more, they penetrate right through it, so that one can see what it is in reality . . . When things seem too seductive, strip them naked, behold, face to face, their worthlessness, make it clear how little value they have, and strip from them that appearance of which they are so proud.
>
> VI, 13[20]

Another mode of exact knowledge of objects is the division, either into quantitative or constituent parts.[21] The *Meditations* give an example of the first mode of division:

---

[i] [Translators note] French: *en plein corps*. Here, as elsewhere, we follow Michael Chase's translation of Hadot's Marcus, at *Inner Citadel*, 105.

A seductive melody ... you can despise it if you divide it into each of its sounds, and if you ask yourself, regarding each of these sounds taken separately, if you are incapable of resisting them; if you are, you would be filled with shame. The same thing will happen if you repeat this procedure in the case of the dance, by decomposing it into each movement or each figure; and the like about the *pankration*.[j] In general, then, and with the exception of virtue and its effects, remember to head as quickly as you can for the parts of a process, in order, by dividing them, to get to the point where you despise them. Transpose this method, moreover, to life in its entirety.

XI, 2[k]

It is in this method of analysis of 'continuous' realities which divides them into quantitative parts that one of the themes dearest to Marcus Aurelius originates: the transience of the present moment.[22] The thought we have just quoted counsels in effect: 'Transpose this method [of decomposition into moments] to life in its entirety.' And we see Marcus Aurelius apply it concretely: 'Do not allow yourself to be troubled by the representations of an entire life' (VIII, 36). In the same way as it is an illusion to represent to oneself a song as anything more than a sequence of notes, or the dance a sequence of successive figures, it is a disastrous mistake to let oneself be disturbed by the global representation of one's whole life, by the accumulation of all the difficulties and tests that await us. Our life is, finally, infinitely divisible, like any continuous reality.[23] Each instant of our life vanishes when we want to seize it: 'And the present will be much diminished, if one strives to circumscribe it' (VIII, 36).[l] Hence the counsel of Marcus

---

[j] [Translators note] I.e. the ancient form of wrestling.

[k] [Translator's note] Compare the translation of Maxwell Staniforth (London: Penguin, 2004), 139:

> You can soon become indifferent to the seductions of song or dance or athletic displays if you resolve the melody into its several notes, and ask yourself of each one in turn, 'Is this that I cannot resist?' You will flinch from admitting it. Do the same to each movement or attitude of dancers, and similarly with the athletes. In short, save in the case of virtue and its implications, always remember to go straight for the parts themselves, and by dissecting these achieve your disenchantment. And now, transfer this method to life as a whole.

[l] [Translator's note] The first clause of Hadot's translation reads: *Le présent se rapetisse au maximum*, which literally would read: 'the present shrinks to the maximum'. In this case, we follow the more parsimonious English translation ('will be much diminished') of Francis Hutcheson and James Moor. Following Chase's general practice in *Inner Citadel*, we translate 'delimiter' here as 'circumscribe'.

Aurelius', repeated many times: 'Circumscribe the present' (VII, 29). That is to say: try to grasp how infinitesimal the instant is in which the future becomes past.

The method employed here consists in isolating through thought a moment from the temporal continuum, then to infer from the part to the whole: of a song, that it is only notes; of a life, that it is only fleeting instants. We rediscover the application of the same principle in some of the 'pessimistic' declarations that we cited earlier. One goes from a moment to the whole of life, from the tedious spectacles of the amphitheatre to all of the duration of existence (VI, 46); from the repugnant aspect of bath water to the totality of the instants of life (VIII, 24). What legitimizes such reasoning? It is the idea that the course of time does not change anything of the content of reality: that is to say, that the entirety of reality is given at each instant or, put differently, that duration is entirely homogenous. The best illustration of this conception is the following thought:

> Consider how many different things are produced in each one of us in an infinitesimal moment, as much in the bodily as in the psychological domain. And then you will not wonder so much that very many, or rather all the effects of nature are produced at the same time in this unity and this totality which we call the cosmos.

> VI, 25

The other mode of division consists in distinguishing the essential components of the object or the event. This is why at several places, Marcus Aurelius enumerates the questions that we ought to pose regarding each thing which is presented to us. These questions are four in number and correspond closely to what are usually called the Stoic 'categories': what is the material element of the thing? What is its causal element? What is its relationship with the cosmos? What is its natural duration?[24] The outcome of this method is to situate the event or object in a 'physical' perspective, in the general frame of physical science. For example, [consider] this thought:

> I consist of a causal and a material principle. Neither of these shall be annihilated; as they were not made out of nothing. But each part of me will be integrated by its transformation into another part of the universe; and that, again, into some other part; and thus to infinity.[25]

> V, 13

In this perspective, the birth and death of the individual become moments of the universal metamorphosis in which nature takes pleasure (IV, 36)[m] and which it gives as a task to itself (VIII, 6). The vision of the impetuous river of universal matter and of the infinite time which carry away human lives is, therefore, ultimately connected to this method of division. Because of it, any event which presents itself, whether suffering, injury or death, loses its purely human signification in order to be connected to its true physical cause, the original will of Providence and the necessary enchainment of causes that results from it.[26] 'Whatever happens to you was prepared for you in advance from all eternity, and the network of causes has woven together your substance and the occurrence of this event for all time' (X, 5).

[3 The cosmic perspective and greatness of soul]

The method proposed by Marcus Aurelius thus totally changes our manner of evaluating the objects and events of human life. When people want to evaluate things, they habitually apply a system of purely human values, often inherited from tradition and falsified by passionate elements. This is what Marcus Aurelius calls the *tuphos*, the swelling of opinion (VI, 13). One could thus say that the method of 'physical' definition, in a certain sense, aims to eliminate anthropomorphism, if one intends by this term the human, all-too-human dimension that people add to things, when they represent them:

> Don't tell yourself anything more than what your primary representations tell you. If you've been told: 'So-and-so has been talking behind your back,' then this is what you've been told. You have not, however, been told that 'Somebody has done a wrong to me.'
>
> VIII, 49

An objective fact is presented to our consciousness: someone has said something. This is the first representation. But most people add to it a second representation, coming from inside of themselves, expressed in an inner discourse: 'this calumnious speech is an injury to me'. To the judgement of existence is then added a judgement of value: a judgement of value

---

[m] [Translator's note] Here, Hadot uses the term *plaisir*.

which, for Marcus Aurelius and the Stoics, has no grounds in reality, since the sole evil which a person can possibly suffer is the moral fault which they themselves commit:

> Dwell thus upon the first representation [i.e. judgements of existence], and add nothing to them, from within [i.e. judgements of value]; and no harm befalls you. Or, rather, add something only inasmuch as you have familiarized yourself with each of the events which happens in the world.
>
> VIII, 49

There are, here, two stages: first of all, to hold to the first representation, to the one which we could call 'naive'; that is to say, to stick to the definition of the object or event taken in itself, without adding a false value to it. Then, second, one attributes to the object or event its true value, relating it to its natural causes: the will of Providence and the will of the human being. We see appearing here a theme dear to Marcus Aurelius: that of the familiarity of human being with Nature. The sage who practises the method of 'physical' definition finds everything 'natural', because he has familiarized himself with all the ways of Nature: 'how ridiculous, like a stranger to the world, is he who is surprised at anything which happens in life!' (XII, 13); 'whatever happens, is as natural and customary and familiar as a rose in the spring, or fruit in summer' (IV, 44).

It is finally in the cosmic perspective of universal Nature that objects and events are to be situated:

> You will open up a vast field for yourself as you embrace the totality of the cosmos in your thought, conceive everlasting eternity, and consider the rapid metamorphosis of each individual thing; how short the time from its birth to its dissolution; how immense the span of time before its birth and after its dissolution.
>
> IX, 32

The vision of the soul[n] comes to coincide with the divine perspective of universal Nature.[27] In the same way that we breathe the air which surrounds us, we must think with the cosmic Thought in which we are bathed.[28]

This transformation of the gaze due to the practice of the 'physical' knowledge [*connaissance*] of things, is nothing else than greatness of soul. In the text cited above (III, 11), Marcus Aurelius says this explicitly: 'nothing

---

[n] [Translator's note] Original: *regard*, which might also be translated as 'gaze' in context.

is more capable of producing greatness of soul than the power to examine methodically and truthfully every object which may present itself to us in life' (III, 11). Marcus Aurelius does not give a long definition of this virtue. At most, he notes that the term *hyperphrôn* (one could translate this as 'noble' or 'magnanimous') implies 'the raising of the thinking part above any sweet or violent emotions of the flesh, above fame, above death, and all such things' (X, 8). Such a definition is close to the one which the Stoics traditionally gave of magnanimity: 'greatness of soul is the virtue or the knowledge [*savoir*] which elevates us beyond what can happen to good men as much as to bad';[29] that is to say, above what the technical language of the Stoics calls 'indifferent' things. For the Stoics, indeed, things which were neither good nor bad were indifferent. For them, the sole good was virtue, the sole evil was vice. Virtue and vice depended upon our will and were in our power. But all the rest – life, death, riches, poverty, pleasure, sadness, suffering or renown – do not depend upon us. These things, independent of our will and thus foreign to the opposition of Good and Evil, were therefore be considered indifferent. They befall good and wicked men indifferently, on the basis of the initial decision of Providence and the necessary interconnection of causes.

To say that the method of 'physical' definition engenders greatness of soul amounts to saying that it makes us realize that everything that is not virtue is indifferent. One of Marcus Aurelius' thoughts explicitly underlines this:

The power of living well is seated in the soul; if it be indifferent toward things which are indifferent. One will be indifferent to indifferent things, if one considers each of these things according to the method of division and definition;[30] remembering that none of them is capable of giving birth to an evaluation concerning its subject and that it cannot reach us, but that things remain still, while it is us who form judgements about them.

XI, 16

The signification of the method that we are studying here appears in a new light. To define or divide the object in a purely 'physical' manner, in a way which is conformable to the 'physical' part of philosophy, is to lift off the false value that human opinion attributes to it. It is thus to recognize the object as 'indifferent', that is to say as independent of our will but dependent on the divine will. Consequently, it is to make it pass from the petty and banal sphere of human interests to the ineluctable sphere of the order of nature.

Here one should notice the formula, 'to be indifferent towards indifferent things'. It seems that not every Stoic would have accepted it. Indeed, the Stoics admitted that a choice was possible amongst indifferent things, and that certain of them were 'preferable' by reason of their greater or lesser conformity with nature. They preferred, for example, peace to war, the salvation of the nation to its destruction. But the formula, 'to be indifferent to indifferent things', recalls the definition of the goal of life according to Aristo of Chios, the heretical Stoic of the third century before Christ: 'to live in a disposition of indifference with regards to indifferent things'.[31] Aristo wanted to say by this that, apart from virtue, there are no things preferable by nature: things could only be preferable in virtue of circumstances.[32] As Joseph Moreau has shown, Aristo wanted to be absolutely faithful to the fundamental principle of Stoicism which recognizes one sole Good, one sole value, which is that of virtue.[33] He maintained that reason was capable of recognizing its duty in each circumstance without need of the knowledge [*connaissance*] of nature. Now, we know that it was the reading of Aristo's writings which provoked the conversion of Marcus Aurelius to philosophy.[34]

Let us specify the sense that Marcus Aurelius gives to this indifference of indifferent things. It consists in not introducing a difference;[o] it is the equanimity of the soul and not any lack of interest or attachment. Indifferent things are not without interest for the sage. On the contrary – and this is the principal benefit of the method of 'physical' definition – from the moment when the sage has discovered that indifferent things do not depend on human will, but on the will of universal Nature, they become infinitely interesting for him. He accepts them with love, but all of them with an equal love. He finds them beautiful, but all with the same admiration. This is one of the essential aspects of the greatness of soul, but it is also the point upon which, whatever influence he may have been exposed to, Marcus Aurelius differs profoundly from what we know of Aristo of Chios. The latter rejected the physical part of philosophy,[35] since he wanted to found duty in a way which was independent of the knowledge [*connaissance*] of nature. On the contrary, Marcus Aurelius founded greatness of soul and the indifference to indifferent things on the contemplation of the physical

---

[o] [Translator's note] Hadot's expression, which becomes increasingly central as the chapter proceeds, is: *ne pas faire de différence*. Our translation here, of 'to introduce differences', follows Chase's at Hadot, *Inner Citadel*, 109, where he talks of the power of assent as 'introduc[ing] value differences' in a closely related context. Later, Hadot will use the plural *faire des différences*: this is literally to 'make differences', which is not a standard English usage, or perhaps to 'differentiate' between different (kinds of) things.

world. The spiritual exercise of physical definition, to which we dedicate the present study, corresponds to the putting to work of the physical part of Stoic philosophy.

The close link between magnanimity and knowledge of nature is found in a very particular way in Seneca.[36] In the preface of his treatise *Natural Questions*, Seneca reflects on the utility of this physical research; this will be, precisely, to cultivate greatness of soul: 'The virtue to which we aspire produces greatness, because it liberates the soul, prepares it for the knowledge of celestial things and renders it worthy of sharing the divine condition.'[37] On this point, the Stoics join the Platonic tradition inaugurated by the famous text of the *Republic*[38] that Marcus Aurelius himself cites in the following form: 'To he who possesses greatness of soul and contemplates the totality of time and being, can you believe that human life can appear to him as something great?' (VII, 35).[39] Greatness of the soul is tied here to a sort of flight of the spirit far from earthly things. Yet, even though Marcus Aurelius implies that he is situating himself within the Platonic heritage by citing this text, it remains true that his conception of the speculative foundations of greatness of the soul is finally radically different from the Platonic theme of the imaginative flight of the soul. Stoicism, indeed, furnishes to Marcus Aurelius a physics of the singular event, of the *hic et nunc*, and it is this physics which, above all, grounds the virtue of greatness of soul.

The present event that the method of the quantitative analysis of the temporal continuum renders nearly evanescent, rediscovers what one could call an infinite value by the method of analysis into essential components. Indeed, if one analyses its causes, each event appears as the expression of the will of Nature which is unfolded or reflected in the interconnection of causes which constitute Fate. 'Circumscribe the present': this is ultimately to liberate the imagination from emotional representations of regret and hope, to thus liberate oneself from useless anxieties or worries. But it, is above all, to truly practice an exercise of the 'presence of Nature', in renewing at each instant the consent of our will to the Will of universal Nature. Thus, every moral and philosophical activity is concentrated in the instant:

> The following is enough for you: your present value-judgement, as long as it is objective; your present action, as long as it is accomplished in the service of the human community; your present inner disposition, as long as it finds its joy in every conjunction of events brought about by the external cause.
>
> IX, 6

Seen in this perspective, one could say that things are transfigured. One no longer introduces a 'difference' between them:[p] they are equally accepted, indeed equally loved:

> The Earth loves! She loves the rain! And the venerable Ether? It loves, too! The Universe, too, loves to produce that which must occur. And I say to the Universe: I, too, love – along with you. Don't we say: 'such-and-such loves to happen'?
>
> X, 21[40]

Just now,[q] everything seemed banal, tedious, even repugnant. Because of the eternal repetition of human things, duration was homogenous: each instant contained everything possible. Now, however, what was boring or terrifying assumes a new aspect. Everything becomes familiar for the man who identifies his vision with that of Nature: he is no longer a stranger in the universe. Nothing astounds him, because he is at home 'in the beloved City of Zeus' (IV, 29).[r] He loves each event – that is to say, each present instant – accepting it with benevolence, gratitude and piety.[41] The word *hileôs*, dear to Marcus Aurelius, expresses well this inner atmosphere and it is with this word that the *Meditations* ends: 'Depart with serenity, for he who sets you free is himself filled with serenity' (XII, 36, 5).

The transformation of the gaze therefore brings a reconciliation between man and things. Under the gaze of the man familiar with nature, everything reacquires a new beauty, and it is a realist aesthetic that Marcus Aurelius develops in the following thought:

> We must also bear in mind things like the following: even the accessory consequences of natural phenomena have something graceful and attractive about them. For instance: when bread is baked, some parts of it develop cracks in their surface. Now, it is precisely these small openings which, although they seem somehow to have escaped the intentions which presided over the making of the bread, somehow please us and stimulate our appetite in a quite particular way. Or take figs as an example: when they are perfectly ripe, they split open. In the case of ripe

---

[p] [Translator's note] As above, *faire différence*, to 'introduce' or, more literally, 'make [a] difference'.

[q] [Translator's note] Original, *tout à l'heure* Hadot is referring, using *enargeia*, to the beginning of the article where he discusses Marcus Aurelius' 'pessimistic' assertions. E.g. X, 27; VI, 46.

[r] [Translator's note] See VIII, 15; XII, 1, 5; IV, 23.

olives, it is precisely the proximity of rot which adds a unique beauty to the fruit. Ears of corn which bend toward the earth; the lion's wrinkled brow; the foam trailing from the mouth of boars: these things, and many others like them, would be far from beautiful to look at, if we considered them only in themselves. And yet, because these secondary aspects accompany natural processes, they add a new adornment to the beauty of these processes, and they make our hearts glad. Thus, if one possesses experience and a thorough knowledge of the workings of the universe, there will be scarcely a single one of those phenomena which accompany natural processes as a consequence which will not appear to him, under some aspect at least, as pleasant. Such a person will derive no less pleasure from contemplating the actual gaping jaws of wild beasts than he does from all the imitations which painters and sculptors provide thereof. His pure eyes will be able to see a kind of flourishing maturity in aged men and women, as well as a kind of amiable charm in children. Many such cases will occur, and it is not just anyone who can derive pleasure from them. Rather, only that person who has become truly familiar with nature and her works will do so.

III, 2

[4 The optimism of Marcus Aurelius?]

We are now far from the pessimistic declarations cited at the beginning of our study. And yet, these pessimistic statements form part of the same spiritual exercise as the hymns to the beauty of Nature that we have now come to read. The one and the other correspond in effect to a spiritual exercise which consists in defining, in itself, the object which is present, dividing it into its quantitative or component parts, and of thus considering it according to the perspective proper to the physical part of philosophy. This spiritual exercise of 'physical' definition, precisely, has the effect of making us indifferent before indifferent things; that is to say, of making us cease to introduce differences between things which do not depend upon us, but which depend on the will of universal Nature. No longer to introduce differences means, first of all, giving up attributing to certain things a false value, insofar as they are measured only according to the human scale. This renunciation explains the sense of Marcus's apparently pessimistic declarations. Nevertheless, to no longer make differences means to discover that all things, even those which seem to us repulsive, have an equal value if one measures them in relation to the scale of universal Nature. To no longer introduce differences is to look at things with the same gaze with which Nature itself regards them. This then is the sense of Marcus' optimistic declarations in which the beauty of all natural phenomena is exalted and through which a loving consent to the will of Nature is also expressed. This inner attitude by which the soul does not introduce differences but preserves its equanimity before all things corresponds to greatness of soul.

Was Marcus Aurelius himself then pessimistic or optimistic? Did he suffer from a stomach ulcer?[42] The *Meditations* do not permit us to respond to this question. They make known to us spiritual exercises which were traditional in the Stoic school, but they reveal to us next to nothing about 'the case of Marcus Aurelius'.

Notes

1 Paul Wendland, *Die Hellenistisch-Römanisch Kultur in ibren Beziehungen zu Judentum und Christentum*, 4th ed. (Tübingen: Mohr, 1978), 238.

2 John M. Rist, *Stoic Philosophy* (Cambridge: Cambridge University Press,1979), 286.

3 Eric R. Dodds, *Païens et Chrétiens dans un Àge d'Angoisse*, trad. H.-D. Suffrey (Paris: La Pensée Sauvage, 1979), 43, n. 2 (E. R. Dodds alludes to *Meditations*, VIII, 1, 1; X, 8, 1–2; XI, 18, 5; V, 10, 1).

4 Dio Cassius, *Roman History*, LXX1, 36, 1.

5 Dodds, *Païens et Chrétiens*, 43, n. 2.

6 Robert Dailly and Henri van Effenterre, 'Le Cas Marc Aurèle: Essai de Psychosomatique Historique', *Revue des Études Anciennes*, LVI (1954): 347–365.

7 Dio Cassius, *Roman History*, LXXII, 6, 4.

8 Dailly and van Effenterre, 'Le Cas Marc Aurèle', 354.

9 Dailly and van Effenterre, 'Le Cas Marc Aurèle', 355.

10 One will find in Georg Misch, *Gieschichte der Autobiographie*, I, 2 (Frankfurt am Main: G. Schulte-Bulmke, 1950), 479 ff. not only an excellent presentation of the collected work of Marcus Aurelius, but a fine development concerning his "pessimism". On spiritual direction and exercises in Antiquity, cf. Paul Rabbow, *Seelenführung in der Antike* (Munich: Kösel, 1954); Ilsetraut Hadot, *Seneca und die Griechicsch-Romanische Tradition der Sellenleitung* (Berlin: Walter de Gruyter, 1969) and, by the same author, 'Épicure et l'enseignement philosophique hellénistique et romain', in *Actes du VIIe congrès de l'Association Guillaume Budé* (Paris: Vrin, 1969), 347–353.

11 Ilsetraut Hadot, 'Épicure et l'Enseignement Philosophique Hellénistique et Romain', 349.

12 Diogenes Laertius, *Lives of the Eminent Philosophers*, X, 135.

13 Epictetus, *Discourses*, III 24,103; III, 5, 11.

14 This is the title given to the *Meditations* of Marcus Aurelius. It could be translated as "for himself."

15 Marcus Aurelius, *Wege zu Sich Selbst*, W. Theiler ed. (Zürich: Artemis, 1974), 14.

16 Cf. Epictetus, *Discourses*, II, 18, 12.

17 Cicero, *Tusculan Disputations*, III, 29 and IV, 37. Cf. Rabbow, *Seelenführung*, 60; Ilsetraut Hadot, *Seneca*, 60 ff.

18 Aulus Gellius, *Attic Nights*, XIX, 2; Clement of Alexandria, *Pedagogue*, II, 10, 64, 3. I take the lesson of the manuscripts, *historian*, and I hear it in the sense of "chat (*bavardage*)".

19 Cf. Marcus Aurelius, *Meditations*, VI, 4 & 10; VI, 24; IV, 14.

20 With Rabbow, *Seelenführung*, 328

21 Cf. Anatole France, *Le Livre de mon ami*, XI, in *Oeuvres*, tome 1 (Paris: Gallimard: Bibliothèque de la Pleiade 1984), 515: "My mother used to say that, to detail them, Mrs. Gance's features were not extraordinary. Whenever my mother expressed this feeling, my father would shake his head with incredulity. He was doing without doubt like me, this excellent father: he did not look at the features of Madame Gance in detail. And whatever the detail was, the whole thing was charming."

22 On this theme, cf. Victor Goldschmidt, *Le Système Stoïcienne et l'Idée de Temps* (Paris: Vrin, 1953), 168 ff.

23 In an exact sense, the Stoics go so far as to affirm that time is divisible to infinity and thus that there is strictly speaking no "present". Still, they admitted a "thickness" (*platos*) of the present [as it is] lived by human consciousness. And precisely the human consciousness can "delimit the present", which has a double sense: on the one hand, to separate what depends upon us (the present) from what does not depend upon us (the past and the future); and on the other hand, to reduce to a passing instant (which nevertheless has a "thickness", however small it may be) a thing which could trouble us: in sum, to divide the difficulties instead of letting oneself be scared by the global representation of all the difficulties of life.

24 Marcus Aurelius, *Meditations*, II, 4; III, 11; IV, 21; VII, 29; VIII, 11; IX, 25; IX, 37; X, 9; XII, 10, 18, 29. The material element corresponds to the first category; the causal element to the second category; the relation to the cosmos to the third (= manner of being, cf. *SVF.* Vol. II, §550); the duration, to the fourth (=manner of relative being). Cf. Otto Reith, *Grundbegriffe der stoischen Ethik* (Berlin: Weidman, 1933), 70 ff.

25   The material element is the body and the *pneuma*, and the causal element is reason.

26   Cf. Marcus Aurelius, *Meditations*, IV, 26; V, 8, 12.

27   Cf. Marcus Aurelius, *Meditations*, XI, 1, 3, and XII, 8.

28   Cf. Marcus Aurelius, *Meditations*, XII, 2.

29   *SVF,* tome. III, §264. On the Stoic notion of the "indifferents", cf. *SVF.*, vol. 1, §47; vol. III, §§70–77 and 117. On the origins and the signification of this notion, cf. Otto Luschnat, 'Das Problem des ethischen Forschritts', *Philologus* 102 (1958): 178–214.

30   I read here *holikôs* with Theiler. If one is to preserve [the term] *holikôs*, one should presuppose that this term means a method for situating the object in the totality of the universe.

31   *SVF.* tome 1, §351.

32   Cf. Sextus Empiricus, *Adversus Mathematicus*, XI, 63.

33   Joseph Moreau, 'Ariston et le Stoïcisme', *Revue des études anciennes* I (1948): 27–48.

34   'Letter of Marcus Aurelius to Fronto', §35, line 12, in Luigi Pepe, *Marco Aurelio Latino* (Naples: Armanni, 1957), 129: "*Aristonis libri me hac tempestate bene accipiuant atque idem habent male: cum docent meliora, tum scilicet bene accipiunt; cum vero ostendunt quantum ab his melioribus ingenium meum relictum sit, nimis quam saepe erubescit discipulus tuus sibique suscenset, quod viginti quinque natus annos nihildum bonarum opinionum et puriorum rationum animo hauserim. Itaque poenas do, irascor, tristum sum,* zêlotopô, *cibo careo.*" On the role of Aristo in the conversion of Marcus Aurelius, compare the *compte rendu* of my course at the *École pratiques des hautes études, V*ᵉ *section, Sciences religieuses. Résumés des Conferences et Travaux* 92 (1983-1984): 331–336. The letter of Marcus Aurelius to Fronto does not relate the "conversion" of Marcus Aurelius, but seems to solidly prove that Marcus had read Aristo. I would now be less affirmative [than I was when first writing this] about the influence of Aristo on Marcus.

35   *SVF.*, vol. 1, §§351–354.

36   Cf. Ilsetraut Hadot, *Seneca*, 115.

37   Seneca, *Naturalis Quaestiones*, I, 6. See also *Letters to Lucilius*, 117, 19. [Translator's note: Compare the differing translation of the passage of the *Natural Questions* by Harry M. Hine (Chicago, IL: University of Chicago Press, 2010), 137: 'The virtue to which we aspire is marvellous not because freedom from evil is in itself wonderful, but because it releases the mind, prepares it for knowledge of the celestial, and makes it worthy to enter into partnership with god.']

38   Plato, *Republic*, 486a. On the theme of "grandeur of soul and contemplation of the physical world", cf. André-Jean Festugière, *Révelations d'Hermé*

Trimégiste, vol. II (Paris: J. Gabalda & Cie, 1944), 441 ff. For a presentation of the whole theme, cf. René-Antoine Gautier, *Magnanimité: L'idéal de la grandeur dans la philosophie paienne et la théologie chrétienne* (Paris: Vrin, 1951).

39 Compare Desmond Lee's translation: "And if a man has greatness of mind and the breadth of vision to contemplate all time and all reality, can he regard human life as a thing of any great consequence?"

40 See equally Marcus Aurelius, *Meditations*, IV, 23 and VII, 57.

41 Marcus Aurelius, *Meditations*, VII, 54.

42 On an analogous problem, cf. Pierre Hadot, 'Marc-Aurèle, était-il opiomane?', *Études de philosophie ancienne*, 97–106.

12 AN INTERRUPTED DIALOGUE WITH MICHEL FOUCAULT: CONVERGENCES AND DIVERGENCES[a]

I met Michel Foucault personally for the first time when he advised me to present my candidature at the Collège de France in 1980. To my great shame, I must admit that at that time I knew his work rather badly, being too absorbed in my own research. From our first encounter – and I was amazed by it – Michel Foucault, on the contrary, told me that he had been an attentive reader of my works, notably of my presentation on '*Epistrophè et metanoia* dans l'histoire de la philosophie' at the Congrès de philosophie de Bruxelles in 1953, and especially my introductory article on 'Exercises spirituels' in the *Annuaire de la Ve section de l'école pratique des hautes études* of the year 1975–6.[1]

From this day onwards, I had the great pleasure to discover for myself – in conversations that were unfortunately too rare, which Foucault himself recalls in the Introduction to *The Use of Pleasure* – Michel Foucault's extraordinary personal presence and intellectual

---

[a] [Translator's note] Hadot's original included this quote as an epigraph: "... philosophy, if at least it remains now what it was in other times, that is to say, an 'ascesis' ..." from Michel Foucault's *L'usage des plaisirs* (Paris: Gallimard, 1984), 15. Due to copyright issues, we are unable to reproduce this here.

acuity.[b] We talked of the Graeco-Roman philosophy of life, and sometimes of the texts of Marcus Aurelius or Seneca. I still regret not having responded with sufficient precision to the question that he posed to me on the exact sense of '*vindica te tibi*' in Seneca's first letter to Lucilius. Unfortunately, his premature death, which came as a shock to all of his friends, interrupted a dialogue that was only just beginning, and from which we would undoubtedly have mutually profited, both from our agreements and also, and above all, from our disagreements. It would take me a long time to be able to precisely examine these agreements and disagreements. For the moment, I must content myself with a brief sketch.

One can observe to what extent our interests and concerns converged by comparing the summaries of Foucault's 1981–2 course at the *Annuaire du Collège de France*[2] and the article, 'Exercises spirituels', of which I have just spoken. One finds, in both, the same themes; be it philosophy as therapy,[c] Socrates and the care of the self, or the different types of spiritual exercises, like the *praemeditatio malorum* and the preparation for death. The same is valid for the 1983 article, 'Self Writing',[3] wherein Foucault takes his point of departure from the examination of conscience in writing, recommended by Saint Anthony to his disciples, which had occupied my attention [in 'Exercices spirituels et "philosophie chrétienne"'].[d] Finally, in 1984, in *The Care of the Self*, the chapter that Foucault devoted to the culture of the self re-examined all of these themes, referring to my researches in the field.[e] Moreover, the idea, 'according to which Christianity took up … a certain number of techniques of self-examination which were already in place in the period of Stoicism',[4] is developed at length in this book, following the path of Paul Rabinow.

---

[b] [Translator's note] See Michel Foucault, *The Use of Pleasure: The History of Sexuality*, Vol. 2, trans. by Robert Hurley (London: Penguin, 1992), 7–8:

> There was also the danger that I would be dealing with documents with which I was insufficiently acquainted. I would run the risk of adapting them, without fully realizing it, to alien forms of analysis or to modes of inquiry that would scarcely suit them. In dealing with this risk, I have benefited greatly from the works of Peter Brown and those of Pierre Hadot, and I have been helped more than once by the conversations we have had and the views they have expressed.

[c] [Translator's note] French: philosophy as *une thérapeutique*.
[d] [Translator's note] See Pierre Hadot, *Exercices spirituels et philosophie antique* (Paris: Albin Michel, 2002), 75–98. In the original, Hadot does not explicitly mention the title of his article, but uses the expression 'ici même (p. 90)', referring to the book which also contains the text, namely *Exercices spirituels et philosophie antique*. We add the title and exclude the page reference to avoid confusion.
[e] [Translator's note] Michel Foucault, 'The Cultivation of the Self', in *The Care of the Self: The History of Sexuality*, Vol. 3, trans. by Robert Hurley (London: Penguin, 1990), 37–68.

For Foucault, as for myself, all of this was not solely an object of historical interest. Foucault writes in the 'Introduction' to *The Use of Pleasure*:

> The 'essay' – which should be understood as the assay or test by which, in the game of truth, one undergoes changes, and not as the simplistic appropriation of others for the purpose of communication – is the living substance of philosophy, at least if we assume that philosophy is still what it was in times past, i.e., an 'ascesis', *askêsis,* an exercise of oneself in the activity of thought.[5]

This is how Foucault conceived philosophy at the end of his life, as Paul Veyne's article, 'Le dernier Foucault et sa morale' ['The Final Foucault and his Ethics'], confirms:

> The idea of styles of existence played a major role in Foucault's conversations and doubtless in his inner life during the final months of a life that only he knew to be threatened. Style does not mean distinction here; the word is to be taken in the sense of the Greeks, for whom an artist was first of all an artisan and a work of art was first of all a work. Greek ethics is quite dead [...]; but he considered one of its elements, namely, the idea of a work of the self on the self, to be capable of reacquiring a contemporary meaning, [...] the self, taking itself as a work to be accomplished, could sustain an ethics that no longer supported by either tradition or reason; as an artist of itself, the self would enjoy that autonomy that modernity can no longer do without. 'Everything has disappeared', said Medea, 'but I have one thing left: myself.'[6]

Foucault's 1983 interview with Hubert Dreyfus and Paul Rabinow also highlights this 'aesthetics of existence' which was Foucault's last conception of philosophy, but which also very possibly corresponds to the philosophy that he concretely practiced throughout his life.[7]

For my part, I recognize in this work of the self on the self, this exercise of the self, an essential aspect of the philosophical life: philosophy is an art of living, a style of life which engages all of existence.

However, I would hesitate to speak with Foucault of an 'aesthetics of existence', both concerning antiquity and regarding the task of philosophy in general. As we have seen, Foucault understands this expression as indicating the meaning that our life is the work that we must undertake.

The word 'aesthetics' evokes for us moderns very different resonances than the word 'beauty' (*kalon, kallos*) had in antiquity. Indeed, the moderns tend to represent the beautiful as an autonomous reality independent of good and evil, whereas for the Greeks, on the contrary, the word [*kalon, kallos*] when applied to human beings normally involved a moral value, as, for example, in the works of Xenophon and Plato that Foucault cites.[8] In fact, what the ancient philosophers sought was not primarily 'beauty' (*kalon*), but the good (*agathon*); Epicurus as much as the other philosophers. Especially in Platonism and Stoicism, the good is the supreme value: 'the souls of worth despise being for the sake of the good, when they spontaneously put themselves at risk for the sake of their homeland, for those whom they love, or for virtue'.[9] This is why, instead of a 'culture of the self', it would be better to speak of the 'transformation', 'transfiguration' or 'surpassing[f] of the self'. In order to describe this state, one cannot avoid the term 'wisdom', which, it seems to me, appears very rarely, if ever in Foucault. Wisdom is that state at which the philosopher will perhaps never arrive but towards which he aims, by striving to transform himself in order to go beyond his present state. It is a mode of existence which is characterized by three essential aspects: peace of mind (*ataraxia*), inner freedom (*autarkeia*) and, except in the sceptics, cosmic consciousness:[g] that is to say, the process of becoming aware of belonging to the human and cosmic Whole, a sort of dilation or transfiguration of the self which realizes greatness of soul (*megalopsychia*).

Curiously, Foucault, who gives so much place to the conception of philosophy as therapy, does not seem to remark that this therapy is aimed, above all, at procuring inner peace: that is to say, at delivering the individual from the anxiety provoked by the preoccupations of life and the mystery of human existence: the fear of the gods and the terror of death. All the schools agree on the goal of philosophy, to attain inner peace, even if they diverge when it comes to setting the means to attain this goal. For the Sceptics, the spiritual exercise par excellence is the suspension of judgement (*epochê*); for the dogmatics – that is, all other ancient schools – one can only accede to inner tranquillity by developing the awareness that one is a 'natural' being, which is to say that one is, in some way, a part of the cosmos, and that

---

[f] [Translator's note] Hadot's term, a vitally important one for him, is *dépassement*. This can mean 'to go beyond', 'to exceed', 'to overcome' (including in the sense of Nietzsche's 'self-overcoming'), 'to overtake', 'to go over', as well as in some contexts, to 'transcend'. Following Michael Chase, we will translate it with forms of the verbs 'to surpass', 'to exceed' or 'go beyond'. It is important to note, however, that in other textual places, Hadot uses the term 'transcendence' referring to the same idea. Indeed, it would be legitimate to translate the French phrase here as 'transcendence of the self'.

[g] [Translator's note] Literally, from: *conscience cosmique*. See Chapter 3 above, and for this threefold distinction, Chapter 10.

one participates in the event of universal existence. It is a matter of seeing things from the viewpoint of universal nature, of putting human affairs in their true perspective. In this way, one attains to greatness of soul, as Plato had already said:

> The pettiness of mind is incompatible with the soul which must tend continually to embrace the whole and the universality of the divine and the human ... Do you think that a soul habituated to great thoughts and the contemplation of the totality of time and being can deem this life of man a thing of great concern? Such a man will not suppose death to be terrible or fearsome.[10]

In Platonism, as well as in Epicureanism and Stoicism, the liberation from anxiety is thus obtained through a movement by which one passes from individual, passionate subjectivity to the objectivity of a universal perspective. It is a matter not of the fashioning of a self as a work of art, but on the contrary of a surpassing of the self, or at least of an exercise by which the self is situated within this totality and experiences itself as one part thereof.

Another point of divergence between Foucault and I concerns this question: beginning from which historical moment did philosophy cease to be lived as a work of the self on the self (whether to realize the self as a work of art or to go beyond[h] it in universality)?

My position is that this rupture occurred in the Middle Ages at the moment when philosophy becomes auxiliary to theology and when the spiritual exercises are integrated into Christian spirituality, becoming independent of the philosophical life. Modern philosophy has rediscovered little by little, and only ever partially, the ancient conception of philosophy.[i] Foucault, by contrast, makes Descartes responsible for this rupture: 'Before Descartes, a subject could not have access to the truth except by first realizing upon himself a certain work which rendered him able to know the truth.'[j] But, according to Descartes, 'in order to accede to the truth, it suffices that I am any subject capable of seeing what is evident'. Thus, 'evidence replaces ascesis'.[11] I am not completely sure that this is exact. Descartes has written, precisely,

---

[h] [Translator's note] Here, again, it would be legitimate to read the expression 'se dépasser dans l'universalité' as 'to transcend oneself in universality'.

[i] [Translator's note] See Chapters 1 and 3 above.

[j] [Translator's note] Compare: 'In European culture up to the sixteenth century the problem remains "What is the work which I must effect upon myself so as to be capable and worthy of acceding to the truth?" To put it another way: Truth always has a price; no access to truth without ascesis ...' Foucault, at Dreyfus and Rabinow, *Michel Foucault*, 251–2.

Meditations, and this word is very important.[k] Concerning these *Meditations*, Descartes advises his readers to dedicate a number of months, or at least a number of weeks, to 'meditate' the first and second meditations, in which he speaks of universal doubt, then of the nature of the mind.[12] This clearly shows that for Descartes also, 'evidence' can only be recognized on the basis of a spiritual exercise. I think that Descartes, like Spinoza, continues to be situated within the ancient tradition of philosophy conceived as the exercise of wisdom.[13] In this way, one sees the difficulty there would be in writing a history of the ways in which philosophers have represented philosophy.

My reflections here can only skim over the problems posed by Foucault's work and my intention is to revisit them one day in a more detailed and thorough way. I would only like to stress here how much I regret the fact that our dialogue was interrupted.

For my part, even less than Foucault do I have the pretension of proposing general and definitive solutions to the philosophical problems of our time. I would only confess that, in the same way that Foucault sought in the last years of his life to realize an 'aesthetics of existence', so the ancient idea of philosophy as a way of life, as the exercise of wisdom and as the effort towards developing a living awareness of the totality, is for me still valuable and relevant today. And I consider it as a sign of the times – striking and unexpected in my eyes – that at the end of the twentieth century, Michel Foucault, myself and certainly many others, at the conclusion of totally different trajectories, came together in this vital rediscovery of ancient experience.

Notes

1   Pierre Hadot, 'Spiritual Exercises', in *Philosophy as a Way of Life*, trans. M. Chase (London: Wiley-Blackwell, 1996), 79–125. This article was initially presented in the *Annuaire de la Ve section de l'école pratique des hautes études* in 1975–1976.

2   Michel Foucault, 'The Hermeneutics of the Subject', in *Ethics, Subjectivity and Truth: The Essential Works of Michel Foucault 1954–1984*, vol. 1, ed. Paul Rabinow, trans. R. Hurley et al. (London: Penguin, 2000), 93–106.

3   Originally published as Michel Foucault, 'L'écriture de soi', *Corps écrit* 3 (1983), 3–23. [Translator's note: Michel Foucault, 'Self Writing', in *Ethics, Subjectivity and Truth*, 207–222].

---

[k] [Translator's note] It is important to note that this issue is equally complex in Foucault. For example, in the same text, Foucault says: 'Second, we must not forget that Descartes wrote "meditations" – and meditations are a practice of the self', Foucault, at Dreyfus and Rabinow, *Michel Foucault*, 252.

4   Hubert Dreyfus et Paul Rabinow, *Michel Foucault, un parcours philosophique* (Paris: Gallimard, 1984), 349. [Translator's note: English edition: Hubert Dreyfus and Paul Rabinow, *Michel Foucault: Beyond Structuralism and Hermeneutics*, 2nd edn (Chicago, IL: University of Chicago Press, 1982), 244]: "Now, we can see that in this activity of the self on itself, the ancients developed a whole series of austerity practices that the Christians later directly borrowed from them. So, we see that this activity became linked to a certain sexual austerity which was subsumed directly into the Christian ethic. We are not talking about a moral rupture between tolerant antiquity and austere Christianity.' Or, 'I do not think that the culture of the self disappeared or was covered up. You find many elements which have simply been integrated, displaced, reutilized in Christianity" (250). Hadot seems to be referring to the following reflection, by Rabinow, in the 'Afterword': "Foucault, in contrast, when he deals with Christianity narrows genealogy to the appropriation of one already organized set of practices (techniques of self-examination) as the form for another already functioning set of concerns (self-decipherment for the sake of salvation)" (262).

5   Foucault, *L'usage des Plaisirs*, 15 [Translator's note: Following here the translation in Foucault, *The Use of Pleasure*, 9].

6   Paul Veyne, 'Le dernier Foucault et sa morale', *Critique* 471–472 (1986), 939. [Translator's note: Our translation follows that by Arnold I. Davidson and Catherine Porter, 'The Final Foucault and his Ethics', *Critical Inquiry* 20, no. 1 (1993): 1–9.]

7   Dreyfus and Rabinow, *Michel Foucault, un parcours philosophique*, 330–331. [Translator's note : English translation, 231, 235.]

8   Foucault, *L'usage des Plaisirs*, 103–105.

9   Saloustios, *Des dieux et de morale*, vol. 3, trans. Gabriel Rochefort (Paris: Les Belles Lettres, 1960).

10 Plato, *Republic*, 486a–b.

11 Dreyfus and Rabinow, *Michel Foucault*, 345.

12 René Descartes, *Réponse aux seconde objection (Contra les . . . Méditations)*, in *Oeuvres de Descartes*, eds. Charles Adam and Paul Tannery (Paris: Vrin, 1982), IX, 1, 103–4: "it is not enough to have envisaged a time, it is necessary to examine [the subject of the meditation] often and consider it at length so that the habit of confounding intellectual things with the corporeal . . . can be effaced by a contrary habit of distinguishing them, by exercise over several days." Cf. 'The Divisions of the Parts of Philosophy in Antiquity' [Chapter 6] in this volume.

13 René Descartes, *Principes de la philosophie*, 'Préface' in *Oeuvre de Descartes*, IX, 2–3: 'Philosophy signifies the study of wisdom.' See Spinoza, *Ethics*, V, prop. 42, scholia.

PART FIVE

ENDS

13 THE END OF PAGANISM

The end of paganism is a spiritual, social and political phenomenon which lasted from the first until the ninth century. One sees the first symptoms of it in the religious reforms of the emperor Augustus which reveal the existence of a crisis in collective consciousness. However, it will take nine centuries for the last hotbed of Hellenic paganism to fade away in Laconia. It is thus a matter of a slow process which knew alternating periods of acceleration and deceleration, flux and reflux. We generally suppose that paganism was vanquished and totally destroyed by Christianity. The historical reality was probably much more complex. Indeed, one could legitimately ask oneself if the disappearance of paganism, or at least its radical transformation, would not have unfolded by itself, without the intervention of Christianity. The economic difficulties of the Roman empire, beginning from the third century, the unification of the Empire and the divinization of the emperor, as well as the development of a theology of a supreme and transcendent God, and the appearance of a spirituality dominated by the refusal of the sensible world – we can see that all these factors at work in paganism after the first century CE would perhaps have sufficed to lead the ancient world to a political, social and spiritual state close enough to what would become the Byzantine empire. By its own natural evolution, paganism would perhaps have arrived at this hieratic conception of the world and the emperor which characterizes the thought of the Byzantine empire. In any case, in order to characterize the phenomenon that we will analyse here, more than an end of paganism, it would be necessary to speak of a fusion of Christianity and paganism. Indeed, although after a violent political and spiritual struggle, Christianity prevailed over paganism, it is, nonetheless, true that – according to an historical process which seems to be repeated in different epochs – the two adversaries mutually contaminated each other in the ardour of the struggle.

The political, social and psychological aspects

The fundamental fact, which influenced all of paganism's evolution beginning from the first century, was the foundation of the Roman Empire. Moreover, this is a phenomenon that carried forwards the enterprise of Alexander [the Great], which gave birth to the Hellenistic spirit in its causes and effects.

At first sight, one could think that the power of the emperor served by its nature to maintain and to sustain ancient religion. But this same power, in fact, by demanding universal and absolute recognition, was led to profoundly modify the spiritual universe which was specific to traditional paganism.

In the first place, political constraint in religious matters had gradually replaced the [once widespread] spirit of religious tolerance. Ancient religion was absolutely not unified: it included a great variety of cults, of beliefs specific to different cities, nations or brotherhoods. Nevertheless, because of the centralizing action of the emperors, the Graeco-Roman world tended towards becoming a single nation. An intense intercommunication was set in place. The cults became blended and, beyond this, the divinities themselves were confounded and unified. But, above all, the cult of Rome and the emperors became in some way a sort of religion of the state. This is the precise point that underlies the persecutions of the Christians. From the point when the empire became aware of the growing power of the new religion, repression became more and more violent, as in the reigns of Decius from 249 CE and of Diocletian from 303 to 311 CE. After the conversion of Constantine, the Christian emperors inherited this intolerance. Christianity, in its turn, gradually became the religion of the state, with the anti-pagan measures being made progressively more and more severe. The aristocracy and the people rallied to the triumphant religion by conformism or fear.

In the second place, the imperial power itself increasingly took on a religious character. Outlined by the living Augustus, the organisation of the cult of the emperors is developed under Caligula, Nero, Domitian, Commodus and Aurelian, until Diocletian, who demands the *adoratio* of his subjects like an oriental sovereign and establishes a court ceremony which, moreover, the Byzantine monarchy will preserve and reinforce. As we have seen, the cult of the emperors introduced into traditional paganism a new element of constraint and obligation. But, above all, it gave birth to an ideology which would totally transform the religious representations of ancient religion. In effect, the image of royal power will come to be projected into the absolute. From this moment onwards, one will represent the divine world according to the model of the imperial monarchy. In the same way as the empire is dominated by a sovereign who transcends all of his subjects, even the most highly placed, so the divine world must be crowned by a supreme and transcendent God, inaccessible and ineffable, without direct relations to the universe. On the other hand, royal power is, on this earth, the intermediary and mediator between God and human beings. Projected into the absolute, this representation leads to the idea of a divine Mediator, a second God that the transcendent God uses in order to create and govern the world. This is why many panegyrists of the emperor will give to him the traits of the Platonic Demiurge, who irradiates[a] over the sensible world the laws that he first contemplated in the divine model. Finally, the imperial power concentrated in the monarch is diffused across multiple intermediaries, reaching the very limits of the empire. In the same way, divine power, which has its origin in the transcendent God, is diffused and extended across the subordinate divinities in order to fill the universe. The imperial ideology thus leads to a systematization of paganism: a transcendent God, situated beyond or above all the other gods; a second God, Mediator and Organizer; and, finally, a unique divine Power which assures the continuity of the divine world and the reciprocal interpenetration of all the intermediaries. This systematisation leads, in a certain measure, to the 'end' of ancient religion. Indeed, it ultimately corresponds to a hierarchical monotheism. It will be a monotheism, because divine Power is concentrated in the figure of a transcendent and unique God; and a hierarchical monotheism, because the divine Power is diffused across a whole hierarchy of subordinate powers, from the second God to the gods, angels and human beings. One arrives at a sort of representation of a

---

[a] [Translator's note] The original: *faire rayonner* is of difficult translation. *Rayonner* has the Platonic or Neoplatonic sense of emanation, like the light that is radiated by the sun. Hadot's phrase is very interesting: the laws emanate or irradiate from the Demiurge. But the latter is active in this process, as a mediator between the divine and the world: he *makes* the laws emanate and spread throughout the world. The Demiurge is what links the world to the divine models: indeed, it is the Demiurge who makes the laws emanate to the world. The (neo)Platonic metaphor appears again in the next sentence: the diffusion of the Emperor's power to the periphery of the Empire is like the light that goes from the centre or source of light to the periphery which is illuminated by the centre.

celestial and political hierarchy which is not very distant from that of the Byzantine monarchy, in which the emperor, symbol of the transcendent God, is the incarnation on earth of the Son of God or the mediating *Logos*. In this evolution of paganism towards a hierarchical monotheism, the attempts at the instauration of a solar theology are very significant. The emperor Aurelian will be its promotor and the Neoplatonic philosopher Porphyry will compose a dedicated treatise in order to show that all of the Gods are ultimately subordinate to the solar power. This is a typical example of the need for unification and systematization which is manifest in the last phase of the history of paganism.

One could say that, up to a certain point, the imperial monarchy had need of a monotheistic ideology. It was in the nature of things that a monarchy based on divine right would gradually replace the principate of popular origin. Augustus had already prepared the way for Constantine, both politically and religiously. The unique emperor could only be the image of a unique God. Eusebius of Caesarea, Constantine's theologian, strongly underlined this: 'Constantine was the first to recognize the dominion of a single God over the world, while himself, assuming sole domination over the Roman world, governed all human beings.' One sole King, one God, one Empire: such is the logic of this historical development.

The economic and social factors equally played an important role in the 'end' of paganism. First, the pagan cults could only be practiced intensively in a state of public prosperity and with the support of the State. Indeed, the upkeep of the temples, sacerdotal colleges, as well as the realization of sacrifices and ritual games demanded heavy expenses. Beginning from the third century CE, economic regression befell the empire at the same time as a grave political crisis. It is precisely in this epoch, as Johannes Geffcken has noted,[b] that the decadence of pagan religious life began to manifest itself. The sanctuaries are closed, festivals disappear. The phenomenon accelerated under the Christian emperors. Indeed, the support of the State for the institutions of the ancient religion is progressively withdrawn. There will come a moment – and this is what notably occurred in the second half of the fourth century – when only the offerings of particular individuals or the support of local aristocrats attached to the past allowed the ancient customs to survive.

---

[b] [Translator's note] Hadot is probably referring to Johannes Geffcken, *Der Ausgang des Griechisch-Römischen Heidentums* (Heidelberg: Carl Winters, 1929). Hadot does not give references to the ancient and modern texts he cites in this chapter. Where possible, we will offer references to the modern authors and texts to which Hadot refers in translator's notes. Otherwise, following the original, we will adduce the text only.

The Roman aristocracy was for a long time under the Christian emperors the last bastion of pagan resistance. In opposition to Constantinople – the new Christian Rome founded by Constantine – ancient Rome, the eternal Rome, defended the idea that it represented and the divinity that it incarnated. 'We struggle for the institutions of our ancestors, for the destinies and the sacred rights of our nation': this is what Symmachus will declare to the Christian emperor, to ask him to return the altar of Victory into the court of the Senate of Rome.^c Multiple inscriptions which date from the end of the fourth century reveal that a number of characters from the Roman aristocracy took pride in their numerous initiations into the different mystery cults, their multiple sacerdotal offices and religious titles. The epitaph dedicated by Aconia Fabia Paulina to her husband Agorius Praetextatus is the most famous and the most typical. In the East, it is, above all, amongst the rhetors and philosophers from the schools in Athens and Alexandria that pagan resistance and the fidelity to ancestral traditions is concentrated. Like in the closed circles of the Roman aristocracy, an ardent religious fervour appears to have reigned in these small groups. But these movements of resistance remain on the margins of the whole of political and social life. Moreover, the Christian emperors created a new aristocracy by elevating to high office^d people who did not belong by birth to the senatorial class. Little by little, it became customary to rally to the official orthodoxy. 'To abandon the altars of the gods, this is the new manner of proceeding in the court,' Symmachus wrote. The political, economic and social disruptions which accompany the end of Antiquity contributed very significantly to the disappearance of the ancient religion.

To these evolving factors, we must add the profound transformation of religious consciousness and of the collective mentality which, beginning in the Hellenistic period, does not cease accelerating until the end of Antiquity. A certain common affective tonality undoubtedly characterizes this entire epoch. It is found as much amongst the pagans as amongst the Christians, amongst the Neoplatonists as amongst the Gnostics. In order to define this psychological phenomenon, certain historians have spoken with some exaggeration of a 'nervous depression', others of a crisis of 'anxiety'. Nearly all have deplored the 'decline of rationalism' which is manifest during this period. It is perhaps not exact to consider this vast transformation as a morbid phenomenon. It is true that there is a psychological crisis, but it is

---

^c [Translator's note] Symmachus appealed to the emperor Valentinian II in 384 CE to have the Altar of Victory restored to the Senate in Rome. His request was denied.

^d [Translator's note] The *clarissimat* was an honorific distinction in the high Roman Empire, tied to the senatorial office. The Latin title is *vir clarissimat*.

caused by an eminently positive phenomenon: the rising awareness of the 'self'[e] or the discovery of the value of individual destiny. The philosophical schools, especially the Epicureans and Stoics, then the Neoplatonists, came to assign a growing importance to the responsibility of moral conscience and the effort to attain spiritual perfection. All of the great metaphysical problems: the enigma of the world, the origin and the end of humanity, the existence of evil and the fact of freedom, are posed in the light of the destiny of the individual. But the necessary price of this becoming aware[f] is evidently a heavy one: it engenders a spiritual tension, an anxiety, a disquietude. The crisis is not limited to small philosophical circles. It manifests itself also amongst the masses. The individual becomes attentive to his salvation, here below, as well as after death. In his body and in his soul, he feels himself menaced by evil powers. The world appears to him haunted by evil demons who act directly on the human imagination and attempt to take possession of human bodies. Moral life takes the form of a struggle between good and evil demons. Also, the sensible world assumes a dangerous and hostile aspect. Human beings feel themselves estranged and isolated. In his studies on the phenomenology of Gnosticism, Henri-Charles Puech has clearly shown how this impression of estrangement from the world could lead to the Gnostic solution. Evil powers also populate the beyond. The individual fears to encounter them in his voyage after death. A proliferation of magical practices follow from this fear, attested to by numerous magical papyri which have been preserved. Exorcists and magicians claim to conjure up the hostile powers. But, above all, it is the mystery religions which claim to bring salvation to uneasy human souls. Whether it is a matter of the mysteries of Isis, the Venus of Egypt, Adonis, the Venus of Syria, Attis, the Venus of Phrygia or Mithra, the Venus of Iran: these religions procure for their followers the impression of participating in the ancestral wisdom of the barbarians, the comforting support of a fervent community, and initiations capable of striking the imagination, as well as hopes of becoming immortal and of deification: in a word, the certainty for the individual of being protected here below and saved in the beyond. One must read book XI of Apuleius' *Metamorphoses* in order to understand all the fervour that a divine figure such as Isis could inspire. Isis was a true Madonna, to whom this prayer is addressed: 'Eternal and holy saviour of human kind,[g] filled with eternal benevolence to comfort mortals, it is the

---

[e] [Translator's note] French: '*moi*'.

[f] [Translator's note] The original is: *prise de conscience*.

[g] [Translator's note] *Salvatrice* being the feminine of 'savior', for which there is no English equivalent.

soft tenderness of a mother to which you bear witness to all the unhappy in their misery.' Nevertheless, not all souls were seduced by this religious sentimentalism. Some wanted to secure the certainty of their individual salvation in a theory which offered to account with precision for the origin and the fate of the soul. Certain amongst them demanded this theory from Platonic philosophy. The latter, in teaching the pre-existence of souls to their sensible existence, explained the presence of the human soul bound to the body by way of a fall, a captivation or a forgetting. They also taught the method to deliver us from this life of imprisonment in the flesh.[h] Most importantly, they secured for the philosopher the certitude that his true reality was exterior to this world and that his true self was instead to be located in the eternal plane of divine Thought, dwelling constantly in the transcendent world. This will be the teaching of Plotinus:

> If we must dare to say what appears just to us, contrary to the opinion of others, it is not true that any soul, not even our own, is entirely immersed in the sensible; there is within it something which always remains in the spiritual world.[i]

Others sought this explanation in Gnosticism. In a mythical form, the different Gnostic doctrines narrated the destiny of the soul: souls fell into the sensible world following a drama which was external to themselves. An evil Power was held to have created the sensible world and the souls, denizens of the spiritual world, thereby found themselves imprisoned despite themselves. With the end of the world and the destruction of the evil Power, their ordeal would come to an end. They would return into the spiritual world definitively. Neoplatonism, Gnosticism, the mystery religions, are different responses to a single question: 'Who are we? Where do we come from? Where are we going to?' These responses are never purely theoretical; they demand of the individual a 'conversion', that is to say, a total upheaval of their being, an effort to return to their true self and to the transcendent reality in which it remains grounded (*epistrophê*);[j] a radical transformation of one's way of life and thinking (*metanoia*). Conversion is 'a new birth', whether it is a philosophical or Gnostic conversion, an initiation into the mysteries or a Christian baptism. According to the priest of Isis who appears in book XI of Apuleius' *Metamorphoses*, those who are

---

[h] [Translator's note] The adjective here is: *charnelle*. Literally, this could be 'fleshly imprisonment', which would be unusual in English.
[i] [Translator's note] The quote comes from Plotinus, *Enneads*, IV, 8, 8.
[j] [Translator's note] See Chapter 5 above.

about to be initiated into the mysteries 'would somehow be born again through the providence of Isis, and will be placed in a new path of life, that of salvation'. Thus, new religious categories dominate the thought of the entire period: those of fall and return, death and rebirth, sin and conversion.

Theology

The rise of theology (in the sense of 'scientific theology') from the Hellenistic period onwards, is a further phenomenon which indicates the existence of the crisis of which we have been speaking. In the fifth and fourth centuries BCE, there was not properly speaking any theological literature. When Plato or Aristotle speak of 'ancient theologians', they understood by this the poets who composed fables concerning the gods. 'Theology', in the sense of a 'scientific discourse on the gods' only emerges in certain parts of Plato's *Laws* and in Aristotle's *Metaphysics*, before being developed in Stoicism and Neoplatonism. In the last centuries of paganism, the manuals and treatises dedicated to this matter are extremely abundant. One of the first great systematic manuals which had a great importance for posterity is that of Varro, composed in the first century BCE. His *Antiquitates rerum divinarum*, following a remarkably ordered plan, treats of sacred figures, sacred places, sacred times, sacred actions and objects (the gods). We can see, once again, in Cicero the trace of Stoic theological treatises, and we can ourselves form an idea of this literary genre because of the *Summary of the Traditions of Greek Theology* composed by Cornatus in the first century [CE]. We possess equally the works of Plutarch, the discourses of Maximus of Tyre or of Dion Chrysostom, which investigate particular theological problems. In the third century CE, Porphyry, Plotinus' disciple, writes a *Philosophy Drawn from Oracles*, a treatise *On the Statues of the Gods*, a further treatise *On the Sun*, all of which are studies in pagan theology. Above all, his *Letter to Anebon* is a sequence of aporias relating to the sacred rites and manifestations of the gods. The Neoplatonic philosopher Iamblichus responds to this *Letter to Anebon* with a *Treatise on the Mysteries* which develops a very systematic and coherent pagan theological doctrine. In the tradition of Iamblichus, one finds a veritable little pagan catechism in the treatise *Of the Gods and the World* composed by Sallustius, a contemporary and friend of the emperor Julian. Sallustius dedicates many discourses to theological subjects (like the Mother of the gods and the Sun-King). But it is with Proclus that the tradition of systematic theology issuing from Iamblichus attains its culmination. His *Platonic Theology* is an edifice of grand proportions which, according to his initial plan, aimed to expound successively the fundamental propositions concerning the gods, then all the degrees of the divine hierarchy, and finally the characters of the gods mentioned in the Platonic dialogues.

One could think that this efflorescence of pagan theology in the first centuries of our era is the sign of a strengthening and development of paganism. In fact, this is not the case. Already the theological enterprise of Varro betrays a crisis of conscience. Above all, with the Stoic and the Neoplatonic philosophers, there is a rationalization and systematization of religious notions which they empty of their traditional contents in order to reduce them to a philosophical 'science'. We will, nevertheless, have occasion to remark that certain principles of pagan theology were taken up by Christian theology. This reflects how pagan theology evolved in the direction of a hierarchical monotheism, notably under the influence of the imperial ideology.

Pagan theology gradually took on the form of a systematic teaching, according to a determined plan, in relation to the following points: the sources of revelation, the parts of theology, the methods specific to each part, the fundamental principles of theological reasoning, the relations between the gods, and the relations between the gods and human beings. This plan is already recognizable in the time of Stoicism, but it was developed in all its amplitude by the Neoplatonic philosophers who gave to Stoic principles a new content, by transposing them from the physical to the metaphysical plane.

Pagan theology thus recognizes three sources of revelation concerning the gods: *logos*, *mythos*, *nomos*; that is, reason, mythology and law. First of all, there exist in all human beings innate notions, derived from Nature or universal Reason: these 'sparkles'[k] of *Logos* allow a first knowledge of the existence and the nature of the gods that philosophy will seek to develop and to elevate to a scientific level. To this natural revelation is added the revelation offered by the gods to certain inspired men, by preference at the origins of different peoples. They were, on the one hand, legislators like Minos or Lycurgus; on the other hand, poets such as Musaeus, Orpheus or Homer. To these originary revelations are finally added the oracles of the gods expressed in different manners in the different sanctuaries. But most of the time, these oracles are related to concrete problems, or give foreknowledge of future events or of the will of the gods. This doctrine of the sources of revelation has great historical importance. Indeed, it means that for the pagan theologian the truth is revealed and that truth and tradition, reason and authority are confounded. On this point, pagan and

---

[k] [Translator's note] French: *'étincelles'*.

Christian theology are in perfect agreement. It results from this that theology can only be the exegesis of a revealed given, preserved in the laws, myths and the writings of philosophers or sacred texts.

These different sources of revelation correspond to different modes of knowledge of divine things. By the development of innate notions, human beings can arrive at rational knowledge of the gods as the causes of physical or spiritual phenomena. This is rational theology, sketched by Plato in the *Timaeus* and the *Laws*, developed by Aristotle, oriented in an exclusively physical sense by the Stoics, which the Neoplatonists then brought back to the metaphysical plane. One could think that this rational theology is a systematic construction, without an exegetical character. However, already in Plato and Aristotle, and, above all, in the Stoic and the Neoplatonic philosophers, it is related to a revealed given that one finds in the writings of previous philosophers (the pre-Socratics and Plato), in poetic myths, laws and national traditions, as well as in the oracles and gods. The magnificent systematic edifices of the Neoplatonic philosophers are constructed through commentaries on Plato or the *Chaldean Oracles*. We are in the presence of an essentially exegetical mode of thought.

This introduces us to the problem of the relations between rational knowledge of the gods and the other modes of knowledge of divine things. These other modes of knowledge exist by themselves, independently of rational theology. On the one hand, in the mythical stories, human beings know the gods under the forms that the latter wanted to assume in human imagination. On the other hand, in the laws or customs of cities, people learned to know the modes of prayer and sacrifice according to which the gods want to be honoured. There is, in this, a direct knowledge of the divine which apparently does not require the elaboration of a rational theology. These two modes of knowledge represent mythical and civil theology. Mythical theology is poetic in nature; civil theology has an historical or juridical character. But civil and mythical theologies can become the object of rational theology, which will involve the exegesis of the given revealed content in these two theologies.

This encounter – or this conflict – between rational theology on the one hand, and the civil and mythical theologies on the other hand, played a very important role in the end of paganism. The intervention of reason in the domain of myths and ancestral customs necessarily had to provoke a spiritual crisis: the myths appeared to be irrational or unworthy of the idea that one should have of divinity, and religious laws appeared to be absurd. Faced with civil and mythical theology, rational theology has to choose between two attitudes: rational critique or justification. The former prevails, above all, in the two centuries that preceded our era: one finds its trace in the writings of Cicero in particular, to the point that the defenders of paganism at the end of the third century CE will come to desire, according to the Christian apologist Arnobius, to forbid the reading of the writings of the great Roman orator. The rational justification involved translating into the terms of 'rational theology', whether physical or metaphysical, the language of the myths and religious customs. This was the work of the Stoic and Neoplatonic allegorists.

Whether it critiques the civil and mythical theologies or attempts to justify them rationally, rational theology never pretends to supplant them. Whether it considers these theologies totally false or whether it claims to uncover their truth, rational theology always maintains that these two theologies are good for the people and useful to the city. One must submit oneself to these traditions which are necessary for maintaining the morality of the lower classes in their duties, as the historian Polybius remarks. The religious practice of the 'rational theologians' or the philosophers has also had very diverse degrees of intensity. Certain philosophers considered religious practice to be unworthy of the sage, because he is able to reach God directly by the spiritual elevation of his thought. Others, on the contrary, strove to observe as religiously as possible the traditional rites, because they considered them to respond to the explicit will of the gods. At the end of antiquity, the first attitude – as we will have occasion to underline – is that of Plotinus and Porphyry. The second attitude is that of Iamblichus, Proclus and the Neoplatonic school in Athens. But, whatever the practical attitude of the rational theologian was, the very existence of a rational theology puts paganism in danger. Whether one identifies the gods with the forces of nature, like the Stoics, or with the Platonic Ideas, like the Neoplatonic philosophers, one removes from the traditional gods their numinous character, orienting oneself instead towards a physical or metaphysical monotheism.

The theological work of Varro, undertaken with the evident aim of religious restoration, allows us to see these dangers to traditional paganism. Varro himself is a rational theologian, which is to say that he gives a cosmological interpretation to the Graeco-Roman religious myths. However, in order to save Roman religion, he undertakes a work of 'civil' theology: that is to say, restoring a historical sense to the traditional rites and names of the gods. As opposed to the rational and mythical theologies of Greek origin, civil theology will be purely Roman, thanks to him. Nevertheless, Varro does not free himself from the religious representations of rational theology. If he wants to restore 'civil' theology, it is because he fears that the gods will perish from the negligence and forgetting of his fellow citizens. This means that for him the gods of civil theology, the traditional gods of Rome, exist only in the consciousness of the Romans: as representations with no reality except in the thought of human beings. If Varro wants to save them, it is exclusively for political reasons. It is only the gods of rational theology, that is to say, the cosmic forces, who in his eyes have substance and reality.

The methods of rational theology vary according to the objects to which they are applied. When they take for their object mythical theology, they utilise the allegorical method, based upon which they discover in the 'fable' a teaching concerning physical processes (if the theology is of Stoic inspiration), or a teaching concerning the origin of the Ideas and the intelligible Models (if the theology is of Neoplatonic inspiration). When rational theology is exercised in an autonomous way, it rather uses the analogical method (the definition of divine attributes by analogy with the highest quality[l] of things[m]) or the negative method (definition of divine attributes by negation of all conceivable qualities).

Rational theology itself has its own fundamental dogmas. They had been defined by Plato in the *Laws* and we rediscover formulations of them until the end of paganism: the gods exist, they take care of human beings, and their justice is inflexible. These fundamental dogmas are the points of departure for the essential demonstrations of theology: the proof of the existence of gods, the theory of providence and free will, and the doctrines on prayer and retribution.

We must now specify the role of rational theology in the religious evolution which led paganism to its end. Beginning from the first century of the Christian era, rational theology, above all, took the form of a justification and an apology of the pagan myths and rites. But the philosophical elements which were used to achieve this end led, in fact, to the elaboration of a hierarchical monotheism, in such a way that polytheism could no longer represent anything but a sort of conventional language without any actual content.[n]

---

[l] [Translator's note] Hadot here addresses a procedure that will appear again in Christian theology. For instance, Aquinas uses this logic in the *a posteriori* proofs of the existence of God: if we see beauty, goodness, etc. in the sensible world, then there must be a supreme or 'maximum' form of beauty, goodness, etc. Moreover, in the discussions concerning apophatic and cataphatic methods in theology in the Middle Ages, a way to speak of God's attributes without reducing them to human categories (and thus, taking into consideration the arguments of negative theology) was the superlative method: e.g. if at issue is the attribute X in some being[s] in the world (let's say good), God is necessarily more-than-X, because his goodness cannot be fully understood or captured in human language.

[m] [Translator's note] French: *en portant au maximum* ...

[n] [Translator's note] The original is: *veritable contenu.*

The Stoics had posed the principle of the fundamental unity of all the gods. However, for them, the gods were but different names for the same cosmic power. Varro expresses this doctrine in the following way:

One must maintain that all of the gods and Goddesses are the one Jupiter, whether as parts of God or powers of God. All this universal life is that of a single living being, which contains all of the gods as powers, members or parts.

Jupiter is thus conceived as the original and reasonable fire which, in unfolding his activity, successively becomes the other elements – air, water and earth – to which, according to the principles of Stoic allegory, the different gods correspond. The total intermixture which constitutes the substance of the universe remains intact and unchanged, but certain powers predominate over others at a determined moment of the cosmic period[o] and other powers are contained within the dominant power according to the mode which is proper to it: the gods are all contained in Zeus, according to the mode proper to Zeus, and in Hera, according to the mode proper to Hera. This is the principle of denomination by predominance. This principle will be taken up in Neoplatonic theology, where it will be transposed onto the metaphysical plane, so that the gods correspond to Platonic Ideas, rather than different physical elements. Kronos, Rhea and Zeus, for example, will stand in relation to each other in the same way that could support the relation between the Platonic Ideas of being, life and intelligence. A single intelligible substance will abide in all three. Precisely because this intelligible substance is constituted by being, life and intelligence, it will be called, respectively, Kronos, Rhea or Zeus, according to the moment of its self-constitution in which being, life or intelligence most predominates. We must underline the following fact: this is exactly the same theological principle which allows certain Christian theologians, notably Marius Victorinus, to give an account of the consubstantiality and distinction of the divine hypostases in the Trinity. The Father is predominantly being, the Son is predominantly life and the Holy Spirit is predominantly intelligence.[p] But the three are present in all three, according to the mode proper to each.

This significant convergence is equally verified if one examines the doctrine of the divine hierarchy. Stoicism already knew the notion of a

---

[o] [Translator's note] French: *période cosmique*.

[p] [Translator's note] Hadot wrote his doctoral thesis on this figure; published as Pierre Hadot, *Marius Victorinus: Recherches sur sa vie et ses œuvres* (Paris: Collection des Études Augustiniennes, 1971).

progressive degradation of the divine power, originally concentrated in fire, then distended little by little into air, earth and water. In Neoplatonic theology, the degradation of divine power results from the augmentation of multiplicity. Concentrated in the original and absolute One, divine power is diffused and unfolds itself,[q] first at the level of thought and then at that of soul, which are unified multiplicities, to be then, finally, dispersed into the sensible world and in matter. We rediscover here, then, the representations of imperial ideology. The One is the transcendent and inaccessible God. Thought or *Logos* is the second God, the Mediator which communicates the power of unity to the multiplicity of beings. A single divine power is thus diffused across all the degrees of reality. So, here again, we must underline that this theology is not solely that of pagans like Numenius or Plotinus or Porphyry. It is equally the theology of the Christians, Origen and Eusebius of Caesarea. They also distinguish between 'God', the transcendent Father, and the *Logos*, for which the word 'God' is no longer a proper name, but an attribute. This *Logos* has the same function as the second god of the pagan Theologians. It creates and rules the world, while the transcendent God remains immobile and without contact with matter. Both for the pagans as for the Christians, we can note the existence of the same theology, which is a hierarchical monotheism.

It is the same type of theology which we find in an apocryphal volume entitled *The Chaldean Oracles*, which was composed in the era of Marcus Aurelius by Julian 'the Chaldean' and Julian the Theurgist. These oracles would become, for the Neoplatonic philosophers after Plotinus, a sacred Writing as venerable as the works of the divine Plato. Again, we find in this text a transcendent God: the Father, whose Intellect and Will, originally combined with him, are put to work and thus conquer an independent reality, during the process of the creation of the intelligible World. The universal Soul, engendered by the Father, spreads the waves[r] of life in the sensible world. One could say that all Neoplatonism, from Iamblichus to Damascius, is born from the effort which it was necessary to make in order to reconcile the sacred Writing[s] that *The Chaldean Oracles* represented with the interpretation that Plotinus gave to this other sacred Writing, Plato's texts. Whereas the *Oracles* spoke of a transcendent God who possessed an Intellect and a Will, for Plotinus the transcendent God is absolutely One and simple, without having within him the least trace of the duality that the

---

[q] [Translator's note] Original: *détendi*.
[r] [Translator's note] French: *répand les flots*.
[s] [Translator's note] Hadot here capitalizes: *Écriture*. This indicates an analogy with 'Scripture'.

presence of an Intellect would imply. In the eyes of Plotinus, the Intellect did not pre-exist in the first God. It resulted only from the original One, by a process of emanation and conversion which engenders all of the intelligible World. All Neoplatonists, except perhaps Porphyry, remain faithful to this idea of an absolutely simple first Principle, transcending all multiplicity and duality, even that kind of duality which could be found in an Intellect which thinks itself. Relatively to this first Principle, the God of the *Oracles*, with its Intellect and Will, is placed at an inferior order of rank. These three entities serve as the model of the hierarchy of triads which in the eyes of the Neoplatonic philosophers constitute the structure of the world: 'rest', 'procession', 'conversion'; or 'being', 'life', 'intelligence'; or again, 'finite', 'infinite', 'mixture of finite and infinite'. These triadic schemes will serve to construct a vast system within which the materials[t] taken from Plato, the Orphic traditions, the *Chaldean Oracles*, the Greek myths, will be systematized: all the gods being ranked after the transcendent One according to the successive plans of 'Henads', 'intelligible gods', 'intelligible and intellective gods' and 'purely intellective gods'. These are vast artificial constructions which no longer have a close relationship with the content of the ancient beliefs that they aimed to defend.

Piety and the mystical pagans

In what regards God, we strongly hold these four principles: faith, truth, love and hope. We must believe that there is no salvation except in conversion towards God; and, when one has believed, one must place all of one's zeal in knowing the truth about God; and once this knowledge is acquired, one must be filled with love for Him whom we have known; and when one is thus filled with love, one must nourish one's soul throughout all one's life with beautiful hopes.[u]

One might well think that these lines were written by a Christian. They are, however, extracted from the *Letter to Marcella* by the famous adversary of Christianity, the philosopher Porphyry. We can observe here the extraordinary metamorphosis of paganism in the last centuries of its existence. If one recalls the profession of faith of Goethe's Faust one could say that, in what concerns their fundamental 'sentiment', the pagans and Christians of the last centuries of paganism are extraordinarily close:

---

[t] [Translator's note] Here: *données*, more literally 'givens'.
[u] [Translator's note] Porphyry, *Letter to Marcella*, 24.

So great is the eternal mystery, fill your soul with it, and if by this sentiment you are happy, call it what you like: Happiness! Heart! Love! God! I myself do not have any name for it. The sentiment is all, the name is only the smoke and sound which veils the heavenly fire!

In this evolution of the pagan religious sentiment, the representation of a transcendent God, situated beyond all of the other gods, plays a fundamental role. This unique God, source of all divinity and of all being, which transcends all gods, absolutely ineffable, unknowable, is an unfathomable mystery, which fascinates souls in love with the absolute. Already from the first century CE, if the fragment which is reported to us by Eusebius of Caesarea is authentic, there is Apollonius of Tyre, a neo-Pythagorean, whose biography written by Philostratus is a beautiful example of pagan hagiography. Apollonius explicitly ties the notion of a transcendent God to the exigency of a spiritual cult: to the first God, which is One and separated from everything else, one will not offer any material sacrifice, but the elevation of one's thought, which is the highest part of our being. Porphyry, in his treatise *On the Abstinence from Animal Food*, takes up and develops this doctrine. To the God which is above all things, it is unnecessary to offer either incense, sacrifice, or audible speech, but one must adore him in silence. Only the elevation of one's soul towards him is a sacrifice worthy of him. The philosopher is the priest of the transcendent God; he is thus superior to the priests of particular gods. Only the philosopher knows how we must honour the transcendent God and reach him deep in one's heart. This doctrine probably allows us to explain the anecdote that Porphyry recounts to us in *The Life of Plotinus*. Another disciple of Plotinus, Amelius, who was devout and liked to offer sacrifices, wanted to take his master to the temple. Plotinus answered: '[i]t is for the gods to come to me, not for me to go to the gods'. This response clearly means that Plotinus considered himself to be in a direct and immediate relation to the transcendent God, superior to all of the other gods. Plotinus and Porphyry aspire, in effect, to a union without intermediary with the supreme God. It is a matter of the unitive experience that the moderns call 'mystical ecstasy'. Porphyry relates that during the six years that he lived with him, Plotinus attained the supreme goal four times, namely: the union with the first and transcendent God. A large part of Plotinus' work, nevertheless, preserves the marks of these mystical experiences. This desire for an experiential and unitive contact with the core of being will remain present in all of the Neoplatonic tradition. Damascius, who was one of the last leaders of the school of Athens, relates to us that his master Isidore did not want to adore the statues of the gods, because he wanted, above all, to approach the gods who are hidden 'within': that is to say, as Damascius tells us, in the secret of absolute Unknowing.[v] This absolute Unknowing is the state of which Damascius speaks at the beginning of his great treatise, *On the Principles*. It is the state in which we find ourselves faced with the Absolute, absolutely ineffable, without relation with us, which is no longer even the Principle, insofar is it transcendent and separated.[w] Nevertheless, this One, this Absolute, this transcendent and ineffable God, unique and separate, that one can only reach by abandoning all form, determination, concepts, discourse and all personality, by an ecstasy which brings being back to its source, is far, indeed, from the gods of the ancient religion.

Nevertheless, these Neoplatonic philosophers consider themselves to be fervent pagans. Plotinus, it is true, seems to have been dismissive of religious practice and Porphyry, for his part, had on this subject a somewhat hesitant attitude. The latter's *Philosophy Drawn from Oracles* is a treatise on pagan devotion; while his *Letter to Anebo* is a sequence of *aporias* concerning the cult of the gods. Porphyry seems to have thought that the religious practices were a means for the salvation of non-philosophers, whereas the philosopher, priest of the supreme God, should dedicate himself to the spiritual cult of the transcendent God. Porphyry enunciates the fundamental maxims of this spiritual cult in relation to the Neopythagorean tradition, in his *Letter to Marcella*:

> In every action, every work, every speech, you should have the sentiment of the presence of God who observes and who is watching [over you] ...
> The sole temple worthy of God is the intelligence of the sage ...
> It is not the language of the sage, which is precious before God, but his works: because the very silence of the sage honours God; as for the fool, he must offer prayers and sacrifices, he defiles the Divinity.[x]

Plotinus and Porphyry seem to have considered philosophy as a sort of transcendent religion, that of the supreme God. But their successors, the Neoplatonic philosophers of Syria and Athens had a wholly different conception of the relationships between philosophy and religion. They will place beyond philosophy what they call 'hieratic': that is to say, sacred operations, the strict observance of rites and sacraments desired by the

---

[v] [Translator's note] French: *Inconnaissance absolue*.

[w] [Translator's note] The Absolute is so transcendent and separate that it cannot even be called a principle anymore: it is beyond principle, it is more-than-principle.

[x] [Translator's note] These quotes coming, respectively, from Porphyry, *Letter to Marcella*, 12, 11, 16.

gods. Iamblichus was the theoretician of 'movement' in his *Treatise on the Mysteries*. For him, the position of Plotinus and Porphyry is utopian. Only a small number of men in the evening of life can hope to attain union with the transcendent God. Human nature is too corrupt because of its union with the body, to normally be able to aspire towards union with this supreme beatitude. The only way which is open towards the divine world is therefore that which the gods themselves have fixed. It can appear repugnant to our reason, which understands neither the sense of rites, nor even the names that the gods want us to pronounce in the ceremonies. But, precisely, it is necessary to renounce the intelligence for the sake of faith. We must carry out the rites without understanding them, because their effects surpass our intelligence. Their efficacy does not depend on our reason, nor on our consciousness: it is contained within the sacraments themselves. These reflections make us think irresistibly of certain formulations of Pascal concerning religious practice.

These theories were abundantly put into place in the schools of Alexandria and Athens between the fourth and sixth centuries, and in certain Roman aristocratic milieus at the end of the fourth century. The *Letters* and *Discourses* of the emperor Julian, the *Life of the Sophists* written by Eunapius, the *Life of Proclus* by Marimus, the *Life of Isidore* by Damascius, abound with edifying anecdotes that instruct us on the piety of these intellectual milieus. These devoted pagans practice fasting with fervour, make pilgrimages to famous sanctuaries and practice sacrifices, divination and ritual baths. They are attentive to all the divine warnings, to the dreams, mysterious signs, miraculous cures and multiple testimonies to divine benevolence. They believe in exorcisms and visions of the future in mirrors. One is surprised to find such credulity, naivety and superstition amongst men who, otherwise, were remarkable logicians and metaphysicians. But in the second century, Lucian in *The Lover of Lies, or The Doubter* had already depicted the representatives of Platonic, Aristotelian and Stoic philosophical schools of the time as sharing this superstitious naivety. The tradition, we see, was firmly established. However, with these last Neoplatonic thinkers, religious practice is accompanied by nearly ecstatic religious sentiment. Damascius recounts to us, for example, that Heraiscus was capable of physically sensing if the statue of a god was really animated by divine power: he would suffer a wound to his heart under the effect of a divine possession, his body and his soul would leap with enthusiasm.

The life of these last faithful pagans is not only filled by the supernatural and the marvellous. It is regimented according to a puritanism and a hatred of the sensible world which are very distant from the ancient religion. In these milieus, a deep horror reigned concerning everything related to sexual realities. Heraiscus suffered a headache if he found himself near to a woman having her period and the philosopher Hypatia cures a disciple of his passion for her by showing him sheets covered in her menstrual blood. The ideal of these pagan circles is the angelic life: 'whoever is truly hieratic', says Proclus, 'shines like an angel in all of his virtue'. The 'angelic' life was also a term employed by Christians of this period to designate the monastic life. Pagans and Christians aspired then to the same ideal, to flee this world. It is true that, persecuted by the Christian emperors and taking refuge in metaphysical abstractions, the last pagans had become, in their turn, strangers here below.

Paganism and Christianity: The struggle

'Strangers here below': this was precisely the reproach made to Christians in pagan polemics. 'The figure of this world passes [away].' Was Christianity not, in its origins and at its root, an eschatological doctrine? Salvation approaches, the end of days is imminent, the kingdom of God will manifest itself, a new heaven and a new earth will be created, the new Jerusalem will descend from the skies. Christianity, because of this fundamental inspiration, is necessarily the negation of the present world in its political, social, economic and even physical structure. The pagan philosophers clearly sensed this, and one could say that this was the fundamental reproach they bore towards Christianity, whether their polemic is situated on the political and historical plane or on that of metaphysics.

In the first place, one could even think that a large part of the pagan philosophers' argumentation against Christianity was uniquely inspired by a conformist mentality, by a blind respect for the established order and received customs. Christianity, they underline, is hardly attractive: it lacks prestige, heroism, splendour. Jesus, at the moment of his trial and death, did not conduct himself as a sage or a divine man. He let his face be spit upon and was crowned with thorns. He did not defend himself with any vigorous and strong discourse, but let himself be insulted like a criminal at the crossroads. He died in an ignominious torture. His famous resurrection took place in the presence of poor women and simpletons. The apostles were rustics and unfortunate wretches, who followed Christ in their naivety. Their end was as shameful as that of Christ. Christian propaganda, in any case, has always been addressed by predilection to people without culture, the poor, inspiring scorn in them for the truly noble life and for worldly wealth. In Christianity, there is thus no place for the essential values of Hellenism: heroism, eloquence, beauty and science.

Other than this, Christians are reduced to 'enemies of the human race'. They refuse to integrate themselves into the life of the city and the religious and cultural traditions which give them their cohesion. Nevertheless, Celsus notes, they eat, drink, marry and participate in the joys of life as necessary evils which are inherent to it. They thus profit from the political and social order. They should, therefore, pay a just honorific tribute to the emperors who watch over this order and they should fulfil the duties that life imposes. If they refuse to accept the traditions and the morals of the nation in which they live, they should at the least go into exile and renounce participating in common life. In the *Octavius* of Minucius Felix, the pagan interlocutor in the dialogue speaks of Christians as a 'people who hide themselves and who flee the light'.

Behind these reproaches, there is more than the habitual hostility of people towards individuals who might trouble the established order in one way or another. There is also, in fact, an entire philosophy of history. To refuse the national religious traditions is to be condemned to error; it means to separate oneself from the divine in order to be blinded by human inventions. In fact, according to paganism, the truth has been revealed to ancient humanity by Nature. At the origins of each people, there are divine men – legislators, poets, kings or inspired philosophers like Linos,[y] Musaeus, Orpheus, Homer and Pythagoras amongst the Greeks. Moreover, each people is guided by a distinct 'genius', god or daemon, the inspiration for and guardian who inspires and guards the laws, traditions, morals, beliefs and national rites. The more ancient a religious or philosophical doctrine is, the closer it is to the primitive state of humanity in which Reason was still present in all its purity, which means to say the more true and venerable it is. Historical tradition is thus the norm of truth: truth and tradition, reason and authority are identified. This is why Celsus entitled his polemical work against the Christians: *True Logos*. He intends by this the 'ancient Norm', 'True Tradition'. This traditionalism is, moreover, resolutely pluralist. The Greeks and Romans are not the only ones to possess precious religious traditions. The Egyptians, Chaldeans, Indians and Hebrews were also nations which were inspired by the gods at their origins. Any tradition, however venerable it may be, cannot claim to possess the truth alone. The truth is spread under diverse forms to all of the peoples and no one nation is the sole depository of divine secrets. 'To such a great mystery, it is not

---

[y] [Translator's note] The text reads 'Linos', but the context renders this improbable; Hadot is perhaps referring to Minos.

possible to arrive by a single path,' Symmachus will say at the end of the fourth century. A century before, Porphyry had already affirmed that he does not know any path to salvation which was universally valuable for all people. When the pagans reproach the Christians for not integrating into the life of the city and for refusing the ancient traditions, they accuse them at the same time of lacking historical roots, and of being separated from the living sources of truth.

It is interesting to observe the Christian reaction to this argument. When Christianity triumphed politically, and became itself a national religion, it would come to oppose to this conservative traditionalism a decided progressivism. With Ambrose, it will speak of a necessary evolution, of progress and of inevitable maturation; with Prudentius, it will rail against the blind fidelity of the pagans to antiquated customs. However, in the first centuries of the Christian era, the apologists take up a different attitude, accepting the postulate of their adversaries. For them, truth becomes identified with tradition and antiquity. They affirm precisely that they represent the most ancient tradition of humankind, and that this tradition is the only true one, while all of the others only deform this primitive and unique revelation. Christian apologists inherited this mode of argumentation from the Jewish apologists. But they complement them by demonstrating that the Christian Church is the only and true legitimate inheritor of the Hebraic tradition; that it is the true Israel and that it alone comprehends the significance of the Law and the Prophets.

Pagans and Christians were thus embroiled in a vast chronological discussion. Each sought to show that its tradition was older than that of the adversary. One attempted thus to date, respectively, Moses and the legislators, poets and founders of religions amongst the different peoples. From this perspective, one can see the ideological importance of the edited chronologies, whether those of the pagans like Phlegon of Tralles or of the Christians like Julius Africanus, Hippolytus or Eusebius of Caesarea.

Porphyry and the emperor Julian place the discussion on another terrain. They do not contest the antiquity of the Jewish people. Porphyry will even go so far as to draw upon the testimony of the mysterious Sanchuniathon, who allegedly lived prior to the Trojan war, to confirm the fact of this antiquity. However, they contest the Christians' right to appropriate for themselves the history of a people whose national traditions they do not respect. Porphyry and Julian admit fully the legitimacy and value of Jewish traditions. The God of the Jews is recognized in his place in the pantheon of humanity. Nevertheless, [they claim,] the Jews were wrong in their wish to make their national God a universal God. As for the Christians, they have no right to call upon a tradition to which they are unfaithful; from the Jews, they have conserved only the sour mood.[z] Moreover, Porphyry submits the Jewish sacred Scripture to a very close historical critique. On the one hand, these writings are written much later than they have been presented as having been written. On the other hand, nothing links these texts to Christianity:

> Nothing survives of Moses: one says that all his works have been destroyed with the Temple. What exists under his name has been composed eleven hundred and eighty years after his death, by Esdras, in a very imprecise manner. And are these writings in which Christ is designated a God, God-Logos, or yet again, Creator of the World, written by Moses? Who has spoken of the crucifixion of Christ?

Porphyry shows equally that the *Book of Daniel* is a prophecy composed *post eventum*, not in the times of Cyrus, but in the times of Antiochus Epiphanes. On this point, Porphyry prefigures the conclusions of modern textual criticism.

Porphyry submits the evangelical writings to the same acute critique. He studies the New Testament very attentively and does not let any contradiction nor any incoherence pass, whether it is a matter of the genealogies of Christ, the accounts of the Passion or of the Resurrection. He insists on the lack of intelligence of the Apostles, the rivalries and the quarrels between Peter and Paul, the deformation of the teachings of Jesus. These critiques reflect[aa] very probably the same fundamental intention. It is a matter of showing to the Christians that their religion lacks historical foundations; that it cannot even be assured of the authenticity of its own traditions, despite their being historically recent.

In this discussion, pagans and Christians thus have an analogous conception of the truth. It is for them a historical fact of divine origin: a revelation given by God to humanity at a given moment. It follows from this that their conceptions of philosophy and theology are identical: human thought could only be exegetical, which is to say that it must strive to interpret an initial given: the revelation contained in myths, traditions and the most ancient laws.

In the eyes of the pagans, Christians do not have a true historical place. This spiritual situation has metaphysical reasons. The Christian doctrine, in its original content, was totally opposed to Hellenic metaphysics. By the

---

[z] [Translator's note] Original: *aigre.*
[aa] [Translator's note] French: *correspondent.*

time when Christianity began to develop, the pagan philosophical schools which remained alive – that is to say, Stoicism and Platonism – commonly agreed upon the following axioms: first of all, in virtue of his goodness, God cannot cease to act and to exercise his creative thought; second, in virtue of his rationality, God can only think an entirely determined system of Ideas or of Reasons which was, therefore, finite and immutable. It follows from this that the World must at the same time be finite and infinite; finite in its structures and infinite in its duration. Finite in its structure, the World will contain a finite number of essences or souls. Infinite in its duration, which is a result of eternal divine thought, the World will be subject either to an eternal movement (of which the stars provide the best model) or to an eternal cycle of births and destructions: with the number of essences, souls or 'reasons' remaining rigorously identical within each of these periods. The Creator of Hellenic metaphysics is a good king whose power is limited by the Law (the Universe of Ideas, Reason) to which he is himself submitted. His work, the sensible World, is without doubt, according to the Platonic philosophers, inferior to the immutable World of the Ideas. But it emanates from it; it is its copy, and it is thus the most beautiful and perfect of its kind.

For the pagan polemicists, Christians imagine God as a capricious tyrant and they despise the sensible World, whose existence is totally irrational, according to their doctrines. They believe, indeed, that God has accomplished and will accomplish a totally unpredictable and arbitrary sequence of actions: the creation of the world in a moment of time, the election of the Jewish people, the rejection of the Jewish people, the Incarnation, the Resurrection and finally the destruction of the world. Proclus will ask the Christians:

Why did God suddenly bring himself to accomplish the creative act, since he had been inactive for an infinity of time? Was it because of the idea that this [creation] would be best? In that case, did he ignore what was best until then? If he did so … it is rather strange; and if, on the contrary, he did know it, why then did he not begin [the act of creation] earlier?

The election of the Jewish people is equally totally irrational. Why did He leave the worshippers of idols in the most complete ignorance for myriads of time, and then only manifest Himself to a small people who only live in a small part of Palestine? This is what the emperor Julian stressed. Celsus, however, already compared both Jews and Christians to a group of earthworms who claim to be the sole object of divine attentions:

We are those to whom God reveals in advance and presages all things; neglecting the universe and the course of the stars, without taking care of this vast earth, it is for us alone that he governs, and with us alone that he communicates by his messengers ... It is for us that all has been created and everything is organised in order to serve we alone.

That God has decided at a given moment to incarnate Himself is also, and doubly irrational. Why did He leave humanity for so many centuries deprived of the benefits of revelation, and why did He permit so many souls to be lost? Above all, how and why did God have need to incarnate Himself? Is not He present everywhere? Has He need to show himself as a parvenu who wants to show off before the mob? If God descends in person towards humanity, He disrupts the order of all the universe. He subjects Himself to change, which is impossible, and even more, to a change in the direction of what is inferior. The idea of the end of the world is even more inadmissible. On this point, it is Porphyry who levels the most vigorous criticisms. How will it be possible that the Creator made 'the figure of this world pass [away]'? Must we suppose that He had not been able to give to creation in the first moment a form adequate and appropriate to the universe and that He was only able to perceive this after the fact? Why then this unfathomable decision to change?

Finally, the resurrection also disrupts the order of the universe. It interrupts the ordered succession of creatures, and the laws of transformation of the elements. Porphyry summarizes the essential parts of these objections in the following terms:

> One will say: 'God can do everything.' But that is not true. God cannot do everything. He cannot make two times two one hundred and not four. For his power is not the only rule of his acts and of his will. He also wants things to have their intrinsic rule and he observes the law of this order.

Contamination

Let us specify that by 'contamination' we mean the process by which paganism or Christianity were brought to adopt ideas or behaviours characteristic of their adversary. The contamination of Christianity by paganism began very soon in the history of Christianity. It was in some way necessarily bound to the missionary character of Christianity. In order to translate its message within the universe of Graeco-Roman thought, nascent Christianity was forced to adapt itself to pre-existing cultural and artistic forms, awaiting until much later to merge with the political and social forms of the ancient world. The contamination was facilitated by the very fact of the evolution of paganism of which we have spoken: the ancient religion transformed itself little by little in virtue of political, social, ideological and philosophical causes. It evolved towards a hierarchical monotheism, towards mysticism and devotion. It is into this neo-paganism that Christianity had intimately merged.[bb] It borrows from it the very idea of theology, the theological methods and principles, the very idea and the methods of mysticism. The pagan polemicists reproach the Christians for these theological borrowings. They denounce their disguised polytheism. The notion of the 'Son of God' seems to them incompatible with a monotheism which pretends to be absolute. The emperor Julian played an active role in underlining this inconsistency: it sufficed for him to evoke the quarrels of Christian theologians of his time discussing the subject of the resemblance or lack of resemblance which could exist between God and his Son. Moreover, the Christian apologist Eusebius of Caesarea, for his part, related the doctrines of Plotinus and Numenius concerning the First and Second God to the Christian teaching concerning the relationship between the Father and the Son. On the other hand, as Porphyry remarked, did not the Christian doctrine of the angels imply an implicit polytheism? The angels, were they not, like the gods, powers[cc] subordinated to the Supreme God and charged by Him with a particular function in the administration of the universe? Indeed, it is true that certain remarks of Origen concerning the angels differ little from the pagan teaching on the subject of the gods, the elements and the nations. After Constantine's conversion, the phenomenon of contamination is prolonged and even intensified. Indeed, the Christian emperors inherit the ceremonial of the court inaugurated by Diocletian, but also, and above all, the imperial ideology. The figure of Christ and that of the emperor tend to be superimposed. Christ was conceived as a transcendent emperor, surrounded by the celestial court, and as a mediator between God and human beings, but the emperor himself became like another Christ, a sort of incarnation of the *Logos*. Neoplatonic philosophy, even though it was resolutely pagan, more and more impregnated Christian theology. Proclus' hierarchical universe served as a model for the celestial and ecclesiastical hierarchies of Pseudo-Dionysus. Hierarchy and hieraticism, two notions which summarize the essence of dying paganism at its end, are also two notions

---

[bb] [Translator's note] The original is: *mêlé*.
[cc] [Translator's note] Again, it is: *puissances*.

that could serve to define the Byzantine Christian world. The contamination between neo-paganism and Christianity reaches in these notions its highest degree.

In the opposite direction, the contamination of paganism by Christianity is effected much more slowly and in a more limited way. In the first centuries, one could note in the pagan milieus certain fairly superficial attempts at assimilating Christian elements. The emperor Alexander Severus, for instance, makes a place for Christ in his pantheon. A certain Mara Bar Serapion, in a letter written in Syriac, compares Christ, whom he calls the 'sage king' of the Jews, with Socrates and Pythagoras. Even though all three had been put to death by their fellow citizens, all three have survived: Socrates, because of Plato; Pythagoras, because of the statue which was erected in his honour; and Christ, in the laws that he promulgated. Even more important than these fugitive rapprochements is the phenomenon of symbiosis which is produced in certain periods, notably after the conversion of Constantine, in the first half of the fourth century in Rome: when pagan and Christian images, pagan and Christian usages peacefully coexist, for example in the Roman calendar of 354 CE. This symbiosis corresponds to a certain ideal of tolerance that in the same period the philosopher Themistius and, somewhat later, the historian Ammianus Marcellinus will nobly defend. Ammianus, an admirer of the emperor Julian, will reproach him for his repressive measures against the Christian rhetors. Additionally, he does not hide a certain admiration for the Christian religion, but will himself profess a sort of 'neutralist monotheism'. Certain pagans even hold a measure of veneration for Christ. This symbiosis between Christianity and paganism is sometimes established in the inner recesses of individual consciences. The most extraordinary example is that of Synesius, the disciple of Hypatia (the pagan philosopher) and Christian bishop of Cyrene. His *Hymns* could as well be considered as inspired by the trinitarian Christian doctrine as, on the contrary, representatives of a pagan theology that one could link to Porphyry's tradition. Concerning many of the figures of this epoch, one could well ask whether they are Christians or pagans. This is the case of Ausonius and Claudian: officially Christians, they remain essentially pagans in their poetic inspiration. Paganism and Christianity are equally juxtaposed in the personality of Boethius: there is hardly any trace of Christianity in the *Consolation of Philosophy*! For a long time, doubt surrounded the authenticity of his theological writings.

Christian thought had little influence on pagan thought. All the same, one can recognize that the pagan polemicists were brought to accept the Christian problematic, in order to refute it. It is possible, for example, that Celsus elaborated his philosophy of history expressly so as to respond to that of the Christian Justin, as has been shown by Carl Andersen.[dd] One could perhaps also discern in Plotinus a certain manner of presenting the myth of Kronos and Zeus, using a Christian vocabulary, with the intention of better refuting the Gnostic Christian doctrine of the fabrication of the world by a God-creator. Porphyry seems to have gone the farthest in this direction. Iamblichus, in fact, reproaches him for having made an appeal, in the *Letter to Anebo*, to the opinion of atheists, that is to say, Christians, who think that all divination is the work of evil demons. Porphyry probably considered that this opinion of the Christians merited a serious examination. Nevertheless, one must not think, as several historians have done, that the evocation by Porphyry of the virtues of faith, hope and love which is found in the passage of the *Letter to Marcella* is drawn from Christianity. This would be to misrecognize the evolution of paganism of which we have spoken above: a similar doctrine is found in several pagan texts, notably the *Chaldean Oracles*.

It is Christian institutions which most fascinated the pagans. The religious reforms of the emperor Julian are the best proof of this. Already at the beginning of the fourth century, Maximinus Daia had attempted to reorganize the pagan priesthood on the model of the Christian Church, constituting them in some way as ecclesiastical provinces directed by a metropolitan centre. Julian goes much farther than this. Not only does he take up the idea of Maximinus Daia, but, above all, he desires that the new pagan Church imitate the Christian Church in its different liturgical, catechistic and charitable activities. Even if it is a little tendentious, the testimony of Gregory of Nazianzus on this subject does not lack interest: [had he succeeded,] Julian would have wanted to institute in all cities a religious teaching concerning 'Hellenic', that is, pagan belief. This would have given to the listeners moral and mystical exegeses of the pagan myths. He would have equally wanted to establish liturgical prayers, and public penitence for sinners. He wanted to found refuges, hospices and sanctuaries for young women, as well as monasteries and places reserved for contemplation. Many of the emperor's letters reveal his intention of imposing on the pagan clergy a discipline analogous to that which existed in the Christian clergy. The priests must lead an irreproachable life. They will refrain from licentious readings and from frequenting theatres and circus games. All their activity will be consecrated to the life of prayer, to philosophical reading, to the recitation of hymns in honour of the divinities, and to missionary and charitable tasks:

[dd] [Translator's note] Carl Andersen, 'Justin und der Mittlere Platonismus', *Zeitschrift für die Neutestamentaliche Wissenschaft* 44 (1952–3): 157–95.

What has contributed most to the development of atheism (that is to say, Christianity) is humanity towards strangers, the care for the burial of the dead and a simple solemnity of life. This is what we must occupy ourselves with, without any dissimulation.

Julian believed he was defending the ancient religion. Nevertheless, on the one hand, the philosopher-emperor, in wanting to give to paganism the organization of the Christian Church, reveals the profound influence exercised by the Christian education he had received in his childhood. On the other hand, the religion which he thought to restore was not the old pagan religion: it is a philosophical monotheism, expressed in the language of Greek mythology. What confirms most clearly the profound transformation of ancient religion is the very fact that Julian was able to form the idea of imposing the institutions of the Christian Church upon paganism. It was necessary, in order for this to be the case, that paganism become a body of doctrine and fixed dogmas, furnished with a systematic theology and a precise moral doctrine. This is exactly what the Neoplatonism of Iamblichus had brought to Greek religion. But this was already the end of paganism and the emergence of a new religion – this neopaganism which would be revived in the Renaissance in the hearts of many of the humanists and to which Gemistus Pletho attempted to give a concrete existence at Mystra.

14 MODELS OF HAPPINESS PROPOSED BY THE ANCIENT PHILOSOPHERS

Divine Beatitude

For the ancients,[1] 'the Blissful ones' (*makares*) was somehow a name proper to the gods who 'have an easy life', as Homer sang.[2] This beatitude consisted for them in immortality, endless youth, and a life eternally filled with pleasures, festivals and feasts. Yet, little by little, under the influence of nascent rationalism, a moral dimension was introduced into the representation of the gods. One can note the first signs of this in Hesiod, then amongst the pre-Socratics and tragic poets.[3] But it is with Plato and Aristotle that this theological shift is consummated. Plato's Creator in the *Timaeus* is good and generous and wishes all [the] things which he engenders to be as good and similar to himself as possible. This is because the world he fashions is itself a blessed god,[4] because it is in harmony with itself: 'alone, solitary, capable in virtue of its excellence of being united to itself, without need of anything else, an object of knowledge [*connaissance*] and friendship for itself, able to be fulfilled by itself'. It is likewise in actively thinking of itself that Aristotle's God finds its happiness and its joy, because it thereby exercises the most excellent and most independent activity.[5]

Six centuries later, in the third century CE, Plotinus' divine world is again a world replete with happiness and light. After having successively described the One, supreme principle of all things, then the divine Intellect which thinks itself, then the divine Soul which contemplates this Intellect, Plotinus concludes: 'Such is the life, blissful and without trouble, that the gods lead.'[6] For him, the banquets of the gods of which the myth of Poros and Penia in Plato's *Symposium* speak symbolize divine beatitude.[7] Plotinus cites the Homeric expression 'to have an easy life'[8] to designate the life of the gods in this spiritual world: 'only good beings are happy, and this is why the gods are happy'.[9] Happiness, for these spiritual beings, consists precisely in their *being* 'spiritual': that is to say, distant from matter, knowing themselves in purity and transparency. Above all, this happiness consists in the fact that they are in contact with the One-Good[a] which transcends them and from which they emanate. The Good itself exceeds all awareness and all happiness.[b]

Like the God-World of the *Timaeus*[c] or Aristotle's conception of the Intellect, the gods of Epicurus are beings of perfect beauty who live in peace and serenity. Far from being pure Thought, they have a human form, even if it is diaphanous and ethereal. And their beatitude is founded in their wisdom and virtue which secure for them a total absence of trouble and an eternity of pleasures. The gods, according to Epicurus, did not create the world and they have no influence on its evolution or on human affairs, since the world is produced by a fortuitous combination of atoms. Like the Homeric gods, the Epicurean gods live in perfect serenity; their state is even better than the poet's gods, because the former take part, passionately, in the quarrels of men. Epicurus' gods do not have to occupy themselves with human affairs and the government of the world. Epicurus, in fact, proposes a notion of the divine which is purer than that of other philosophers like Plato or the Stoics, to the extent that his gods are not enchained and absorbed in the task of governing of the world. They are without relation with other things, finding absolute happiness in their pure perfection.[10]

Participation in divine beatitude

The idea that it is possible for human beings to participate in divine beatitude predates philosophical reflection. Ancient religious festivals already involved, first and foremost, communion in the joy of the gods. As Plato will say: 'for the good man, to sacrifice to the gods and to enter

---

[a] [Translator's note] French: *l'Un-Bien*.
[b] [Translator's note] Hadot's verb here is *dépasser* and we have translated *conscience* here as 'awareness'.
[c] [Translator's note] Literally, Hadot's term is: *Dieu-Monde*.

without ceasing into relation with them through prayer, offerings and all the features of the divine cult is the most beautiful, as well as the best and surest path to beatitude'.[11] This is because men intensely feel the presence of the god in these moments of collective joy:

> Through pity for our race which is by nature given over to pain, the gods have instituted, as breaks in the middle of our labours, the alternation[d] of festivals which are celebrated in their honour, and they have given us, as companions for these celebrations, the Muses, Apollo Musagete [Leader of the Muses] and Dionysus.[12]

Moreover, the denomination 'the blissful [or blessed] ones' accorded to the inhabitants of 'the Isles of the Blessed' clearly shows that the ancients thought that certain men, by their exceptional virtue, could merit a beatitude akin to that of the gods: 'those who die after an entirely just and holy life go after their death to the Isles of the Blessed where they remain, sheltered from all troubles, in perfect happiness'.[13]

With the rise of philosophy, the way in which men could participate in divine beatitude comes to be defined in a more precise manner. In this perspective, one can without totally opposing them distinguish two great tendencies: on the one hand, the Socratic tradition, for which participation in divine happiness is founded on the presence of God in the human soul and is ultimately realized through the love of the Good; on the other, the Epicurean attitude, which is very complex and that we will try to define later.

Even though we know little about the historical Socrates, the testimonies of Plato and Xenophon allow us to glimpse that he loved to speak of a divine presence, the famous *daimôn* which manifested itself in his inner life: 'a certain voice which, when it makes itself heard, always deters me from what I was about to do'.[14] Moreover, Socrates will forever remain the model of the philosopher who prefers the moral good over all the other human goods and over life itself,[15] and who declared:

> The greatest of goods for a man is every day to discuss virtue and the other subjects of which you hear me talk about when I examine others and myself; and a life which is not submitted to such an examination is not worth living.[16]

Plato and Aristotle remain fundamentally faithful to this profound Socratic orientation, but they intellectualize it considerably. For them, the

---

[d] [Translator's note] Original: *alternance*.

moral life that the inner god inspires is not solely a virtuous life but also a life of contemplation. At the end of the *Timaeus*, Plato thus declares: 'he who takes care of the divine that is within him, to maintain in perfect order the *daimôn* which lives within them in order, he necessarily is extremely happy'.[17] But it appears in this context that it is, above all, in governing[e] his thoughts and in applying them to divine things that a man can achieve this extraordinary happiness.

For Aristotle, at the same time that the divine in the world is, at its summit, like the object of love which moves the heavens, it is also pure Intellect which thinks itself. Likewise, the divine in human beings is the intellect, the mind. We are thus led to the fundamental paradox, according to which, what is most essential in man transcends the merely human.[f] Accordingly, man will find his happiness in the life which suits him to the highest degree and which is, nevertheless, superhuman: the life of the mind. 'The more our contemplation is developed, the more our happiness grows.'[18] The supreme happiness of the human being is thus a divine beatitude that we can only achieve exceptionally: 'this state of joy that we only possess at rare moments, God has it always'.[g] Let us add that, in his realism, Aristotle well knows that no man can achieve this happiness without the health of the body, which is assured by a requisite minimum of nourishment and care. This is also a man who, precisely, estimates that it is preferable to attach himself to a minimum of such external goods.[h]

For Plotinus, human happiness is founded in the divine presence within the soul, and in the impulse[i] of the soul towards the Good. What one glimpsed already in Plato and Aristotle will therefore appear in Plotinus even more clearly, namely, the connection between the divine presence and love of the Good. Plato and Aristotle indicate that the divine presence of the spirit within the soul is insufficient by itself to assure the happiness of human beings. It is also necessary to become aware of this presence, 'to take care'[j] of this inner deity and to thereby rise to the life of the spirit. This divine presence was understood as a call to the love of the Good: that is to say, to the conversion of one's entire being towards the divine Spirit. To express this configuration, Plotinus finds the most striking formulae: 'the

---

[e] [Translator's note] The verb is: *régler*.
[f] [Translator's note] This paradox is explored in relation to the sage in 'The Figure of the Sage' above.
[g] [Translator's note] Aristotle, *Metaphysics*, 1072 b28.
[h] [Translator's note] Aristotle, *Nicomachean Ethics*, 1179 a.
[i] [Translator's note] Original: *élan*.
[j] [Translator's note] Original: '*prendre soin*'.

Spirit is simultaneously a part of ourselves and that towards which we elevate ourselves'.[19] More than this: 'Thus the Supreme, as containing no otherness, is always present with us; but we are only present in it once we reject everything that distances us from it and when we put otherness away'.[20] It is the famous principle of Pascal's thought: 'you would not have searched for me if you had not already found me'. It is the unconscious presence of the Divine in us which makes us love it and seek it out. The divine presence and love of the Good are, therefore, intimately linked together. Yet, for Plotinus, it is not enough only to say that happiness is a participation in the life of the Spirit within us. For him, the soul has an even higher vocation, even if it is only rarely realized. For, according to Plotinus, if the Spirit is good, it is not *the* Good. Essentially, for Plotinus, the happiness of self-consciousness and of the relation to the self which characterizes the life of the Spirit is something finally inferior. The Good itself is beyond happiness, because it has need of nothing, even of itself. It is not good to itself, but it is solely the Good of others. Therefore, the soul will not become content only by being united with the Spirit in privileged moments but will feel, with the Spirit, in moments that are even more rare and exceptional, the presence of the Good itself in a 'loving fervour', as Plotinus says.[21] The supreme happiness for the soul is thus an experience which one could qualify as mystical. It is characterized, amongst other things, by an immense joy. It suffices for the soul to be with Him,[k] 'so great is the joy at which it is arrived'.[l]

In a certain sense, one could detect in Plato, Aristotle and Plotinus a kind of hedonism: the life of the Spirit and the love of the Good are accompanied by a spiritual enjoyment[m] and joy. It is remarkable that, in the Socratic tradition, Stoicism, for its part, represents an admirable effort to purify the moral intention as far as possible of all motivations exterior to the love of the Good, and thus of all hedonism, even spiritual. Certainly, the Stoics also founded the happiness of man on the presence of God in the soul and on the love of the Good: 'the sacred spirit resides within ourselves, which observes and controls our bad and our good actions'.[22] As Epictetus comments:

You carry God everywhere with you … and yet you ignore him …, it is within yourself that you carry him and you do not realise that you sully this divine presence by impure thoughts and inappropriate actions.[23]

---

[k] [Translator's note] Here, we respect Hadot's choice of pronoun [*Lui*].
[l] [Translator's note] Plotinus, *Enneads*, VI, 7, 34, 38.
[m] [Translator's note] Original: *jouissance*.

One therefore also finds amongst the Stoics the same paradox that we saw in Aristotle and Plotinus. God is at the same time ourselves, to the extent that we are a spark or fragment of him, as well as something which is more than ourselves, towards which we must return ourselves: a norm of inner and transcendent Reason, according to which we ought to live. Indeed, the Stoics affirm more clearly and explicitly than Plato, Aristotle and Plotinus that there is no other happiness or pleasure than virtue itself, the moral good itself, which is its own reward. Clearly, for the Stoics, there is no other good than the moral good, that is, the efficacious and complete will to do good. All the rest is indifferent, deprived of intrinsic value. Therefore, the Stoic sage is absolutely free with regards to everything. As examples of indifferent things, the Stoics enumerate life, health, pleasure, beauty, power, wealth, fame and noble birth and their opposites: death, illness, pain, ugliness, weakness, poverty, obscurity and base birth. All these things are neither good nor evil and as such do not bring for us either happiness or misery. We will not develop here what the Stoics call the theory of duties: the manner in which, to allow the good will to find a matter for exercise, they attempted to formulate a code of practical conduct which accorded a relative value to things which in principle were indifferent like health, family or the city. It suffices here to have underlined the Stoic moral purity. Epictetus or Marcus Aurelius, who are the legatees and the culmination of the ancient Stoic tradition, remarkably formulate the fundamental attitudes of the Stoic in relation to the different domains of reality. The moral good consists, first of all, in judging well in each circumstance of life, in holding to a strict objectivity in all of them; then, in accepting with piety those events which do not depend upon us and which are destined for us by Providence; and, finally, in acting with justice and in the service of the human community in matters which do depend upon us.[24]

Epicurus, for his part, depicted the participation of human beings in divine happiness in a completely different way to the extent that, for him, happiness resides neither in the moral good nor in the exercise of thought, nor even in action, but in pleasure. The unhappiness of people is caused by the fact that they fear what they need not fear, and that they desire things which are not necessary for them to desire and which escape them. Their life is for these reasons consumed by unjustified fears and unsatisfied desires. This is why Epicurean physics will precisely deliver people from these fears, by showing them that the gods are not to be feared, since they play no role in the course of the world and dwell themselves in perfect serenity. As for death, since it is total dissolution, it is not a part of life. The Epicurean is delivered from insatiable desires by learning to distinguish between desires which are natural and necessary, like eating and drinking; desires that are natural and not necessary, like the pleasures of love; and those which are neither natural nor necessary. The satisfaction of the first and the renunciation of the last – and, eventually, of the second also – will suffice to assure serenity. 'The cries of the flesh are "not to be hungry", "not to be thirsty", "not to be cold". Whoever enjoys this state and the hope of enjoying it rivals God himself in happiness.'[25] Such an ethics can seem at first glance very materialistic. But to a more attentive examination, it supposes a great delicateness of the soul which is reflected in the Epicurean representation of the serenity of the Gods. Epicurean piety, as André-Jean Festugière has shown, is one of remarkable purity of sentiment: 'it is by the gods above all that voluptuousness is born in the heart of man'.[26] This thought can be related to religious festivals. There, as we have said, not only does the sage find the joy of which we have spoken earlier in the presence of the gods. Furthermore, as the Epicureans say:

> he [the sage] admires nature and the condition of the gods, and he strives to approach it, he aspires to touch it, to live in [this condition], and he names the sages friends of the gods and the gods friends of the sages.[27]

Moreover, since the gods for the Epicureans are not occupied with human affairs, the sage will not invoke them in order to obtain any benefits. Instead, he will find his happiness in contemplating their serenity, thereby joining them in their joy. The love of the gods, for Epicurus, is the love of their beauty and perfection. Paul Decharme refers to this as 'pure love'.[28] The sage will find his happiness in taking the gods as models in order to live himself in perfect serenity and purity of soul. He does this by disciplining his desires, by examining his conscience and by accepting the fraternal correction of the Epicurean community bound together by bonds of an intense friendship. Epicurean happiness, like that of the gods, amounts perhaps to the pure pleasure of existing.[29]

Egoistic forms of happiness?[n]

Are the models of happiness described by ancient wisdom egoistic? One could perhaps think this is the case by rereading the descriptions I

---

[n] [Translator's note] Literally: '*Bonheurs égoistes?*'

have just briefly given. Historians and philosophers have not failed to make this charge. It, indeed, seems that certain of these models of happiness are reserved for an elite: those few capable of realizing Aristotelian contemplation or Plotinian ecstasy, for example. But, above all, doesn't it seem that each of these models of happiness seem to be aimed exclusively at the perfection of isolated individuals?

In fact, the problem is complex. First, one cannot deny the 'missionary' character of many of the great ancient philosophies: 'missionary' in the double sense of 'to receive a mission from the divinity' and 'to try to convert others'. Socrates is again the fundamental model. He presents himself as 'the man who has been assigned to the Athenians by the will of the gods, to stimulate them like a gadfly'.[30] 'I speak to the poor and to the rich without distinction':[31]

> I am a man who was given to the City by the deity: ask yourselves if it is humanly possible to neglect, as I have done, all one's personal affairs [...] for all of these years, and that only occupy myself with you [...] urging you to become better ...[32]

Epicurus was presented by his disciples as a god amongst men or the saviour of humanity. Each Epicurean then became, in his or her turn, a missionary like that Diogenes, who, in the town of Oenoanda in Lycia (in the south-west of Turkey) in the third century CE, engraved a gigantic inscription recounting the main lines of the Epicurean doctrine, so as to make known its message of salvation to his fellow citizens and future generations.[33] All of antiquity stands as testimony to the extraordinary diffusion of the Epicurean doctrine. The originality of the Epicurean school lay in trying to convert all men, even those uncultivated and without any particular intellectual formation, and also to admit into its ranks slaves, women, and even courtesans like that Leontion, a disciple of Epicurus, represented in an ancient painting 'in meditation'.[34]

Stoic philosophy also did not refuse to address slaves and women and all human beings in general. We recall on the subject this judicious remark of Georges Rodier:

> The Stoics wanted ... virtue and happiness to be made accessible to all; they wanted them to be so in this world ... But, for that, it necessary that the world we live in is as beautiful and as good as possible, and thus not opposed to any imagined superior world ... It is necessary that no other realities exist than those which are offered to our eyes in the azure breast of Zeus.[35]

The idea of a missionary philosophy is also not absent from Stoicism, to the extent that it was always connected to Cynicism. After Diogenes, the Cynics were always ardent propagandists, addressing themselves to all classes of society, preaching by example, denouncing social conventions and proposing a return to the simplicity of the life according to nature. Epictetus, in a certain way, depicts the Cynics as the monks of Stoicism. The Cynics are the envoys, the messengers, the spokespeople of God amongst men and according to Epictetus, philosophy is the testimony (*martus*) of God.[36]

It is true, on the other hand, that the Platonism of Plato or Plotinus, or again Aristotelianism, were philosophies reserved for an elite cultivated in all the sciences.

So, can one not then say that the models of happiness conceived by the ancient philosophical schools remain fundamentally egotistic proposals of individual perfection, attained by the withdrawal of the self and flight from the world? Finally, I think that we must respond with a 'no' to this question.

Let us start with the simplest point. It is evident that, the Stoics, for whom happiness is found in a moral good which involves, as constitutive parts, the dedication to the life of the community, the practice of justice and love towards other men, cannot be presented in this way. But isn't Epicurean happiness egoistic? It is true that Epicurean serenity and the refusal to get involved in the worries of the City could authorize certain suspicions regarding Epicureanism. But the missionary inspiration of Epicureanism, the considerable role that friendship plays in it and the constitution of communities in which the members help each other spiritually and materially – these are all facts which suffice to refute the representation of Epicureanism as an egoistic form of hedonism.

As for Plato and Aristotle, the concern for politics and the improvement of the City suffice to preserve them against this reproach of 'egoism'. But what about Plotinus? What, after all, can we say of a work which, in the presentation that is given of it by Porphyry, Plotinus' disciple, ends with these lines:

> Such is the life of the gods and of divine and happy men: the separation from all things [from] here below, a life which feels no pleasure in these inferior things; the flight of the alone towards the Alone.[37]

This flight of the alone towards the Alone has often been interpreted as a narcissistic attitude, a withdrawal of the self into itself, the *Seul*, which is the One or the Good, being, in fact, nothing other than [my]self.° Unfortunately,

---

° [Translator's note] Literally, the *moi* (me).

we cannot undertake a lengthy discussion of this problem here. Let me say solely that it is essential to the Plotinian mystical experience that it is, on the one hand, an experience of the self, to the extent that is a revelation of one's interiority; and, on the other hand, that it is also an experience of the Wholly Other, to the extent to which it pushes against the limits of the relative, of language, of the sayable and the thinkable, and presses up towards the Absolute with which it is, precisely, impossible to fully identify. One cannot qualify such an experience as 'egoistic'.

Such, too briefly described, are the different models of happiness proposed by the philosophical schools of antiquity. The Christians will not forget them. The Stoic conception of happiness will, on the contrary, be taken up in the monastic and ascetic traditions. It is, actually, in no way extraordinary that when the famous Father Ricci wanted to proselytize Christianity to the educated Chinese in 1605, he composed a *Livre des 25 paragraphes*,[38] as a sort of catechism of rules for happiness based largely upon paraphrased translations from the *Manual* of Epictetus, adapted to Christianity and Confucianism. As for the Platonic, Aristotelian and Plotinian models of happiness, the important role that they played in the formation of Christian mystical experience is well known.

Notes

1   This chapter originally appeared in *La Vie Spirituelle*, t. 72 (1992), pp. 33–43. It was republished in Pierre Hadot, *Études de Philosophie Ancienne* (Paris: Les Belles Lettres, 2010).

2   Homer, *Iliad*, I; 339; VI, 138; *Odyssey*, IV, 805. On the sense of "happiness" (*makar-*) in Antiquity, see Gerhard Kittel & Gerhard Friedrich, *Theologisches Wörterbuch zum Neuen Testament* (Stuttgart: W. Kohlhammer, 1933), article "Makar".

3   Cf. the book, already 'ancient', but still interesting, of Paul Decharne, *La Critique des Traditions Religieuses chez les Grecs, des origins au temps de Plutarque* (Paris: Alphonse Picard et Fils, 1904) and, in the collection *Entretiens sur l'Antiquité Classique*, ed. H. J. Rose et al, vol. 1: *La Notion du Divin, Depuis Homère Jusqu'à Platon* (Vandoeuvres-Genève: Fondation Hardt, 1954).

4   Plato, *Timaeus*, 34b.

5   Aristotle, *Metaphysics*, 1072 b28.

6   Plotinus, *Enneads*, I, 8, 1, 25.

7   Plotinus, *Enneads*, III, 5, 9, 39.

8   Plotinus, *Enneads*, V, 8, 4, 1.

9 Plotinus, *Enneads*, III, 2, 4, 47.

10 Cf. André-Jean Festugière, *Epicure et ses Dieux*, 2nd ed. (Paris: Presses universitaires de France, 1968), 71–100; Bernard Frischer, *The Sculpted Word* (Berkeley: University of California Press, 1982), 83–84.

11 Plato, *Laws* IV, 716d.

12 Plato, *Laws*, II, 653d.

13 Plato, *Gorgias*, 523 b2.

14 Plato, *Apology*, 31d.

15 Plato, *Apology*, 29d.

16 Plato, *Apology*, 38a.

17 Plato, *Timaeus*, 90c.

18 Aristotle, *Nicomachean Ethics*, 1178b.

19 Plotinus, *Enneads*, I, 1, 13, 7.

20 Plotinus, *Enneads*, VI, 9, 8, 33.

21 Plotinus, *Enneads* VI, 7, 35, 24. [Translator's note: Here, the expression is: *ivresse aimante*.]

22 Seneca, *Letters to Lucilius*, 41, 2.

23 Epictetus, *Discourses*, II, 11–14

24 Cf. Pierre Hadot, 'Une clé des *Pensées* de Marc Aurèle: les trois *topoi* philosophiques selon Épictète', *Les Études Philosophiques* (1978), 225–239.

25 Translated into French at Festugière, *Épicure et ses dieux*, 44.

26 Cf. Festugière, *Épicure et ses dieux*, 97 (fragment 385 a, in Hermann Usener, *Epicurea* (Leipzig: Teubne, 1887), 355, 6. [Translator's note: Hadot uses the *voluptué* here rather than *plaisir/s*.]

27 Usener, *Epicurea*, 258, 15, fragment 386, cited by Festugière, *ibid.*, 98.

28 Decharme, *La Critique*, 257.

29 On the life led at or in the Epicurean school, see Norman W. De Witt, *Epicurus and his Philosophy* (Minneapolis: University of Minnesota, 1954), 9 and Wilhelm Schmidt's article 'Epicurus', in *Reallexikon für Antike und Christentum,* vol. V (Stuttgart: Hiersemann, 1962), col. 740–755.

30 Plato, *Apology*, 30e.

31 Plato, *Apology*, 32b.

32 Plato, *Apology*, 31a–b.

33 A complete edition with Italian translation of these fragments is found in Angelo Casanoca, *I frammeni ai Diogene d'Enoanda* (Florence: Università degli studi di Firenze, 1984).

34 Pliny the Elder, *Naturalis Historia*, 35, 99 & 144. On the diffusion of Epicureanism, see Cicero, *De Finibus*, II, 14, 27: "Epicurus has moved not solely Greece and Italy, but again all the Barbarian world," and De Witt, *loc cit.*, 26–27 and 329. According to Lactantius, *Institutions Divines*, III, 25, 4, women, slaves, and the ignorant were admitted into philosophy by the Stoics and Epicureans.

35 Georges Rodier, *Études de philosophie grecque* (Paris: Vrin, 1926), 254–255, cited by Victor Goldschmidt, *Le Système Stoïcien et l'Idée de Temps* (Paris: Vrin, 1977 [3rd edn]), 59, n. 7.

36 Epictetus, *Discourses*, III, 22; and see Armand Delatte, 'Le Sage Témoin dans la Philosophie Stoïco-Cynique', in *Bulletin de la Classe des Lettres* (Bruxelles: Académie Royale de Belgique [5e Série, vol. 39], 1953), 166–186.

37 Plotinus, *Enneads*, VI, 9, 11, 48. [Translator's note: We here translate *le seul* as 'the alone', and *Le Seul* as 'the Alone'. The term *seul* can signify, as an adjective, 'lonely', 'alone', 'only' or 'sole'. Here the adjective is being hypostasized to translate Plotinus' thought. 'Lonely' connotes an anthropomorphic dimension that could be misleading here; while the One at issue here is 'alone' beyond the Ideas, but not the 'only' or 'sole' hypostasis in Plotinus' system.]

38 Cf. Christopher Spalatin, 'Matteo Ricci's Use of Epictetus' *Encheiridion*', *Gregoranum* 56 (1975): 551.

REFERENCES

Modern editions of ancient texts

Aelius Aristide, *Discours Sacrés: Rêve, religion, médecine au IIe siècle après J.-C.*, ed. by A. J. Festugière, Paris: Macula, 1986.

Albinus, 'Eisagôgê', in *Platonis Opera*, V I, ed. by Karl Friedrich Hermann, Leipzig: Novi Eboraci Apud Harperos Phatres, 1853.

Albinus (Alcinous), 'Didaskalikos', in *Platonis dialogi decundum thrasylli tetralogias dispositi*, ed. by Karl F. Hermann, Leipzig: Teubner, 1880.

Alexander of Aphrodisius, *Alexandri Aphrodisiensis in Aristotelis Topicorum Libros octo commentaria*, ed. by Maximilian Wallies, Berlin: G. Reimer, 1891.

Ambrose, *Apologie de David*, ed. and trans. by Pierre Hadot and Marius Cordier, Paris: Éditions du Cerf, 1977.

Anonymous Prolegomena, ed. by Leonard G. Westerink, Amsterdam: Prometheus Trust, 1962.

Aristotle, *Metaphysics*, in *Aristotle in 23 Volumes*, Vols 17 and 18, trans. by Hugh Tredennick, Cambridge, M A: Harvard University Press, and London: William Heinemann Ltd, 1933, 1989.

Aristotle, *Nicomachean Ethics*, trans. by H. Rackham, Loeb Classical Library 73, Cambridge, M A: Harvard University Press, 1926.

Boethius, Anicius Manlius Severinus, *De Topicis Differentiis*, trans. by Eleanore Stump, Ithaca, N Y: Cornell University Press, 1978.

Diogenes Laertius, *The Lives and Opinions of the Eminent Philosophers*, trans. by Charles D. Jonge, London: H. G. Bohn, 1853.

Diogenes of Oeneanda, *Eliae in Porphyrii Isagogen et Aristotelis Categorias Commentaria, Commentaria in Aristotelem Graeca*, ed. by Adolfus Busse, Berlin: Georgii Reimeri, 1900.

Epictète, *Entretiens*, Livre I, ed. and trans. by Joseph Souilhé, with the collaboration of Amand Jagu, Paris: Les Belles Lettres, 1943.

Epictetus, *Discourses*, trans. by Thomas Wentworth Higginson, New York: Thomas Nelson & Sons, 1890.

Epictetus, *Discourses*, trans. by George Long, London: G. Bell and Sons, 1890.

Epictetus, *Discourses, Books 1–2*, Trans. by W. A. Oldfather, Loeb Classical Library 131, Cambridge, M A: Harvard University Press, 1925.

Epictetus, *Discourses and Selected Writings*, trans. by Robert F. Dobbin, London: Penguin, 2008.

Epicurus, *Epicurea*, ed. by Hermann Usener, Leipzig: Teubne, 1887.

Hermes Trismegistus, *La Révélation d'Hermès Trismégiste*, Tome II, *Le Dieu cosmique*, ed. by André-Jean Festugière, Paris: Les Belles Lettres, 1948.

Hippocrates, *L'oeuvre de Hippocrate*, Tome IX, trans. by Émile Littré, Paris: J. B. Baillière, 1861.

Ioannis Stobaei Anthologium, Vols 1–5, ed. by Curtius Wachsmuth and Otto Hense, Berlin: Weidmannsche Buchhandlung, 1884–1912.

Isocrates, *Discours*, Tome III, ed. and trans. by Georges Mathieu, Paris: Budé, 1966.

Lucian, *Hermotimus, or the Rival Philosophies*, trans. by H. W. Fowler and F. G. Fowler, in *The Complete Works of Lucian*, Oxford: Clarendon Press, 1905.

Lucian, *Hermotimus ou les Sectes*, trans. by Eugène Talbot, Paris: Hachette, 1857.

Lucretius, *On the Nature of Things*, trans. by W. H. D. Rouse, revd by Martin F. Smith, Loeb Classical Library 181, Cambridge, MA: Harvard University Press, 1924.

Lucretius, *On the Nature of Things*, trans. by A. E. Stallings, London: Penguin, 2007.

Marcus Aurelius, *Marco Aurelio Latino*, ed. by Luigi Pepe, Naples: Armanni, 1957.

Marcus Aurelius, *Meditations*, trans. by Maxwell Staniforth, London: Penguin, 2004.

Marcus Aurelius, *Wege zu Sich Selbst*, ed. by W. Theiler, Zürich: Artemi, 1974.

Marcus Aurelius Antoninus, *The Meditations of the Emperor Marcus Aurelius Antoninus*, trans. by Francis Hutcheson and James Moor, ed. and with an 'Introduction' by James Moore and Michael Silverthorne, Indianapolis, IN: Liberty Fund, 2008.

Marcus Tullius Cicero, *On Ends*, trans. by H. Rackham, Cambridge, MA, and London: Harvard University Press, 1931.

Marinus, *Vita Procli*, ed. by Jean François Boissonade, London, Rome, Paris: Lipsiae: Weigel, 1814.

Origen, *In Canticum Canticorum*, in *Origenes Werke*, Vol. 8 (GCS 33), ed. by W. A. Baehrens, Berlin: C. Hinrichs, 1925.

Platon, *Phédon*, ed. and trans. by Léon Robin, Paris: Belles Lettres, 1952.

Porphyry, *La vie de Plotin*, Tome II, ed. by Luc Brisson et al., Paris: Vrin, 1992.

Porphyry, *Porphyrii Isagoge et in Aristotelis categoris commentarium*, ed. by Adolfus Basse, Berlin: G. Reimer, 1887.

Porphyry, *Sententia*, ed. by Erich Lamberz, Leipzig: Teubner, 1975.

Proclus Diadochus, *Commentarium in Platonis Parmenidem*, in *Procli Opera Inedita*, ed. by Victor Cousin, Paris: Augustus Durand, 1864.

Proclus Diadochus, *Commentary on the First Alcibiades of Plato*, ed. by Leendert G. Westerink, Amsterdam: North-Holland Publishing, 1954.

Proclus, *Theologie Platonicienne*, ed. and trans. by Henri-Dominique Saffrey and Leenert G. Westerink, Paris: Les Belles Lettres, 1986.

Saloustios, *Des dieux et de morale*, Tome 3, trans. by Gabriel Rochefort, Paris: Les Belles Lettres, 1960.

Seneca, Lucius Annaeus, *Natural Questions*, trans. by Harry M. Hine, *The Complete Works of Lucius Annaeus Seneca*, Chicago, IL: Chicago University Press, 2010.

Simplicius, *Simplicii in Aristotelis Categorias Commentarium*, ed. by Karl Kalbfleisch, Berlin: Reimer, 1907.

Simplicius, *Simplicii in Aristotelis Physicorum Libros Quattuor Priores Commentaria*, ed. by Hermann Diels, Berlin: G. Remeiri, 1882.

Teles, *Teletis Reliquiae*, 2nd edn, ed. by Otto Hence, Tübingen: G. Olms, 1909.

Theon of Smyrna, *Expositio Rerum Mathematicarum ad Legendum Platonem Utilium*, ed. by Eduard Hiller, Leipzig: Tuebner, 1878 [1966].

Titus Lucretius Carus, *The Nature of Things: A Metrical Translation*, trans. by William Ellery Leonard, London, Paris and Toronto: J.M. Dent & Sons, 1916.

Modern references

Allier, Raoul, *Psychologie de la conversion chez les peuples non-civilisés*, Paris: Payot, 1925.

Andersen, Carl, 'Justin und der Mittlere Platonismus', *Zeitschrift für die Neutestamentaliche Wissenschaft* 44 (1952–3): 157–95.

Aubenque, Pierre, *Le problème de l'être chez Aristote*, 2nd edn, Paris: Presses Universitaires de France, 1966.

Beierwaltes, Werner, *Proklos*, 2nd edn, Frankfurt-on-Main: Klostermann Vittorio GmbH, 1979.

Bénatouïl, Thomas, 'Stoicism and twentieth-century French philosophy', *Routledge Handbook of the Stoic Tradition*, ed. by John Sellars, 541–62, London: Routledge, 2015.

Benjamin, Walter, *Oeuvres choisies*, trans. by M. de Gandilac, Paris: Julliard, 1959.

Berkeley, George, *Alciphron; or, The Minute Philosopher: In Seven Dialogues Containing an Apology for the Christian Religion Against Those Who are Called Free-Thinkers*, London: J. and R. Tonson and S. Draper, 1752.

Berkeley, George, *Oeuvres choisies de Berkeley*, Tome 2, ed. and trans. by André-Louis Leroy, Paris: Presses Universitaires de France, 1965.

Billete, André, *Récits et réalités d'une vonversion*, Montréal: Presses de l'Université de Montréal, 1975.

Bloch, Jules, *Les inscriptions d'Asoka*, Vol. 8, Paris: Collection Émile Senart, 1950.

Blumenberg, Hans, *Paradigmen zu Einer Metaphorologie*, Bonn: Suhrkamp, 1960.

Bonhöffer, Adolf Friedrich, *Epiktet und die Stoa*, Stuttgart: Ferdinand Enke, 1890 [reprint 1968].

Bréhier, Émile, *Chrysippe et l'ancien stoïcisme*, Paris: Presses Universitaires de France, 1951.

Bréhier, Émile, *Études de philosophie antique*, Paris: Presses Universitaires de France, 1955.

Bréhier, Émile, *Histoire de la philosophie*, Tomes 1–2, Paris: Presses Universitaires de France, 1961.

Bruns, Georg Hermann Ivo, *De Schola Epicteti*, Kiel: Kiliae, 1879.

Brunsvicg, Léon, *De la vraie et de la fausse conversion*, Paris: Presses Universitaires de France, 1950.

Casanoca, Angelo, *I frammeni ai Diogene d'Enoanda*, Florence: Università degli studi di Firenze, 1984.

Castree, Noel, 'Review in brief: *The Veil of Isis: An Essay on the History of the Idea of Nature*, by Pierre Hadot, translated by Michael Chase', *Cultural Geographies* 14, no. 3 (2007): 477–8.

Celenza, Christopher S., 'What counted as philosophy in the Italian Renaissance? The history of philosophy, the history of science, and styles of life', *Critical Inquiry* 39, no. 2 (2013): 367–401.

Chase, Michael, Stephen R. L. Clark and Michael McGhee (eds), *Philosophy as a Way of Life: Ancients and Moderns – Essays in Honor of Pierre Hadot*, Oxford: John Wiley, 2013.

Chelini, Jean and Henry Branthommer (eds), *Histoire des pélerinages non chrétiens: Entre le magique et la sacré*, Paris: Hachette, 1987.

Chemiss, Harold, *Die Ältere Akademie*, Heidelberg: C. Winter, 1966.

Chenu, Marie-Dominique, *Introduction à l'étude de saint Thomas d'Aquin*, Paris: Institut d'Études Medievales, 1954.

Cooper, Anthony Ashley, Third Earl of Shaftesbury, *Exercices*, ed. by Laurent Jaffro, Paris: Aubier, 1993.

Cooper, John M., *Pursuits of Wisdom: Six Ways of Life in Ancient Philosophy from Socrates to Plotinus*, Princeton, NJ: Princeton University Press, 2012.

Cooper, John M., 'Socrates and philosophy as a way of life', in *Maieusis: Essays in Ancient Philosophy in Honour of Myles Burnyeat*, ed. by Dominic Scott, 20–42, Oxford: Oxford University Press, 2007.

Corneanu, Sorana, *Regimens of the Mind*, Chicago, IL: University of Chicago Press, 2011.

Croissant, Jeanne, *Aristote et les mystères*, Liége: Droz, 1932.

Dailly, Robert and Henri van Effenterre, 'Le cas Marc Aurèle: Essai de psychosomatique historique', *Revue des Études Anciennes* 56 (1954): 347–65.

Davidson, Arnold I., 'Introduction: Pierre Hadot and the spiritual phenomenon of ancient philosophy', in Pierre Hadot, *Philosophy as a Way of Life: Ancients and Moderns: Essays in Honour of Pierre Hadot*, trans. by Michael Chase, 1–46, London: Wiley-Blackwell, 1995.

Davidson, Arnold L. and Catherine Porter, 'The final Foucault and his ethics', *Critical Inquiry* 20, no. 1 (1993): 1–9.

de Coulanges, Fustel, *The Ancient City*, Botache: Kitchener, 2001.

De Roy, Olivier, *L'intelligence de la foi en la Trinité selon Saint Augustine*, Paris: Études Augustiniennes, 1966.

De Waelhens, Alphons, *La philosophie de Martin Heidegger*, Louvain: Nauwelaerts, 1942.

DeWitt, Norman W., *Epicurus and His Philosophy*, Minneapolis, MN: University of Minnesota Press, 1954.

Decharne, Paul, *Entretiens sur l'antiquité classique*, Tome 1, in *La notion du divin, depuis Homère jusqu'à Platon*, ed. by H. J. Rose, Vandoeuvres-Genève: Fondation Hardt, 1954.

Decharne, Paul, *La critique des traditions religieuses chez les Grecs, des origins au temps de Plutarque*, Paris: Alphonse Picard et fils, 1904.

Delatte, Armand, 'Le sage-témoin dans la philosophie stoïco-cynique', *Académie Royale de Belgique, Bulletin de la Classe des Lettres* 39 [Bruxelles, 5e série] (1953): 166–86.

Denton, Peter H., 'Review of *The Veil of Isis: An Essay on the History of the Idea of Nature*', *Essays in Philosophy* 12, no. 2 (2011): 363–71.

Derrida, Jacques, 'Plato's Pharmacy', in Jacques Derrida, *Dissemination*, trans. by B. Johnson, 61–3, Chicago, IL: University of Chicago Press, (1981).

Descartes, René, 'Préface', in *Oeuvres de Descartes*, Tome 9, ed. by Charles Adam and Paul Tannery, Paris: Léopold Cerf, 1904.

Descartes, René, 'Réponse aux Secondes Objections (Contra les . . . Meditations)', *Principes de la philosophie*, in *Oeuvres de Descartes*, Tome 9, ed. by Charles Adam and Paul Tannery, Paris: Léopold Cerf, 1904.

Dodds, Eric R., *Païens et chrétiens dans un âge d'angoisse – Aspects de l'expérience religieuse de Marc-Aurèle à Constantin*, French trans. by H.-D. Suffrey, Paris: La Pensée Sauvage, 1979.

Domański, Juliusz, *La philosophie, théorie ou manière de vivre?: Les controverses de l'Antiquité à la Renaissance*, avec une préface de Pierre Hadot, Paris, Fribourg (Suisse): Editions Universitaires, 1996.

Dostal, Robert J., 'Pierre Hadot, *The Veil of Isis: An Essay on the History of the Idea of Nature*, Originally published as *Le Voile d'Isis: Essai sur l'histoire de l'idée de Nature* (Paris: Gallimard, 2004)', *Bryn Mawr Classical Review* 2007.03.25.

Dreyfus, Hubert and Paul Rabinow, *Michel Foucault: Beyond Structuralism and Hermeneutics*, 2nd edn, Chicago, IL: University of Chicago Press, 1982.

Dreyfus, Hubert and Paul Rabinow, *Michel Foucault: Un parcours philosophique*, Paris: Gallimard, 1984.

Dupréel, Eugène Gustave, 'La pensée confuse', *Annales de l'École des Hautes Études de Gand* 3 (1939): 17–27.

Düring, Ingemar, *Aristoteles*, Heidelberg: Bibliothek der Klassischen Altertumswissenschaften, 1966.

Düring, Ingemar, 'Aristoteles und die Platonische Erbe', in *Aristoteles in der Neueren Forschung*, ed. by Paul Moraux, Damstadt: Wissenschaftliche Buchgesellschaft, 1968.

Ernout, Alfred and Léon Robin, *Lucrèce, De la nature, Commentaire*, Vol. II, Paris: Les Belles Lettres, 1962.

Eckermann, Johann Peter, *Gespräche mit Goethe*, Westbaden: Insel-Verlag, 1955.

Evans, John D. G., *Aristotle's Concepts of Dialectic*, Cambridge: Cambridge University Press, 1977.

Festugière, André-Jean, *Epicure et ses Dieux*, 2nd edn, Paris: Presses Universitaires de France, 1968.

Festugière, André-Jean, 'L'ordre de lecture des dialogues de Platon aux Ve–VIe siècles', *Mus. Helv.* 26 (1969): 282–96.

Festugière, André-Jean, *Révelations d'Hermé Trimégiste*, Tome 2, Paris: J. Gabalda & Cie, 1944.

Fiordalis, David (ed.), *Buddhist Spiritual Practices: Thinking with Pierre Hadot on Buddhism, Philosophy, and the Path*, Berkeley, CA: Mangalam, 2018.

Flynn, Thomas, 'Philosophy as a way of life: Foucault and Hadot', *Philosophy and Social Criticism* 31, nos 5–6 (2005): 609–22.

Force, Pierre, 'In the teeth of time: Pierre Hadot on meaning and misunderstanding in the history of ideas', *History and Theory* 50, no. 1 (2011): 20–40.

Foucault, Michel, 'L'écriture de soi', *Corps écrit* 3 (1983): 3–23.

Foucault, Michel, *L'usage des plaisirs*, Paris: Gallimard, 1984.

Foucault, Michel, *Le souci de soi*, Paris: Gallimar, 1984.

Foucault, Michel, *Michel Foucault: Beyond Structuralism and Hermeneutics*, ed. by Paul Rabinow and with an Afterword by and an Interview with Michel Foucault, 2nd edn, Chicago, IL: University of Chicago Press, 1982.

Foucault, Michel, 'Self writing', trans. by R. Hurley and Others, in *Ethics, Subjectivity and Truth: The Essential Works of Michel Foucault 1954–1984*, Vol. 1, ed. by Paul Rabinow, 207–22, London: Penguin, 2000.

Foucault, Michel, *The Care of the Self: The History of Sexuality*, Vol. 3, trans. by Robert Hurley, London: Penguin, 1990.

Foucault, Michel, 'The cultivation of the self', in *The Care of the Self: The History of Sexuality*, Vol. 3, trans. by Robert Hurley, 37–68, London: Penguin, 1990.

Foucault, Michel, 'The hermeneutics of the subject', trans. by Hurley and Others, in *Ethics, Subjectivity and Truth: The Essential Works of Michel Foucault 1954–1984*, Vol. 1, ed. by Paul Rabinow, 93–106, London: Penguin, 2000.

Foucault, Michel, *The Hermeneutics of the Subject: Lectures at the Collège de France 1981–1982*, ed. by Frédéric Gros and trans. by Graham Burchell, London: Picador, 2005.

Foucault, Michel, *The Use of Pleasure: The History of Sexuality*, Vol. 2, trans. by Robert Hurley, London: Penguin, 1992.

France, Anatole, *Le livre de mon ami*, in *Œuvres*, Tome 1, Paris: Gallimard: Bibliothèque de la Pleiade, 1984.

Friedlander, Paul, *Plato*, Princeton, NJ: Harper & Row, 1973.

Friedman, George, *La puissance et la sagesse*, Paris: Gallimard, 1970.

Friedrich, Caspar David and Carl Gustav Carus, *De la peinture de paysage*, Paris: Klincksieck, 1988.

Frischer, Bernard, *The Sculpted Word*, Berkeley, CA: University of California Press, 1982.

Gadamer, Hans-Georg, *Wahrheit und Methode*, 2nd edn, Berlin: Akademie Verlag, 2011.

Gaiser, Konrad, *Protreptik Und Paränese Bei Platon Untersuchungen Zur Form des Platonischen Dialogs*, Stuttgart: Kohlhammer, 1959.

Gaiser, Konrad, *Platons ungeschriebene Lehre: Studien zur systematischen und geschichtlichen Begründung der Wissenschaften in der Platonischen Schule*, Stutgart: Klett-Cotta, 1963.

Gaiser, Konrad, 'Plato's enigmatic lecture "On the Good"', *Phronesis* 25 (1990): 5–17.

Gaukroger, Stephen, *Francis Bacon and the Transformation of Early-Modern Philosophy*, Cambridge: Cambridge University Press, 2001.

Gautier, René-Antoine, *Magnanimité: L'idéal de la grandeur dans la philosophie Paienne et la théologie chrétienne*, Paris: Vrin, 1951.

Geffcken, Johannes, *Der Ausgang des Griechisch-Römischen Heidentums*, Heidelberg: Carl Winter, 1929.

Gigante, Marcello, *La bibliothèque de Philodème et l'épicurisme romain*, Paris: Les Belles Lettres, 1987.

Gladigow, Burkhardt, *Sophia und Kosmos*, Hildesheim: Georg Olm, 1965.

Goblot, Edmond, *Le vocabulaire philosophique*, Whitefish, MT: Kessinger Publishing, 2009 [1901].

Goethe, Johann Wolfgang von, *Geschichte der Farbenlehre*, Yearbook of the Goethe Society XI, 1949.

Goethe, Johann Wolfgang von, *Italian Journey*, trans. by W. H. Auden and E. Meyer, London: Penguin: 1962.

Goethe, Johann Wolfgang von, *Voyage en Italie*, Paris: Omnia, 2011.

Goldschmidt, Victor, *Le système stoïcien et l'idée de temps*, Paris: Vrin, 1977.

Goldschmidt, Victor, *Les dialogues de Platon*, Paris: Presses Universitaires de France, 1947.

Goldschmidt, Victor, *Métaphysique, histoire de la philosophie, Recueil d'études offert à F. Brunner*, Neuchâtel: Éditions de la Baconnière, 1981.

Goldschmidt, Victor, 'Remarques sur la méthode structurale en histoire de la philosophie', *Métaphysique et Histoire de la Philosophie, Recueil d'Études offert à Fernand Brunner*, ed. by Fernand Brunner and Gilbert Boss, 213–40, Neuchâtel: Editions de la Baconnière, 1981.

Goldschmidt, Victor, 'Sur le problème du "Système de Platon"', *Revista Critica di Storia della Filosofia* 5 (1950): 169–78.

Goldschmidt, Victor, 'Temps historique et temps logique dans l'interprétation des systèmes philosophiques', *Actes du XIeme Congrès International de Philosophie* 12 [Bruxelles] (1953): 7–13.

Goulet, Richard (ed.), *Dictionnaire des philosophes antiques*, Paris: CNRS, 1983.

Goulet-Cazé, Marie-Odile, 'L'arrière-plan scolaire de la *Vie de Plotin*', in Porphyry, *La vie de Plotin*, Tome 1, 231–80, dir. Luc Brisson and Jean-François Pradeau, Paris: Vrin, 1982.

Graeser, Andreas, *Die Logischen Fragmente des Theophrast*, Berlin: De Gruyter, 1973.

Graeser, Andreas, *Zenon von Kition*, Berlin: De Gruyter, 1975.

Grimal, Pierre, *Les jardins romains*, Paris: De Boccard, 1943.

Groethuysen, Bernard, *Anthropologie philosophique*, Paris: Gallimard, 1952.

Hacking, Ian, 'Almost Zero', *London Review of Books* 29, no. 9 (10 May 2007): 29–30.

Hadot, Ilsetraut, *Arts libéraux et philosophie dans la pensée antique*, Paris, 1984.

Hadot, Ilsetraut, 'Épicure et l'enseignement philosophique hellénistique et romain', *Actes du VIIIe Congrès de L'Association Guillaume Budé*, 347–53, Paris: Vrin, 1969.

Hadot, Ilsetraut, 'La division néoplatonicienne des écrits d'Aristote', in *Aristoteles – Werk und Wirkung. Mélanges Paul Moraux*, Tome 2, 249–85, Berlin: Walter de Gruyter, 1967.

Hadot, Ilsetraut, 'La figure du guide spirituel dans l'antiquité', in Pierre Hadot, *La philosophie comme éducation des adultes: Textes, perspectives, entretiens*, 323–60, Paris: Vrin, 2019.

Hadot, Ilsetraut, *Le problème du néoplatonisme alexandrin*, Paris: Études Augustiniennes, 1976.

Hadot, Ilsetraut, *Seneca und die Griechisch-Römische Tradition der Seelenleitung*, Berlin: De Gruyter, 1969.

Hadot, Ilsetraut, *Sénèque: Direction spirituelle et pratique de la philosophie*, Paris: Vrin, 2014.

Hadot, Ilsetraut, 'The Spiritual Guide', in *Classical Mediterranean Spirituality*, ed. by Arthur H. Armstrong, 436–59, London: Routledge & Kegan Paul, 1986.

Hadot, Ilsetraut, 'The Spiritual Guide', in *World Spirituality*, Vol. 15, *Classical Mediterranean Spirituality*, 44459, New York: 1986.

Hadot, Ilsetraut, 'Tradition stoïcienne et idées politiques au temps des gracques', *Revue des Études Latines* 48 (1970): 133–79.

Haldane, R.B. and J. Kemp, 'Will and Representation/Preface to the First Edition', available at: https://en.wikisource.org/wiki/The_World_as_Will_and_Representation/Preface_to_the_First_Edition (accessed 6 June 2019).

Hankey, Wayne J., 'Philosophy as way of life for Christians? Iamblichan and Porphyrian reflections on religion, virtue, and philosophy in Thomas Aquinas', *Laval Théologique et Philosophique* 59, no. 2 [*Le Néoplatonisme*] (Juin 2003): 193–224.

Happ, Hein, *Hyle: Studien zum Aristotelischen Materie-Begriff*, Berlin: De Gruyter, 1971.

Harrison, Peter, *Territories of Science and Religion*, Chicago, IL: University of Chicago Press, 2014.

Hartmann, Hans, 'Die Stuktur der idogemanischen Sprachen und die Entsehung der Wissenschaft', in *Sprache und Wissenschaft*, ed. by Joachim Jungius, Göttingen: Vandenhoeck & Ruprecht, 1960.

Havelock, Eric A., *Aux origines de la civilisation écrite en Occident*, trans. by E. Escobar Moreno, Paris: Maspero, 1981.

Havelock, Eric A., *Preface to Plato*, Cambridge, [MA]: Harvard University Press, 1961.

Hellwig, Antje, *Unterschungen zur Theorie der Rhetorikbei Platon und Aristoteles*, Göttingen: Vandenhoeck & Ruprecht, 1973.

Hermann, Karl-Friedrich, *Platonis Opera*, VI, Leipzig: Novi Eboraci Apud Harperos Phatres, 1853.

Hirzel, Rudolf, 'De Logica Stoicorum', *Satura Philologica, Festschrift Hermann Souppe*, Berlin, 1879.

Hoffman, Ernst, 'Epikur', in M. Dessoir, *Die Geschichte der Philosophie*, Vol. 1, 223–35, Wiesbaden: Ullstein, 1925.

Horn, Hans-Jürgen, 'Antakolouthie der Tugenden und Einheit Gottes', *Jarbuch fur Antike und Christentum* 13 (1970): 3–38.

Hunter, Ian, *Rival Enlightenments: Civil and Metaphysical Philosophy in Early Modern Germany*, Cambridge: Cambridge University Press, 2001.

Inwood, Brad, 'Introduction', in Lucius Annaeus Seneca, *Selected Philosophical Letters*, Clarendon Later Ancient Philosophers, xi–xxiv, Oxford: Oxford University Press, 2010.

Inwood, Brad, 'Review of John Sellars, *The Art of Living: The Stoics on the Nature and Function of Philosophy*', *Notre Dame Philosophical Reviews* 2004.04.04. Available at: www-site https://ndpr.nd.edu/news/23760-the-art-of-living-the-stoics-on-the-nature-and-function-of-philosophy/ (accessed November 2015).

Irrera, Orazio, 'Pleasure and transcendence of the self: Notes on "a dialogue too soon interrupted" between Michel Foucault and Pierre Hadot', *Philosophy and Social Criticism* 36, no. 9 (2010): 995–1017.

James, William, 'The varieties of religious experience', *Gifford Lectures*, 1902, New York: Random House, 1929.

Jaspers, Karl, *Nietzsche: Introduction à sa philosophie*, French trans. by Henri Niel, Lettre-Préface by Jean Wahl, Paris: Gallimard, 1950.

Jünger, Friedrich Georg, 'Wort und Zeichen', in *Die Sprache*, Dumstadt: Wissenschaftliche Buchgesellschaft, 1959.

Kant, Immanuel, *Critique of Judgment*, trans. by W. S. Pluhar, Cambridge, MA: Hackett Publishing, 1987.

Kant, Immanuel, *Critique of Practical Reason*, ed. and trans. by M. Gregor, Cambridge: Cambridge University Press, 1997.

Kant, Immanuel, *The Groundwork for the Metaphysics of Morals*, ed. and trans. by Allen Wood, New Haven, CT, and London: Yale University Press, 2002.

Kant, Immanuel, *Vorlesungen über die Philosophische Encyclopädie*, in *Kant's Gesammelter Schriften*, XXIV, 8–9, Berlin: Deutsche Akademie der Wissenschaften zu Berlin, 1980.

Kerford, George B., 'The image of the wise man in Greece before Plato', in *Mélanges Verbeke, Images of Man in Ancient and Medieval Thought*, 18–28, Leuven: Leuven University Press, 1976.

Kerford, George B., 'What does the Wise Man know?' in *The Stoics*, ed. by John M. Rist, 125–36, Berkeley, CA: California University Press, 1978.

Keysser, Christian, *Eine Papua-Gemeinde*, Neuendettelsau: Freimund-Verlag, 1950.

Kia-Hway, Lion, *L'esprit synthétique de la Chine*, Paris: Presses Universitaires de France, 1960.

Kim, Alan, 'Pierre Hadot, *The Veil of Isis: An Essay on the History of the Idea of Nature*', *Notre Dame Philosophical Review* 2007.05.06. Available at: https://ndpr.nd.edu/news/the-veil-of-isis-an-essay-on-the-history-of-the-idea-of-nature/.

Kittel, Gerhard and Gerhard Fredrich , 'Makar', in *Theologisches Wörterbuch zum Neuen Testament*, Stuttgart: W. Kohlhammer, 1933.

Krämer, Hans-Joachim, *Der Ursprung der Geistmetaphysik*, Amsterdam: Grüner, 1967.

Krämer, Hans-Joachim, *Platonismus und Hellenistische Philosophie*, Berlin: De Gruyter, 1971.

Lamb, Matthew, 'Philosophy as a way of life: Albert Camus and Pierre Hadot', *Sophia* 50 (2011): 561–76.

Laplanche, Jean and Jean-Bertrand Pontalis, *Vocabulaire de la psychanalyse*, Paris: Presses Universitaires de France, 2007 [1967].

Lausberg, Heinrich, *Handbuch der literischen Rhetorik*, Munich: Max Hueber Verlag, 1960.

Le Blond, Jean-Marie, *Loqique et méthode chez Aristote*, Paris: Vrin, 1939.

Le Corre, René, 'The prologue of Albinus', *Revue Philosophique* 81 (1965): 28–38.

Leeow, Gerardus Van der, *La réligion dans son essence et ses manifestations*, Paris: Payot, 1970.

Leisegang, Hans, *Denkformen*, 2nd edn, Berlin: De Gruyter, 1951.

Leshout, Henri van, *La théorie plotinienne de la vertu: Essai sur la genèse d'un article de la* Somme theologique *de Saint Thomas*, Freiburg: Broché, 1926.

Luschnat, Otto, '*Das Problem des ethischen Fortschritts in der Alten Stoa*', *Philologues* 102 (1958): 178–214.

Lynch, John P., *Aristotle's School: A Study of a Greek Educational Institution*, Berkeley, CA: University of California Press, 1972.

Maier, Friedrich, 'Der Sophos Begriff. Zur Bedeutung, Wertung und Rolle des Begriffs von Homer bis Euripid', PhD dissertation, München, 1970.

Marcus, N. Tod, 'Sidelights on Greek philosophers', *Journal of Hellenic Studies* 77, no. 1 (1957): 132–41.

Marx, Karl, *Economic and Political Manuscripts of 1844*, trans. by Martin Milligan, Moscow: Progress Publishers, 1959.

Mauss, Marcel, *The Gift: The Form and Reason for Exchange in Archaic Societies*, London: W.W. Norton, 1990.

Mehat, André, *Essai sur les stromates de Clement of Alexandria*, Paris: Éditions du Seuil, 1966.

Meillet, Antoine, 'Comptes rendu', *Bulletin de la Société de Linguistique de Paris* 32 (1931): 23.

Merlan, Philip, *From Platonism to Neoplatonism*, The Hague: Nijhoff, 1960.

Merleau-Ponty, Maurice, *Phénomenologie de la Perception*, Paris: Gallimard, 1945.

Merleau-Ponty, Maurice, *Phenomenology of Perception*, London and New York: Routledge, 2005.

Michel, Alain, *Rhétorique et philosophie chez Cicéron*, Paris: Presses Universitaires de France, 1960.

Michelet, Jules, *Journal*, Tome 1, ed. by P. Veillaneix, Paris: Gallimard, 1959.

Mignucci, Mario, *L'Argomentazione Dimonstativa in Aristotele*, Vol. 1, Padova: Editrice Antenore, 1975.

Misch, Georg, *Gieschichte der Autobiographie*, Frankfurt am Main: G. Schulte-Bulmke, 1950.

Montesquieu, Charles-Louis de Secondat, *Cahiers I (1716–1755)*, Recueillis et présentés par Bernard Grasset, Paris : Grasset, 1941.

Moraux, Paul, 'La joute dialectique d'après la huitième livre des *Topiques*', in *Aristotle on Dialectic: The Topics*, ed. by Gwilym E. L. Owen, 277–311, Oxford: Oxford University Press, 1968.

Moreau, Joseph, 'Ariston et le stoïcisme', *Revue des Études Anciennes* 1 (1948): 27–48.

Mureşan, Valentin, 'Filosofia ca mod de viaţâ sau despre relaţia filosofie-biografi', *Revista de Filosofie Analiticâ* 4, no. 20 (Iulie–Decembrie 2010): 87–114.

Nicholson, Marjory Hope, *Mountain Gloom and Mountain Glory: The Development of the Aesthetics of the Infinite*, New York: Cornell University Press, (1959).

Nietzsche, Friedrich, *Considérations Inactuelles*, Tome 3, French trans. by G. Bianquis, Paris: Aubier-Montaigne, 1966.

Nietzsche, Friedrich, *The Gay Science*, ed. and trans. by Walter Kaufman, New York: Vintage, 1974.

Nock, Arthur D., *Conversion: The Old and the New in Religion from Alexander the Great to Augustin of Hippo*, Oxford: Oxford University Press, 1933.

Nussbaum, Martha, *Therapy of Desire*, Princeton, NJ: Princeton University Press, 1993.

Parain, Brice, *Recherches sur la nature et les fonctions du langage*, Paris: Gallimard, 1942.

Pascal, Blaise, *Of the Geometrical Spirit*, in Blaise Pascal (1623–62), *Minor Works: The Harvard Classics, 1909–14*, trans. by O. W. Wright, New York: P.F. Collier & Sons, 1909–14.

Perelman, Charles, *Rhétorique et philosophie*, Paris: Presses Universitaires de France, 1952.

Perret, Jacques, 'Le bonheur du sage', in *Hommages à Henry Bordon*, 291–8, Bruxelles: coll. Latonus [Tome 187], 1985.

Pigeaud, Jackie, *La maladie de l'âme*, Paris: Les Belles Lettres, 1981.

Pigliucci, Massimo, *How to Be a Stoic: Using Ancient Philosophy to Live a Modern Life*, New York: Basic Civitas Books, 2017.

Pohlenz, Max, *Die Stoa*, Göttingen: Vandenhoeck & Ruprecht, 1959.

Rabbow, Paul, *Seelenführung: Methodik der Exerzitien in der Antike*, Munich: Kösel, 1954.

Raphael, Fred and Gérard Siebert, M. Join-Lambert, T. Fahd, M. Simon and F. Rapp, *Les pélerinages de l'antiquité biblique et classique à l'occident medieval*, Paris: Gauthner, 1973.

Rapin, Claude, Pierre Hadot and Guglielmo Cavallo, 'Les textes littéraires grecs de la Trésorerie d'Aï-Khanoum', *Bulletin de Correspondance Hellénique* 111 (1987): 244–9.

Reith, Otto, *Grundbegriffe der stoischen Ethik*, Berlin: Weidman, 1933)

Richard, Marie-Dominique, *L'enseignement oral de Platon*, Paris: Éditions du Cerf, 1986.

Rist, John M., *Stoic Philosophy*, Cambridge: Cambridge University Press, 1979.

Robert, Jeanne and Louis Robert, 'Bulletin épigraphique [note critique]', *Revue des Études Grecques Année* 84–401–403 (1971): 397–540.

Robert, Louis, 'De Delphes à l'Oxus: Inscriptions grecques nouvelles de la bactriane', *Comptes Rendus de l'Académie des Inscriptions et Belles Lettres* 112, no. 3 (1986): 416–57.

Robin, Léon, *La théorie des idées et des nombres*, Paris: F. Alcan, 1908.

Robin, Léon, *Platon, Phédon*, Paris: Belles Lettres, 1952.

Rodier, Georges, *Études de philosophie grecque*, Paris: Vrin, 1926.

Romilly, Jacqueline de, *Histoire et raison chez Thucydides*, Paris: Belles Lettres, 1956.

Rousseau, Jean-Jacques, *Reveries of a Solitary Walker*, trans. by Peter France, London: Penguin, 1979.

Ryle, Gilbert, 'Dialectic in the Academy', in *New Essays on Plato and Aristotle*, ed. by Renford Brambough, 39–68, London: Routledge & Kegan Paul, 1965.

Sabbatucci, Darrio, *Essai sur le mysticisme grèc*, Paris: Flammarion, 1982.

Sargant, William W., *Physiologie de la conversion religieuse et politique*, Paris: Presses Universitaires de France, 1967.

Schaerer, René, *La question platoniciennes*, Paris: Neuchâtel, 1969.

Schlumenger, Daniel, L. Robert, E. Benveniste and A. Dupont-Sommer, 'Une Bilingue Gréco-Araméenne d'Asoka', *Journal Asiatique* 246 (1958): 1–48.

Schmid, Wolfgang, 'Epikur', in *Reallexikkon für Antike und Christentum*, Tome 5, Stuttgart: Hiersemann, 1994.

Schmid, Wolfgang, 'Götter und Menschen in der Theologie Epikurs', *Rheinisches Museum* 94 (1951): 97–156.

Schmidt, Wilhelm, 'Epicurus', in *Reallexikon für Antike und Christentum*, Vol. V, cols 740–55, Stuttgart: Hiersemann, 1962.

Schneider, Klaus, *Die Schweigenden Götter*, Hildersheim: G. Olms, 1966.

Schrijvers, Petrus Hermanus, *Horror ac Divina Voluptas: Études sur la poétique et la poésie de Lucrèce*, Amsterdam: A. M. Hakkert, 1970.

Sellars, John, '*De Constantia*: A Stoic spiritual exercise', *Poetics Today* 28, no. 3 (2007): 339–62.

Sellars, John, 'What is philosophy as a way of life?', *Parrhesia* 28 (2017): 40–56.

Sharpe, Matthew J., 'How it's not the Chrysippus you read: On Cooper, Hadot, Epictetus, and Stoicism as a way of life', *Philosophy Today* 58, no. 3 (2014): 367–92.

Sharpe, Matthew J., 'Socratic ironies: Reading Hadot, reading Kierkegaard', *Sophia* 55 (2016): 409–35.

Sharpe, Matthew, 'To not forget: Pierre Hadot's last book on Goethe: Pierre Hadot, *N'oublie pas de vivre: Pas de vivre: Goethe et la tradition des exercises spirituels* (Albin Michel, 2008)', *Parrhesia: A Journal of Critical Philosophy* 15, no. 22 (2015): 106–17.

Sharpe, Matthew J., 'What place discourse, what role rigorous argumentation? Against the standard image of Hadot's conception of ancient philosophy as a way of life', *Pli* (2016): 25–54.

Snell, Bruno, *Leben und Meinungen der Sieben Weisen: Griechische und Lateinische Quellen*, München: Heimeran-Verlag, 1952.

Souilhé, Joseph, 'Introduction á *Épictete*', *Entretiens*, Paris: Belles Lettres, 1949.

Spalatin, Christopher, 'Matteo Ricci's use of Epictetus', *Encheiridion*, *Gregoranum* 56 (1975): 551–7.

Stenzel, Julius, *Kleine Schriften zur Griechischen Philosophie*, Darmstadt: H. Gentner, 1957.

Strauss, Leo, *Persecution and the Art of Writing*, Chicago, IL: University of Chicago Press, 1948.

Tchouang-Tseu, *Philosophes taoïstes*, Paris: Gallimard, Bibliothéque de la Pléiade, 1980.

Testa, Federico. "Towards a History of Philosophical Practices in Michel Foucault and Pierre Hadot". *Pli* (2016): 168–190.

Theiler, Wilhelm, 'Review', *Gnomon* 5 (1929): 307–17.

Throm, Hermann, *Die Thesis: Ein Beitrag zu ihrer Entstehung und Geschichte (Rhetorische Studien)*, Université de Lyon: Persée, 1938.

Throm, Hermann, *Die Thesis*, Paderborn: F. Schöningh, 1932.

Toynbee, Arnold J., *La civilisation à l'epreuve*, Paris: Gallimard, 1951.

Valéry, Paul, *Varieté*, in *Oevures*, Tome 1, Paris: Bibliothèque de la Pléiade, 1957.

Van Der Leeuw, Gerard, *La religion dans son essence et ses manifestations: Phénomenologie de la religion*, Paris: Payot, 1948.

Vernant, Jean-Pierre, *Mythe et pensée chez les Grecs*, Tome 1, Paris: F. Maspero, 1971.

Veyne, Paul, 'Le dernier Foucault et sa morale', *Critique* 471–2 (1986): 933–41.

Voelke, André-Jean, *La Philosophie comme thérapie de l'âme: Études de philosophie Hellénistique*, 'Preface' by Pierre Hadot, Paris: Vestigia, 1994.

Warneck, Joh, *Die Lebenskräfte des Evangeliums. Missionserfahrungen Innerhalb des Animistischen Heidentums*, Berlin: M. Warneck, 1908.

Weil, Éric, *Logique de la Philosophie*, Paris: Vrin, 1974, 1985.

Wein, Hermann, 'Sprache und Wissenschaft', in *Sprache und Wissenschaft*, in *Philosophie als Erfahrungswissenschaft*, Dordrecht: Springer, 1965.

Wendland, Paul, *Die Hellenistisch-römanisch Kultur in Ibren Beziehungen zu Judentum und Christentum*, 4th edn. Tübingen: Mohr, 1978.

Whorf, Benjamin Lee, *Language, Thought, and Reality*, New York: Technology Press of MIT, 1956.

Wieland, Wolfgang, 'Aristoteles als Rhetoriker und di Exoterischen Schriften', *Hermes* 86 (1958): 332–46.

Wieland, Wolfgang, *Die Aristotelische Physik*, Göttingen: Vandenhoeck & Ruprecht, 1962.

Wieland, Wolfgang, *Platon und die Formen des Wissens*, Göttingen: Vandenhoeck & Ruprecht, 1982.

Williams, Bernard, 'Do Not Disturb', *London Review of Books* 16, no. 20 (October 1994): 25–6.

Witt, Reginald E., *Albinus and the History of Middle Platonism*, Cambridge: Cambridge University Press, 1937.

Texts by Pierre Hadot

'Ancient spiritual exercises and "Christian philosophy"', in *Philosophy as a Way of Life: Ancients and Moderns: Essays in Honour of Pierre Hadot*, trans. by Michael Chase, 126–44, London: Wiley-Blackwell, 1995.

Discours et mode de vie philosophique, Paris: Les Belles Lettres, 2014.

'Etre, vie et pensée chez Plotin et avant Plotin', in *Entretiens sur L'Antiquité Classique*, Tome 5, 105–57, Genève: Fondation Hadt, 1960.

Études de patristique et d'histoire des concepts, Paris: Belles Lettres, 2010.

Études de philosophie ancienne, Paris: Belles Lettres, 2010.

'Exercices spirituels', *Annuaire de la Ve section de l'École des Hautes Études* 84 (1977): 25–70.

Exercices spirituels et philosophie antique, 3e édn, Paris: Albin Michel, 1992, 2002 [1981].

'Forms of life and forms of discourse in ancient philosophy', in *Philosophy as a Way of Life: Ancients and Moderns: Essays in Honour of Pierre Hadot*, trans. by Michael Chase, 49–70, London: Wiley-Blackwell, 1995.

'Heidegger et Plotin', *Critique* 145 (Juin 1959): 339–56.

Introduction aux 'Pensées' de Marc Aurèle: La citadelle intérieure, Paris: Librairie générale française, 2010 [1998].

'Jeux de langage et philosophie', *Revue de Métaphysique et de Morale* 67, no. 3 (1960 [1962]): 330–43.

La citadelle intérieure: Introduction aux Pensées de Marc Aurèle, Paris: Fayard, 1992, 1997.

La philosophie comme éducation des adultes: Textes, perspectives, entretiens, Paris: Vrin, 2019.

'La physique comme exercice spirituel ou pessimisme et optimisme chez Marc Aurèle', *Revue de Théologie et de Philosophie* 3rd Series [Troisième série] 22 (1972): 225–39.

Le Voile d'Isis: Essai sur l'histoire de l'idée de Nature, Paris: Gallimard, 2004.

'Marc-Aurèle: Était-il opiomane?', in *Études de philosophie ancienne*, 97–106, Paris: Belles Lettres, 2010.

Marius Victorinus: Recherches sur sa vie et ses œuvres, Paris: Collection des Études Augustiniennes, 1971.

Marius Victorinus, Traités théologiques sur la trinité, text established by P. Henry, introduction, translation and notes by P. Hadot, 2 vols, Paris: Éditions du Cerf, 1960.

N'oublie pas de vivre: Goethe et la tradition des exercices spirituels, Paris: Éditions Albin Michel, 2008.

'"Only the present is our happiness": The value of the present instant in Goethe and ancient philosophy', in *Philosophy as a Way of Life: Ancients and Moderns: Essays in Honour of Pierre Hadot*, trans. by Michael Chase, 217–37, London: Wiley-Blackwell, 1995.

'Philosophie, dialectique, rhétorique dans l'antiquité', *Studia Philosophica* 39 (1980): 139–66.

Philosophy as a Way of Life: Ancients and Moderns: Essays in Honour of Pierre Hadot, trans. by Michael Chase, London: Wiley-Blackwell, 1995.

'Philosophy, exegesis, and creative mistakes', in *Philosophy as a Way of Life: Ancients and Moderns: Essays in Honour of Pierre Hadot*, trans. by Michael Chase, 71–8, London: Wiley-Blackwell, 1995.

'Physique et poésie dans le *Timée* de Platon', *Revue de Théologie et de Philosophie* 115 (1983): 113–33 (also in *Études de philosophie ancienne*, 277–305).

Plotin: Ou la simplicité du regard, Paris: Gallimard, 2008 [1963].

Plotin, ou la simplicité du regard, 1929–2011.

Plotin, Porphyre: Études Néoplatoniciennes, Paris: Belles Lettres, 2010.

Plotinus, or the Simplicity of Regard, trans. by Michael Chase, Chicago, IL: University of Chicago Press, 1996.

Porphyre et Plotin, Tome 1, Paris: Études Augustiniennes, 1968.

Porphyre et Victorinus, Paris: Études Augustiniennes, 1968.

'"Préface" to Yoko Orimo's translation of the *Shôbôgenzô of Dogen*', in Pierre Hadot, *La philosophie comme éducation des adultes: Textes, perspectives, entretiens*, 239–46, Paris: Vrin, 2019.

'Spiritual exercises', in *Philosophy as a Way of Life: Ancients and Moderns: Essays in Honour of Pierre Hadot*, trans. by Michael Chase, 79–125, London: Wiley-Blackwell, 1995.

The Inner Citadel: The Meditations of Marcus Aurelius, trans. by Michael Chase, Cambridge, MA, and London: Harvard University Press, 1998, 2001.

The Present Alone is Our Happiness: Conversations with Jeannie Carlier and Arnold I. Davidson, trans. by Marc Djebillah and Michael Chase, 2nd edn, Stanford, CA: Stanford University Press, 2011.

The Veil of Isis, trans. by Michael Chase, Cambridge, MA: Harvard University Press, 2008.

The Veil of Isis: An Essay on the History of the Idea of Nature, trans. by Michael Chase, Cambridge, MA: Belknap Press of Harvard University Press, 2006.

'The view from above', in *Philosophy as a Way of Life: Ancients and Moderns: Essays in Honour of Pierre Hadot*, trans. by Michael Chase, 240–3, London: Wiley-Blackwell, 1995.

'Une clé des *Pensées* de Marc Aurèle: Les trois *topoi* philosophiques selon Épictète', in *Exercises Spirituels*, 2nd edn, 165–92, Paris: Albin Michel, 2002 [1978].

What is Ancient Philosophy? trans. by Michael Chase, Cambridge, MA: Belknap Press, 2002.

INDEX LOCORUM

INDEX OF PROPER NAMES